"Henning Wrogemann's *Intercultural Hermeneutics*, the first in a groundbreaking three-volume introduction to mission studies, is a remarkable study of a key advance in the study of world Christianity. Refusing to avoid the difficult questions of culture, syncretism, inculturation, and identity, Wrogemann presents the reader with a kaleidoscope of expressions and themes found within the world Christian communion and with positive methodological steps by which this diversity might be understood in its difference. The more theoretical considerations, focused on semiotics, discourse, and cultural theory, are amply illustrated with living examples of intercultural encounter. A range of voices and church bodies all contribute to a vision remarkable in scope that directs our attention to the gospel in its movement across every boundary. This three-volume series will prove to be a landmark in the study of mission."

John G. Flett, Pilgrim Theological College, author of *Apostolicity*

"This is a book of dazzling breadth and truly remarkable depth of scholarship. It offers a foundational approach that, if taken seriously, will influence mission studies in profound and significant ways."

Stephen B. Bevans, professor emeritus, Catholic Theological Union

"This comprehensive study of the emerging field of intercultural theology charts a pathway for discussing both normative and descriptive issues arising from cultural difference. Wrogemann carefully builds a theoretical structure using Western philosophical hermeneutics, theologies, and anthropologies. He then shows how that framework can facilitate conversation among theologians and mission partners on seemingly incommensurable issues such as demon possession, healing, syncretism, and gender theologies. A rich dialogue with African theologians on critical topics such as inculturation, Christology, and contextuality establishes the veracity of this approach, allowing for a diversity of expressions of Christianity from around the world. This well-crafted work promises to become definitive for global discourse in intercultural and mission studies."

Frances S. Adeney, professor emerita of evangelism and global mission, Louisville Presbyterian Theological Seminary, board member, The American Society of Missiology, author of *Women and Christian Mission*

"For some time now an important conversation on mission studies and intercultural theology has been developing in Germany that is largely unknown in the English-speaking world. In this extensive study (the first of three volumes) Henning Wrogemann has provided a valuable introduction to these conversations. His proposal of intercultural hermeneutics as a comprehensive method that accounts for culture as a complex field of action where actors appropriate the gospel in multiple contexts, along with the case studies he provides, offers fruitful suggestions of ways mission theology in the West can move beyond the impasse of current discussions of contextualization."

William Dyrness, Fuller Theological Seminary, author of *Insider Jesus*

"*Intercultural Theology*, Volume 1, *Intercultural Hermeneutics* is filled with insight, erudition, and analytical wisdom. In this fine book, Henning Wrogemann lays a firm foundation for two more volumes that together with this one introduce the field of intercultural theology/mission studies. The comprehensiveness of the vision on offer is impressive, as Wrogemann ranges widely across theological disciplines, cultural studies, postcolonial scholarship, and discourse theory. Many examples drawn from the experience of the church in Africa in particular enhance the accessibility of what remains throughout a substantive study of world Christianity and ecumenical theology."

Stanley H. Skreslet, F. S. Royster Professor of Missions, Union Presbyterian Seminary, Richmond, Virginia

INTERCULTURAL THEOLOGY *Volume One*

INTERCULTURAL HERMENEUTICS

Henning Wrogemann

TRANSLATED BY *Karl E. Böhmer*

IVP Academic

An imprint of InterVarsity Press
Downers Grove, Illinois

InterVarsity Press
P.O. Box 1400, Downers Grove, IL 60515-1426
ivpress.com
email@ivpress.com

English edition ©2016 by Henning Wrogemann
Original German edition ©2012 by Gütersloher Verlagshaus, a division of Verlagsgruppe Random House GmbH

Original title: Lehrbuch Interkulturelle Theologie/Missionswissenschaft, Band 1: Interkulturelle Theologie und Herrneneutik. Grundfragen, aktuelle Beispiele, theoretische Perspektiven, *by Professor Henning Wrogemann* ©2012 by Gütersloher Verlagshaus, a division of Verlagsgruppe Random House GmbH, München, Germany.

InterVarsity Press® is the book-publishing division of InterVarsity Christian Fellowship/USA®, a movement of students and faculty active on campus at hundreds of universities, colleges and schools of nursing in the United States of America, and a member movement of the International Fellowship of Evangelical Students. For information about local and regional activities, visit intervarsity.org.

All Scripture quotations, unless otherwise indicated, are the author's translation.

Figure 4: Virgin of Guadalupe, circa 1700. Google Art Project / Wikimedia Commons.

Cover design: Cindy Kiple
Interior design: Beth McGill
Images: Ekely/iStockphoto

ISBN 978-0-8308-5097-6 (print)
ISBN 978-0-8308-7309-8 (digital)

Printed in the United States of America ∞

InterVarsity Press is committed to ecological stewardship and to the conservation of natural resources in all our operations. This book was printed using sustainably sourced paper.

Library of Congress Cataloging-in-Publication Data
A catalog record for this book is available from the Library of Congress.

P	24	23	22	21	20	19	18	17	16	15	14	13	12	11	10	9	8	7	6	5	4	3	2
Y	39	38	37	36	35	34	33	32	31	30	29	28	27	26	25	24	23	22	21	20			

For Andra, Julia, Sarah, and Ellen

Contents

Preface to the English Edition (2016)

In the twenty-first century, Christianity has become a global religious configuration with many regional variations. These variations within Christianity imply that local Christian actors are allowing local contexts to shape their message and way of life to a significant extent. At the same time, tensions arise because the values and behaviors of one context, such as West Africa, sometimes clash with those of a different context, such as India. This directs our attention to intercontinental and intercultural relationships between the various Christian churches and movements in Africa, Asia, the two Americas, Europe, Oceania, and elsewhere: Who gets to decide what is "Christian," and on what basis? Does "Old Europe" possess the superior authority on the grounds of its centuries-old doctrinal tradition, or do the churches in other continents possess the superior authority because they have greater missionary vitality and are perhaps more contextual?

This brings us to the research area of the discipline that has come to be known in European countries as "intercultural theology." What is intercultural theology all about? For starters, it is about developing awareness of the wealth of differences in the global scene when it comes to the Christian way of life. It begins with something as simple as appreciating and understanding the outlandishness of churches and congregations in other cultures. In other words, this is about the issue of intercultural hermeneutics. After all, differences exist not only between various confessions and denominations but also between various cultural forms of the same denomination, such as between Baptist entities in the Congo, Thailand, and North America. What do these forms look like? Is it possible for "theology" to be expressed in songs, dances, and rituals? To what extent may theological doctrines differ from each other?

But intercultural theology, understood as an intercultural hermeneutics of Christian entities worldwide, is about more than just appreciating the differences. It is also concerned with what constitutes the *unity* or at least the *commonality* within intercultural ecumenism. In this regard, we will need to address some issues which are being discussed in North America under the heading of "World Christianity." Still, *intercultural theology* places a different emphasis, since its aim is not to play the Christianities of other continents off against the European history of Christianity but rather to help people progress beyond binary interpretive models and to come to a better understanding. But how is this to be substantiated theoretically?

The present first volume of my *Intercultural Theology* addresses issues of intercultural hermeneutics.[1] It deals with contextual theologies from various continents and contexts, articulated in a variety of media. In addition, it addresses the issue of ecumenical cohesion. We must first become aware of the many differences between local Christianities before we can get a general idea of what constitutes Christianity as a global religious configuration (irrespective of what the individual observer may believe to be true or normal).

The second volume will proceed to cover the contextual diversity of Christian missions worldwide. Differences exist not only between various forms of Christian worship, ritual acts, ideas of moral values, and forms of socioethical-political involvement, but also between various configurations of Christian missions, Christian life witness, and Christian proclamation. Continental European universities locate the discipline of intercultural theology in the tradition of mission studies. Globally, the Christian religious configuration continues to exert a strong missionary influence and to cross boundaries to this effect. Never in the history of Christianity have there been as many missionaries as there are today. Never have there been such diverse modes of operation.

It is essential that people become aware of this in order to counteract stereotypes that tend either to see Christian missions in a negative light, as

---

[1]The German title for the three-volume set is *Textbook on Intercultural Theology/Mission Studies*. The individual volumes have the following titles: *Intercultural Theology and Hermeneutics—Foundations, Contemporary Examples, Theoretical Perspectives* (vol. 1); *Mission Theologies of the Present—Global Developments, Contextual Profiles, and Ecumenical Challenges* (vol. 2); *A Theology of Interreligious Relations—Religious-Theological Paths of Thought, Cultural Science Inquiries, and a Methodologically New Approach* (vol. 3).

is often the case in European societies today, or to misinterpret them trium-phalistically. Intercultural theology is tasked with studying these forms, analyzing them, and doing mission theology by attempting to come up with substantive, locally appropriate answers and by communicating these amid the wealth of different contexts and positions.

But there is more. The third volume of this textbook will speak to another issue, namely to that of interreligious relationships. The quest to understand the Other should not only be pursued among Christians of different cultures with respect to the *forms* of Christian churches, congregations, and move-ments, nor only with respect to the *modes of operation and the goals* of dif-ferent Christian missions, but also with respect to *other religious configura-tions* and their followers. From a religiocultural perspective, societies are becoming more and more pluralistic today. But how are we to deal with this diversity? How can we appreciate the religious Other and at the same time be sure of our own respective faith traditions and ways of life? What do we mean when we speak of dialogue, identity, witness, recognition, and plu-rality? What factors actually play a role in interreligious relationships—various media, perhaps? What claims to validity are people making, for in-stance, when it comes to civil society? In a globalized world, people of different religions and cultures can no longer avoid each other. They have no choice but to work together respectfully. But this does not mean surren-dering one's own principles of faith.

The three volumes of this textbook are written in the awareness that the discipline of intercultural theology[2] will fundamentally determine the future of theological education in all parts of the world. It is not sufficient merely to describe global Christianity from a historic perspective. This is about much more than that. It is about seeking *to understand* as far as possible the variations among local Christianities, their forms and contexts, and their missions and interreligious relationships. This calls for a *descriptive* approach.

---

[2]In the German academy, the discipline is identified as "intercultural theology/mission studies" (*Interkulturelle Theologie/Missionswissenschaft*). This double label became common in German-language scholarship around 2005 in response to the fact that *mission studies* or *missiology* had become a source of misunderstanding. Using both terms retains continuity with previous mis-sion studies while also clarifying the relationship with religious studies and theology in general. It also serves to address the reality of religious pluralism and the significance of the global context for theological thought. See the discussion about this in chapter two.

Then again, this is about factoring ourselves into the equation and taking a theological position with respect to these discourses. This in turn calls for a *normative* approach. After all, if the intercultural theologian were *to refuse* to take a position, then she might well be accused of attempting to take a neutral position from which to study all the other phenomena as mere "research objects." This would factor her own views out of the equation and eliminate the possibility of criticism by other brothers and sisters. That is to say that, in this sense, intercultural theology thrives on the tension occasioned by a descriptive and a normative approach. For this reason, it resorts to an *academically responsible* methodology, drawing from the fields of religious studies, mission studies, and cultural studies. At the same time, it uses approaches from the *theology* of mission, the theology of religion, and the theology of ecumenism. This means that intercultural theology takes a new approach that builds on the tradition of mission studies and pursues it in a new way.

At this point I would like to express my heartfelt gratitude to the translator of this book, Dr. Karl E. Böhmer, and to InterVarsity Press for publishing it under the IVP Academic imprint.

Henning Wrogemann
Wuppertal, Germany
Epiphany 2016

Preface to the German Edition (2011)

Christianity is a global religious configuration, yet the mainstream media seldom take notice of its diversity and beauty, its problems and profundities, and its strengths and challenges. But the same is also true with regard to Christian churches and congregations. In Europe, Christianity is regarded as a religion that has more or less grown old and stale, to which the poor church attendance, the many churches that have been sold, and the declining membership figures bear eloquent witness. At the same time, fairly little notice is taken of the presence of Christians in other continents in general. In the area of theological studies, the discipline dedicated to both the study of the outward appearance taken by the Christian presence outside Europe and its subject matter also led a marginal existence until very recently. It is only as of recently that change has begun to take place.

This new emphasis was long overdue for a number of reasons. First, today's globalized world demands knowledge and awareness of both transnational and transcontinental interrelationships as an essential part of basic education, be it in the areas of history, politics, or economy (to name just three). Correspondingly, for the purpose of theological orientation the student must become familiar with Christianity as a *global religious configuration with many cultural- and context-specific variations*, of which the formative vigor often clearly transcends the older categories of confessional profiles. Besides, there is no need to emphasize that taking notice of foreign brothers and sisters accords with an ecumenical orientation of the Christian faith. Many interrelationships, such as political and societal events in countries in Africa, Asia, Latin America, and Oceania, are almost impossible to understand without knowledge of the religiocultural agents that are at work—including the Christian congregations and churches.

A look at European societies and their contexts in turn reveals that *a plurality of Christianities is already present there too in the form of immigrant congregations*. It is estimated that in the urban area of Hamburg, for instance, more Christians from Africa, Asia, and Latin America attend the worship services of their congregations on any given Sunday than German Christians do those of the state churches and of other German churches. From the perspective of intercultural ecumenism on a transcontinental and intercultural level, the question at issue is one of ecumenical scope, perception, and solidarity; closer to home, in terms of local and regional proximity, the question at issue is one of on-site intercultural-ecumenical cooperation.

A particular expertise is needed for the observation and analysis of these phenomena, an expertise that is introduced into the spectrum of theological disciplines by the subject of intercultural theology/mission studies. It goes without saying that research methods from the areas of cultural and religious studies are brought to bear as well. At the same time, this subject concerns itself with researching the *dissemination modalities of various religious configurations as well as their mission awareness*. Thus it studies mission as an interreligious phenomenon (even though the term *mission* has only limited application to other religious configurations or to various movements or institutions within them). By providing analyses in this domain, the subject contributes both to the analysis of society and, in a more general sense, to the research of conflict and conflict resolution from the perspective of mission and religious studies. *In the context of culturally and religiously pluralistic societies, the scientific analysis of the agents of civil society in this sense (religious groups, movements, or institutions may certainly be understood to be such) and of their specific motives, self-justification, behavioral patterns, and networks makes an indispensable contribution to the perception of societal realities.* Furthermore, mission studies research is of singular importance for the understanding of societal processes in other countries and continents. It is astonishing to observe that, in the European context, the subject of mission leads a marginalized existence and that the term is still shunned in many places, while in other countries and contexts, expansion efforts by religious agents have increased dramatically. Religious agents and their missions are therefore of considerable relevance, not only socially but also politically (in very diverse forms). There is a significant need for research in this area.

Beyond what was said above, there is a growing interest in the issue of relationships between the religions. In the past, such issues were frequently discussed under the rubric of a "theology of religion." The subject of intercultural theology/mission studies has long made important contributions to this subject area in the form of field research and individual studies. Such research continues to be of considerable significance for the future, since it presents a correction to the tendency that continues overly to predominate in the European context, namely to discuss such issues merely on the level of intellectual reflection. In this regard it is possible to open up new, more comprehensive, more up-to-date, and often more realistic perspectives on the basis of material from the intercultural-interreligious domain.

These few remarks touch on only a limited number of aspects that will be discussed in this three-volume textbook on intercultural theology/ mission studies. The present first volume is dedicated to the subject of *intercultural theology and hermeneutics*. It is soon to be followed by a second volume on *mission theologies of the present* and by a third on *a theology of interreligious relations*. The textbook is intended for those studying to become pastors or teachers; for interested readers in congregations, churches, schools, and institutions in the area of intercultural social work; for colleagues in the area of ecumenical mission work, such as those serving in academic departments or in mission institutes; and beyond that for the general public.

At this point, I would like to thank the people who accompanied me during the past two decades on my journeys in the area of intercultural ecumenism and local interreligious relationships, including many longstanding friends and colleagues. They helped me again and again to see the world with different eyes. In addition, I would like to express my gratitude to my coworkers in two mission institutes, first the Evangelical-Lutheran Mission in Lower Saxony (ELM), where I served for six years, and then also the United Evangelical Mission (UEM), with which I am currently cooperating extensively. Many of you provided me with insight into the issues of your life and your work. I would also like to thank my doctoral and habilitation supervisor, Heidelberg scholar in mission and religious studies, Prof. Dr.

Theo Sundermeier, who was and continues to be a source of inspiration and encouragement to me.

For their many pointers and proofreading efforts, my gratitude goes to my former assistant, Dr. Gudrun Löwner (Bangalore); to my doctoral candidates, Sören Asmus and Detlef Hiller; and also to my current assistant and habilitation candidate, Dr. John Flett. The complete work is dedicated to my family, who have patiently endured up until now the times of my absence and who accompany my work with loving interest.

Henning Wrogemann
Wuppertal, Germany
November 2011

PART I

Intercultural Theology

What Does This Mean?

The Gospel of Life
in the Midst of Cultures

An African Case Study

The research area of intercultural theology comprises worldwide Christianity, i.e., that religious configuration that is currently represented by more than two billion followers in all parts of the globe and that has found its expression in a plethora of regional and local varieties of Christianity. Intercultural theology/mission studies focuses its attention on those processes of exchange in which new forms of Christianity arise in a given place, on the one hand, and in which Christian churches, congregations, and movements exert an influence on the cultures, contexts, and societies in that place, on the other. In addition, it investigates how these various Christianities—in the form of churches, congregations, networks, and individual people— enter into a relationship with one another, be it on a local, regional, or transnational level. A striking example from the area of intercultural encounters will preface the subsequent explanations by way of illustration. This example will serve as the basis for an introduction to important, determining issues for the subject of intercultural theology/mission studies.

How Pastor Mastai Drives Out Evil Spirits in His Congregation in Dar es Salaam

The Kimara Lutheran Parish is located in Dar es Salaam, Tanzania. Dar es Salaam is a large port city near the island of Zanzibar on the Indian Ocean, a city of currently about four million residents. The Kimara Lutheran Parish is located near the city next to a major arterial highway. It comprises a modern edifice, containing both the church building on the second floor and various congregation rooms on the first. The façade is white, the roof a radiant light blue. From the spacious parking lot, we enter the lower part of the building, proceeding through a hallway into an anteroom. Around thirty persons are gathered here, mostly women, generally young and middle aged, and also a few men and a few elderly people. We pass through the waiting room and enter the pastor's office. Reverend Willy Samuel Mastai is a young man in his early thirties, perhaps, of the athletic type, wearing plain clothing, shirt not tucked in. The room conically tapers toward the pastor's desk owing to the form of the building. While the more spacious part is tiled, the tapering part is carpeted. A few chairs line the otherwise bleak walls; the many barred windows are open. It is sunny outside. Palm fronds sway in the breeze. The desk is rather cluttered; behind it stands a shabby cupboard with a few files, on top of it a few trophy cups.

All day long people have been calling on the pastor, looking for advice and help. We—a colleague from Germany, a local pastor of the Lutheran church, and myself—are briefly greeted as guests, followed by a likewise brief introduction to what is about to happen. Then Reverend Mastai again turns to his tasks: pastoral care, prayers for healing, and exorcisms. The next person seeking help is allowed to enter. Some of the people outside have been waiting for four hours already, as the pastor briefly explains. The middle-aged woman is smartly dressed; rings and earrings reveal that she probably belongs to the middle class. She takes off her shoes and positions herself in front of the pastor with a touch of bashfulness. A short conversation in Kiswahili follows. We three visitors are invited to stand in a circle and lay hands on the woman, on her shoulders. The pastor says an audible prayer for healing, perhaps two minutes long; a brief exchange of words takes place, and the woman leaves. A young man comes in; after a brief explanation, a prayer for blessing is spoken over him, and he leaves. It seems he did not want anything more than a blessing. In the meantime, the pastor's phone, which he had deposited on his desk, keeps ringing every few minutes. The pastor is in great demand. A middle-aged woman enters; the pastor sits down on his chair, the woman next to him. A somewhat more extensive exchange takes place, and then the pastor dismisses the woman. While she leaves he explains that it concerns relationship problems, it would take a while, and a special session would be necessary.

Then an older woman comes in, poorly dressed, thickset, and corpulent. The pastor already knows the woman. He estimates that this is the fourth time she has come. It seems that she suffers from the indwelling of evil spirits. The woman positions herself in front of the pastor. He instructs her in a few words to look him in the eyes, while he himself stares at her with a very grave expression. Half a minute. One minute. One and a half minutes. The woman repeatedly evades his gaze; she looks at the floor or past him. Abruptly, Reverend Mastai then lifts up his hand and places it on the woman's forehead and the upper part of her face. The exorcism begins, for only if she had matched his gaze would it have been an unmistakable sign that the spirit had left the woman already. The state of possession is not yet over; the evil spirit is still present within her. Therefore the pastor begins to say the prayer of exorcism.

He prays out loud; his voice sometimes grows louder and then softer again. Again and again the demand is repeated for the evil spirit to depart in Jesus' name: "In the name of Jesus, the mighty Savior"—the same words are repeated eight times, ten times, fifteen times. The woman's body is seized with convulsions; she hugs herself, contorts herself, with her eyes closed or occasionally rolling about. She falls backwards; we bystanders catch her, only just managing to prevent her from hitting the floor. Choking noises ensue; sometimes she emits a loud scream; the woman is again seized with convulsions as if trying to spit something out. She is foaming at the mouth, trembling and contorted. Then she comes to again, takes four steps sideways, bent over, to where a little plastic bowl with sand is ready; she spits. Presumably, this kind of spitting out takes place frequently. The cellphone on the desk rings and rings. No one pays any attention to it. Again and again the pastor casts a searching look at the woman, continually saying new prayers of exorcism over her, accompanied by the murmuring of his colleague, who is also a pastor but who maintains a low profile except for the murmured prayer. After a few minutes, the exorcism is over. The pastor asks the woman whether she feels any better; she nods casually, does not say much—and leaves. All of a sudden, everyday normality resumes—or at least, that is how I experience it as an observer.

More persons are led in and treated in a similar fashion.[1] For the most part, these are women. Besides the prayers of exorcism, which sometimes

---

[1] It must be noted, first, that the pastor receives no compensation for his healing services at all and, second, that such prayers for healing and exorcism also form part of the worship services from time to time.

transition into a loud, intermittent series of commands, little physical contact occurs; when it does, then it does so especially in the area of the forehead and head and in the form of laying hands on the upper abdomen of the female patients or by pressing on this area with the hand. The female patients repeatedly sink backwards or fall all the way to the floor. After a number of such treatments, Pastor Mastai takes a break. When asked why women in particular make use of these treatments, he answers that this is probably due to the women being under stress in this country's social system, which remains a patriarchal one. He establishes a connection to the activity of the spirits by pointing out that these strains impose suffering on the women and that this suffering in turn makes them vulnerable and therefore receptive for the activity of evil spirits. After these impressions, we now leave Reverend Mastai and his congregation in Dar es Salaam and ask some pertinent questions.

AN OBSERVER ASKS CRITICAL QUESTIONS FROM A EUROPEAN PERSPECTIVE

Let us imagine a European person observing these events. It may be assumed that the scenario that was just depicted would initially cause some disconcertment for her. There was the trembling by someone who was "possessed," the screaming, the choking, the spitting—she might think it was slimy and rather disgusting. Dealing with demons is not an everyday occurrence in Western society, but rather something relegated to the domain of horror movies, a marginalized topic barely good enough for the often bloodthirsty spine-chillers of the cinema. But even in these movies, the subject of demons is usually depicted as restricted to a few persons, while here in Dar es Salaam it is obviously something that concerns many people. This raises the question of the doctrine of demons and society: Is this not a matter of having relapsed into the ritual language of the old tribal religions? Is this not a case of a conventional, traditional, and almost "medieval" devotional practice? Or is this not somehow also a modern phenomenon—after all, it occurs not in the country but in a city with more than a million inhabitants? And if the latter is the case, then in what sense is it modern? With regard to the people involved, our observer could go on to ask: Does this constitute an irrational or a rational manner of action? In short, from a European perspective one might well ask: Is this ordinary or extraordinary? Backward or modern? Irrational or rational?

Now our observer hails from the realm of a Christian environment. In addition, as a church elder, hers is a decidedly ecclesiastical perspective. She asks herself: Is this practice actually still *Christian*? Or is this a case of an illegitimate commingling of religions (which would need to be labeled with the corresponding technical term, *syncretism*)? Does this not constitute a reemergence of the religious practice of the old tribal religions, which had been overcome by Christianity long before? With regard to her congregation in Germany, she asks herself: Is this practice actually still *Lutheran*? As far as she knows, no exorcisms are performed in the German Lutheran mainline churches anymore, and especially not in connection with pastoral care. What value does this religious practice then have for the larger reality of the Lutheran church in Tanzania? Is this not something practiced by the Pentecostal churches (our German church elder once heard a presentation about the Pentecostal movement), in which healing, miracles, and the exorcism of spirits play a far greater role worldwide than in other Christian churches? Or, put more critically, she might ask herself: Is what is happening here "authentic"—or is it not rather some form of charlatanry? In short, from a European Christian perspective, one might well ask, Is this syncretistic or Christian? Pentecostal or Lutheran? Authentic or fake?

These questions reflect a European preconception strongly determined by the thinking of the Enlightenment. The basic assumption is that practically every phenomenon of our realm of experience may be explained scientifically. Physical suffering may be explained by means of an examination and treated with surgeries and medications; mental illness may likewise be explained by means of anamnesis and treated with corresponding psychological or medicinal therapy. This way of thinking determines not just everyday life in Western society but also life in the church: in worship services, congregation activities, and diaconal institutions, a "rational" manner of action sets the tone throughout—that is to say, one that does not account for the interference of any evil powers (spirits, demons, etc.). This is the reason for our church elder's impression that Pastor Mastai's "treatments" constitute a premodern, irrational, syncretistic, and perhaps disingenuous practice, one that is in no way "Lutheran" in the normal sense, "Reformed," or somehow "evangelical."

All of this leads to another dilemma, namely to the *ethical question*: Can the practice of Pastor Mastai be condoned? From a European perspective, should the man not be made to understand that what he is doing is profoundly prescientific? Should one not insist that these poor people do not need some strange arcane rites but rather psychological treatment, and that they need it not from a pastor but from an academically trained psychotherapist? Is this not, more than anything else, an ostensible case of deferring the problems? Could it not be that many symptoms even result from mental illnesses, which are impossible to diagnose medicinally? Is it not irresponsible summarily to administer "spiritual" help to the people when *real* help is needed instead? Is it not necessary first to consider the social causes that might be behind the mental disorders of many women, such as the unemployment of the husband who constantly beats his wife, or the excessive demands made on her as a result of too many children, or something similar? Would social programs not therefore be much more effective than this kind of pastoral activity? And, if nothing else, is it not one's Christian duty to help people by (among other things) helping them come to know the truth, and does this not also mean interpreting the actual state of affairs *correctly*? Are people not delivered from their fears when they come to understand that it is not evil spirits that are the cause for certain phenomena, but simply a complex of interrelated factors that may be described scientifically?

These ethical questions might well lead to the formulation of *ethical challenges* for ecclesiastical cooperation, and our church elder, who simultaneously also serves as a delegate of her church body (and, being a church parliamentarian, she therefore also has a vote), wonders whether she should not propose this to a committee as a topic for discussion: in the framework of the worldwide Christian community (global ecumenism), this might serve as an example to demonstrate the value of mutual assistance. Thus, for instance, one might invite the pastor to study in Germany in order for his views on spirit beliefs to be corrected by means of scientific theory construction. Or one could design projects to facilitate development cooperation with the intent of addressing the social problems that evidently either give rise to or reinforce the belief in possession. One could help the Lutheran churches in Tanzania augment their diaconal activities, and one could contribute to their theological education by deploying European theologians in order to maintain the Lutheran profile of these churches or to reclaim it. We now leave our church elder to her further deliberations and turn to the Tanzanian pastor.

How Pastor Mastai Experiences Germany: Reciprocal Questions from an African Perspective

Pastor Mastai comes to Germany on a theological scholarship program. He stays for a few weeks. Germany, the land of Martin Luther and the Reformation. Pastor Mastai is very excited. After settling in, he observes that there are many things that impress him. The scope of diaconal activity in Germany is wide: hospitals, welfare service centers, and consulting centers—everything seems well organized. The buildings are in good shape, and everything appears very professional. True, he had also heard that the Christian faith life in Europe leaves much to be desired, and he also knows congregations in Tanzania and other African countries that have already sent African missionaries to Europe,[2] but his firsthand impressions leave him with questions.

Worship services in his congregation are attended primarily by young people. There is always a large group of children present, and most of them take part in Sunday school. In Germany, children are seldom seen at worship services, according to his impression, and although the church buildings are beautiful and sometimes awe inspiring, those attending are usually in their sixties or older. And the worship services are very orderly, quiet, predictable, and—as far as he is concerned—exceptionally brief. Pastor Mastai wonders what the believers actually expect from God. Germany is a Christian country, but on Sunday mornings, the streets are deserted. Pastor Mastai begins to ponder. During a conversation he picks up on a term that he heard in a presentation and asks me whether Christianity in Germany is not "syncretistic." He explains,

> It says in my Bible that Jesus drove out evil spirits, healed people, and performed miracles—that Jesus helps us! But the people in this country do not believe that anymore, not even those in the churches. But if the Bible

---

[2]Andreas Heuser, "'Odem einzuhauchen in verdorrtes Gebein . . . ': Zum Missionsverständnis ausgewählter afrikanischer Kirchen in Hamburg," in *Theologie—Pädagogik—Kontext: Zukunftsperspektiven der Religionspädagogik; Wolfram Weisse zum 60. Geburtstag*, ed. Ursula Günther et al. (Münster: Waxmann, 2005), 269-85.

proclaims the truth, how then can you not believe in it any longer? You believe in science, not in the Bible anymore! You have exchanged the truth of the Bible for technology. And that is syncretistic.

These few observations suffice to show how difficult intercultural encounters can be. After all, the persons in our case study both accuse each other of syncretism, taken to mean either an illegitimate "commingling of religions" (the accusation that African Christianity adopts aspects of traditional superstitions) or alternatively a commingling of the Christian message with elements of other worldviews (the accusation that by their blind faith in science, European Christians abandon the truth claim of the Bible).

On the Relevance of the Subject of Intercultural Theology/Mission Studies

The case study demonstrates how different the perspectives of two people can be who both belong to one and the same Christian denomination (the Lutheran denomination), while each belongs to a different culture (Tanzanian culture, German culture). The relevance of the subject of intercultural theology/mission studies thus also lies in the need for an analysis of these contrasting perspectives and for them to enter into conversation with each other. This is a matter of intercultural and interreligious understanding as a prerequisite for mutual appreciation, for peace, and for cooperation in societies marked by already great and ever-increasing cultural plurality. This subject devotes itself to these topics and thereby introduces an intercultural, interreligious, and ecumenical perspective into the instruction of theology. This perspective flows from the self-understanding of the Christian faith traditions themselves, inasmuch as the declaration by Jesus Christ that the kingdom of God is at hand exercises a claim on *all* people.

In what follows, a number of the subject's analytical perspectives will be discussed against the backdrop of the case study provided earlier (naturally without being exhaustive). It should be noted here already that the discipline of intercultural theology/mission studies initially utilizes descriptive methods. That is to say, methods of analysis deriving from the areas of religious and cultural studies are brought to bear. In a second step, an inquiry is made on the basis of these findings into how the phenomena that were described may be interpreted from a theological perspective. Value-oriented (normative) aspects play a significant role in this regard. Methodologically, however, the two perspectives remain separate from each other.[3] Let us then consider some of the issues raised, doing so from the perspectives of religious studies, mission history (especially in the sense of the history of the theory of religion and mission theology as well as of its practical implementation), intercultural theology, and intercultural hermeneutics.

With regard to the phenomena of possession and to exorcistic practices in the region of the megacity of Dar es Salaam, intercultural theology/mission studies initially makes use of *religious studies analyses.* These include the following questions: (1) What form did the traditional religion presumably take in a certain area (such as that of a certain ethnic group in the region of present-day Dar es Salaam) and at a certain point in time (since religiocultural configurations constantly change)? Furthermore, which social structures and which family relationships were present? Which types of economy prevailed? Which ecological factors played a decisive role? Which rites were carried out? How was the social hierarchy structured? Which symbolisms were in place? To which mythological narratives was the origin of the ethnic group or the tribe attributed? How did the structures change in the context of colonial history and after meeting representatives of both Muslim and Christian religious configurations? (2) Which elements of the belief in demons and of exorcistic practices may be observed today, and from where precisely might they derive? If the older tribal traditions have for the most part ceased to exist, if only certain set pieces of these traditions continue to feature in the lifeworldly knowledge of people, and if at the same time set pieces from Islamic and Christian traditions have been added, then what meaning do people perceive in certain symbolisms, or what do they even perceive to be meaningful? For instance, the figure of a "Satan" as a counterpart to the divine power was unknown in most African tribal traditions; Islam and Christianity introduced the concept and thereby also the contraposition between good (God) on the one hand and evil (Satan) on the other, which is a comparatively recent phenomenon in Africa, religiohistorically speaking.

---

[3]The definition of the relationship, though, is far more complex—which remains to be demonstrated.

Having raised these few issues, let us turn now to the theological ones. We will initially examine them from the perspective of mission history. The following will need to be analyzed: (1) Which religiotheological and missiological preconceptions prevailed among the various denominations and their missions in this area (Tanzania)? How did Baptists, Lutherans, members of Roman-Catholic religious orders, Presbyterians, and others perceive and interpret the tribal religions that were foreign to them? Which methods of operation did they adopt in order to enter into a relationship with the members of these religious traditions? And which methods of operation verifiably remain in use by various denominations to this day? (2) Or did a fundamental change take place in recent years? And if yes, from where do the corresponding influences derive? Conservative Lutheran missionaries, for instance, firmly repudiated exorcisms and the belief in spirits. The permeation of exorcistic practices into Lutheran congregations may be observed to have taken place only long after Tanzania's independence, predominantly under the influence of growing Pentecostal groupings and churches in Tanzania.

From the perspective of mission history, then, the central question of this theological issue may be formulated as follows: Which theology of religion and which mission theology did the European missionaries advocate, and how were they received and implemented in the churches? In addition, we also need to raise the genuinely theological (i.e., normative) primary questions of intercultural theology/mission studies, namely: (1) Which texts of the Christian tradition (the Bible) do the representatives of various Christian religious configurations (in this instance, Tanzanian Lutherans vis-à-vis German Lutherans; naturally, dialogues between Tanzanian Lutherans, Pentecostals, and Roman Catholics are also conceivable) cite in order to substantiate their practice? Moreover, is this citation warranted? Thus, which Christian practice is legitimate, permitted, acceptable, and valuable—or, alternatively, which is questionable or even inadmissible? (2) And what happens, or what would happen, if Christians of the same cultural tradition but of different denominations dissented strongly on a given topic? How about if they came from diverse cultural backgrounds?

This problem introduces the *issue of intercultural hermeneutics*. First, (1) we must inquire into the basic hermeneutical and cultural-semiotic interpretation:

What exactly does a member of one culture *perceive to be a sign* when encountering a different culture? For instance, did our German church elder notice that a sign system of *looks* is present during such an exorcism? The exorcist looks into a person's eyes for a long time; if the person looks elsewhere and avoids the exorcist's gaze, then he interprets it as a certain sign that the person is possessed. But there are also other, entirely different sign systems that are normally of no interest to European observers. Thus the earth itself can serve as a sign system, one that cannot be charted, subdivided, sold, or possessed *qua* land registry office, but that rather *constitutes* the life and the tradition of a tribe. Another example is that of time, which for other cultures does not advance in regular units, as it does according to European conceptions, but which has the *power to determine outcomes* for better or for worse, depending on the time of day or celestial alignment. (2) Thus one issue is the question as to what precisely is perceived to be a sign, i.e., as conveying meaning; in addition, whenever misunderstanding or lack of understanding occurs between cultures, the special problem presents itself of how intercultural understanding is actually possible in the first place. (3) A further challenge arises especially in the area of intercultural relationships between, say, Christians from Germany and those from Tanzania, namely the challenge of determining who actually has *the authority to interpret the exchange.* If, for instance, there are two different interpretations of exorcistic practice, both representing commonly held, culturally accepted interpretations and both claiming to stand on the authority of the witness of the biblical and Christian traditions—who then gets to decide which side is right? And if no such authority exists, what form could the process take in which both sides attempt to reach an understanding? And if it should happen that no understanding can be reached, how then could ongoing intercultural-Christian, i.e., ecumenical, relationships be *sustained*?[4] At what degree of separation can one still speak of "one" Christian religion? Or is there rather a plurality of Christian religious configurations?

The case study above may have shown that the area of discussion of the subject of intercultural theology/mission studies requires a methodologically varied toolset to arrive at an analysis, whereby a clear distinction needs

---

[4]On this point, see chapter twenty-four, and especially under the heading "Toward an Ecumenical Appreciation of Plurality: Maintaining Contact from a Distance."

to be made between a descriptive approach and a reflection about normative subject matter. Furthermore, it has become clear that the area under discussion potentially comprises all the places where the Christian presence is located on earth. At the same time, just as in all other scientific domains, a single individual is only able to acquire in-depth knowledge about a small segment, even if many basic themes of the subject of intercultural theology/ mission studies have a broader importance, since they serve as cross-cutting themes for a variety of otherwise different cultural contexts. Before addressing a representation of these basic issues in the course of this treatise, we will first need to discuss the term *intercultural theology*.

2

Intercultural Theology

A Primer

First-time students of intercultural theology will initially want to know what the general definition of the term is and which books are useful for an in-depth study of the topic. The following remarks are thus conceived as an introduction that provides an initial elucidation of the term and that points out some important book series and publications at the same time. Naturally, the wealth of material allows only a very limited selection in this regard. The overview is intended to provide interested readers with an initial introduction, enabling them then to pursue their specific interests.

INTERCULTURAL *THEOLOGY*: THEOLOGICAL CONCEPTIONS FROM THE THIRD WORLD?

Since the mid-1960s, the book trade has featured an increasing number of books on the subject of what is termed "intercultural theology" (*Interkulturelle Theologie*) today. For the most part, these books are about "local theologies," thus for instance specifically about African or Asian Christian theologies. As far as the literature goes, these theologies are in many respects a relatively recent phenomenon. For the study of the subject of intercultural theology, this literature is groundbreaking indeed. Whether it is also sufficient will need to be discussed at a later point. For now, a brief overview of some selected publications will suffice.

The volumes from the 1970s and 1980s especially document the wealth of contextual theologies, thus for instance Asian theology as evidenced by Choan-Seng Song's (b. 1929) *Third-Eye Theology*,[1] South Korean Minjung

---

[1]Choan-Seng Song, *Third-Eye Theology: Theology in Formation in Asian Settings* (Maryknoll, NY: Orbis Books, 1979).

theology as represented by Byung-Mu Ahn (1922–1996),[2] African theology as represented by John S. Pobee (b. 1937),[3] or the politically themed *Black Theology* in the context of the South African apartheid regime.[4] The same objective is pursued by Roman Catholic theologians such as the Africans Jean-Marc Ela (1937–2008)[5] and O. Bimwenyi-Kweshi (b. 1939),[6] the Sri Lankan Aloysius Pieris (b. 1934),[7] and the South African Charles Villa-Vicencio (b. 1931).[8]

It is evident that around the mid-1990s, after about thirty years of intensive theological labor of writing contextual works and about twenty years after the founding of the Ecumenical Association of Third World Theologians (EATWOT) in the year 1976, it was possible to make an initial appraisal. For an exchange between theologians from the Third World, the reader is referred to the anthology *Third World Theologies: Commonalities and Divergences.*[9]

Of course the titles presented here constitute only a very small selection, which is not surprising in light of the magnitude of world Christianity and the corresponding plurality of its contexts.[10] Besides, we provided only references to *source documents* of what may be described by the broader term "intercultural theologies." However, in order better to be able to systematize and thus understand such theologies, more comprehensive analyses of the relevant cultural and contextual interrelationships are needed from the areas of mission studies and religious studies. This raises the question as to how the most comprehensive definition of the term *intercultural theology* might be obtained.

---

[2]Byung-Mu Ahn, *Draußen vor dem Tor: Kirche und Minjung in Korea; Theologische Beiträge und Reflexionen,* Theologie der Ökumene 20 (Göttingen: Vandenhoeck & Ruprecht, 1986).

[3]John S. Pobee, *Toward an African Theology* (Nashville: Abingdon, 1979).

[4]Basil Moore, ed., *Black Theology: The South African Voice* (London: C. Hurst, 1973).

[5]Jean-Marc Ela, *Ma Foi d'Africain* (Paris: Karthala, 1985). For an English translation, see *My Faith as an African* (Maryknoll, NY: Orbis Books, 1988).

[6]Oscar Bimwenyi-Kweshi, *Discours Théologique Négro-Africain: Problème des Fondements* (Paris: Présence Africaine, 1981).

[7]Aloysius Pieris, *Fire and Water: Basic Issues in Asian Buddhism and Christianity* (Maryknoll, NY: Orbis Books, 1996).

[8]Charles Villa-Vicencio, *A Theology of Reconstruction: Nation-Building and Human Rights,* Cambridge Studies in Ideology and Religion (Cambridge: Cambridge University Press, 1992).

[9]K. C. Abraham, ed., *Third World Theologies: Commonalities and Divergences, Papers and Reflections from the Second General Assembly of the Ecumenical Association of Third World Theologians, December, 1986, Oaxtepec, Mexico* (Maryknoll, NY: Orbis Books, 1990).

[10]See for instance John C. England et al., eds., *Asian Christian Theologies: A Research Guide to Authors, Movements, Sources,* 3 vols. (Maryknoll, NY: Orbis Books, 2002–2004).

INTERCULTURAL THEOLOGY: ECUMENISM IN FULL, PLEASE, NOT JUST IN PART!

Speaking with people interested in global ecumenism, one may easily get the impression that the readers of representative literature (i.e., of books from a certain area that have been translated) often tend to come away with very one-sided appraisals of country-specific contexts. Thus in the 1980s there was strong interest in the Korean Minjung theology in particular, a political liberation theology that arose in the context of the South Korean military dictatorship. The great number of publications on the subject could easily lead one to believe that the majority of South Korean Christians belong to the political Minjung theology movement. This was and continues to be an error, however, since the overwhelming majority of Korean churches are characterized by a staunch conservatism that might be described as ranging from "evangelical" to "fundamental," to use Western nomenclature. Yet these churches have not received any significant attention, neither by the German nor by the English book market. The most probable reason for this is that scholars from the German and Anglo-Saxon sectors considered these churches to be less than spectacular and that during these years they did not fit in well to the atmosphere of liberation theology favored by the ecumenists associated with the World Council of Churches.

Naturally, this should not be seen as a challenge to the propriety of such theological movements and characterizations. Yet there are clearly communication barriers present here that impede an appreciation of ecumenism as a whole. The theological positioning in the so-called conciliar process, which called for a commitment to justice, peace, and the integrity of creation, for example, easily led people unilaterally to become critical of or completely disregard other forms of Christian faith and life, of congregation activities, and of ecclesiastical structures. Efforts to engage other Christians or to challenge them to mutual conversation despite or even precisely because of their frequently very different positions fell by the wayside. Typical examples include the stereotype held by European Christians that the churches in the Pentecostal movement lack sufficient sociopolitical engagement and are thus partly to blame for the injustice in many contexts. Conversely, a widespread prejudice exists among Christians from Pentecostal congregations and churches to the effect that faith in the historic churches is "dead" and that those belonging to them remain Christian in name only.

In addition to the two factors discussed above—a distorted perception of respective contexts arising from a one-sided representation in the literature, on the one hand, and an unwillingness to recognize the validity of other Christian positions, on the other—one may also list as a third factor the internal dynamics of the academic pursuit of theology. Discussing intercultural theology in the sense of a fully developed theological discipline is a distinctive aspect of theological instruction at institutions of higher learning, i.e., colleges and universities. In this regard, theologians from both the southern and northern hemispheres are eager to demonstrate that their own theological efforts are compatible with the international academic discussion. This calls, first, for the adoption of succinct positions (frequently stated in an exaggerated fashion); second, for their presentation in the form of academic articles or monographs; third, for the adoption of internationally established jargon (often including very abstract terminology); and last, for the effort to attract attention within the structures and idiosyncrasies of the international theological "market" and, along with it, the effort to be recognized as belonging to the theological elite.

These efforts are laudable, for they benefit the Christian religion; by stimulating an intercultural theological dialogue, they provide a countermeasure to the centrifugal forces prompted by Christianity's ever-increasing differentiation. Otherwise the various local Christianities would be in constant danger of absolutizing themselves, taking themselves and their particular cultural and contextual profiles for granted. Let us take the interreligious dialogue, for example. At times, Christians in Germany see the parameters of the dialogue between Christians and Muslims very differently from Christians in Egypt. Thus I have frequently heard the criticism that Egyptian Christians do not hold a "real" dialogue but that they just "curl up into a ball" and assume a defensive posture. What was meant was that dialogues on the subject of theological doctrine seldom took place in Egypt. My impression was that a superficial and "very German" understanding of dialogue predominated, one that was oriented primarily to the exchange of arguments, to rationality, and to theological content. Yet these people did not consider the possibility that *dialogue* may also refer to something entirely different, something that does not take place on a rational level; that nonverbal dialogues, for instance, might take place by means of the *symbolism of official meetings*.[11] It will suffice to point out that it is only possible to counteract and revise the absolutizing of one's own understanding (in this case that of *dialogue*) by means of intercultural exchange. In this regard, intercultural theological discourses play a significant role on the international level, yet at the same time they constitute only a fraction of what is meant by *intercultural theology*, as this example may demonstrate.

The subject area of intercultural theology has to do with the fundamental issue of what precisely is meant by *theology*. This in turn means: *It has to do with the question of the forum—of the media—in which theology manifests itself.* Thus the research topic for intercultural theology also includes the attempt to define the term *theology*. This book intends to show that theology may not only be condensed into rational theorems, speeches, sermons, articles, books, creeds, and written texts. Such an understanding of theology would be insufficient and would contribute little toward the understanding of intercultural phenomena. Rather, theology expresses itself in the proverbs of everyday life and in certain rituals like, say, festivals, processions, forms of meditation, and others. The inner space of a Reformed church, painted white and empty except for a table and a pulpit, breathes theology and is an expression of theological convictions. The same goes to the same extent for an Orthodox church, filled for its part with an overabundance of icons, candles, crosses, billows of incense smoke, polyphonic singing, and a worship event that—almost like a theatrical play—is a figurative representation of the events of salvation, with a story that is portrayed and roles that are played by actors such as priests, deacons, and assistants. When seen as a whole, the latter constitutes a highly complex ensemble of symbols, a particular sign language of faith. How much more careful, then, should we not be—to go beyond these examples of European Christian traditions, with which we are more or less familiar—when observing the expressions of Latin American, Oceanian, African, or Asian Christians, so that we may begin to comprehend what they mean?

---

[11]At festivals of great significance, say, when representatives of other religions express greetings at official locations. Such meetings usually convey a great deal of symbolism (who arrives with which delegation, who speaks with whom for how long at which place, etc.) and communicate nonverbal messages. These make it possible to draw conclusions about the current state of interreligious relationships.

What, for instance, is the theological meaning of Christian social structures? Or consider the interpretation of church as the community of Christians as expressed in the form of tribal kinship relations: Is it possible for aspects of the gospel to be expressed *within* these affiliations? Or what about Western congregations, in which Christians interact not as members of family groups but rather as individual persons, almost like separate atoms constituting one corporate society? How about the titles and honorifics used for Jesus Christ? May a title used in the New Testament such as "Son of God" be applied to Christ in a context where a categorical distinction is made between the status of father and son, i.e., where the son always occupies a position *below* that of the father? What is to be done in those contexts where people do not conceive of God as being "up there" somewhere but rather view *the earth* as representing the divine? How about the position of women, the role of rituals such as fasting and tithing, the understanding of Christian involvement in society, issues of war and peace, the nature of love and justice, the way the Bible is understood, or the understanding of what a "brother," a "soul," or "salvation" is? Fundamental differences exist with regard to these things that depend on one's cultural context, religious environment, and particular Christian confession or denomination. And of what then does the Christian essence consist that unites all Christians worldwide? *One of the fundamental tasks of the subject of intercultural theology/mission studies is to take into account the broad scope of world Christianity. This prohibits it from being limited to a particular confession's concept of ecumenism, and it also prohibits it from being limited to certain forms of the Christian essence associated with the milieu of the World Council of Churches (no matter how significant these may be). That which is different, otherwise, or offensive (such as fundamentalist movements, congregations, or churches) must also be investigated in order to ascertain its particular views. In this regard, it is not uncommon for the conventional approaches of intercultural theology to fall short.*

INTERCULTURAL THEOLOGY: A NEW TECHNICAL TERM, ITS POTENTIAL, AND ITS LIMITATIONS

From the wealth of literature on the term *intercultural theology* we will survey only a small selection at this point. The identity of the person who popularized the term remains a subject of debate. The term undoubtedly gained in popularity through the work of Birmingham mission scholar Walter Hollenweger, especially through his three-volume anthology of essays, *Interkulturelle Theologie*.[12]

Meanwhile, in the English-speaking domain the technical term *world Christianity* came to be used more and more. Educational institutions where this was the case include Yale, Harvard, Princeton, and Union Theological Seminary in New York. Hope University in Liverpool may serve as an example from the UK.[13] In recent decades, eminent theologians from the southern hemisphere were called to serve as chairs at these institutions—for example, Lamin Sanneh (b. 1945) from Gambia.[14] While on the one hand this development does demonstrate an "internationalization" of theology to a certain degree (albeit to a very limited one in reality), on the other hand—and this is the other side of the coin—it augments the brain drain from the countries of the south. In other words, the most distinguished theologians of the south may be found serving at educational institutions of the north. To be sure, the decision in each case is a personal and a legitimate one; seen on the whole, however, the development is unfortunate, considering the state of education in a number of countries in the south.

Let us return to the subject of intercultural theology. This term came to be used more and more to replace the older technical term *mission studies*. For a time, the subject's raison d'être was called into question. As a result a number of suggestions were made aimed at safeguarding at least the subject

---

[12]Walter J. Hollenweger, *Interkulturelle Theologie*, vol. 1, *Erfahrungen der Leibhaftigkeit*; vol. 2, *Umgang mit Mythen*; and vol. 3, *Geist und Materie* (Munich: Chr. Kaiser Verlag, 1979–1988). For the longest time, no relevant publications were brought out under the title "Intercultural Theology." This has begun to change. See the thorough and multifaceted introduction by Klaus Hock: *Einführung in die Interkulturelle Theologie* (Darmstadt, Germany: Wissenschaftliche Buchgesellschaft, 2010). In contrast, V. Küster almost completely restricts his focus to academic treatises by contextual theologians associated with the EATWOT. See Volker Küster, *Einführung in die Interkulturelle Theologie* (Göttingen: Vandenhoeck & Ruprecht, 2011). See also Richard Friedli et al., eds., *Intercultural Perceptions and Prospects of World Christianity*, Studies in the Intercultural History of Christianity 150 (Frankfurt: Peter Lang, 2010), as well as the anthology of contributions by colleagues associated with the University of Birmingham, such as Allan Anderson or Kirsteen Kim: Mark J. Cartledge and David Cheetham, eds., *Intercultural Theology: Approaches and Themes* (London: SCM Press, 2011).

[13]At the University of Basel in Switzerland, the former chair for mission studies was recently renamed the "Professorship for Non-European Christianity" (*Professur für Außereuropäisches Christentum*).

[14]He later taught in Ghana and then at various educational institutions in the UK and the United States.

matter. Thus Werner Ustorf, for example, suggests subordinating mission studies to various other scientific disciplines in future and relegating it to the status of a mere research *theme*, as it were. I believe, however, that this approach simply leads to the dissolution of the subject (in question), that it is neither required as far as the content is concerned nor desirable with a view to the institutions concerned. Besides, there has been strong international resistance to the intention to abandon the term *mission/mission studies*.[15]

In a response formulated as early as 2005, representative professionals from the area of religious studies/mission studies belonging to the Academic Association for Theology (*Wissenschaftliche Gesellschaft für Theologie*) and to the board of directors of the German Society for Mission Studies (*Deutsche Gesellschaft für Missionswissenschaft*) proposed the dual designation "intercultural theology/mission studies" in a position paper.[16] The following section will be devoted to the discussion of which term is better suited for the subject and on what grounds.

INTERCULTURAL THEOLOGY OR MISSION STUDIES?

As a technical term, the older designation *mission studies* seems to have fallen on hard times. In German-speaking areas, the term *mission studies* appears to have been eclipsed by the term *intercultural theology*. In the abovementioned joint paper by the board of directors of the German Society for Mission Studies and the professional group from the domain of religious studies/mission studies associated with the Academic Association for Theology, the terms *intercultural theology* and *mission studies* were combined very deliberately by means of a forward slash. This conjunction ensured

---

[15]See Ken Christoph Miyamoto, "A Response to 'Mission Studies as Intercultural Theology and Its Relationship to Religious Studies,'" *Mission Studies* 25, no. 1 (2008): 109-10; Susan Smith, "A Response to Re-naming Mission as 'Intercultural Theology' and Its Relationship to Religious Studies," *Mission Studies* 25, no. 1 (2008): 111-12; and Francis Anekwe Oborji, "Missiology in Its Relation to Intercultural Theology and Religious Studies," *Mission Studies* 25, no. 1 (2008): 113-14. Cf. Wissenschaftliche Gesellschaft für Theologie and Deutsche Gesellschaft für Missionswissenschaft, "Mission Studies as Intercultural Theology and Its Relationship to Religious Studies," *Mission Studies* 25, no. 1 (2008): 103-8.

[16]These groups included religious scholars and mission scholars such as Dieter Becker, Michael Bergunder, Andreas Feldtkeller, Klaus Hock, and Henning Wrogemann. See German Society for Mission Studies, *Fachgruppe Religions- und Missionswissenschaft der Gesellschaft für Wissenschaftliche Theologie und Vorstand der Deutschen Gesellschaft für Missionswissenschaft, Mission Studies as Intercultural Theology and Its Relationship to Religious Studies*, www.dgmw.org /MissionStudies.pdf (accessed January 8, 2015).

that the new central concept of intercultural theology was clearly identified with regard to its origin. In this way, mission studies was redefined as intercultural theology.

Whether this term is more appropriate than the older one essentially depends on the audience one has in mind. As far as *institutional politics* are concerned, i.e., within the institutional framework of theological faculties and university committees, the term *intercultural theology* has the incontestable advantage that it emphasizes the interculturality of theology. From a global perspective, theology is pursued everywhere. This means that the subject is just as concerned with contributing to an adequate understanding of theological traditions from Africa, Asia, Latin America, and Oceania, for example, as it is with reflecting on this exchange itself and on how it is determined by its own context. The stereotypical association of mission with narrow-mindedness, arrogance, bias, etc., is thereby preempted. This makes it easier to explain the purpose of the subject and the need for education in this subject area. After all, *intercultural* may be used to signify not only those phenomena that are related to the plurality within one particular society (keywords: migration, diversity, etc.), nor only those related to the cultural diversification among diverse expressions of Christianity on a global level (keyword: context-specific instantiations of the Christian presence), but also a broad spectrum of phenomena of an interreligious nature (for instance, relationships between Christians and Muslims, and particularly within the parameters of an intercultural comparison).

Even though the term may offer many advantages with regard to institutional politics, it must be recognized that semantically the relationship between intercultural theology and religious studies remains somewhat indistinct. *To put it briefly, the point is that the subject matter of intercultural theology is not entirely "theological."* From the perspective of researchers in religious and cultural studies, theology is usually considered as reflecting the study of the theological positions of their *own* respective fields. Seen from this perspective, theology has a uniformly normative character. This, however, conflicts with the claim to methodological neutrality commonly made by researchers in the fields of religious and cultural studies. In this respect, the advantage of the term *mission studies* is evident: the emphasis is placed on the term *studies*, which may be understood on the one hand as a purely descriptive, scientific endeavor, i.e., as a description of social phenomena in the area of religious and cultural studies that is as neutral as possible in terms of its worldview.[17] In terms of African Initiated Churches, for instance, it is necessary initially to undertake a purely descriptive study of the family relationships, the historical genesis of social formations, of internal and external labelling processes, etc. Anything "theological" that serves as an object of study must first be interpreted in light of a context that has been apprehended in a purely descriptive manner. In this approach, the enterprise of scientific study is characterized by the principle of neutrality.[18]

On the other hand, the term *studies* may also be understood as the *scientific analysis of theologically normative argumentation*. In this sense, as is generally known, Paul Tillich called for the preservation of semantic clarity, methodological clarity, and logical clarity in order to satisfy the criteria for the scientificity of the endeavor. With this in mind, systematic theology is positional, for it is predicated on the Christian self-understanding within a given context; it is also coterminous with scientific study, for it offers a methodologically replicable and thus generally communicable analysis of the subject matter. Substantiations and argumentations may be scrutinized both generally and methodologically in order to verify their intelligibility, theological construction, coherence, and sufficiency. The term *studies* may therefore be understood in both a descriptive and a normative sense. In contradistinction, the term *mission* indicates the subject area: *it concerns the expansion of Christian religious configurations, on the one hand, and the plans, efforts, and forms of expansion within the local context (in both qualitative and quantitative dimensions), on the other*. Seen from this angle, the term *mission studies* is the more comprehensive one, to which—to list just three examples—the terms *intercultural theology* (the analysis and description of contextual expressions of Christianity), *theology of mission* (theologically normative and contextual argumentation for Christian expansion), and *theology of religions* (defining the relationships between

---

[17]For more on this topic, see Andreas Feldtkeller, "Mission aus der Perspektive der Religionswissenschaft," *Zeitschrift für Missionswissenschaft und Religionswissenschaft* 85 (2001): 99-115.
[18]See Theo Sundermeier, "Zum Verhältnis von Religionswissenschaft und Theologie," in *Religion—Was ist das? Religionswissenschaft im theologischen Kontext: Ein Studienbuch*, 2nd ed. (Frankfurt: Lembeck, 2007), 273-306.

Christian claims to validity and those of other religions) may be subordinated. These subordinate terms in turn call either for a descriptive analysis or for a positional reflection as far as their theologically normative content is concerned.

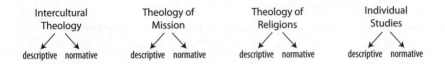

Intercultural Theology	Theology of Mission	Theology of Religions	Individual Studies
descriptive normative	descriptive normative	descriptive normative	descriptive normative

descriptive = analyses from the areas of religious and cultural studies
normative = theological-positional analysis, interpretation, and evaluation

Figure 1. Mission studies

A third aspect must also be considered, namely the way in which various Christian configurations worldwide understand themselves. In light of the fact that there have never been more Christian missionaries worldwide than there are today, it must be admitted that the custom of harboring a skeptical attitude toward mission is evidently a phenomenon associated with a limited geographical area (predominantly that of Europe).[19] In other words, mission critics from the European context constitute only an extremely small minority within worldwide Christianity. In Europe, too, the interest in mission is intensifying among churches from the entire spectrum of confessions and denominations. The scientific study of the concepts, activities, and outcomes associated with this interest is thus of great importance. From this perspective, *mission studies* is probably the more appropriate term, since the term *intercultural theology* does not sufficiently cover the phenomenon of mission, i.e., expansion. Conversely, the dual designation *intercultural theology/mission studies* seems to offer a good solution, since it makes provision for both institutional and content-related aspects.

---

[19]This becomes evident not only in light of the many *newer mission societies*, but also of the global increase in mission studies research. This is attested by the various *societies for mission studies research*, for instance, of which only a small selection is listed here: the German Society for Mission Studies (DGMW, founded in 1918); the International Association of Mission Studies (IAMS, founded in 1972); the Southern African Missiological Society (SAMS); the Korean Society for Mission Studies; the American Society of Missiology (founded in 1972); the Fellowship of Indian Missiologists (founded in 1991); the Asian Society for Missiology; and the Central and Eastern European Association for Mission Studies.

THE OBJECTIVE AND BASIC LAYOUT OF THIS BOOK

This book aims at providing an introduction to the principal themes of the subject of intercultural theology/mission studies so as to illuminate the broad scope of the research. It is concerned with *intercultural ecumenism*, not just with a narrow conception of ecumenism limited by a Eurocentric perspective or by the perspective of denominational studies. It is concerned with all of the many forms of expression of the Christian faith instead of merely concentrating on doctrinal and written theology. It aims at a comprehension that is as holistic as it is critical and that seeks to question the apparently self-explanatory correlation between the self and the other.[20] Therefore, part two begins by addressing the issue of what it means to understand in the general sense and what intercultural understanding means in particular. In so doing it covers the subject areas of semiotics (1), understanding (2), the other (3), and culture (5) as well as the phenomena of religious symbols (4) and of the symbolic language of everyday coherencies (6). This is done using examples that are both tangible and relevant. The theoretical principles are "brought to life" throughout by means of examples. *The basic hypothesis of this book is that understanding is only possible when the interdependency between the concept of understanding and the understanding of culture becomes clear.*

In part three, various types of contextual theology are discussed using examples of churches and Christian movements from the African continent. This limitation makes it possible to address fundamental issues of contextual theology while avoiding the pitfall of merely jumping from one continent to the other in a kind of "name hopping." After (1) the introduction, various perspectives are presented: (2) contextual theologies by theologians from the mainline churches, (3) contextual concepts by women, (4) contextual theologies by the so-called evangelicals, and (5) contextualizations at the grassroots level. The last section aims to demonstrate how the respective theologies are not merely determined by the African contexts but also and particularly by the discourse positions of those who formulate them.

---

[20]It must be expressly noted that the literature references have been kept to a reasonable minimum in this book. Providing more comprehensive information would have gone beyond the scope of a textbook.

Part four addresses historical perspectives, for the topics of gospel, cultures, missions, and foreign encounters are as old as Christianity (in its many cultural manifestations) itself. Here various basic models of a missionary understanding of culture and religion are identified, each of which served in a formative manner for long periods of time (sometimes for centuries). This concerns first (1) colonial contexts in what later came to be known as Latin America; then (2) the model of the conversion of the individual, using the missions of the Moravian Brethren as an example; (3) the model of mission as the ennoblement of the foreigner; (4) indigenization; and (5) the appropriation model. The goal is to demonstrate how other cultures are either rejected or viewed with indifference, as being in need of ennoblement, or as being worthy of preservation, and alternatively, in the last model, how the recipient culture is viewed as a significant contributor to the process of cultural encounters.

Having presented a large number of examples, part five proceeds to discuss a number of theoretical concepts that are of substantial importance for the subject of intercultural theology/mission studies. These are (1) the term *inculturation* and its variants; (2) the term *syncretism*; (3) theoretical approaches from the domain of *postcolonial studies*, such as hybridity or transculturality; (4) the term *ecumenism*; and (5) terms related to various contexts that may serve as cross-cutting themes, such as *reconciliation, development, ecology,* and *gender.* Finally, (6) some thoughts from the subject areas of systematic theology and the theology of mission are presented with the aim of providing an outlook on anticipated challenges. It must be expressly noted that themes emphasizing either the theology of mission or the theology of religions/interreligious dialogue are only touched on in the present volume, since these themes are to be addressed at length in volumes two and three of this textbook series.

PART II
....

Intercultural Hermeneutics and
the Concept of Culture

In order to provide an introduction to the subject of intercultural theology/
mission studies, let us begin with the question, How does intercultural understanding actually take place, and how is it even possible for it to take
place? After all, something must first be understood before it can be described. This chapter will begin by (1) illustrating what it actually means "to
understand," using an example. This will be followed (2) by a brief overview
of the Western history of the study of understanding (hermeneutics). After
all, intercultural understanding within the domain of Christian religious
configurations has a long history to look back on, which in turn makes it
possible to locate one's own position. Having been sensitized to the concept
of understanding, we will proceed (3) to discuss the concept of culture. Here
we will need to examine the relationship between the problem of interculturality (which presupposes a multiplicity of cultures) and the phenomenon

of globalization. Does globalization not lead different cultures to become more and more alike? Will the problem of interculturality not therefore resolve itself in the foreseeable future? Using some true-to-life examples, we will demonstrate that this is highly improbable. The following section will (4) address the issue of the intercultural-interreligious exchange and the problem that it is impossible to exchange symbols without exercising power. Put differently, if cultures and religions encounter each other in ever more intense ways and through an ever greater array of multimedia, how then do they dissociate themselves from one another in order to maintain their own identity? These issues lead (5) to a discussion of the concept of culture itself, for the question as to what intercultural understanding is depends on the definition of the term *understanding*, on the one hand, and the definition of the term *culture*, on the other. In short, the point is that the concept of culture itself suggests to what extent intercultural understanding is actually possible. Then we will use a variety of examples in order to demonstrate from the perspective of cultural semiotics how many things (such as space, clothing, or time) may carry "meaning" for people from other cultures. We will also aim to demonstrate from the perspective of discourse theory how certain forms of the stylization of cultures constitute a kind of cultural foreignness. Finally, I plead for an intercultural hermeneutics, in which the dimensions of semiotics and discourse theory converge.

3

Intercultural Hermeneutics

Introduction

Let us then turn to the study of intercultural understanding. From the wide variety of possible theories, we will initially select and use the approach of cultural semiotics. Since various forms of the Christian faith express themselves within the models that prevail in their own respective cultures and contexts, our attention is directed to the question as to what exactly members of other cultures even perceive as being significant, i.e., as being signs.

HERMENEUTICS AND THE THEORY OF SIGNS (SEMIOTICS)

Semiotics is the theory of signs (from the Greek *semeia*, signs).[1] At issue here is not just how signs are to be interpreted, but rather the far more fundamental problem of how something *may come to function* as a sign for a certain person. Issues of semiotics thus constitute an important subdomain of the subject of intercultural hermeneutics. This may be explained using the example of written texts. For instance, the so-called classic hermeneutics is concerned with the interpretation of *written* texts inscribed on things like stones, leather, or paper. Written texts are artifacts, thus artificially produced objects. As the reader seeks to understand them, the principal question is, What induced the author to write the text? It is thus—either consciously or unconsciously—assumed that there was intentionality present, that there was a reason for writing. Thus the fundamental enquiry of hermeneutics reads, What did the author intend to say with the text, and how may one identify the meaning that the author intended?

---

[1]Umberto Eco, *A Theory of Semiotics* (Bloomington: Indiana University Press, 1979).

If the object of analysis is a mathematics text, then it may still be a rather simple exercise to identify the content of the text and the intention of its author. Yet this exercise becomes far more difficult when it comes to narrative texts, for it may very well be that the author's intention is not easily discernible. For in addition to its literal meaning, i.e., to its factual declaration, the text might also be meant, say, ironically, i.e., the intention might be to create the impression of a double entendre. Or the text might have been intended to be funny, which, however, presupposes knowledge of what might have been considered to be funny at the time of the author or—as far as the writer's personality is concerned—knowledge of what she personally might have considered to be funny. It is altogether difficult to ascertain the conceptual significance of poetic texts, for poetry often aims to evoke changes in mood. For instance, when Georg Trakl writes, "Powerful is the silence in stone" (*Gewaltig ist das Schweigen im Stein*), then we are faced with the problem of whether it is even legitimate to ask the question as to what that means. Does this statement contain meaning, or does its meaning not perhaps consist in eliciting a mood? And what criterion might be applied to determine which mood is the "appropriate" one? After all, all people are different and therefore also surely sense very different moods within themselves according to their respective origins and their social, cultural, or biographical contexts. At least, one may assume this to be so, for it is impossible to know for sure.

What can we say about understanding, then, especially when texts are concerned? In this context, coming from a semiotic perspective, we affirm that written texts may rather easily be understood to the extent that their method of production indicates *that they are conveying something that is intended to be understood in the first place*. No matter what response the poem evokes in people, it was created with the purpose of expressing the mood of the author and of eliciting moods in other people, or else it would not have been written. This is evident even if the question as to whether it is possible to ever "appropriately" understand a poem must remain open.

This is only the initial point of departure for semiotic inquiry, however, for semiotics is not only concerned with the interpretation of signs but also—as we said—with how something comes to serve as a sign for human beings (to whom we restrict ourselves here) in the first place. After all, things may function as signs without an entity intentionally (willfully) designating these things as signs. A popular example for this is fire: if lightning strikes a forested area, if a forest fire is kindled, and if smoke begins to rise, then someone who sees the smoke from a distance understands the smoke as a sign that a fire is burning over there. Her reaction will presumably be to run away in order to escape the fire. Thus in this instance, one thing (the smoke) comes to function as a sign for another thing (the fire), which it *signifies*. The woman does not see the fire as such; the smoke leads her to conclude the existence of a (large) fire, even though the two things are not identical. Now, the fire was, however, caused by the lightning strike, and thus there was—in contrast to written texts—no subject present who intentionally manufactured or used this sign. Yet this means that an element from the woman's surroundings came to function as a sign for her. How is this possible?

Loosely speaking, one might say that it is within the realm of possibility for the world to be full of signs and that people only need to know how to decode them. Speaking more precisely, it is the regularities occurring in the world that allow people to gain experience. If things keep on repeating themselves while people observe them, then as soon as people detect the regularity, such things begin to function as signs for them. Smoke implies the presence of fire, for where fire comes into being there is always smoke as well, regardless of how clearly or indistinctly it may be seen. When trees are covered with hoarfrost it implies that it was below freezing during the night. Ice on the pond implies that the water below is very cold. The world can thus come to serve people as signs in a variety of ways.

Yet it is important to make distinctions, for the fire might have been kindled by a lightning strike, in which case it would not serve any other referential function. However, the fire might also signify the presence of other people, for instance when smoke in the border region between two feuding tribes implies that members of the other tribe have lit a campfire. When there is a war going on as well, then the smoke possibly means danger for the members of the opposing tribe, even though the smoke is not intentionally being used as a sign. The question as to whether something functions as a sign must therefore be expanded to include the aspect of in which context something comes to function as a sign and for which purpose. For the smoke in this example only functions as a sign of danger when a state of war exists between the two aforementioned tribes. The context here merely determines the meaning that members of the one tribe detect in the signal (the smoke). Beyond that, however, smoke may also be intended to function as a means of the transmission of signs, for instance when a signal fire is lit on purpose, or even more clearly when smoke signals are used as a certain code to transmit words or associations, for then the smoke signals become a text.

Accordingly, from a semiotic perspective, the object of smoke may have many different causes. If caused by an accidental lightning strike, it would have no human agent. When functioning as a sign of a campfire, it would have been caused by a human agent, even though it might not have been intended to function as a sign. If the smoke was produced by a signal fire, then it was intentionally created for the purpose of transmitting signs, i.e., the smoke is something that transmits content—and thus a text—by making use of a code established between different people. In the last example, the smoke actually comes to function as a very specific kind of writing system, just as, for instance, certain knots were used as a writing system in South American cultures, for example by the Aztecs.

How Are Semiotic Codes "Discovered"?

Once these correlations have become clear, another question presents itself: In what way are people influenced by their culture to read their surroundings, i.e., to experience them in *a meaningful way* according to certain interpretive paradigms? We have already seen that it is possible to identify as signs things not caused by human agents. This identification may be highly individual, i.e., someone interpreting certain things or events as signs; but one can only talk about it in a meaningful way when at least two people agree on what may be understood as a sign. Thus signs may only be detected when they are redetected, and this presupposes a number of people perceiving the signs according to the same *semiotic code*.

Now, it is of critical importance for the study of intercultural understanding *to begin by admitting even the possible existence* of a wide variety of such semiotic codes, for in light of the diversity of cultures it is impossible to "know" them all. Thus one would need to devote attention to discovering patterns of encoding and decoding signs among foreign cultures. We will need to address such patterns presently. Also important is the question as to what actually constitutes the "semiotic energy," as cultural studies expert Aleida Assmann has pointed out. Put differently, what makes a person perceive something as a sign? According to Assmann, it is particularly human fear.

> Fear . . . engenders a world in which all things function as agents of threat and persecution. Goethe's *Erlkönig* is a case study of this feverish condition which replaces the familiar world with a foreign and hostile one. "The night a thousand monsters made," as it says elsewhere; but the transformation of an oak tree in the fog into a mighty giant is not a product of the night, but of fear.[2]

The semiotic question is therefore no longer whether it is actually "true" that a threat exists ("It's just an oak tree, after all . . ."), but rather what functions as a sign for somebody: what does he perceive to be a sign or, from another person's perspective, what does someone "turn into" a sign. What one person might "overlook" as an unspectacular aspect in his perception of the world, another might perceive as a sign that is as obvious as it is threatening. At this point, it will be helpful to incorporate the semiotic question into the domain of intercultural understanding. *We will use the subject of demonology as an example and make frequent references to it. We will, however, first interpolate another example that will be more familiar to the European culture in order to meet the reader where she is. Both examples are concerned with the question, according to which paradigms of perception are things or events actually perceived as signs? In other words, which paradigms lead to the assumption of meaningfulness, of semiosis?* Let us begin with the example from a European context:

> The Hansen family lives in Hamburg. It consists of a father, Victor; a mother, Sophia; and two children, Thomas and Mary. The father works in a law firm in the city center, the mother works at home as a computer specialist, and the children still go to school. One day, as the children are both out and about in the city center, they happen to notice their father coming out of the entrance to a multistory house. His face is red, he is sweating a little, and his clothing

---

[2]Aleida Assmann, "Geschmack an Zeichen: Homo interpres und die Welt als Text," *Zeitschrift für Semiotik* 12, no. 4 (1990): 359-70 (quotations drawn from 373 and 366). The translation of Goethe's phrase *Die Nacht schuf tausend Ungeheuer* supplied above is by Edgar Alfred Bowring in *The Poems of Goethe: Translated in the Original Metres, with a Sketch of Goethe's Life* (London: John W. Parker and Son, 1853), 77.

is in a state of disarray. He looks to the left and to the right, adjusts his clothing, walks to the nearest train station, and waits there for his train. A little later, a woman leaves the house. She looks over at Victor, greets him; he greets back; she gets into her car, which is parked at the side of the road, and drives off. The children look at each other quizzically. Why?

They see a whole ensemble of signs that combine to form a story in their perception. What are the signs they see? First, there is the fact that both children believe their father to be at work, while here they see him at a *place* where he cannot work, for the house in question is a private residence (place). Second, there is the fact that their father had not mentioned any plans to relocate, which indicates that he is *keeping something secret* from the family (mode). Third, he leaves the house with an elevated body temperature, as signified by the red color in his face and by the circumstance that he is sweating; therefore he must have been engaged in an activity that was physically demanding (physical condition). Fourth, his clothing is in a state of disarray, which conceivably implies getting dressed or undressed, or at least engaging in strenuous activity (clothing). Fifth, he turns to the left and to the right, which is probably an indication that he wants to avoid being seen (manner). Sixth, a woman leaves the house a little later, who he evidently seems to know (person of reference). Six signs that combine to arouse the children's suspicions.

> The children come home and report. Their mother is irritated but tries not to let it show in front of the children. No, says Sophia, she does not want to speculate but rather intends to ask her husband to explain himself. Victor returns home that evening. When asked to explain himself, he becomes a little annoyed. The children think: Does Victor have the audacity to become annoyed despite his misconduct? Meanwhile Sophia continues to wait. Victor explains. He is sorry for the secretiveness, he says; actually, no one was supposed to know about this. It has to do with Sophia's birthday, Victor continues; since she likes to dance so much, while he himself was unable to do so, he secretly enrolled in dancing lessons from Mrs. Schneider at the dance school Schneider and Wille. The dance studio is in the house. There are only five persons taking lessons. This was the last lesson, and next week he wanted to surprise Sophia with an evening of dancing together. The children are speechless; Sophia is relieved.

So much for the first example. From a semiotic perspective, it is interesting to observe that there are various paradigms of perception concurring here that may be described as "diagnostic" and "investigative" forms of reading (to use Aleida Assmann's terminology).[3]

Diagnostic and Investigative Reading

Diagnostic reading includes understanding certain phenomena to function as signs for certain facts and circumstances. The red color of Victor's face, for instance, may be read diagnostically as indicating an increase in blood circulation: more blood enters the outer capillaries, which causes the face to become red. So far, so correct. The only question, then, is what caused this increase in blood circulation. Was it perhaps an illness that led to fever? Was it sporting activities? Or—as was presumed in this case—an affair? Diagnostic reading thus associates sign and signified in a close interrelationship. Tooth pain implies tooth decay, a bluish bruise indicates a possible blow, etc. In contrast, investigative reading may not resort to such a narrow conceptual link. It is not like a medicinal compendium that lists all manner of bodily symptoms, which are then associated with certain illnesses.

In the process of investigative reading, that which allows the *phenomena to be read as signs* is a *story*. And a person's imagination conceives, tests out, and attempts to extrapolate how this story took place exactly. The abovementioned phenomena of the place, the secretiveness, and the sweating are combined in the children's thought processes heuristically into the sequel of a story. The more everything combines to "make sense," the surer the children become that they are able to read the phenomena correctly. That this was not the case, however, is something the children only realize afterwards. Thus Victor did not look around because he wanted to avoid being seen but simply because the street he had to cross had a high volume of traffic, and therefore his looking to and fro was mandated by the need to maintain road safety. Thus here the children interpreted something as a sign (of Victor's internal

---

[3]"The medicinal diagnostician proceeds semantically; he locates the meaning of his signs in a lexicon of established correlations between appearances and significances. The investigator proceeds syntactically; he investigates the meaning of signs by adding contingent, isolated elements together to form the structure of a necessary coherency. The things become signs in an ad hoc manner by means of the (re-)construction of a story, in which they are assigned their significant place." Assmann, "Geschmack an Zeichen," 364.

state), of duplicity or of the father's bad conscience, although in reality it was no sign at all, since Victor only wanted to cross the street with a good conscience. Investigative reading thus seeks to construct a story by way of trial, in order to decode things that have been observed and that suggest themselves to be significant, so as to unlock their meaning.

In view of investigative reading, Assmann assumes a basic attitude of suspicion as a given: as a result, all manner of things, facts, and circumstances are "eyed" suspiciously to see whether they actually constitute secret clues, whether things that would otherwise "have nothing to say" and are thus unrelated are now suddenly invested with meaning. The suspicion bears on the "innocence" of the objects, facts, and circumstances: if they were "innocent," then they would just be present, but if they are invested with meaning, then they indicate the presence of a story that has remained hidden up until then. Everything, even the smallest trifle, can become an important sign.

These semantic insights help us better to understand intercultural phenomena like the phenomenon of demonology. Namely, if people perceive their environment as being influenced by powers, spirits, and demons, then from an intercultural perspective the observer—who does not believe in spirits and demons himself—is able to ask the question: Which paradigms of perception do these people believe to be "significant," and which aspects of reality serve to carry meaning for them? For the domain of intercultural hermeneutics, this theme is significant and should not be underestimated. Which paradigms do other people believe to be encoded in their social world? Just one example: A man is sitting in front of his hut in South Africa. Suddenly, a white beetle comes crawling out of the hut. The man sees the beetle and keeps track of it. Much later he will recount how the spirit of an ancestor was at work in this white beetle, and he will tell stories of what he experienced while the ancestral spirit was leading him. The bottom line is that many beetles are simply beetles, but under certain circumstances common phenomena (like beetles) become signs. We will have more to say about this later.

What Does It Mean to "Understand"? A Primer

Let us first leave the field of semiotics for a bit and return to the question of understanding. We will do so by trying to get a grip on what actually is meant by the term *understanding*.[4] Some believe that misunderstanding is the norm and that in contrast, understanding is the exception. Whether one agrees with this opinion depends entirely on what one understands by "understanding." Some believe that understanding in the ultimate sense is impossible—and there are good reasons to make this claim. We may demonstrate this by using as an example the account of the couple, Victor and Sophia, and their children, Thomas and Mary. Who understood what in this story? First of all, as far as the general facts are concerned, this little story recounts events that are supposed to have taken place in twenty-first century Hamburg. It may be understood as an unplanned observation of the father carried out by his children. The observation arouses their suspicion, which he is able to allay during the conversation at home. Thus the outward facts and circumstances seem to be clear for the present.

Yet there may be deeper dimensions to the text, as demonstrated, for instance, by the question, Who composed the text, and with what intention? Is this a description of an actual event, for example, or is it a literary text?

In the latter case, the text would certainly contain hidden intentions. For example, one could then understand the names as signs (they were certainly not understood in this way beforehand). They would constitute an encrypted code that would catch only the eye of those with an at least rudimentary grasp of the Greek and Latin languages. In this case, the (Latin) name Victor would be read in terms of its literal meaning as signifying a "winner" (whatever the author might have meant by that). The name of the mother, Sophia, comes from Greek and means "wisdom." This would make good sense, because Sophia's character is portrayed as adopting a wait-and-see attitude, as not prejudging, and in this sense as being "wise" indeed. This leaves the names Thomas and Mary.

Yet as far as these names are concerned, the semiotic codes of "symbolic names" and "knowledge of Greek"/"knowledge of Latin" would no longer suffice, for the names Thomas and Mary might also carry other, nonlingual connotations. A profound biblical knowledge might tentatively be more

---

[4]We are unable at this point to go into the details of the hermeneutical discussion of recent years. For more on this issue, see, for instance, Hans-Georg Gadamer, *Wahrheit und Methode: Grundzüge einer philosophischen Hermeneutik*, 3rd ed. (Tübingen: Mohr, 1972). For an English translation of Gadamer's book, see *Truth and Method*, rev. ed. (London: Bloomsbury Academic, 2013).

helpful in this regard. In the New Testament, there is a certain Thomas among the disciples of Jesus of Nazareth, known in the Christian tradition as "doubting Thomas." The Gospel of John records that he doubted the resurrection of Jesus Christ and that it was only Jesus' resurrection body and the stigmata (the marks of the nails inflicted during the crucifixion on his hands and feet) that convinced Thomas that Jesus had truly risen. This association (Thomas = doubter) would match the character of the boy named Thomas, who doubts his father. Interpreting the name Mary would be a more difficult exercise, however, for there are a number of women by the name "Mary" in the books of the New Testament, such as Mary the mother of Jesus or Mary of Magdala.

Let us summarize. Simply understanding the course of events might not be enough fully to understand the story; one must also consider whether the author intended it as a description of an actual event or as a literary text. Furthermore, it becomes clear that if the latter is the case, then additional codes need to be applied (linguistic proficiencies, knowledge of the biblical traditions) in order to identify other possible signs and to interpret them. But this would by no means be the end of it. Biographical knowledge of the author would also be needed to prove whether the text was intended in the literal sense only, in the sense of social criticism, or in an autobiographical sense. And if in an autobiographical sense, does the narrative contain evidence of attempts to conceal or gloss over anything? Is it possible to pick up overtones of irony? Would one thus only understand the story if one read and relived it from the perspective of the author himself? And who would truly be able to do so? Is it possible for everyone to relive it, or is it only possible for those who are married and have children themselves, first, and second, who come from Germany? After all, the story might very well have different connotations for people from Saudi Arabia or Brazil. And what about the time period? For example, would a German person from the early Middle Ages be able to understand what the story is actually about, or perhaps a Chinese person from the time of the Ming Dynasty?

So many questions. A feasible way to approach some of the problems highlighted here (to say nothing of solving them!) might be to revisit the basic meaning of the concept of understanding. In what follows, I join Thomas Haussmann in identifying two meanings for it. I take understanding to mean "to grasp," "to comprehend," on the one hand, and "to empathize," "to relive," on the other.[5] Even this distinction indicates that no matter how the concept of understanding is conceived, it always connotes a gradual procedure. Applying this to our example of the story of Victor and Sophia, to begin with it indicates that understanding may take place either on a superficial or on a more profound level. This liberates the concept of understanding from the false dichotomy between understanding and not understanding.

Moreover, it is helpful to distinguish between various objects of understanding. This may significantly help us to achieve clarity as we reflect on the subject of intercultural understanding. Haussmann proposes a differentiation between "the understanding of language," "the understanding of the course of events," "the understanding of facts, circumstances, and events," and the "understanding of expressions of experiencing and feeling."[6] Let us briefly discuss these aspects. The *understanding of language* demands a number of presuppositions and abilities in terms of "grasping" and "comprehending." One must be able to hear spoken words, read written words, and grasp the literal meaning of a sentence. Thus meaning must be elicited by applying language proficiencies, knowledge of the context of the speech act, and an awareness of the speaker's psychological attitude. Let us apply this to Victor as he explains his actions to his wife and children. Thomas, Mary, and Sophia understand the words he is speaking, but things already begin to get tricky when it comes to the context of the speech act. After all, the children understand the words in a context akin to that of a courtroom (for they still consider their father to be guilty), whereas Victor is probably trying to clear up a misunderstanding instead. As the children look at Victor, they initially interpret his psychological attitude (as the speaker) as audacity. Later they will realize that this was not the case and therefore that the semiotic code they used (interpreting the father's angry reaction as "audacity")

---

[5]Thomas Haussmann, *Erklären und Verstehen: Zur Theorie und Pragmatik der Geschichtswissenschaft* (Frankfurt: Suhrkamp, 1991), 136. It might be appropriate to add the critical remark at this point that by making this distinction, Haussmann is in danger of sweeping the problem of understanding out of the way by definition. In reality, the difference between grasping and understanding is not as clear-cut as Haussmann makes it out to be. Nevertheless, this approach is quite helpful in clarifying the terminology at hand.

[6]Ibid., 137-46. Besides the category of facts, circumstances, and events, Haussmann's differentiation is adopted from that of J. Habermas.

was inappropriate, for Victor's angry reaction was in fact an expression of disappointment that his plan to surprise his wife had been rendered null and void by the children's accidental observation. The anger, as the children also later realize, was thus not a sign of audacity but an expression of frustration.

We have been speaking of understanding in the sense of "grasping" and "comprehending." Now, for the *understanding of language*—with which we are still concerned here—it is not necessary to "understand" in the sense of "to reexperience"; and even if it were possible to relive a situation in some partial sense, it would not guarantee successfully understanding it in and of itself. It would rather be only a *helpful resource*. After all, the person trying to reconstruct the situation ("let me put myself in the subject's place") does so by calling to mind experiences of her own that she *believes* to be analogous to those of the subject. These, however, cannot possibly constitute the object that is to be understood or that was understood. Attempting to put oneself in another person's shoes in order to try to relive what the other person felt is clearly an endeavor subject to limitations. Even if I have experienced what it means to have a headache, I cannot know what that means to someone else, for headaches come in many varieties; and the same thing is true for people's tolerance of suffering, which raises the possibility that some people might describe even slight discomfort as "painful." The upshot is that it is actually impossible to relive something, for there is no entity that could calibrate the genuineness of doing so. After all, I am just as unable to enter the body and spirit of another person as other people are with regard to me.

Let us now proceed to the second object, the *understanding of the course of events*. What goes for the understanding of language also goes for the understanding of the course of events. While it might well be possible to comprehend the actions of a depressed person, for example, it is nevertheless impossible to understand (in the sense of reexperiencing) how a depressed person feels, because a person who is not depressed can hardly begin to imagine how a depressed person feels. In terms of the third possible object, *the understanding of facts, circumstances, and events,* understanding in the sense of empathizing or inwardly reexperiencing is also not possible. These things too must be grasped or comprehended. At most, one might try to reproduce people's motivation or impulses that have been brought about by facts, circumstances, or events or, conversely, that lead to them ("Why on earth would she have done that?").

For the fourth category, of "understandable" objects, though—the *expressions of experiencing and feeling*—empathy can be very helpful. It may help one person to "grasp" what motivated the other. Even in this case, however, empathy does not constitute understanding in and of itself; it is merely a helpful resource toward understanding. In this sense too understanding must be interpreted as "comprehension," not as "empathetic reconstruction." Strictly speaking, the latter is not even possible. To use the example of inter-religious dialogue, it is hardly possible for a Christian to inwardly reexperience what reciting the suras means to a practicing Muslim who has learnt how to recite the Qur'an in the original Arabic by his sixth year of life. To be sure, people could try to find analogies within their own realm of experience, such as their familiarity with the text of Psalm 23 ("The Lord is my Shepherd; I shall not want . . ."), fostered from early childhood on. Yet such analogies are not coterminous with understanding itself (in the sense of inwardly re-creating something); they may simply help one to grasp that these Qur'an texts are obviously very important to the Muslim. This implies that understanding would have been achieved in the sense of grasping the motivational structures in play. Conversely, however, understanding in the sense of empathetic inward re-creation must be recognized as a gradual process, the culmination of which is ultimately unattainable.

We see that when it comes to the concept of understanding, it makes good sense to distinguish between the different objects of understanding. As we do so, we recognize that understanding is possible, at least in the sense of "grasping" and "comprehending," while we conclude that understanding in the sense of "reliving" is ultimately impossible. And so it is: if the text about Victor, Sophia, and the children had indeed been intended in an autobiographical sense, then no one would be able truly to understand Victor, for his biographical experiences (which shaped his view of a mother's role or of women) are unique to him. And the same is true for the vitality he senses in his body, his relationship to Sophia, his contacts to other people, the situation in his family and work at the time, his position in terms of ethics, worldview, or intergenerational relationships, his standing in society, the influence of German culture (whatever that may be) on him, and many other things. Therefore, if understanding in the sense of "reliving" and "re-experiencing" is beyond the limit of understanding, then for methodological purposes we must ask how understanding may be achieved within the realm of possibility. Put differently, how may we perceive semiotic codes as comprehensively as possible? The answer may then enable us to "grasp" and "comprehend" what someone from a different culture means in a particular context.

4

The History of Hermeneutics in the West and Interculturality

An Overview

The examples have shown that when dealing with issues of understanding something that is culturally foreign, it is absolutely essential to be mindful of one's own premises and assumptions. For that reason, we will now outline the essential stages of the Western history of hermeneutics. *This will bring into focus the perspective always presupposed by European observers.* In addition, however, the research area of intercultural theology/mission studies is also concerned with another important aspect: if various forms of expression of the Christian faith are to be discussed here, and if Christians worldwide appeal to the biblical texts to justify their own actions, then the question needs to be: How are the books of the Bible themselves actually to be understood? That means that various regional outcomes of biblical exegesis must be brought into dialogue with one another. They must be investigated to ascertain their fundamental method of biblical exegesis and related to the Christian history of biblical exegesis. The following deliberations outline important turning points of the Western history of biblical exegesis and of hermeneutics in general. At the same time, reference is made repeatedly to the subject of demons.

FROM THE EARLY CHURCH TO THE PHILOSOPHY OF THE ENLIGHTENMENT

It is hard to overestimate the importance of the treatise *De doctrina christiana* by church father Augustine of Hippo (354–430) for the history of Christian hermeneutics. Augustine calls for the life of the exegete to conform to Holy Scripture and furthermore for him to be familiar with its wording.[1] In addition, he calls for a distinction to be made between the literal and the figurative sense, whereby obscure passages of Scripture are to be interpreted from the perspective of those that are clear. One should only resort to an *allegorical interpretation* when unable to discern any meaning pertaining to *ethics* or *dogmatics*.[2] Theologian John Cassian (360–430) built on Augustine's distinction and proceeded to develop the *doctrine of the fourfold interpretation of Scripture*, in which he refined the binary division between the literal and the allegorical sense, resulting in a subdivision of the allegorical sense into didactic, ethical, and eschatological aspects. This hermeneutical approach would remain definitive for the next thousand years.[3]

This is not surprising, for on the one hand, the doctrine of the fourfold interpretation of Scripture is helpful—semiotically speaking—for discovering as many levels of meaning as possible, which leads to the identification of a plethora of possible applications in the contexts of congregational life, sermons, pastoral care, and doctrine. On the other hand, it also opens the floodgates to the tendency to become arbitrary. The contrariness of the biblical witness as an expression of the divine act of revelation is in danger of being lost; when interpreted allegorically, it only serves to confirm what the "exegete" already thinks or would like to hear.

The hermeneutical principles of Reformer Martin Luther (1483–1546) may certainly be interpreted as endorsing this criticism. Luther recognized *Holy Scripture alone (sola Scriptura)* as the basis for his criticism of the church. In the face of an excessive number of ecclesiastical traditions, Luther maintained that only Holy Scripture may serve as the basis for Christian doctrine, not tradition (by which he meant primarily the literature of the church fathers, but also a plethora of traditions from the realm of popular religion that threatened to obscure the essence of the gospel). For all intents and purposes, the Roman Catholic Church had until then allocated equal

---

[1]On the basis of a reliable text in the original language, i.e., Hebrew and Greek, if possible.

[2]The rule of faith (*regula fidei*) is to serve as a summary of the core content of Scripture. It is evident that Augustine takes it for granted that exegetes will struggle with comprehension.

[3]Intensified attempts were made during the age of the Renaissance and humanism (from the fifteenth to the sixteenth centuries) to regain a more literal understanding of biblical statements. These were flanked by efforts to secure more precise Hebrew and Greek original texts vis-à-vis the Latin Vulgate. However, such attempts were limited to the sphere in which ecclesiastical doctrine was formulated.

authority to Holy Scripture and to the traditions of the church. This made it possible to legitimize on the basis of tradition all manner of additional traditions not found in the Bible. In contrast, Luther insisted on the primacy of Holy Scripture.

Luther maintained that Holy Scripture is not to be interpreted by the church, but that *Holy Scripture interprets itself instead.* In concrete terms, this means that the church does not stand above Scripture—in the sense that it possesses the monopoly of interpretation (as the inspired church)— but rather that the church *comes to stand below Scripture,* for it is a church of the Word. The church is and continues to be a creature of the divine Word (*creatura verbi*) and must allow itself to be criticized by the biblical message.[4] But why may Holy Scripture be interpreted in such a relatively simple manner?

There is both an external and an *internal clarity in Holy Scripture.* The interpretation of Scripture—according to Luther—constantly demonstrates the existence of these two kinds of clarity. The *claritas externa,* on the one hand, is the external clarity relating to the wording and the grammar. The *claritas interna,* on the other hand, is the ever-present internal clarity relating to the gospel that may be understood with the help of the Holy Spirit, the true hermeneut (interpreter) of Scripture. The general principles hold that *obscure passages are always to be interpreted from the perspective of those that are clear,* that *writings are to be elucidated within their respective contexts* (for instance, Romans passages within the overall context of Romans), and that the *literal sense is to take precedence.*[5] In so doing, Luther restricted the practice of allegory and pleaded for a philological and historical interpretation of the text, whereby the confessions of the early church are applied as an aid to orientation. The interpretive criterion is the center of Holy Scripture. This center in turn is constituted by "what

---

[4]This calls into question the authority of the magisterium of the church (especially that of the councils), for now *Holy Scripture comes to serve as the norm of the church* (and not vice versa). The principle that "Scripture interprets Scripture" has extensive consequences in terms of church politics, for now the hierarchy of the church is stripped of its putative authority on the basis of Holy Scripture. Criticism of the church is based on Scripture.

[5]According to Luther, God's Word as communicated in Scripture is directed *at human beings in the form of an address* made up of both *law and gospel.* It empowers the *hearers to bear witness for God.* Another important principle is the rule that *the Old Testament is to be understood from the perspective of the New Testament.*

promotes Christ" (*was Christum treibet*). Put differently, the witness to Christ makes up the center of Scripture for both the New Testament and the Old Testament. Yet it must be emphasized that Luther's scriptural hermeneutics was not conceived as a fixed system.[6]

From the eighteenth century onward, the *philosophy of the Enlightenment* paved the way for the increasing prevalence of a rationalistic interpretation of the world. The world came to be perceived as an entity functioning according to certain fundamental laws. Our task is to recognize them. From the perspective of the field of semiotics, Aleida Assmann concludes,

> Since the modern period began, the world has fallen silent.—The world (in the sense of something to be interpreted, deciphered, and understood) is seen as belonging to a prescientific, archaic way of thinking. Modern people are characterized not least by having learned no longer to demand meaning from their environment. They no longer perceive the environment as a book to be read at random. Galilei claimed that the book of nature was written in geometric figures; in contrast, the modern-day natural sciences believe it to be encoded in formulas. In either case, however, access via the path of direct understanding is barred. Within the sphere of the natural sciences and technology, nature has been indifferentized, objectified, demystified, and therefore also semiotically neutralized. The world has lost its power to signify; no one is able to read it anymore, "ever since the *Methodus* of René Descartes and the *Ars Critica* of Jean LeClerc came to serve as the basic primers," as Hamann succinctly put it. The discovery of empirically verifiable laws of nature has made the world safer and more predictable, but also more muted. This new security was achieved in part by the abolition of the signs and wonders which had kept people restless, always ready to pay attention.[7]

Rationalistic thought was thus markedly typified by *anthropocentrism*. Human insight was seen as the basis of knowledge, whereas in contrast, the authority of the established traditions was called into question more and

---

[6]The significance of Luther's scriptural hermeneutics may be seen in the reaction of the Roman Catholic Church to the Reformation event. The Catholic Council of Trent (1545–1563) determined that only the *Latin Bible translation* (the *Vulgate*) constitutes the authoritative canon, not a German translation of Hebrew and Greek original texts. *Scripture (the Bible) and tradition (the church fathers) are placed on the same level.* The interpretive lens continues to comprise the doctrine of the fourfold interpretation of Scripture. This was an effort to fortify the magisterial traditions of the church.

[7]Aleida Assmann, "Geschmack an Zeichen: Homo interpres und die Welt als Text," *Zeitschrift für Semiotik* 12, no. 4 (1990): 359-70, 362, 373.

more. This way of thinking was predetermined by a *critical approach*, namely the refusal to take anything for granted any longer and the insistence on evaluating everything (which is what it literally means "to criticize"). It was hoped that the sought-for increase in insight would lead to a fundamental improvement of the situation. This amounts to the rationalistic thesis of *a fundamental perfectibility of the world.*[8] Scientific thought led to ever more rapid increases in knowledge and understanding, such as Newton's mechanics and a wide variety of other discoveries and inventions. The dominant principle was that of the *experiment*, i.e., an experimental setup allowing for the same calculated results to be reproduced ad libitum. The *idea of the demonstrability* of hypotheses was based on the concept of *repeatability* (and therefore of verifiability) by means of experiments. On the basis of demonstrability, the result was an accentuation of the dimension of experience and of the notion of regularity. From this perspective, extraordinary experiences such as the miracles attested in the biblical writings came to be questioned more and more. This led to the question, If these miracles did not actually happen, to what extent can the biblical writings still be considered to be "true"? A possible solution to this question will now be provided using the example of theologian Ernst Troeltsch.

ANALOGICAL HERMENEUTICS: THE EXAMPLE OF ERNST TROELTSCH

Ernst Troeltsch (1865–1923) was one of the best-known representatives of the so-called history of religions school (*Religionsgeschichtliche Schule*) and of cultural Protestantism. He outlined what he considered to be the indispensable principles of historical-critical methodology.[9] The *principle of criticism* states that Holy Scripture is to be interpreted just like every other work of world literature. It is not just what one derives from tradition that is considered to be true; authoritative truth must be recognized by the individual on the basis of a subjective critical examination. The *principle of analogy* maintains that only those elements in the sources may be considered

---

[8]See Horst Möller, *Vernunft und Kritik: Deutsche Aufklärung im 17. und 18. Jahrhundert* (Frankfurt: Suhrkamp, 1986).
[9]Ernst Troeltsch, "Über historische und dogmatische Methode in der Theologie," in *Zur religiösen Lage: Religionsphilosophie und Ethik*, 2nd ed., vol. 2 of *Gesammelte Schriften* (Tübingen: J. C. B. Mohr, 1922), 729-53.

historically probable that may also be found in the present circumstances of life by analogy (which is not the case for miracles, resurrections, etc.). According to Troeltsch, all historical events are to be considered as fundamentally comparable. Loosely speaking, one might say that what is inconceivable today can also not have happened in the past, no matter what the historical record may claim.

In addition, the *principle of correlation* asserts that all historical events are to be extrapolated from within their contexts. That is to say that it is not legitimate to claim special status for some or other part of history, for instance for some act of God that suddenly, inexplicably, and miraculously interrupts the course of history. Finally, Troeltsch's *principle of personality* allows for something new to take place in history albeit only through the mediation of especially original individual personalities, as was the case for instance with the great founders of religion such as Buddha, Jesus, or Muhammad. Less original people then become their followers by picking up on this newness and imparting it to others. The result is that the ripple effect of their impact may be traced throughout the history of humanity.

Rationalistic apologeticists attempt to explain miracles by means of natural events so as to both defend the historicity of the Bible stories and simultaneously do justice to the scientific worldview. In contrast, Troeltsch takes the radical consequences of the scientific worldview seriously and does not even attempt to explain the miracles of the Bible. On the contrary, he views the impact of the contribution of religious personalities as being transmitted in history *within the consciousness* of the people inspired by them (in movements and religious configurations). In a sense, the attempt to identify the literal meaning and to verify the historicity of the recounted events is abandoned. The actual events are relocated into the inner life of the religious personalities and—in their wake—of the believers. *The analogical aspect of this approach consists in perceiving that which is alien in history in accordance with one's own experiences.* The historical-cultural divide is bridged; the distance is dismissed by means of an allegedly uniform experience of faith. On the one hand, the *difference* in worldview is recognized; on the other hand, however, it is claimed that an *analogy* exists in terms of the perception of faith.

EXISTENTIAL HERMENEUTICS: THE EXAMPLE
OF RUDOLF BULTMANN

Marburg New Testament scholar Rudolf Bultmann (1884–1976) was undoubtedly one of the most significant theologians of the twentieth century. With regard to the interpretation of New Testament texts, Bultmann dedicated himself to answering the question how it is actually possible for Christians to understand these texts today when many of the stories which they tell contradict the modern perception of reality. Bultmann believed that hardly anybody anticipates God to intervene in the world directly any longer. In fact, it is almost impossible to reconcile the world of miracles, angels, spirits, and demons with the scientific worldview, a worldview that seeks to identify reasonable causes for everything that happens. In this modern worldview, everything works according to the principle of cause and effect, which may be described scientifically. But let us allow Rudolf Bultmann to speak for himself. In his book *Jesus Christus und die Mythologie*,[10] he states: "Modern human beings can no longer accept these mythological concepts of heaven and hell; in the scientific conception of the universe, the terminology of 'above' and 'below' has become meaningless, although the idea of the transcendence of God and of evil continues to have meaning." While Bultmann explicitly states that the idea of "evil" continues to have meaning for people, he did believe that people today are unable to associate with the New Testament accounts that speak of Satan and evil demons. Admittedly, some people might conclude that these stories are simply to be rejected as false, possibly to be deleted from the New Testament, or simply to be labeled as anachronistic and ignored along the lines of, "They don't mean anything to anybody anymore!" Bultmann, however, deemed this conclusion to be misguided. He believed, rather, that these stories may be understood today in a figurative or metaphorical sense. A deeper sense appertained to the stories, which was directed at the existential understanding of human beings. Here he adopted the term *existential* from the so-called existential philosophy, especially from that of philosopher Martin Heidegger (1889–1976).

---

[10]Page references are provided with respect to Rudolf Bultmann, *Jesus Christus und die Mythologie: Das Neue Testament im Licht der Bibelkritik*, 5th ed. (Gütersloh, Germany: Gütersloher Verlagshaus, 1980). For an English translation, see *Jesus Christ and Mythology* (1958; repr., London: SCM Press, 2012).

The word *existence* is usually used to refer to nothing more than the presence of things. For instance, in common parlance we say, "That house over there has existed for ages."

Yet in existential philosophy the term *existence* does not refer to the presence of things but rather to the understanding of the existence of the human being.[11] For instance, it concerns the fact that human life is *finite*, ending at death, and that human beings are therefore permanently confronted with such questions as to how to organize their life, or what things or activities are to take precedence, as they ask the question, "How do I allocate my time?" or, "Am I wasting my time when I do this?" According to Heidegger—and Bultmann follows suit in this regard—the existence of the human being means both her *concern* for herself and the question every human being asks herself, "What constitutes me? What constitutes my existence in terms of my uniqueness, my ego?" On the one hand, people have the attitude that they do not want to distinguish themselves from others, that they want to conform to others in the sense of what "people" do, how "people" behave, or what "people" think about a given subject. This is a legitimate need for uniformity (which may provide people with relief). On the other hand, people want to see themselves as unique (at least, that is how it is in the Western world; people from other cultures might feel differently in this regard). The important thing is that Bultmann only wanted to outline the conditions in which people exist; he did not want to say anything about *how* they should live. He saw the answer to the existential question provided in the Jesus stories of the New Testament, in which he recognizes the revelation of God. More on that later.

Now, according to Bultmann, the existential understanding of human beings is fairly similar between all people of all periods. For this reason he sought to circumscribe this supratemporal existential understanding, which is expressed in the New Testament in a very special manner. Bultmann summarizes his interpretation, which he calls his "existential interpretation," as follows:

---

[11]"Existential philosophy attempts to show what it means to exist by distinguishing between the ontology of human beings as 'existence' and the ontology of all other beings not as existence, but merely as *'presence'* (this technical use of the term 'existence' goes back to Kierkegaard). Only human beings are able to have an existence; after all, they alone are historical, i.e. all human beings have their own history. . . . By not answering the question as to the reason for my own existence, existential philosophy relegates my own existence to the domain of my personal responsibility, and in so doing makes me receptive for the Word of the Bible." Bultmann, *Jesus Christus und die Mythologie*, 63-64.

Another example is the idea of Satan and the evil spirits, into whose power human beings have been placed. This conception is based on the experience that even when we ignore all the evil outside of ourselves to which we are subjected, we ourselves are mysterious when it comes to our own actions. Human beings are often driven by passions and not in control of themselves, with the result that indescribable evil bursts forth from them. Here too the conception of Satan as the ruler of the world is an expression of a deeper insight, namely that evil is not only to be found here and there in the world, but that all individual evils represent a single power which ultimately grows out of the actions of human beings to form a spiritual atmosphere which overwhelms everybody. The consequences and effects of our sins become a power which controls us and from which we are unable to liberate ourselves. In our time especially—even though we no longer think mythologically—we speak of demonic powers that rule over history and ruin the political and social life. This kind of language is metaphorical, it is figurative language; but it expresses the insight and the recognition that the evil for which every individual person is responsible has coalesced to become a power which in some strange manner enslaves every member of human society.[12]

Let us note: Bultmann emphasized that although the language of demonic powers is used figuratively, this figurativeness conveys a meaning that may be deconstructed on the level of the understanding of one's own existence. Bultmann stated (1) that human beings are *not* "transparent" to themselves. This concerns the mysteriousness of one's own self. There is something within the human being that he does not experience as a part of himself. "Why did I ever do that?" In the image of possession, this something that is at work "within" the human being is presented as a demon that somewhere, somehow *entered into* the human being.[13] Bultmann went on to state (2) that this "something" is perceived as a power that overwhelms the individual, leading to a disempowerment of the self. The accounts of the New Testament speak of possessed persons being thrown about, falling to the ground, foaming at the mouth, and speaking with a different voice, which

---

[12]Ibid., 18-20. "The talk about the 'acting God' also refers to the events of one's own existence." Ibid., 79.

[13]As far as the nineteenth and twentieth centuries are concerned, one may affirm that this "something" was no longer seen as a demon coming from outside, but—according to Sigmund Freud, for instance—is located in the (repressed) urges of the *id*, which influences the *ego* on an unconscious level.

are all signs of being overwhelmed by evil demons. A modern variant of this feeling of being overwhelmed might be addiction, the compulsion to do something, alcoholism, drug dependency, or illnesses such as kleptomania and others. Furthermore, Bultmann maintained that the condition for its existence (Bultmann users Heidegger's term *existentialia* [*Existentialien*]) is constituted by the circumstance that (3) a power of evil is at work *everywhere*. An atmosphere of evil comes into being that supersedes the individual human being, symbolized perhaps in the New Testament by the image of "Satan and his angels," symbolized perhaps in the twentieth century by fascism, when entire nations fell under the spell of a misanthropic ideology and when many conducted themselves accordingly. Evil is thus understood as a *supraindividual* power. According to Bultmann, this power came into being (4) in a "strange manner," which points to the secretive origin of evil.

Bultmann also referred to the entire procedure of this existential interpretation as "demythologizing." "To demythologize means to deny that the message of Scripture and the church is bound to an old, outmoded worldview."[14] Here Bultmann was concerned with the mass of modern people as a whole, who he wanted to introduce to the enduring meaningfulness of the biblical texts. At the same time, he was aware that not all people share this modern view of the world. "Of course some aspects of primitive thought and superstition continue to survive and to be revived today. Yet it would be a disastrous mistake for the preaching of the church to take notice of whatever had been revived in this way or allied itself with it."[15] Apart from the terms *primitive thought* and *superstition*, which are considered offensive today, it stands out that Bultmann considered these ways of viewing the world to be passé, that he only bargained with a few remnants of this way of thinking and that he perhaps even expected this type of worldview to disappear entirely.

Bultmann believed that the core of the message of the New Testament is that God's Word becomes audible, which summons the human being to

---

[14]Bultmann, *Jesus Christus und die Mythologie*, 37. Elsewhere, Bultmann explains, "*Demythologizing is a hermeneutical method*, i.e. a method of interpretation, a method of exegesis. 'Hermeneutics' is the art of interpretation." Ibid., 50.
[15]Ibid., 39.

entrust himself to God completely.[16] For Bultmann, this Word of God cannot be proven on the basis of history, for only when a human being allows this Word to address him and to grant faith to him, only when he entrusts himself to it completely, *only then can he experience that it is true*:

> The objective historian as such is unable to see that a historical person, Jesus of Nazareth, is the eternal Word, the logos. But it is of all things the mythological description of Jesus Christ in the New Testament that makes it clear that we must see the person and work of Jesus Christ in a way that does not fit into the categories by which the objective historian understands the history of the world, if it be so that the person and work of Christ are to be understood as the divine act of salvation. This is a real paradox. Jesus is a human, historical person from Nazareth in Galilee. His work and his fate play out in world history, and as such they are subject to be investigated by the historian, who may understand them as a part of the ongoing process of history. Nevertheless, such an isolated historical investigation is unable to grasp what God has done in Christ, namely the eschatological event.[17]

This is a seductive theological solution that we do not need to pursue any further at this point. What is important in this context is to respond by asking, "What are we to think about those people who continue to be at odds with Bultmann's presuppositions regarding the validity of a modern worldview? And what are these presuppositions exactly?"

An *initial presupposition* consists in the assumption that a worldview must be inherently consistent, cohesive, without contradiction, and coherent. For Bultmann, this meant an unavoidable choice between either a rational-scientific interpretation of the world or a mythical interpretation of the world. One only allows for the operation of demonstrable causal factors, while the other also counts on the intervention of spiritual and powerful essentialities that miraculously make things happen, such as a demon that brings about someone's death. For Bultmann, it was impossible to have both, causality here

---

[16]"The Word [of God] calls human beings away from their selfishness and the imaginary security which they have constructed for themselves. The Word calls them to God who is beyond the world and beyond scientific thought. At the same time, it calls the human being to his true ego. For the ego of the human being, his inner life, his personal existence, is also located beyond the visible world and beyond rational thought. The Word of God addresses the human being in his personal existence and thereby allows him to be free from the world and from the worry and fear that overwhelm him as soon as he forgets 'what is beyond.'" Ibid., 43.

[17]Ibid., 94-95.

and the miraculous intervention of nonverifiable beings there. Yet many people do not share this presupposition. These are people who sometimes resort to the one (causal) interpretation and sometimes to the other (demonological) depending on the phenomenon. An illness, for example (such as a bladder infection), may then be interpreted as the natural result of temporary hypothermia on one occasion and as the result of bewitchment on another.

Many people sympathize just as little with the *second presupposition*. According to this, phenomena may be interpreted in ways other than either causally or demonologically; it is also possible to employ both interpretive approaches by *combining them with each other*, which Bultmann and others considered impossible. For instance, when I asked the Tanzanian exorcist why it is that approximately 80 percent of those who consider themselves to be bewitched or possessed are women, he answered that this was due to the women being under stress. To my baffled response as to what he meant by that, he provided an explanation that experts would describe as a sociopsychological interpretive approach—that the woman were under stress because of their high workload, their responsibility for the children, or the pressure they experience at home when their husbands, often unemployed themselves, beat or mistreat them. After providing this socioscientific interpretation, to my astonishment the exorcist proceeded to add a demonological one: he explained that their suffering rendered the women weak and vulnerable to evil spirits, for it was now much easier for these to enter the women. Thus in this case a causal explanation is combined with a demonological explanation to form a three-part connection: (1) the women suffer from being overloaded and mistreated = a sociopsychological-causal interpretive approach; (2) the women thereby become weak and vulnerable to "influences" = a medicinal-causal interpretive approach, since a weakening of the body, e.g., of the immune system, verifiably leads to illnesses; (3) the weakening makes it easier for demons to enter the women = a demonological interpretive approach. Contrary to Bultmann's assumptions, people not only resort to a variety of interpretive approaches in everyday life depending on the situation, but also frequently combine both types of interpretive approaches. This shows that Bultmann's approach is too limited to allow for the multiplicity of meaning comprising the statements and behavioral patterns of people of other cultures.

EFFECTIVE-HISTORICAL HERMENEUTICS: THE EXAMPLE OF HANS-GEORG GADAMER

In his book *Wahrheit und Methode,* influential philosopher Hans-Georg Gadamer (1900–2002) directs his attention to the impact of the historical perspective on the process of understanding.[18] This concerns those traditions in which we have always stood.[19] It is imperative to factor into the hermeneutical process the prejudices that are brought to bear in these traditions, because even during the process of understanding itself, meaning is always being tentatively assumed. As Gadamer puts it,

> Anyone wishing to understand a text will always mentally draft a blueprint. He will anticipate a meaning for the whole as soon as an initial meaning presents itself in the text. Conversely, such a meaning only presents itself if one already reads the text with certain expectations of a certain meaning in mind. Understanding what the text says comprises mentally drafting a blueprint which is constantly being revised by the meaning that arises as one continues to make progress.[20]

Gadamer called this process of redrafting and revising the "hermeneutical circle." According to Gadamer, every person stands within a certain horizon. Conversely, every text verbalizes such a horizon. Understanding comes about when the horizons merge. Put differently, understanding is only possible from within the horizon in which I have always stood. Therefore it is not I who understands; rather, my standing within the horizon makes it possible for me to understand, i.e., my participating in the effective history (*Wirkungsgeschichte*) to which I owe my being. Gadamer writes, "Understanding is to be thought of less as a subjective act than as participating in an event of tradition, a process of transmission in which past and present

---

[18]Hans-Georg Gadamer, *Wahrheit und Methode: Grundzüge einer philosophischen Hermeneutik,* 3rd ed. (Tübingen: Mohr, 1972); for an English translation, see *Truth and Method,* rev. ed. (London: Bloomsbury Academic, 2013). See also "Vom Zirkel des Verstehens," in *Variationen,* vol. 4 of *Kleine Schriften* (Tübingen: J. C. B. Mohr, 1977), 54-61. For a criticism of Gadamer's approach, see Thomas Haussmann, *Verstehen und Erklären: Zur Theorie und Pragmatik der Geschichtswissenschaft* (Frankfurt: Suhrkamp, 1991), 148-75.

[19]"In actual fact, history does not belong to us; rather, we belong to it." Gadamer, *Wahrheit und Methode,* 261. At this point one might reply, "Which history, whose history, and who defines how it is to be understood?"

[20]Gadamer, "Vom Zirkel des Verstehens," 56-57.

are constantly mediated."[21] This assertion is reinforced when Gadamer identifies an ontological element within the circle of understanding: the hermeneutical circle is not to be thought of simply as a methodology but as "an
element of the ontological structure of understanding."[22]

At this point some responses suggest themselves. True, it makes sense that
people always introduce their own preconceptions into the process of understanding, but does Gadamer's rehabilitation of effective history not go
too far? How is it possible to attempt to understand when it is the horizon
itself, as it were, that makes understanding possible? How can other cultures
be understood when in this regard one's own cultural and historical perspective functions as a unit, as it were, from which it is impossible to escape?
And what actually takes place when Western texts are read by members of
other cultures? Do people who come from such traditions then already have
an advantage, so to speak, when it comes to the right understanding? And
how can one claim that such an advantage exists when the German culture
of the early Middle Ages (at a time interval of approximately fourteen
hundred years) may well seem as foreign to the Germans of today as do the
cultures of Oceania, for instance? Does Gadamer not assign too simple a
meaning to the concept of tradition? Should understanding not rather be
understood as a type of negotiation in the sense of establishing a consensus,
namely that various agents agree to understand traditions in as similar a
manner as possible?[23]

Gadamer's approach is eminently suited to illustrate how the concept of
understanding and the concept of culture interrelate, i.e., how each concept
should be differentiated from the other in order to do justice to the problem
of intercultural understanding. Gadamer is correct in emphasizing that it is
impossible to circumvent the role of one's own preconceptions in the process
of understanding and that it must therefore be brought to mind, i.e., integrated into the process of understanding. Simply put, whatever it is that I
perceive, I perceive it through that cultural-historical era–specific lens that

---

[21]Gadamer, *Truth and Method*, 302.
[22]Ibid., 305.
[23]See the criticism by Shingo Shimada and Jürgen Straub in "Relationale Hermeneutik im Kontext
    interkulturellen Verstehens: Probleme universalistischer Begriffsbildung in den Sozial- und
    Kulturwissenschaften—erörtert am Beispiel 'Religion,'" *Deutsche Zeitschrift für Philosophie* 47,
    no. 3 (1999): 449-77.

is particular to me. However, Gadamer's approach is based on the concept of a rather uniform culture, which is concealed in the concept of the horizon. Cultural conditions are nowhere near as uniform as Gadamer suggests, because cultures are also constructs in which various agents contend with one another about what forms a part of one's own identity and what does not. Cultures are not as uniform, self-contained, or inescapable as Gadamer's horizon concept indicates. How is a "merging of horizons" possible against such a background? And why should such a merging of horizons be able to guarantee that I have understood someone else when Gadamer does not even allow my counterpart to have a voice? Gadamer's hermeneutics is oriented toward texts that are unable to dispute the claim that they have been understood. Gadamer's thesis that a text has been understood when a merging of horizons has taken place is therefore highly subjective.

This model will inevitably fail as soon as texts are read interculturally (and all the more when biblical texts are read interculturally) because members of different cultures (traditions and religions) might have a completely different understanding. *But this is no longer a case of the merging of horizons; rather, it is a case of an intercultural hermeneutics of textual understanding, in the sense of an understanding of encounters between members of different cultures.* For then it also concerns those *criteria that members of other cultures invoke as a benchmark of correct understanding,* for instance the criterion of *having received the spirit* (i.e., inspiration, which is often the case among Pentecostal Christians), the criterion of *social tolerance* (by analogy, a Confucian proverb states that truth is whatever benefits society), the criterion of *corporeal experience* (whatever brings about healing is true), or the criterion of *meditative awareness training* ("truth" in the sense of the highest possible level of meditative consciousness, which is the case in a number of Buddhist traditions). Gadamer's hermeneutics addresses the important issue of the prejudices that play a role in the process of understanding. This, however, can only prompt us critically to question what Gadamer insinuates "tradition" to be: Who gets to define what tradition is? Which interests are paramount, which traditions are simply invented (in the area of *postcolonial studies,* the *invention of traditions* is an important keyword) and to what purpose, and which traditions are misused against whom?

Cultural-Semiotic Hermeneutics: The Example
of Clifford Geertz

Let us now turn from the area of philosophical hermeneutics to the hermeneutical approach of the US-American ethnologist Clifford Geertz (1926–2006). As an ethnologist, Geertz was of course aware of the problem of the cultural experience of something foreign. He asked the critical question, "What happens to *verstehen* [understanding] when *einfühlen* [empathy] disappears?"[24] Geertz's wording indicates that he was thinking of German discussions on the topic of hermeneutics. He proposed that "understanding" does not mean "putting oneself into someone else's skin [*sic*]," since the phenomenon that is to be understood is not located within people somehow but rather in the public sphere of human interaction. In short, *whatever is culturally meaningful is also public and observable.* Let us consider a few examples.[25]

According to Geertz, it is not necessary to attempt "to get yourself into some inner correspondence of spirit with your informants"; rather, understanding them demands "seeing their experiences within the framework of their own idea of what selfhood is." This becomes possible when the ethnographer attempts to identify and to understand *the experience-near concepts unself-consciously used by the informants in day-to-day life*, concepts that the actors generally use without recognizing "that there are any 'concepts' involved at all" because they take them for granted. This results in a shift in perspective. "The ethnographer does not, and, in my opinion, largely cannot, perceive what his informants perceive. What he perceives, and that uncertainly enough, is what they perceive 'with'—or 'by means of,' or 'through' . . . or whatever the word should be."[26]

The focus is on determining the conceptions that are expressed in social interaction and are therefore "public." "Understanding" therefore consists

---

[24]Clifford Geertz, "'From the Native's Point of View': On the Nature of Anthropological Understanding," *Bulletin of the American Academy of Arts and Sciences* 28, no. 1 (1974): 26-45, quotation drawn from 27; also available online at http://hypergeertz.jku.at/GeertzTexts/Natives_Point.htm (accessed January 21, 2015).

[25]Geertz lists various generic formulations such as "inside" versus "outside" perspectives, or "emic" versus "etic" analyses, but then goes on to state that the issue is whether the ethnographer is describing a culture using experience-near or experience-distant concepts. Experience-near concepts threaten to leave ethnographers lost in the details, whereas the more abstract experience-distant concepts are, the more meaningless they become. See Geertz, "From the Native's Point of View," section one.

[26]Ibid.

not of imagining oneself to be someone else but of searching out and analyzing symbolic forms. Geertz demonstrates this using the example of how people define themselves as "persons," comparing the Western concept of person with those of the Javanese, the Balinese, and the Moroccans. The following holds true for the Western definition:

> The Western conception of the person as a bounded, unique, more or less integrated motivational and cognitive universe, a dynamic center of awareness, emotion, judgment, and action organized into a distinctive whole and set contrastively both against other such wholes and against its social and natural background, is, however incorrigible it may seem to us, a rather peculiar idea within the context of the world's cultures. Rather than attempting to place the experience of others within the framework of such a conception, which is what the extolled "empathy" in fact usually comes down to, understanding them demands setting that conception aside and seeing their experiences within the framework of their own idea of what selfhood is. And for Java, Bali, and Morocco, at least, that idea differs markedly not only from our own but, no less dramatically and no less instructively, from one to the other.[27]

Geertz shows that for the Javanese context, the "sense of what a person is" is lived out in constellations—that are essentially religious—that may crudely be described using contrasting pairs such as "inside" and "outside" or "refined" and "vulgar." Outside, for instance, has "nothing to do with the body as an object"; rather, it refers to a part of human life that is outwardly observable and to which "refined" is to correspond. The word may also be defined to mean "smooth," "exquisite," and "pure." "Inside" has nothing to do with the conception of a "soul" or anything of the sort. It does not refer "to a bounded unit at all, but to the emotional life of human beings taken generally. It consists of the fuzzy, shifting flow of subjective feeling perceived directly in all its phenomenological immediacy but considered to be, at its roots at least, identical across all individuals, whose individuality it thus effaces."[28] Correspondingly, within this cultural context—to put it in simplified terms and to focus on just one single aspect—"person" refers not to an encapsulated whole but to the realization of what it means to be "a human being." It does not concern individuality but rather the aspiration

---

[27]Ibid.
[28]Ibid., section two.

to correspond to what "being human" means, which in turn manifests itself in the most even balance of feelings and actions.

As he attempts to define what "person" may mean, Geertz notes some other marked differences in connection with attributive appellations that he observes in the area of what is today Morocco. Here a person is not designated with a definitive name; rather, names are used relationally. That is to say, a person is observed only within the context of her relationship to some possible "we-group."

> A man I knew who lived in Sefrou and worked in Fez but came from the Beni Yazgha tribe settled nearby—and from the Hima lineage of the Taghut subfraction of the Wulad Ben Ydir fraction within it—was known as a Sefroui to his work fellows in Fez, a Yazghi to all of us non-Yazghis in Sefrou, an Ydiri to other Beni Yazghas around, except for those who were themselves of the Wulad Ben Ydir fraction, who called him a Taghuti. As for the few other Taghutis, they called him a Himiwi.[29]

Thus here identities that are publicly assessed are always determined with regard to the context and not by themselves, i.e., as autonomous subjects.

There are other conceptions of subjectivity, for instance among certain tribes that hold that people "share their fates with *doppelgänger* beasts" (such as the man who has a bat as his totem animal), such that the fates of both are linked together in a kind of reciprocal connection. Geertz believed that it was important for these forms of personhood to be accessible via the public use of symbols. "Accounts of other peoples' subjectivities can be built up without recourse to pretensions to more-than-normal capacities for ego effacement and fellow feeling."[30] Geertz uses this terminology to distinguish between understanding in the sense of "empathizing" on the one hand and understanding in the sense of "comprehending" on the other. Even though it has been proven that empathy is ultimately impossible, it is very well possible to comprehend why or how a person or a group acts. Accordingly, at issue here is the comprehension of events, actions, and motives.

This makes it clear that the hermeneutics espoused by Geertz is primarily oriented *toward the informants* and to the manner in which they themselves

---

[29]Ibid., section four.
[30]Ibid., section five.

describe their own reality, which concepts they use to do so, etc. This information is accessible in the public use of signs (language, rituals, behavioral patterns, etc.). In order to describe it, it is not necessary to attempt to identify any allegedly covert fundamental laws; rather, the task is to determine certain regularities by means of "thick description." The interpretation of a culture thus takes place to the greatest possible extent within its own forms of expression; what it means to members of other cultures is explained in a tentative and cautious manner. We will later need to elaborate on Geertz's concept of culture as well as on the criticism leveled against his approach from a postcolonial perspective. At this point it will suffice to point out, first, that Geertz understood cultures as relatively homogenous units; second, that the political dimension hardly played any role in this approach; and third, that he paid little attention to the manner in which cultural signs may be misused for purposes of ideological manipulation.

IDEOLOGY-CRITICAL CULTURAL HERMENEUTICS: ROLAND BARTHES, THE COMAROFFS, AND ERVING GOFFMAN

As early as 1957, in his book *Mythologies*, French literary scholar Roland Barthes (1915–1980) presented an interpretation of culture from a semiotic perspective.[31] Here Barthes distinguishes between object language and metalanguage, observing that objects that appear to be quite ordinary at first glance also convey additional messages or may be understood to do so potentially. Barthes defines a myth as something that lends to things the appearance of ordinariness in such a way that it seems inherent. As Barthes puts it, "Here we have arrived at the actual principle of myth: It transforms history [i.e., an accidental occurrence or object] into nature [i.e., a given having an appearance of necessity]."[32] *When signs function as myth, Barthes sees in them a manipulative aspect, something that distorts and must be*

---

[31]Roland Barthes, *Mythologies* (Paris: Éditions du Seuil, 1957); for an English translation, see *Mythologies: The Complete Edition, in a New Translation*, trans. Richard Howard and Annette Lavers (New York: Hill and Wang, 2012); for a German translation, see *Mythen des Alltags* (Frankfurt: Suhrkamp, 1964). Page references will be provided here with respect to the German translation.

[32]Barthes, *Mythen des Alltags*, 113. For more on Barthes, see Dirk Quadflieg, "Roland Barthes: Mythologe der Massenkultur und Argonaut der Semiologie," in Stephan Moebius and Dirk Quadflieg, eds., *Kultur: Theorien der Gegenwart* (Wiesbaden, Germany: Verlag für Sozialwissenschaft, 2006), 17-29.

criticized. Such criticism should take place in one of two ways. The first is personally to make others aware of the distinction between the two levels of object language and metalanguage along with personally cultivating as myth-free a way of speaking as possible. The second is to use poetic language to undermine the seemingly customary meaning allocated to things. For when language is no longer used for the purpose of depicting reality, it will prove resistant to any attempts at disambiguation.

The analyses of Roland Barthes may be elucidated using a simple example. In the 1950s, a cover page of the magazine *Paris-Match* featured the following ensemble of signs in a photo that seemed perfectly ordinary: a *Tricolore*, and in front of it a dark-skinned French soldier.[33] According to Barthes, in terms of object language the only features serving as signs are the things themselves, i.e., the dark-skinned soldier and the flag behind him, or more precisely, the flag of the French nation. Yet it is within the specific situation (the phase of decolonization) that the significance of the image becomes clear. First, it illustrates the greatness of the French nation; second, the corresponding pride of its citizens, and to be even more precise, of its citizens who—and this is the third point—are recognized as citizens irrespective of their skin color. Even though the picture seems to signify something very ordinary, it has an additional, greater meaning; something more is being suggested and in a way that is almost no longer recognizable for what it truly is, namely—we might paraphrase Barthes here—a kind of manipulation. In this case, the manipulation consists of the suggestion that the perpetuation of the French colonial empire is justifiable. The picture is thus understood in the context of French colonial ideology.

In his early works, Barthes interprets many objects belonging to day-to-day culture, such as car brands, women's clothing, and others, examining them with a view to identifying their unique significance, i.e., that which these objects may be observed to signify within a societal context in his opinion. Semiotics for the purpose of cultural criticism. In the world of today this type of cultural criticism might apply especially to the products of advertising agencies, for instance when a certain product is very obviously designed to correspond to the way of life or to the desires of a very

---

[33]Barthes, *Mythen des Alltags*, 95.

particular consumer group. Yet the criticism also applies to national symbols, such as historical events that are stylized as expressions of a nation's character or its historic mission. To sum up, with respect to a cultural-semiotic hermeneutics à la Clifford Geertz, Roland Barthes points out that signs may well be imbued with an excess of meaning intended for manipulative purposes.

Meanwhile, the downside to this approach may be demonstrated using an example from the area of postcolonial studies. After all, it is easily possible for this approach to degenerate into a hermeneutics of arbitrariness. The example: In the two-volume work *Of Revelation and Revolution: Christianity, Colonialism, and Consciousness in South Africa*, authors John Comaroff and Jean Comaroff attempt to describe various mentalities in the context of European colonialism and Christian missions.[34] They do so by applying a hermeneutics of suspicion to the sources: What is *not* being said in the sources? What is being glossed over? Are there intimations or hints at what is *really* going on or at the mindsets *behind the texts*? This work undoubtedly opens up new perspectives, yet it has also elicited very critical responses, especially with regard to the way in which it handles source materials. Irving Hexham has provided a detailed refutation of the work, pointing out how the Comaroffs—in his opinion—distort and misuse historical sources.[35] He claims, for instance, that the Comaroffs use the sources to extrapolate a missionary ideology, attempting to validate it using the examples of *health* and *life in the home*, or using themes like *the body, the perception of the body, sexuality,* and *conceptions of order* and *of the controllability of the world* in general.

---

[34]John Comaroff and Jean Comaroff, *Of Revelation and Revolution: Christianity, Colonialism, and Consciousness in South Africa*, 2 vols. (Chicago: Chicago University Press, 1991–1997).

[35]Irving Hexham, "Violating Missionary Culture: The Tyranny of Theory and the Ethics of Historical Research," in Ulrich van der Heyden and Jürgen Becker, eds., *Mission und Gewalt* (Stuttgart, Germany: Franz Steiner Verlag, 2000), 193-206. The list of critical appraisals also includes Rodney Elphick, "South African Christianity and the Historian's Vision," *South African Historical Journal* 26 (1992): 182-90, especially 186-87. Elphick criticizes that the Comaroffs simply left out important theological themes of the discourse between missionaries and the indigenous population, themes that undoubtedly had an effective history of their own. Another example is Clifton C. Crais, "South Africa and the Pitfalls of Postmodernism," *South African Historical Journal* 31 (1994): 274-79, especially 278-79. Crais concludes "that the Comaroffs' deconstruction of these texts becomes synonymous with the consciousness of the colonized. There is thus a powerful and problematic conflation that defers an engagement with other sites, other texts, that may reveal a past that is more open-ended, more disjointed, and more interesting" (278).

It will suffice to adduce just one example at this point. The Comaroffs refer at one point to an observation by missionary Robert Moffat (1795–1883) regarding the health implications of the African custom of mothers carrying their children in leather pouches on their backs.[36] In this regard, Moffat writes that the children wet the pouches. Because of the cold wind, the children frequently contracted pneumonia. Meanwhile, the Comaroffs interpret Moffat's observation first as an expression of his belief that the physical proximity between mother and child is a source of illness, and second as an example of typical European "social engineering," addressing things in the interests of order, health, and cleanliness.[37] Moffat is thus stylized as an example of an allegedly widespread colonial perception, of a consciousness formation that ostensibly had serious consequences for the colonial territories. In contrast, South African Irving Hexham finds that the Comaroffs are obviously unable to comprehend the harsh realities of rural life in Africa, and that from a medicinal perspective, Moffat's observation is accurate. This means, as Hexham infers, that the Comaroffs frequently take source materials (like the Moffat quotation in this instance) out of their context, alter them, or reinterpret them, thereby pressing them into service as warrants for a(n otherwise not explicitly apparent) "missionary/colonial ideology" of the nineteenth century. The source material is mined to provide material with which to shore up a preexisting theory ("colonial ideology"). So much for the example.

From the perspective of cultural hermeneutics, the bottom line is that it is assuredly correct that cultural symbolisms may be employed—either consciously or unconsciously—for manipulative purposes, as Roland Barthes's example indicates. However, if we apply Barthes's distinction between signs of the first order and signs of the second order to the Comaroffs, then it becomes apparent that a hermeneutics of arbitrariness may easily insinuate itself into the analysis. After all, in this example the Comaroffs read signs of

---

[36]Moffat served as a missionary for the London Missionary Society in southern Africa from 1816 onwards.

[37]With regard to Moffat's observations in this regard, the Comaroffs write, "The warm closeness of an African mother's body did not protect or nurture. It was a source of sickness. The management of mundane bodily functions in the name of order, health, and cleanliness was a major feature of European social engineering throughout the nineteenth century—both at home and abroad." Comaroff and Comaroff, *Of Revelation*, 2:336.

the first order (Moffat speaks about African children wetting the leather pouches in which they are being carried on the backs of their mothers and supposes that wetness and cold often lead to the contraction of pneumonia) and interpret them under the suspicion that they contain meaning of the second order (which would mean that Moffat represents a colonial European ideology fixated on cleanliness and order, that he is therefore unable to tolerate the physical proximity between mother and child that he observes, and that he interprets it by resorting to a pseudo-medicinal explanation that might well also serve to express his intent to put a stop to such African cultural practices). The only problem is that it is difficult to attest this interpretation of the Comaroffs using historical sources and cultural practices. There is an acute danger that this alleged colonial ideology (as claimed by the Comaroffs) could be read into all kinds of possible contexts and statements. The attempt at an ideology-critical hermeneutics thus falls prey to the suspicion of being ideological itself.

The works of Erving Goffman (1922–1982) take the same line as the approach of Roland Barthes. Goffman asserts that the interaction between people depends on the manner in which a person seeks to control the image she presents of herself. When interacting with others, people resort to a façade, suppressing those aspects of their "self" that might prove deleterious in light of the particular role expectations of others.[38] In other words—to apply the terminology of the theater—something is being performed "front stage" while something else is being concealed "backstage." Something similar happens in situations where doctors pretend to be unfazed by diagnoses in front of the patients but express their apprehension as soon as they are among themselves. Now, such stylizations usually take place in what Goffman calls "ensembles," i.e., specific associations of people with something in common (e.g., career, role, or position). Here the object is to control the outward impression, which in turn implies maintaining inward secrecy of certain aspects. In contradistinction to Roland Barthes's approach, that of Goffman may be bolstered from the perspective of cultural semiotics by

---

[38]See Erving Goffman, *Frame Analysis: An Essay on the Organization of Experience* (New York: Harper & Row, 1974); Goffman, "The Interaction Order," *American Sociological Review* 48, no. 1 (1983): 1-17. See also Heinz-Günter Vester, "Erving Goffman's Sociology as a Semiotics of Postmodern Culture," *Semiotica* 76, nos. 3-4 (1989): 191-203.

inquiring after those culture-specific forms of expression that manifest something akin to secrecy (what is to be considered secret, by whom, and in what way? Why and for what purpose is it being kept secret?).

Goffman went on to develop a more progressive theory of "frames," in which he points out that human interactions must initially be understood within "primary frameworks," while there might also be other frames modifying the primary framework in question. It is therefore only possible to understand an interaction correctly when it is clear whether it concerns a primary framework or one that has been modified, such as a joke, a game, a ritual, or a trick. Semiotically speaking, the aim is to understand phenomena as signs that indicate such an alteration. For instance, when does an ordinary frame become a more playful frame? And what are the signs within a certain culture that indicate that an alteration has taken place? Accordingly, signs do not just exist on the level of the signified but also on the level of a second order, which signifies how the signified is to be understood. Goffman distinguishes between five frameworks that modify the original frame: *pretending-as-if, competition, ceremony, putting-something-into-a-different-context*, and *special types*.

The joke may serve as a touchstone for how well someone is able to understand a different culture, for here it becomes clear that there are not just certain signs to be understood per se but that in addition those semiotic codes are also being transmitted that indicate that the phenomenon in question is to be understood within a different frame—i.e., as a joke. Such signs that indicate a different frame may be very subtle, such as a minor change in the tone of voice to indicate overtones of irony, of imitating someone else, and the like.

Our deliberations have indicated how helpful a cultural-semiotic hermeneutics may be to shed light on actions and thought that are foreign to us. This always presupposes the existence of a considerable variety of cultural formations, however, one that needs to be negotiated hermeneutically. The following two sections will speak to how this variety is precisely to be understood, how it comes about, how it is maintained, and how cultural formations and claims to power relate to each other.

5

Globalization and Interculturality

Is "Foreignness" Dying Out?

Cultural scientist Klaus P. Hansen recently mused about whether, in an age of globalization, cultural foreignness is doomed to extinction.[1] Is it not true that cultural paradigms are becoming more and more analogous worldwide? In many industrialized nations, the product range of brand-name clothing is very similar; it goes without saying that whether in central Africa, Greenland, or Brazil, mobile phones have become just one more facet of everyday life; computer networks are globally interconnected, along with the corresponding jargon and the specialized codes, which are usually exchanged in English. Seen against this backdrop, what continues to be so special about foreignness? Besides, media like television and the Internet constantly feature all kinds of lifestyles and cultural practices, and one click of a mouse button can bring up the—at least from one's own perspective—quirkiest and most unique elements of other cultures, be it in the form of images, texts, or video clips. It is not difficult for instance to find YouTube videos of miraculous healings, of various forms of Buddhist meditation, of recordings of Muslim pilgrimage festivals in Egypt, or of séances by followers of Umbanda in Brazil. But when does this lead to alienation anymore? When does foreignness still come across as something incomprehensible, distant, enchanting, enticing, frightening, or mystifying? And is this actually the true concern of intercultural hermeneutics?

The exotic side of foreignness is always predicated on some kind of "experiential thrill." But what happens when role players in the media vie for the attention of media users in so many different ways that this attention,

---

[1]Klaus P. Hansen, *Kultur und Kulturwissenschaft: Eine Einführung*, 3rd ed. (Tübingen: A. Francke Verlag, 2003), 334.

this experiential thrill, becomes the focus of a kind of continuous media barrage as the sole advertising strategy? Does this not lead to the diminishing of these effects? Does the thrill not give way to oversaturation and fatigue at some point? Does the permanent inundation of stimuli not lead to a tendency by the recipients to isolate themselves? How is it then still possible to discern between foreignness and the attempt by the media to resort to alienation in order to attract attention?

In this context, it is not only the issue of the media that is significant but also the issue of boundaries. Do people notice foreignness especially at the boundaries between peoples and ethnicities, i.e., where different cultures encounter one another? Our own personal vacation experiences certainly seem to suggest this as we cross the border and enter a country where we do not understand the language. Here foreignness is initially perceived in the sense of incomprehensibility, for the people say something that is unintelligible to somebody who does not speak the language. The same will probably be true in terms of the customs and conventions of the people and of their way of doing things. Europeans may sense feelings of foreignness every time they see angry protesters from the Arabic world in the news bearing protest signs featuring slogans written in Arabic lettering. The lack of understanding causes uncertainty and may easily lead to fear.

In this regard, however, some might object that in recent decades this kind of foreignness has seemed to diminish more and more. In almost every country of the world, essential information is presented in linguistic patterns that are globally familiar. These include not only Arabic numbers and English technical terms, but also certain pictograms as may be found on traffic signs as well as the symbols of global corporations and their products, for instance large pharmaceutical concerns, mobile phone companies, automobile companies, food producers, and many others. This makes it possible to have a general knowledge that also ensures the ability to communicate to a great extent in "foreign" countries. So again, we ask the question: Is foreignness on the way out? Put differently, what is the actual "locus" of foreignness?

WHAT IS THE "LOCUS" OF FOREIGNNESS?

That there is no such thing as foreignness (whatever that may be) "per se," i.e., in an abstract sense, soon becomes evident when we consider that the experience of foreignness is always something that affects us personally. Something is foreign *to me*. This makes foreignness a relational term, for the experience of foreignness only takes place within the framework of relationships. Now, one might be tempted summarily to relegate the problem of foreignness to the sphere of the individual and to claim that the experience of foreignness is contingent on the psychological makeup of a given individual. Loosely speaking, this would mean that people who are easily frightened constantly experience foreignness, while those who are fearless and have "nerves of steel" weather all kinds of encounters with ease and find them "interesting" without perceiving them as foreign in the sense of "frightening" or "enchanting." One could also attempt to explain foreignness on a psychological level and see it as a fundamentally human way of perceiving one's surroundings, one fueled by people's unconscious fears that arise from the interplay of specific events or encounters and are perceived as a fear of the unknown, whereas in actual fact—and this is important—it arises from one's own unconscious self. According to this interpretation there is no such thing as foreignness in the outward sense; rather, foreignness is the foreignness within me.[2]

However, individualistic interpretations are unable to account for the circumstance that people experience something like the perception of foreignness collectively. It is *people groups* who experience other people groups as foreign or at least as different. Yet in the transition from contacts by individuals to collective contacts, paradigms of perception undergo a radical change, as research on stereotypes has demonstrated.[3] Thus if foreignness is not conceived as dependent on a person's character structure nor relegated to the psyche almost as a fundamental aspect of human existence, then foreignness must be seen as a kind of human action. Foreignness then comes about as a result of action—to be precise, either the action of perceiving or of portraying. Let us proceed to review some of the insights gained from the research on stereotypes.

---

[2]Sigmund Freud, "Das Unheimliche," in *Werke aus den Jahren 1917–1920*, vol. 12 of *Gesammelte Werke: Chronologisch geordnet*, ed. Anna Freud and Marie Bonaparte (London: Imago, 1947), 229-68. For an ethnopsychological perspective, see Mario Erdheim, "Die Repräsentanz des Fremden: Zur Psychogenese der Imagines von Kultur und Familie," in *Psychoanalyse und Unbewußtheit in der Kultur* (Frankfurt: Suhrkamp, 1988), 237-51.
[3]The standard work on research on stereotypes continues to be Henri Tajfel, *Human Groups & Social Categories: Studies in Social Psychology* (Cambridge: Cambridge University Press, 1981).

THE CONSTRUCTION OF STEREOTYPES AND
AN "INTENTIONAL" FOREIGNNESS

The term *stereotype* implies that a group of people is bracketed together by at least one common characteristic. In and of itself, this is a very normal procedure. According to Aristotle, every classification entails one general common denominator and one specification. We can classify the population of Germany as men and women, as north Germans and south Germans, as academics or tradespersons, and in many other ways. Such a subdivision becomes a stereotype when certain characteristics are allocated to a group. Whereas when individuals come into contact, one person will perceive the other from a variety of reference points, this does not hold true for stereotypes.[4] I know my old friend or my neighbor; I know his name, his character, how he relates to society, his temperament, his characteristics, his foibles, his history, his taste, perhaps his wishes, goals, hopes, and many other things besides. When it comes to stereotypes, however, a de-individualization takes place, which means that groups of people are classified and perceived according to only a very few characteristics. Frequently, the knowledge in question is not gained from or verified by personal experience so much as that it is rather simply established within one's own collective environment. For example, Germans almost always associate the Netherlands with aspects like the ocean, flat land, bicycles, windmills, tulips, cheese, and perhaps Vincent van Gogh, even though many Netherlanders might prefer to vacation in the mountains, not necessarily like cheese, prefer roses, and not know van Gogh. In such cases the individual disappears behind the stereotype.

When it comes to stereotypes, along with the de-individualization there is a certain reduction that takes place: consequently, people from other nations and ethnicities or members of other people groups are perceived only according to a few certain characteristics, while other characteristics are overlooked. This is precisely what makes stereotypes so attractive in terms of political misuse. As a result, one's perception of the world becomes oversimplified. The world that might otherwise seem so confusing becomes simpler, clearer, and more manageable when stereotypes are applied. Stereotypes

---

[4]See Hansen, *Kultur und Kulturwissenschaft*, 322ff.

provide relief by (seemingly, or at least subjectively) simplifying the mass of reference points. In each case, the otherness of the others as defined by a handful of characteristics makes them identifiable, delimitable, and in a certain sense "easier to handle." On this basis people proceed to distinguish between what is familiar and what is foreign, between what is normal and what is abnormal, and between what is right and what is wrong.

In other words, stereotypes are used either to define foreignness on the basis of certain empirical values or to stylize something as foreign and thereby to create the concept of foreignness. In this regard, power interests usually play a very significant role, since these kinds of allocation practices are frequently used to justify one's own actions. Let us consider an inter-religious example from the era of colonialism. This example points to an "intellectual climate" that determined the relationship between European powers and colonial territories for more than a century in various manifestations. This intellectual climate served as a point of reference for the people and organizations operating on an intercultural level during this time, one with which they either agreed or disagreed.

DRAWING UP INTERCULTURAL BORDERS: AN EXAMPLE FROM THE COLONIAL PERIOD

The history of European colonialism is usually divided into the period of early colonialism, the colonial period of the nineteenth century, and finally the age of imperialism that followed the Berlin-Congo conference (1884/85). Imperialism means that the individual European powers, most especially Great Britain, France, Germany, Belgium, and Italy, attempted to annex as many territories as possible. In the wake of these developments, toward the end of the nineteenth and at the beginning of the twentieth centuries, many territories with majority Muslim populations fell under the influence of the colonial powers. The following example is selected from this realm. It is significant that in this case, as in others, the exertion of colonial influence was justified especially using arguments referring to the cultural condition and state of civilization of other religions. One's own culture and civilization were portrayed as superior in every respect, in terms of science, technology, military, civilization, and ethics. In contradistinction, the blame for the backwardness of the territories that had now become colonial possessions was placed squarely on the other religions. Thus what served to justify the annexation was Europe's civilizing mission, in which the Christian religion did not necessarily need to play a specific role, yet in which the denigration of other cultures and religions provided an essential rationale. In the discourse that will be outlined in the following example, it will be shown that stereotypes were used that have remained definitive for many people right up until the present.

EUROPEAN CIVILIZATION AND THE ISLAMIC WORLD: THE BATTLE FOR RATIONALITY

Around the year 1870, a growing number of people began to claim that the responsibility for Europe's scientific and technological discoveries was Europe's alone. They asserted that ideas of progress, the ability to develop, modernity, and scientificity were to be found only in Europe. In contrast, other cultures and religions, including those of the Islamic world, were generally seen as retrogressive. In the case of the Islamic world, it was believed that the basis for this retrogressivity was to be found in the Islamic religion. One famous representative of this movement was French philosopher Ernest Renan (1823–1892). In his 1883 presentation "L'Islam et la science," Renan attempted to demonstrate that Islam is characterized by hostility towards science.[5] He claimed that the idea of progress was unthinkable in Islam. Renan pointed out that science and religion do not necessarily relate to each other as polar opposites; however, he stated, it becomes problematic when either side crosses the boundaries. Yet whereas a new approach had taken place in Christianity since the Reformation, Islam had not reached this point as of yet.

Renan subjects the "Arabic period" of science to a closer scrutiny, posing the question as to whether it is even legitimate to speak of "Arabic" philosophy, art, and science or of "Mussulman" science and civilization. He concludes that as far as the first century of Islam is concerned, this is not the case, whereas a certain amount of latitude was conceded to the pursuit of

---

[5]Ernest Renan, *Der Islam und die Wissenschaft*, ed. Klaus H. Fischer (Schutterwald/Baden, Germany: Wissenschaftlicher Verlag, 1997). For the French original, see *L'Islam et la Science* (1883; repr., Apt, France: L'Archange Minotaure, 2007). See also Albert Hourani, *Arabic Thought in the Liberal Age: 1798–1939* (Oxford: Oxford University Press, 1962), 120-23.

philosophy and science from the rule of the Abbasids (after 750 CE) onward. However, according to Renan, these scientific pursuits were fueled almost exclusively by Greek philosophy and education; the science was passed on for the most part by Christians. Renan believed that Islam played no part in the scientific spirit of this period per se.[6]

According to Renan, from a structural perspective it was the idea of the "dogma that controls society" that put up the greatest resistance to progress.[7] Whereas during the first centuries of Islam, science and philosophy were merely tolerated, they would later be persecuted. On the whole, Islam was deleterious not only to human reason, but also to itself. "By killing science, it killed itself; it condemned itself to an existence of deplorable inferiority in the world."[8] Renan asserted that this was evident in the mindset of many Muslims up to the present.

> To be sure, the Mussulman is essentially characterized by the hate of science and by the conviction that research is useless, frivolous, indeed almost godless, that science such as the science of history is an infringement of the attributes of God, because by concerning itself with the times that preceded Islam, it makes it possible to fall back into the errors that had previously been overcome.[9]

It is easy to recognize that Renan works with a whole range of stereotypes that he seeks to verify historically. The following arguments are foundational both for Renan and for other authors: (a) the Islamic faith is opposed to science, which led to a restriction on scientific research and, concomitantly, on technological progress; (b) Islamic law is considered immutable, and societal development is restricted as a result; and (c) the piety of folk religion

---

[6]"That beautiful scientific movement was nothing but the work of Parsees, Christians, Jews, Harranians, Ishmaelites, and those Muhammadans who were inwardly disgusted by their own religion. It only met with curses on the part of orthodox Muslims." Renan, *Der Islam und die Wissenschaft*, 28.

[7]The claim of rigidity was also made in the field of mission studies—for instance by Gustav Warneck (who G. Rosenkranz called the "father of German mission studies")—to warrant the assertion that in comparison to Christianity, Islam is no "world religion" in the true sense since it possesses no cultural "malleability" (*Anschmiegsamkeit*). Buddhism and Islam are therefore unable to become world religions, for the "Islamic peoples are condemned to rigidification by the religious legalism of their institutions, and Buddhism has only been able to attract passive populaces that had been deprived of their vitality under the pressure of Asiatic despotism." Gustav Warneck, *Evangelische Missionslehre*, 2nd ed. (Gotha, Germany: F. A. Perthes, 1897), 1:81.

[8]Renan, *Der Islam und die Wissenschaft*, 34.

[9]Ibid., 33.

fosters a dependency on religious authorities, which inhibits self-determined actions, which in turn impedes the personal development of the individual into a self-determined personality. It should be expressly noted that famous sociologist Max Weber (1864–1920) advocated similar arguments;[10] the ensuing thought progression may be traced right up to the present, for instance in the work of Bassam Tibi (b. 1944).[11] In the 1980s and 1990s especially, the term *fundamentalism* was heavily debated; many authors tended on the basis of similar stereotypes to accuse Islam, as in "the one Islam" (whatever that may be), of a propensity to fundamentalism. But let us return to the debate of the nineteenth century.

The arguments that have been cited are similar to other interpretive rationales that have been employed within Europe, not with reference to "the one Islam" but rather by Protestant theologians over against Roman Catholic Christianity. Thus representatives of the so-called cultural Protestantism (*Kulturprotestantismus*) such as German theologian Ernst Troeltsch[12] claim that European civilization developed especially on the basis of the Protestant interpretation of the world. In Protestantism it is not the hierarchy of the church and the community that regulate life qua an authority and a regulating power; rather, it is the immediate relationship between the individual believer and God that counts. According to Troeltsch, the Protestant believer is not subject to any law or hierarchy, only to God and his conscience. Besides, since God is regarded as the creator and the world as the creation, it is permissible to study the world on a scientific basis, for in this respect a belief in miracles is immaterial to the interpretation. Thus here one may see paradigms of thought similar to those used with regard to Islam above: (a) the Protestant faith views the world as God's creation, which is

---

[10]For his famous 1904/1905 treatise, see Max Weber, "Die protestantische Ethik und der Geist des Kapitalismus," in *Gesammelte Aufsätze zur Religionssoziologie*, 9th ed. (Tübingen: J. C. B. Mohr, 1988), 1:17-206 (with reference to Islam, see 102). For an English translation, see *The Protestant Ethic and the Spirit of Capitalism: With Other Writings on the Rise of the West*, trans. Stephen Kalberg, 4th ed. (Oxford: Oxford University Press, 2008). See also Toby E. Huff and Wolfgang Schluchter, eds., *Max Weber and Islam* (New Brunswick: Transaction Publishers, 1999); Georg Stauth, *Islam und westlicher Rationalismus* (Frankfurt: Campus, 1993).

[11]Bassam Tibi, *Islam and the Cultural Accommodation of Social Change* (Boulder, CO: Westview Press, 1990). According to Tibi, the development of Islam came to an end at the point of "semi-modernity."

[12]For more on Troeltsch, see Henning Wrogemann, *Mission und Religion in der Systematischen Theologie der Gegenwart* (Göttingen: Vandenhoeck & Ruprecht, 1997), 37-57.

scientifically analyzable. There is no need for miracles (this is directed at the popular piety of Roman Catholics with their veneration of the saints, belief in miracles, etc.); (b) the Protestant faith does not need any ecclesiastical hierarchy and legislation and is thus able to permit, promote, and shape societal change; (c) the Protestant faith is responsible only to God and the conscience and is therefore independent of any ecclesiastical-religious paternalism, which is conducive to the development of an autonomous personality. Here it becomes clear that essential elements of the philosophy of rationalism—autonomous thought, a critical mind, a moral stance, scientificity—are ascribed to essential characteristics of the Protestant faith.

Let us recap: Paradigms of argumentation that Renan and others view as specifically European and therefore as deriving from the Judeo-Christian tradition, and that they bring to bear against that which they call the Islamic religion, are simultaneously applied by the Protestant side in the sphere of inner-European and inner-Christian disputes against Roman Catholic and Orthodox Christianity. A system of binary opposites comes into being: a faith in God and in miracles that is opposed to science versus a faith that favors science; rigid religious laws or a rigid religious hierarchy versus being responsible only to God or one's own conscience; and surrendering to foreign authorities versus critical autonomous thought.

As the disputes went on, the respective opponents picked up on these arguments and in a sense began to mirror them. Case in point is Muslim reformer Muhammad Abduh (1849–1905). It is hardly possible to over-estimate Abduh's contribution to the Islamic development of the late nineteenth and early twentieth centuries: he worked as a scholar, educator, mufti, theologian, and reformer.[13] In his youth he had some negative experiences with the traditional education system of the Qur'anic schools and *madrasas*. Thus it was no accident that he made the reform of the educational system his life's work. How did Abduh explain the weakness of the Islamic world? He assumed that this weakness was to be ascribed to both external factors

---

[13]See especially Gunnar Hasselblatt, "Herkunft und Auswirkungen der Apologetik Muhammed ʿAbduh's (1849–1905), untersucht an seiner Schrift: Islam und Christentum im Verhältnis zu Wissenschaft und Zivilisation" (PhD diss., University of Göttingen, 1968); Yvonne Haddad, "Muhammad Abduh," in ʿAlī Rāhnamā, ed., *Pioneers of Islamic Revival* (London: Zed Books, 1994), 30-63, on 30; Kenneth Cragg, *The Oxford Encyclopedia of the Modern Islamic World*, s.v. "Abduh, Muhammad."

(the hegemony of European powers) and internal factors. He recognized the scientific achievements of the West, for instance the arts, industry, the health care system, order, new political structures, and military power. Yet he believed that this did not imply that Muslims had therefore to subordinate themselves to the West. He publicly and critically remarked that Western liberality only benefits the Europeans. Yet Abduh was also self-critical and admitted that Islamic religious scholars were responsible for many undesirable developments within the Islamic world. Their actions—and this was for Abduh the nub of the matter—had led to the obscuration of the *true Islam*. What was needed was a return to the practice of the early period of Islam, to the time of the ancestors (in Arabic, *as-salaf*), in order to restore the Islamic world to its ancient strength. Because of this basic principle of returning to the ancestors, this school of thought has since come to be designated as Salafism (in Arabic, *salafiyya*).[14]

Concerning Europe, Abduh championed the apologetic hypothesis that almost everything that had contributed to the empowerment of Europe had been derived and appropriated from Islamic sources. Abduh assumed a polemical position against European Christianity as a religion and as a civilization. He resorted to many arguments to dispute the connection between European Christianity and modern civilization. He claimed that Christianity (1) teaches a type of flight from the world, an eagerness to withdraw from the world rather than actively to organize it; (2) is based on a belief in miracles and is therefore opposed to science; (3) confers to clerics' great power over people, leading to paternalism and militating against the freedom of the individual; and (4) teaches that faith is to be received as a gift, which is tantamount to advocating the primacy of irrationality. Among other points of criticism, he also claimed that Christianity (5) treats the value of the family (here he meant the family network) with contempt.

The principles of Islam appear to reflect a conception that is the exact opposite. Thus, according to Abduh, Islam knows only two basic principles, namely the unity of God and the prophethood of Muhammad. Both can be rationally verified. Besides, there is no contradiction between rationality

---

[14]See Henning Wrogemann, *Missionarischer Islam und gesellschaftlicher Dialog: Eine Studie zu Begründung und Praxis des Aufrufes zum Islam (daʿwa) im internationalen sunnitischen Diskurs* (Frankfurt: Lembeck, 2006), 54-83.

and what has been revealed. In cases of doubt, rationality takes precedence. Furthermore, Islam is open to various interpretations. Calling others to the truth of Islam only makes sense if that truth is demonstrable, but not if there is a need to refer to miracles or something similar. Abduh claimed that a religious authority is not necessary since the immediate relationship between God and human beings is one of the fundamental aspects of Islam.[15]

Abduh located this rational view of Islam as a point on a general line of development: according to this view, humanity is steadily moving along a trajectory towards perfection, and this progress is promoted whenever people seek to appropriate the world by means of reason. This essentially evolutionist interpretation, as well as the elements of religion criticism, may be traced back to (among others) influences exerted on Abduh by those authors with whom he grappled most, for instance the evolutionist theories of British social scientist Herbert Spencer (1820–1903), who coined the phrase "survival of the fittest," philosopher Auguste Comte (1798–1857), biologist Charles Darwin (1809–1882), and Enlightenment philosopher Jacques Rousseau (1712–1778).[16] Abduh planned to implement his reform ideas by creating an indigenous education system for all children (both male and female) that featured instruction in arithmetic, reading, writing, and religious education, whereby special emphasis was to be placed on the differences between Islam and Christianity.

In conclusion, it is fair to state that for Abduh, the true Islam of the ancestors (*salaf*) emerges as the superior religion. The downright reformatory principles that Abduh brought to bear against Christianity reflect the paradigms we have described very clearly: (a) it is a matter of referring back to the pure beginnings; (b) it is a matter of the compatibility of revelation and reason; (c) it is a matter of how relevant religion is to a society in terms of scientificity, progress, and ethics; and (d) it is a matter of optimism of progress that views societies as moving along a path of steady improvement.[17]

---

[15]See Hasselblatt, "Herkunft und Auswirkungen," 198-99.

[16]As presented especially in the works of John William Draper (1811–1882), Gustave Le Bon (1841–1931), and Edward Gibbon (1737–1794). See Hasselblatt, "Herkunft und Auswirkungen," 184-99. On the adoption of Islamic traditions, see ibid., 200ff.

[17]Abduh was by no means the only thinker to teach that Islam and modernity are compatible. Other personalities such as Indians Sayyid Ahmad Khan (1817–1898) and Muhammad Iqbal (1877–1938) also provided important impulses in this regard.

With regard to the stereotypes that are employed, we may come to the following conclusions: Both sides engage in a discourse of alterity, for each attempts to characterize the other as different and inferior by pointing to certain characteristics. Both sides are intent on denying each other the credit for the achievements of the civilization in question, such as scientific insights. Thus Renan denies that Muslim civilization has made any advances in scientific knowledge, for those that have been made were made by Christians and Jews within the Muslim world. Abduh on the other hand maintains that every single one of the—historically undeniable—scientific innovations may be traced back to the legacy of Islamic traditions, *of which the Muslims had been deprived*. This may be described as a discourse of disinheritance. *Yet what also becomes clear in the framework of this discussion is that both sides orient themselves by the same perceptions and values, namely religion as the basis of a rational worldview, scientificity, progress, and an ethical and moral way of life based on religious precepts.* This indicates that foreignness is not inherent to these points, since the antagonists both belong to the intellectual elites of their countries and are participating in an international discourse. Consequently one may observe that in this context, foreignness is being stylized. In this regard, another interesting similarity is constituted by the *process of reasoning that distinguishes between the ideal religion and that which actually exists*: Renan, Troeltsch, and Abduh identify as the core of their religion a religious worldview that is clearly distinct from the belief in miracles and the bondage to authority that are inherent to the traditions of folk religion (cults of pilgrimages to graves, of the veneration of saints or of particular religious leaders). Both sides admit the existence of undesirable developments within their own religious traditions (Roman Catholic folk religion on the one side, and Islamic folk religion, especially in the area of the Sufi cult of grave worship, on the other), but they attribute them to other actors (on the one side, the priests and the hierarchy of the church who do not intervene against folk religion, and on the other, the traditional scholars or the Sufi masters). In addition, both are concerned with the restoration of the true religion.

During the colonial period, we also find the implementation of similar paradigms of argumentation in other areas such as India, where criticisms from the domain of neo-Hinduism also take the form of a discourse of alterity. Here too rationality and scientificity are claimed on behalf of one's own tradition, and here too reference is made—as in the case of Islamic actors—to the superiority of one's own traditions in the domain of spirituality. Swami Vivekananda (1863–1902) and Sarvepalli Radhakrishnan (1888–1975) may serve as examples of this approach.[18]

Let us summarize: The views of that which is other and foreign are often stylized, leading to the frequent occurrence of discourses of alterity, as demonstrated above. This insight is of great importance for both intercultural hermeneutics and intercultural theologies, for here too it is not just a matter of understanding and of describing a theological identity but rather and at the same time also a question of power. The following example will demonstrate that stereotypes can also lead to very tangible repercussions, that they can manifest themselves within institutions and thereby create social realities.

The British Empire and "Indirect Rule" in India: The Power of Science

Religious studies research is not just conducted from a quasi-neutral observer perspective; rather, it creates and fashions new possibilities for paradigms of religious relationships. This means that *the research is itself involved in the interreligious and intercultural sphere, and it creates social realities.* In short, *the scientific description of that which is other and foreign creates realities,* no matter whether it is carried out in the area of religious studies, cultural studies, or in models of theologies of religion. The so-called Orientalism debate, for instance, is concerned with the power-political calculi that play or played a role in the description of other cultures and religions. As we have seen, images are not only depicted; they are constructed. Whereas Renan and Abduh in their interaction were essentially concerned with interpretations, in the Indian context Great Britain as a colonial power institutionalized interpretations of that which is other and foreign in the form of laws and structures of colonial administration. That means that the interpretation of that which is foreign (India) led to the creation of certain colonial structures that in turn were intended to alter the actually existing religiocultural-societal framework of India in a lasting manner.

---

[18]See Paul J. Will, "Swami Vivekananda and Cultural Stereotyping," in Ninian Smart and B. Srinivasa Murthy, eds., *East-West Encounters in Philosophy and Religion* (Mumbai: Popular Prakashan Pvt., 1996), 377-87.

Scholar of religious and mission studies Andreas Nehring has used the example of India to demonstrate how the British in the form of the colonial officials of the East India Company influenced the Indian context in the eighteenth century.[19] The British worked together particularly with Brahmins, whom they on the basis of their own perspective (thus biased by certain theoretical presuppositions) viewed as leaders of the Indian society, and therefore whom they elected to engage in dialogue and consultation. On this basis, the British created judicial and bureaucratic systems by which India was to be ruled. To this end they selected certain classical texts from the Indian tradition that they considered to be relevant for India. Here British colonial officials drew on the philological research of European indologists, many of whom had never been in India, however, such as the famous Max Müller (1823–1900). Yet they also did not consider this to be necessary, since they were convinced that they were able to discern the *true nature* of Hinduism, as in "the one Hinduism," by means of the Holy Scriptures of India.

Here a depth hermeneutics from the tradition of Platonic philosophy was taking effect, according to which the true nature of things is to be found in the texts, or more precisely in their depth dimension. From this perspective, texts are generally considered to be the authoritative sources, while the daily life of folk religion is seen as being of lesser value. Deeply held presuppositions are at play here, which reveal preconceptions of religion and culture significantly characterized by the Christian worldview, since factors like scripturality (Holy Scriptures, Bible), uniformness (ecclesiastical magisterium), and doctrinal authority (such as Christian synods or confessional texts) play an important role.[20]

Thus, for instance, the British selected and translated the "Laws of Manu" (the *Dharmasastra*) from Sanskrit, the holy language of India. For according to the will of the British and their "indirect rule" approach to colonial

---

[19]Andreas Nehring, "Religion, Kultur und Macht: Auswirkungen des kolonialen Blicks auf die Kulturbegegnung am Beispiel Indiens," *Zeitschrift für Missionswissenschaft und Religionswissenschaft* 87 (2003): 200–217.

[20]The circumstance that these characteristics did not exist in the Indian religious configurations was simply ignored. Thus, for instance, there were no religious entities overseeing doctrine, no hard-and-fast religious doctrines, a complete lack of uniformity in ritual practice, no founder figures, no Holy Scriptures that were recognized as canonical, and so on. For this reason it is imperative to speak—even today—of Indian religious configurations in the plural, for "the one Hinduism" does not exist, and it clearly never has.

governance, India was to be ruled using "native laws" and by means of in-digenous elites—under British supervision, of course. Both native legis-lation and the establishment of an infrastructure of native authority on the ground would guarantee the appropriateness of the rule, for only in this way could the British Empire be stabilized (after all, Great Britain would have lacked the personnel and the financial means to exercise direct rule).[21]

The work of translation was begun in the year 1771 and consolidated in written form first in 1775 and then again in 1792. This text (the "Laws of Manu") regulates the relationships between the castes in every detail. It speaks of rights and duties, especially of the lower castes. *Previously, however, and this is of fundamental significance, these texts had not been in force every-where in India at all, and especially not in South India, where the caste system took on a very different appearance at the time.*

The English translation efforts thus led them *to orient their politics toward the alleged elite,* on the one hand, and *to neglect the masses of the Indian population,* on the other. The result was that the difference between the literate and the nonliterate now came to be put into effect on the level of society, as it were; that is to say, it now began to play a role (whereas in Africa it was a facet of daily life). The British believed that by issuing these legal writings, they were bringing the true India to the casteless; they pub-lished the *texts* and distributed many copies of them. Furthermore, they appointed mostly *Brahmins* as teachers, judges, and political decision makers, thereby consolidating their power and expanding this system throughout India. None of these things had previously existed to such an extent, neither the knowledge of the "Laws of Manu," nor the influence of the Brahmins, nor the orientation toward the caste system. Yet in this way the "true India" was to be brought to the lower castes, as it were, who were considered to be irreligious and depraved, which was done at their expense, however. At the same time, Christian mission was forbidden because it was feared that it would lead to unrest (the prohibition was issued in 1833), which would have been disadvantageous to the exploitation of the country.

Thus by means of actions taken on the basis of religious studies, an "Indian" system of rule was constructed to the benefit of the British (*indirect*

---

[21]See Andrew Porter, "Religion and Empire: British Expansion in the Long Nineteenth Century, 1780–1914," *Journal of Imperial and Commonwealth History* 20, no. 3 (1992): 370-90.

rule), while the British believed that in so doing they were giving the Indians "what was theirs" (i.e., their own law), as it were.[22] Yet it was only now that the caste system in this sense truly came into being. In addition, a census was held in the year 1871 for the purpose of classifying—i.e., subdividing—all of India according to the four "classic" castes. This made India easier to govern for the British. At the same time, though, India came to be constituted over against Europe as "the other," namely as a country in which—from the British perspective—(a) freedom of the individual was not possible and (b) priests had more power than political leaders. This was of considerable significance for the self-justification of colonial Great Britain, since it enabled the British to see themselves as a modern power as opposed to the "backward" India (over which they ruled by the same token, using this system).

In short, the paradigms of perception with respect to India are similar to those with respect to the Islamic world, namely in a number of ways: First, the Indians are seen to lack individual freedom and responsibility, which is also the case with respect to the Muslims. This shows once again that the Protestant ethics of conscience is seen as an essential aspect of one's own identity (in this case the British-European identity). Second, reference is made to the priests in this context as well, who—according to this argument—prohibit both free thought and thus also progress, in a manner similar to that of the Islamic scholars and Sufi masters. It is legitimate to conclude that both the Islamic world and India are being characterized in similar ways. These characterizations should thus be understood as stylizations of foreignness. *It is important to recognize that such stylizations have led to very real consequences for various societies, cultures, and traditions.*

FOREIGNNESS, INTERCULTURAL HERMENEUTICS, AND DISCOURSE THEORY

It has been demonstrated that frequently foreignness is not just a given; rather, it is stylized and constructed, often very deliberately. Intercultural theology therefore has no choice but to apply insights gleaned from discourse theory. At issue here is the question of who is using which arguments

---

[22]Nehring, "Religion, Kultur und Macht," 204-6.

from which discourse position in order to achieve certain goals. From this perspective, as will be demonstrated later in greater detail, cultures are not to be understood as delimitable uniformities characterized by relative inward uniformity in terms of language, certain values and norms, customs, certainties in everyday life, and so on. Instead, cultures are spaces with constantly moving borders. They are spaces in which various actors are engaged in conflict about what truly defines the "identity" of such a cultural configuration and, one may add, of a certain religious configuration. To pursue intercultural theology thus means to position oneself within the spectrum of such interests and claims to validity expressed using the framework of religiocultural paradigms, either to postulate one's own rationales and their social-cultural-political consequences or to criticize corresponding attempts by others.

In the preceding chapter, questions of intercultural hermeneutics were discussed using examples from the macro level of international, intercultural, and interreligious discourses. In contrast, the following chapter will use an example from the micro level, namely Christian ashrams in India, to ascertain which aspects are to be considered when it comes to the issues of intercultural and interreligious practice, a practice that leads to the condensing of symbols and that manifests itself within such condensations. It will be shown that intercultural theology is not a harmless pursuit, for it is concerned with achieving a successful life of faith and with criticizing those traditions that are harmful to life. This means that whenever intercultural theology is brought to bear, the element of conflict also plays an important role. Using the example of Christian ashrams, we will concern ourselves first with the adoption of symbols from Hindu traditions as efforts toward inculturation. The combination of various religious symbolisms will then be explained using the example of a Christian *gopuram*, which usually serves as the entrance gate to a Hindu temple but in this instance as the entry to a Christian ashram. The next section will discuss the criticism of such inculturation on the part of Hindu activists. Moving on, this criticism will be located within the spectrum of newer Hindu fundamentalist movements, in which religious symbolisms are used to draw boundaries between that which the activists consider to be genuinely "Indian" and therefore acceptable and that which is designated as "non-Indian" and therefore to be prohibited in India. Finally, it will be shown that it is not only a matter of Hindu activists leveling criticism against such Christian efforts at inculturation, but also of Christian movements voicing harsh criticism against such attempts at inculturation. This concerns the protests of the so-called Dalit Christians.

Is Inculturation Permissible?

Concerning Symbolic Forms and Their Use

Inculturation is initially used here in a very general sense to mean that the Christian gospel enters into a relationship with a certain culture. As the divine Word became "incarnate" in the human being Jesus of Nazareth (Jn 1:14), the gospel is now to find its expression and to take effect in the forms of a certain culture in an analogous manner. In this regard we will devote attention to the symbolic forms in which the gospel expresses itself.

THE EXAMPLE OF CHRISTIAN ASHRAMS IN INDIA

Let us take India as an example. India currently has a population of about 1.2 billion people, of whom about 70 percent belong to the Hindu religions, about 13 percent to Islam, and about 2.4 percent to Christianity. Christian congregations therefore constitute a rather small minority. Even though it is presumed that there have been Christian congregations in India for over fifteen hundred years, several churches trace their origins back to the mission work of Roman Catholic missions since the sixteenth century and to Protestant missions since the early eighteenth century. However, the majority of churches in India today came into being as a result of mission work that commenced only after the year 1858. Previously, the British East India Company had prohibited mission activity, fearing side effects that might have proved harmful to business. Since from the end of the nineteenth century onwards many European missions emphasized the cultural differences to the Indian context, many of the Indian churches that came into being as a result of these initiatives partly reflect a European influence, in the form of churches built in a neo-Gothic style, for instance, or in the form of interior fittings such as pews, sanctuary areas, or images that correspond to European prototypes. In the case of many of these churches, one may therefore speak of "inculturation" only to a very limited extent—one would need to define exactly what is meant.

Yet we cannot pursue this topic any further at this juncture. Rather, we are concerned with some of those projects that were begun sporadically since the beginning of the twentieth century and particularly since the 1960s— namely, the founding and organizing of Christian ashrams.[1] Ashrams are religious centers in which meditation is conducted and spiritual instruction is given. Raja Savarirayan aptly summarizes some important aspects:

> There is no institution that reflects the spirit of classical India as purely as does that of the "ashramas." This was originally an expression used for all four ages of life, those of the student, the paterfamilias, the forest hermit, and the itin- erant monk. The expression means something like "stages of intense effort." *The* ashram later came to be regarded as the locus for the third age of life, the hut or the complex of huts used for religious meditation, the forest settlement, e.g. in which the Upanishads [i.e., certain Holy Scriptures of the Hindu tradi- tions] were written. It continues to be the guiding principle for the center of religious life.[2]

Now, a number of Christian centers of meditation selected symbolic forms that are considered meaningful by the Hindu traditions and ad- opted them with some minor changes. These aspects are to be our focus in what follows. This applies first of all to forms of *lifestyle*: in Christian ashrams, spiritual masters and spiritual seekers live according to Indian custom; they go barefoot, eat their meals while seated on the ground, and wear—just like the *sannyasins* of the Hindu traditions—ocher-colored garments. In a number of ashrams, the daily routine is arranged in such a way that times for mutual prayer and reflection are scheduled in the

---

[1]Naturally, we can only elaborate on a few important aspects here in an exemplary fashion. See Ernst Pulsfort, *Christliche Ashrams in Indien: Zwischen dem religiösen Erbe Indiens und der christ- lichen Tradition des Abendlandes*, 2nd ed. (Altenberge, Germany: Oros, 1991). For a more general treatment, see Paul Puthanangady, "Die Inkulturation der Liturgie in Indien seit dem Zweiten Vatikanum," *Concilium* 19 (1983): 146-51.

[2]Raja Savarirayan, "Christliche Ashrams," quoted in Hugald Grafe, *Evangelische Kirche in Indien: Auskunft und Einblicke* (Erlangen: Verlag der Evang.-Luth. Mission, 1981), 295. I consider this description to be an obvious idealization, however.

morning, at noon, and in the evening. In this respect, there is great variation from one ashram to another.

In the Saccidananda Ashram, for instance, which will be our focus in what follows, passages from the biblical writings are read at each of those occasions; in addition, texts from the Hindu traditions are read in the morning, from the Qur'an and from the Guru Granth Sahib (the Holy Book of the Sikhs) at noon, and from texts by spiritual personalities from the Tamil traditions in the evening.[3] But it is also in terms of architecture and interior decoration that symbolic forms were borrowed from the Hindu traditions, such as the *gopuram*, an entrance gate in the form of a tower, as is typical for Hindu temples. The symbolism of such a Christian *gopuram* will now be discussed in a somewhat more detailed fashion. The significance of this ashram for our purposes lies in the fact that it comprises a center for the Benedictine Order within the Roman Catholic Church.[4]

Religious Symbols and Their Interreligious Application

So what do Christian *gopurams* look like, and what symbolism do they use? The image (fig. 2) shows the *gopuram* of the Christian Saccidananda Ashram in Shantivanam, near the south Indian city of Trichy.[5] The barrel-type tower construction with the little tiers built on top is patterned after a Hindu *gopuram* (fig. 3). We may begin by noting the fact that the Hindu *gopuram* has five tiers added on top,[6] while the Christian one has only three. In terms of the symbolism, we single out only the following aspects: three intertwined faces are portrayed in the middle of the *gopuram* known as the Trimurti (meaning the "tri-figure"). Depictions of the Trimurti are frequently found in the Hindu religions, often on posters that are very popular.[7]

---

[3]Pulsfort, *Christliche Ashrams in Indien*, 82.

[4]Like many other religious orders of the Roman Catholic Church, the Benedictine Order is represented in many countries of the world. This adds to the significance of this example, since within one and the same order a great variety of regional and cultural variations of religious life is permitted.

[5]For more on this ashram, see Pulsfort, *Christliche Ashrams in Indien*, 80-88.

[6]There are, however, also smaller ones with, say, three tiers, as well as far larger ones with varying numbers of tiers.

[7]For an example of a Trimurti poster, see the image at this link: www.iitis.de/sites/default/files/ Trimurti_Comparison.pdf. The full poster portrays the three gods Brahma, Vishnu, and Shiva, but also depicts three spiritual masters from the nineteenth and twentieth centuries. For an introduction to the iconography of India, see Anneliese Keilhauer and Peter Keilhauer, *Die Bildersprache*

Figure 2. Christian Ashram gate

The gods are considered to have different functions with reference to the cosmos, with Brahma being seen as the creator, Vishnu as the sustainer, and Shiva as the destroyer. Yet this is only one of the manifold and very diverse religious theories that is of little significance for the religious practice of the general mainstream. A large number of other gods, spirits, forms, and spiritual masters are also venerated. The Trimurti poster clearly and strikingly features a plethora of religious symbols. The basic premise is that each divinity is characterized by certain symbols. The divinity in the poster facing the observer is meant to be Vishnu, identifiable by attributes such as the skin color (blue) or the mark on the forehead (vertical lines). The figure facing to the left is meant to portray Shiva, as may be seen by the mark on the forehead (horizontal lines), for instance, or by the attribute of his riding animal, the Nandi bull, also depicted here. But gestures expressed by the hand position (in Sanskrit, *mudra*) or by objects held in the hands also play a role; for Shiva, for instance, it is the trident (on the right hand side of the image), the shell, or the drum. All things considered, what makes a certain figure identifiable among the various divine forms is a combination of the attributes of (1) the skin color, (2) the clothing, (3) the riding animal, (4) the hand position, (5) the objects held in the hands, and (6) other symbols that connote certain stories of the gods (in Shiva's case, for instance, Mount Himalaya in the background as well as a fountain of water springing up from his head that stands for the River Ganges).

But let us return to the Christian *gopuram* (fig. 2). By comparison, it seems plain. The inscription on it makes reference to the Christian doctrine of the Trinity, i.e., God revealing himself in the Creator, in Jesus Christ, and in the power of the Holy Spirit. This revelation is also referred to as the Triunity, since it refers to the one and only God irrespective of his threeness. This is expressed in the Trimurti figure. A closer look reveals that the countenance facing forward has a beard and masculine features, while the figure with androgynous features facing to the left (from the observer's perspective) also has a beard. The figure facing to the right is portrayed with feminine features and without a beard. In Christian interpretation, this refers to God the Father, the Son, and the Holy Spirit. The Trimurti figure forms both a unit and the upper part of a large cross that leads into the Trimurti figure. The cross itself is brown in color, whereas the Trimurti figure is portrayed in red. In the middle of the cross is a graphic character, namely the well-known Hindu symbol Om.[8]

Figure 3. Hindu *gopuram*

---

[8]The symbol Om (ॐ) is expressed as a meditative intonation (mantra) and simultaneously as a prayer. It is considered to be a symbol of the Vedic revelation. It consists of the three forms, A-U-M, which in turn symbolize creation, preservation, and dissolution, followed by the eternal cycle of new creation, preservation, and dissolution, etc. In this sense, Om is also a symbol for the holistic totality of reality. The syllable *Om* is a unifying symbol common to all the various

Behind the Trimurti figure, a triangle is visible (blue in color), while the pedestal on which the tiers are constructed is stylized—and this is something most Europeans without the necessary background would fail to recognize—as an *opened lotus blossom*.

Let us attempt to interpret what we are seeing. To the practiced eye—to those who have studied both religious configurations, both the Hindu faiths and Christianity—the combination and interconnection of Hindu and Christian symbols is clearly visible. Let us take stock (without intending to be exhaustive) by considering the figurative symbolism, the abstract symbolism, the proportional symbolism, the color symbolism, and the number symbolism. With respect to Christianity, the following aspects are of particular importance: in terms of figurative symbolism, it is the angels (as a minimum); in terms of abstract symbolism, it is the cross and the triangle; in terms of color symbolism, it is the colors red, blue, and white; and in terms of number symbolism, it is the numbers three, seven, and twelve. Admittedly, other religious configurations also view these symbols as meaningful. From the perspective of the Hindu traditions, it is especially the Trimurti figure and the lotus blossom that are important in terms of figurative symbols; in terms of abstract symbols, it is the graphic character for the syllable *Om*; in terms of color symbolism, it is the colors blue, gray, and red, yet beyond those also a whole range of other colors; and in terms of number symbolism, the five and the nine are particularly important, but besides those also an inestimable number of other symbols.

This raises the question of how adherents of the Hindu traditions on the one hand and adherents of Christian traditions on the other see this combination of religious symbols that are drawn from both the Hindu and Christian traditions. What do they see as meaningful? What signs do they see? *The following remarks may serve as an example of an intercultural-interreligious hermeneutics, one that incorporates the aspect of symbolic forms and the plurality of potential correlative constellations within which it is possible to attribute meaning or according to which believers may attribute meaning. It will be shown that a variety of interpretations is possible.*

---

movements of the Hinduism traditions, irrespective of the form of religious use to which it is put by the individual movements. For an introduction to the subject, see Peter Schreiner, *Im Mondschein öffnet sich der Lotus: Der Hinduismus* (Düsseldorf: Patmos, 1998), 84, 92, 123.

From the *perspective of Hindu devotees*, the combination of symbols in the Christian *gopuram* may be read as depicting three divinities; at the same time, common people would probably find it difficult to identify the specific divinities concerned because the attributes typical for Hindu divinities are missing (the color, the riding animal, the hand gestures, the objects that are held in the hands, and the references to narratives about certain divinities such as the Himalaya or the Ganges). As the Trimurti figure in the poster demonstrates, one example of such an attribute might be constituted by the riding animal: the god Shiva is portrayed with his riding animal, the Nandi bull. Other examples of attributes are things that a divinity wears as clothing; in the case of Shiva, this is often an animal skin, which identifies him as an ascetic. Another attribute might be the skin color; in the case of Shiva, this is often gray, for as an ascetic he is covered with gray ash, whereas Vishnu is usually shown with a blue skin color. But in the first instance, those things are considered attributes that the gods hold in their hands, such as in Shiva's case the trident or the shell.

Now in the Christian *gopuram* all of these attributes have been omitted, which for a Hindu devotee begs the question as to which divinities are being depicted here. Conversely, the *sign Om*, the *lotus flower*, and the general *setting of the gopuram* and the ashram lying behind it will probably engender in him a *feeling of familiarity*. Let us turn our attention to the lotus symbol. In general, the lotus flower is considered a *symbol of purity*, for it retains its radiant white, pink, or red color even though it grows out of the muck of water bodies.[9] It symbolizes the possibility of rising above the impurity of the world and of achieving a greater measure of spiritual purity by means of rituals, devotion, or meditation. For the Hindu traditions, these associations play a fundamental role. In the realm of *mythology*, the lotus is considered *the origin of the world*, for it is said that a lotus grew out of the belly button of the god Vishnu, and from this lotus the god Brahma issued, who created the world. In general, the lotus is considered an *ideal of beauty*; hence the expressions "face of a lotus" or "lotus-eyed one" (used with reference to one's beloved). The lotus flower is an attribute of the god Vishnu and his spouse, Lakshmi; the layered composition of its leaves *symbolizes the composition of*

---

[9]See ibid., 10-16.

the world, but it also *symbolizes the spiritual way,* for the body's most important energy center is known as the lotus chakra. The lotus is also significant for the practice of meditation; for instance, the *basic meditative position*
is referred to as the lotus position. This clearly shows that the Indian traditions are unique in allocating a wide range of meaning to the lotus symbol.

However, from the perspective of a Christian believer with a European
background, the symbols of the Om, the lotus (inasmuch as this symbol is
even recognized as such), the Trimurti figure, and the setting of the *gopuram* in particular will probably cause disconcertment. The angels to the
left and to the right will probably seem familiar to the Christian; after all,
angelic figures are frequently found in the baroque churches of Europe.
Also recognizable would be the sign of the cross and the symbol of the triangle. Furthermore, the coloration may be read against the background of
Christian iconography, assuming that the depiction of the Trimurti is perceived as Christian. In this case, the brown color of the cross might be
understood as a reference to the cross of Jesus as the "tree," while the red
color of the Trimurti figure could be seen as symbolizing the love of God,
which expresses itself in the event of the cross and resurrection of Jesus
Christ. The blue color of the triangle could be understood as a reference to
God's otherworldliness, for blue represents the heavens as a symbol of distance, of otherworldliness, of the exaltedness and power of God, just as the
combination of blue and gold represents the night sky and the stars. In this
case—according to this interpretation—this would constitute a portrayal of
the Trinity of God, i.e., of how God originally existed in his transcendence
(blue triangle) and how he may be perceived in the unfolding of his revelation as Creator (Father), Redeemer (Son), and Perfecter (Spirit) in the
story of Jesus Christ for the benefit of us human beings, i.e., as a loving God
(red Trimurti figure).

We could then attempt to decipher the number symbolism, for the *gopuram* features various combinations of threes. Thus one may discern three
levels—the pedestal with its lotus flower symbolism, the level of the images
with the three-figured representations (angels, Trimurti, angels) and the
upper tier with its three raised sections. This would seem to suggest the holy
number nine of the Hindu traditions, whereas other combinations, such as
the arrangement of four groups of three, say, would seem to suggest the

number twelve, which is considered holy in Christian tradition as the symbolic number of perfection. In each case, however, the repetition of the number three would be a clear reference to the Holy Trinity of God—or at least this is what the name of the ashram suggests.

That the proportions are just as important is something we can only suggest at this point. Naturally, the central position of the Trimurti figure underlines the centrality of its status. In addition, this figure is positioned slightly above the level of the angels, while the Trimurti figure is firmly established as part of an ensemble. This truly provides food for thought, for three types of symbolism are being combined here: *while the cross may be an abstract symbol, from the perspective of Christian traditions it also refers to a historical context*, namely to the crucifixion of Jesus of Nazareth around the year 30 CE (according to the Christian reckoning of time). This symbol is couched in a language of its own, since in its capacity as the intersection of two lines, a vertical and a horizontal one, it could evoke many associations, while it refers to a story that provides numerous points of reference for this specific symbolism. *In contrast, the symbol of the triangle is an abstract sign that does not correlate to a historical context*. In the Christian tradition, it represents the Trinity of God, and thus it corresponds primarily to a doctrinal context. Similarly, *from a Christian perspective, even though the figurative depiction of the Trimurti is symbolic, it would also be associated for the most part with a doctrinal context. However, it does intersect with the witness of the New Testament by depicting the presence of God in multiple dimensions.* Now, if one were to focus only on this one ensemble, one could come up with the following interpretation: the three sides or corners of the triangle in blue represent the otherworldliness of God, the three faces in red represent the love of God in his incarnation, and the three long arms of the cross in brown represent the crucifixion of the historical Jesus of Nazareth as the Son of God. When the threefold aspect of the three levels (the arms of the cross, the Trimurti, the triangle) is factored in, the result is a numerical value of twelve, which in Christian symbolism represents God perfecting the world by his power. Yet if one were to focus only on the Trimurti figure and the cross, the cross could be seen as consisting of a total of four arms, three long ones and one short one, resulting in a numerical value of four, all depicted in brown. To this one may add the threefold aspect of the

Trimurti, uniformly presented in red. The result would be a numerical value of seven, which could refer in terms of Christian symbolism to the coming together of God (threeness: Father, Son, and Holy Spirit) and world (fourness: the four compass points). This number represents the *reconciliation* of God and human beings through the event of the cross of Jesus Christ.[10]

These interpretations are all possible, yet they were not all necessarily intended; they are possible but not arbitrary. The special effect created by the interplay of proximity and distance thus might have an impact on people from a wide variety of different traditions: first for Indians from a Hindu context, second also for Christians from a non-Indian context, and furthermore, third also for Indian Christians from "traditional mission churches" who had up until that point been unacquainted with the use of symbols from the Hindu traditions.

In many of the elements, the form of the symbols stays the same, such as the form of the cross, the sign Om, or the lotus flower as well as of the Trimurti figure. *Yet their arrangement clearly varies*, as the investigation of the Trimurti depiction has shown, for instance. For, in this instance, a color change has taken place, since the color red is used for Hindu gods only in very specific instances. It is not typically used for the god Vishnu nor for Shiva, and as far as I know it is also used infrequently for other gods. In contrast, in the Christian tradition and beyond it, the color red is often used as a symbol for, say, fire, energy, dynamism, or love. Second, as we said, it was decided to forgo the use of attributes, and third, the cross symbol was introduced, not in the sense of an attribute but rather as a combination.

Thus it is possible that the continuity of the symbols (lotus, Om, cross) and the discontinuity of their arrangement (combination, colorization, hierarchical composition according to right and left, large and small, high and low) may lead observers and practitioners gradually to adopt a new interpretation of what it might mean. We will revisit this issue later. Suffice it to say at this point that this represents an attempt to inculturate the Christian gospel. It is carried out, first, by religious specialists (priests, monks/nuns, meditators),

---

[10]Reconciliation is symbolized by the addition of world (four) and God (three), which results in the number seven; perfection is symbolized by the multiplication of world (four) and God (three), resulting in the number twelve; and the peak of perfection is achieved by multiplying the number twelve by twelve, resulting in 144.

second, in a very deliberate and considered manner, and third, using architectural forms that are generally characteristic for religious practice and constructed in a durable fashion. This means, fourth, that inculturation is being pursued here as a means to create community, for there must be a community of people to live out these forms of inculturation. Fifth, it is important to note that this form of inculturation is in fact oriented toward the cultural-symbolic forms of a different religiocultural tradition, which calls for a high level of interpretive competence. Sixth, it is therefore legitimate to characterize this effort as an elitist form of inculturation.[11]

My Symbol, Your Symbol: The Dispute About the Legitimacy of Inculturation

It goes without saying that inculturation never takes place in a vacuum. Of course, cultural-societal settings are arenas where power plays are also carried out, and because of this, religious symbols have always played an important role. Symbols are easily identifiable and therefore well-suited to function as a means of expression or evoking a sense of group identity. Then again, they can be used to exclude other people. This happens when individual symbols are used in such a way as to assert the foreignness of others. In India too conflict exists over the use of religious symbols. In this regard, various ideal-typical tendencies may be distinguished. First, we must consider the historical context. After Great Britain had extended its colonial state apparatus over all of India in the year 1856, the colonial administration was expanded and consolidated. In 1880 and 1890, censuses were carried out to this end, which also captured people's caste and religious affiliation. These statistics indicate that in terms of percentages, the number of Christians increased slightly but measurably. This provoked the opposition of Hindu activists who painted a picture of the impending extinction of the Hindu religion and mobilized against both Christians and Muslims and against their activities with regard to the expansion of their faiths.

This discourse took place in the context of nationalist movements, in which these movements raised the question as to the national identity of India. Now, to some extent, Hindu activists associated the national identity

---

[11]For one thing, only a few people live in ashrams, and for another, it is difficult if not impossible to reconcile this form of spiritual practice with the everyday life of the working population.

of India with the Hindu religions and their traditions, which they perceived to be "proto-Indian." This was used as an argument to stylize the Islamic and Christian religions as "foreign" and to stigmatize them. Islam was thus portrayed as a religion of conquest that had been forcefully introduced into India, while Christianity was portrayed as a colonially imported religion. It mattered little that the actual history of religion did not corroborate these stylizations. It is probable that Christianity, for example, was represented in India by as early as the second century, or by the fifth or sixth century at the latest, as new archaeological discoveries demonstrate. Islam for its part did not enter the country by means of the expansion of Islamic systems of rule but rather by the nonviolent efforts of the Sufi orders. On the whole it is believed that the present forms of the Hindu religions, especially Vishnuism and Shivaism, only came into existence at a relatively late point in the timeline of the history of religion.[12]

Nevertheless, in the public discussion Hindu activists insisted that Christianity and Islam are not Indian religions in the true sense, and for this reason they denied them the right to exist in India or at the very least their right actively to promulgate their faiths. In this context, the example of Christian efforts at inculturation may be understood as a type of offer to engage in dialogue or at least as an attempt positively to engage the question as to the "Indian character" of Christianity in its doctrine, forms of expression, and practice. Besides the argument that Christianity has existed in India for over fifteen hundred years, it is also legitimate to point to the willingness on the part of Christians to engage in dialogue. Doing so is not without its problems, however, as statements by Hindu activists demonstrate. These may currently be found in great numbers on the Internet. For instance, the website christianaggression.org reports on a Christian missionary as follows:

> The Christian missionary calling himself *Swami Sachidananda Bharanthi* uses all kinds of Hindu symbols, Sanskrit terminology, and Hindu-Practices in trying to make the christian Gospel understandable in India. Hindu-activists opposing christian mission work in general criticise this approach. On their homepage they say, Bharanthi is *"misquoting Hindu verses, building*

---

[12]Axel Michaels, *Der Hinduismus: Geschichte und Gegenwart* (Munich: C. H. Beck, 1998).

> *Churches that look similar to temples, Ashrams, doing Christian ceremonies*
> *like Hindu festivals, and adopting Hindu names for conversion centers. They*
> [the Christian missionaries] *construct preaching centers which are outwardly*
> *as closely as akin* [sic] *to Hindu Ashrams. Christian evangelists continue the*
> *outward form of Hinduism while adding a new dimension based on the Bible."*
> This is seen to be an effort *"to implement a policy of psycho programming and*
> *mind manipulation to demand the voluntary participation of Hindus for con-*
> *version. The plan is to break the spirit or sap the vitality of Hindus, who con-*
> *tinue to enjoy a spiritual life. It is a trick for exploitation and bondage as well*
> *as to crush Hindus."*[13]

Christian efforts at inculturation are thus interpreted as an activity by which spiritual violence is done to Hindus and that contribute to the destruction of Hindu traditions. Christian adoption of Hindu symbols is rejected and denounced as an ill-advised infiltration method. It should be expressly noted that Christians in Germany have made similar statements using the same argumentation regarding activities by Hindus (such as Hare Krishnas) or Buddhists there. Christians arguing against the criticism by Hindu activists in India may readily refer to the freedom of religion guaranteed by the constitution and thus to statutory law. Yet as far as the perspective of the Hindu activists is concerned, the combination of both paradigms of argumentation demonstrates that they insist on stylizing Christianity as a foreign religion, for on the one hand, they postulate its foreignness, and on the other hand, they firmly reject attempts at cultural rapprochement on the part of Christian actors. In essence this constitutes a form of ideological nationalism that utilizes models of religious argumentation. It is based on the notion of a nation that is uniform in terms of culture and religion—a notion that has never in the history of India even come close to approximating the actual state of affairs yet that keeps on being postulated and thereby reinforced as the end goal.

---

[13]Andreas Nehring, "Hinduismus und Christentum: Begegnung, Konflikte, Brüche," in Mariano Delgado and Guido Vergauwen, eds., *Interkulturalität: Begegnung und Wandel in den Religionen* (Stuttgart, Germany: Kohlhammer, 2010), 247-63. Citation drawn verbatim (except for the additions in square brackets) from 262; it is drawn in turn from Babu Suseelan, "Dishonest Christian Evangelism in Fake Hindu Cultural Garb," www.christianaggression.org/item_display.php?type=ARTICLES&id=1173670155 (accessed February 18, 2015).

The Use of Religious Symbols by the Media in the Discourse on Identity and Exclusion

These phenomena raise the question: Why do Hindu activists place such great emphasis on what happens in some Christian ashrams in India? In order to answer this question, it is necessary to bring to mind the importance of symbolic forms in political discourse. Political theorist Clemens Six has pointed out (and rightly so) that Hindu activists have in recent decades deliberately used symbols from the Hindu traditions to portray India as a uniformly Hindu country in order to stylize other religious configurations, most especially Islam and Christianity, as "foreign" to India. However, since the Hindu traditions encompass such an immensely diverse range of ritual practices, doctrines, and views, these must be reduced to a manageable set of symbols in order to be able to serve as a warrant for India's putative "Hindu identity." To this end, the symbols thus identified must first be intuitive, i.e., recognizable; second, they must be well-known; and third, they must be usable in a political sense.[14]

At the outset, we must point out that the Hindu religions have no centralized institutions. This means that there are for Hinduism no principal founder figures like Buddhism's Gautama Buddha, Judaism's Moses, Christianity's Jesus, or Islam's Muhammad. Second, there is no fixed canon of Holy Scriptures, like the Bible in the case of Christianity or the Qur'an in the case of Islam. Third, there is no authoritative magisterium, i.e., no priestly hierarchy that could vouch for the validity of religious doctrine. Fourth, there is no uniform set of beliefs, nor are there any uniform rituals; rather, a plurality of conceivable religious practices exists. Fifth, the number of different divinities is just as multitudinous; there are thousands of divinities overall, especially local ones, and besides these there are also a number of divinities known on a wider scale, such as Vishnu, Shiva, Krishna, Ganesha, Kali, Durga, or Lakshmi. Small wonder that such a constellation makes it extremely difficult to posit a symbol set that allegedly carries weight for all of India. At any rate, it is evident that up until the mid-twentieth century, no such set existed; and to date, Hindu activists have not succeeded

---

[14]The following observations are drawn from Clemens Six, *Hindu-Nationalismus und Globalisierung: Die zwei Gesichter Indiens: Symbole der Identität und des Anderen* (Frankfurt: Brandes & Apsel, 2001).

in establishing one. Yet the questions remain: Which symbols were selected? Why were these symbols in particular selected? And what attempts were made to make them popular in all of India?

The terse observation will suffice that for Hindu activists, the point of departure is a very specific view of history, which—and this must be emphasized from the outset—does not correspond to the actual history of India. In terms of its actual history, India never was a unified whole, let alone a nation; rather, it was a conglomerate of the most diverse dominions and forms of government. However, in the nineteenth century, after the Indian subcontinent in its entirety finally fell under British colonial rule, the British introduced the idea of the territorial national state into this area. British historians who had internalized this idea then superimposed it onto Indian history, which they proceeded to subdivide into an alleged succession of Hindu overlords, Muslim Mogul lords, and British colonial rule. This division clearly constitutes a stylization of rulership, for the overlordship of the Moguls—to cite just one example—never extended over all of India at any one point in time; rather, this vast territory was ruled by a multiplicity of Hindu rulers and subdivided into rather complicated constellations of many dominions. In addition, the territory was never Islamized; this was never the political aim of the Mogul lords, nor did they ever have the power to do so. Meanwhile, Indian historians adopted this view in order to postulate from an anticolonial perspective the existence of an original age of Hindu lords, a golden age that should now be restored by combating the colonial power and the Muslims on the one hand and by rediscovering the basis (from the viewpoint of religious studies, the *alleged* basis) of Hindu traditions on the other.[15]

---

[15]Ibid., 78-81. It is quite legitimate to speak of "invented traditions" in this instance. A similarly controversial topic is the hypothesis developed in the nineteenth century that claimed that Indo-Germanic tribes referring to themselves as Aryans had immigrated to India from the northwest and had successively subjugated the indigenous population. In South India in particular, people who consider themselves to belong to the original population (Dravidians) have been arguing for some time that they and not the Hindus are the rightful heirs to the land, whereas Hindu activists attempt to document that no such immigration ever took place and that the Hindu traditions should be seen as India's original religious configuration instead. Both sides thus appeal to the principle of seniority, and each side is attempting to prove the legitimacy of its claim on the basis of history. See Michael Bergunder, "Umkämpfte Vergangenheit: Anti-brahmanische und hindu-nationalistische Rekonstruktionen der frühen indischen Religionsgeschichte," in Michael Bergunder and Rahul Peter Das, eds., *"Arier" und "Draviden": Konstruktionen der*

The historical narrative of conflict between the various groups (especially the Hindus and the Muslims) is, as Six rightly states, an invention of tradition, just as the groups it features are an invention, for such uniform groups never existed in history, and they still do not exist today. In the late nineteenth century, Hindu nationalists designated the cow as a holy animal and as a symbol of the putative pan-Indian Hindu tradition. Meanwhile, this tradition was far more widespread in northern India than in southern India. The so-called cow protection movement that sprang up as a result demanded that India's Supreme Court institute a wholesale prohibition from slaughtering cows. Such a prohibition would have particularly affected Muslims and Christians. Now, up until this time it would have been no problem for these groups to eat beef, especially since slaughtering was not done in public. Meanwhile, the postulate that the holy cow represented "the" one Hindu tradition meant that a symbol was effectively being brought into play against Muslims and Christians in general and against the British colonial rulers. The symbol of the cow was used to distinguish insiders from outsiders, friend from foe, and what belonged in India from what did not belong; the aim was to deny the legitimacy of the presence of the British, the Muslims, and the Christians in India in equal measure. Six explains the symbolic value of the cow as follows:

> Firstly, the cow was declared to be the "universal mother" that feeds people and gives life to them. Killing a cow thus came to be seen as matricide in a metaphorical sense. Secondly, the veneration of the cow came to be considered the true heart of Hinduism. This meant that killing a cow was interpreted as a direct attack on the religion as a whole. Thirdly, from the perspective of the actors, the Muslims by virtue of their custom of eating beef were automatically seen as opponents of the Hindus.[16]

Another attempt was made at creating a symbol and institutionalizing its use by harnessing the increasing veneration of the god Ram and by

---

Vergangenheit als Grundlage für Selbst- und Fremdwahrnehmungen Südasiens (Halle, Germany: Verlag der Franckeschen Stiftungen zu Halle, 2002), 135-80, and specifically 135-36.

[16]Six, *Hindu-Nationalismus und Globalisierung*, 82. Six continues, "So it is not surprising that this movement resulted not only in the protection of cows, but also in attacks especially on Muslims and Christians. To a lesser extent, people from the lower castes and the untouchables were also attacked. This clearly demonstrates that social divisions persisted within the newly established Hindu community."

propagating this veneration.[17] As late as the nineteenth century, this god had virtually no followers in southern India. This only changed when Hindu nationalists systematically instituted a series of attempts to stylize the god Ram as the god of all of India and to apply this symbol against outsiders within India (Muslims and Christians).[18] Despite the proven fact of religious history that Christianity has been an integral part of the religious lifeworld and tradition of India for almost eighteen hundred years, despite the fact that local Muslim traditions go back as far as the eighth century, and despite the fact that the religious configurations of, say, the Vishnu cult and the Shiva cult only came into being much later—at least in terms of their current significance and form—representatives of the Hindu traditions continue to stake their claim to all of India on behalf of their allegedly homogeneous religious configuration. This amounts to a deliberate stylization of foreignness: *the intent is to portray one's fellow Indians from the other religious configurations as outsiders.* And now activists press the legend surrounding the god Ram into service in order to stigmatize the other as an outsider. They stylize the birthplace of the god Ram in Ayodhya as the symbol for the unity of the Indian nation. A 1996 paper of the Hindu nationalist party BJP states, "Sri Ram is the unique symbol, the unequalled symbol of our oneness, of our integration, as well as of our aspiration to live the higher values."[19]

Using various campaigns, especially festivals of the gods, pilgrimages, and political announcements, as a divinity Ram was stylized first as fighting for the unity of India and second as a good king and ruler who elevated India by enabling its culture and economy to blossom. Heretofore, the character of this god had been portrayed as even-tempered, but now, by means of hawkish symbolism, he was reinterpreted as a model for combat-ready Hindus and popularized using stickers, posters, and other media. In the religious tradition, Ram is seen as an incarnation of the god Vishnu. The famous epic poem "Ramayana" records the deeds of Ram, the son of a king who marries another king's daughter, called Sita. When Sita is abducted to Lanka (Sri Lanka), Ram saves her with the help of an army of monkeys led

---

[17]Anuradha Kapur, "Deity to Crusader: The Changing Iconography of Ram," in Gyanendra Pandey, ed., *Hindus and Others: The Question of Identity in India Today* (New Delhi: Viking, 1993), 74-109.
[18]Six, *Hindu-Nationalismus und Globalisierung*, 83.
[19]As cited in ibid., 101.

by the monkey general, Hanuman. Subsequently, Ram serves as a just ruler. He finally returns to heaven together with the population of Ayodhya. The city Ayodhya is considered to be the birthplace of the god Ram. Originally a temple was constructed at the site where he was said to have been born, but it was torn down in the year 1528 by the Muslim Mogul ruler Barbar and replaced with a mosque, the Babri Masjid.

As it was, Ayodhya had long served as a city of pilgrimage and as a sacred site for Buddhists, Jains, Muslims, and Hindu devotees. Even after the Babri Masjid was constructed, in fact for centuries afterwards, Hindu devotees were permitted to venerate their god Ram there—most probably outside the temple as such, yet within its proximity and thus on the grounds of the former temple.[20] But from 1855 onwards, violent conflicts began to break out. In 1912 and 1934, for instance, severe unrest erupted concerning these sacred sites. Following India's independence in 1949, the conflict took on a political dimension; in 1984, Hindu activists began publicly to call for the liberation of the site and the reconstruction of the Hindu temple. Hindu activists mobilized thousands of Hindu believers to conduct pilgrimages to Ayodhya in order to lend weight to the demand. The activists stylized the site as the center of India. In the early 1990s, they went on to conduct campaigns that led to the violent destruction of the Babri Masjid. As a result, riots took place that caused thousands of deaths on both sides. Unfortunately, our framework does not permit further discussion of these events.

Of particular interest for our purposes, however, is the use and dissemination of religious symbols. As a site, Ayodhya came to be stylized as the symbol at the heart of the conflict between the (allegedly uniform) groups of Hindus, on the one hand, and the Muslims, on the other. In the 1980s and 1990s, campaigns to this effect were carried out in the media, for instance by *Organiser*, a journal of Hindu nationalist organization Rashtriya Swayamsevak Sangh (RSS), and by means of stickers, posters, flyers, pilgrimages, political announcements, radio broadcasts, movies, and many other media. This is an example of religious symbolism that seems harmless in and of itself but that is imbued—we may recall the discussion regarding Roland Barthes—with a secondary level of meaning. Now the depiction of the

---

[20]Ibid., 92ff.

Hindu god Ram does not just signify a god any longer; it also signifies, on the one hand, the claim that this god represents all Hindu devotees (a claim to validity on the part of Hindu activists that is directed "inward") and, on the other hand, the demarcation of Hindu identity in the face of the others, especially of the Christians and Muslims (a claim to validity directed "outward"). Yet it must be noted that this symbolism actually serves to bring about the demarcation in the first place, that it disseminates it, cultivates it, and in some situations intensifies it.

WHICH CULTURE? THE CRITICISM OF CHRISTIAN ASHRAMS BY DALIT CHRISTIANS

The efforts at inculturation expended in Christian ashrams are criticized not only by Hindu activists but also by Christian movements and churches. A prominent example is constituted by the Dalit Christians, who make up about 80 percent of the Christians in India.[21] Some explanations on the Indian caste system will help us better to understand the protests of the Dalits.[22] Constituting more than 70 percent of the population, the Hindu religions are the dominating force, while Muslims constitute approximately 13 percent and Christians only about 2.4 percent (which nevertheless yields a number of about twenty-eight million people). Even though in terms of numbers India is the largest democracy in the world, Indian society as a whole is still far removed from equal treatment for all people. While the government does seek to improve the lot of the lower classes of society by means of a quota system, these efforts run up against the social structure, which is determined on the basis of religion. The so-called caste system fundamentally determines the subdivision of people according to accidents of birth. While the caste system only provides for four main categories, in

---

[21] For more on the living situation of Dalits, issues of justice, and newer developments, see A. M. Abraham Ayrookuzhiel, "Dalit Theologie: Bewegung einer Gegenkultur," in Johanna Linz, ed., *Gerechtigkeit für die Unberührbaren: Beiträge zur indischen Dalit-Theologie*, Weltmission Heute, Studienheft 15 (Hamburg: Evangelisches Missionswerk in Deutschland, 1995), 51-68.

[22] Andreas Nehring, "Reinheit und Bekehrung. Hindu-Nationalismus, Säkularer Staat und die Anti-Bekehrungsgesetze in Indien," *Zeitschrift für Missionswissenschaft und Religionswissenschaft* 88, no. 3/4 (2004): 232-49. See also Arvind P. Nirmal, "Towards a Christian Dalit Theology," in R. S. Sugirtharajah, ed., *Frontiers in Asian Christian Theology: Emerging Trends* (Maryknoll, NY: Orbis Books, 1994), 27-40.

reality there are thousands of subclassifications among the lower castes.[23] It is not necessary to study this phenomenon in more detail at this point; rather, what is significant for our purposes is the religious justification behind it. An ancient sacred text from the Rig Veda sees society as deriving from the killing and dismemberment of a primordial human being. It states,

> When they divided Puruṣa [the primordial human being] how many portions did they make? What do they call his mouth, his arms? What do they call his thighs and feet? The *Brāhman* [Brahmans] was his mouth, of both his arms was the *Rājanya* [warriors] made. His thighs became the *Vaiśya* [merchants and agriculturalists], from his feet the *Śūdra* [enslaved class] was produced.[24]

The caste system, which is legitimized on the basis of religion, is associated with purity regulations. Ritual purity is passed on within the family and the clan, while ritual impurity is to be avoided. Such impurity is contracted by *eating* with, *touching* or *marrying* people from a lower caste. In practice, this means that marriages are not contracted between castes, no shared meals are held, physical contact is avoided, etc. People from the lower castes have few prospects of social advancement; others discriminate against them. There are approximately five hundred million Shudras, for instance, belonging to the lower caste(s), but below them are those who are not even thought of as belonging to the caste system. These are the lowest of the low, the Dalits.

What does this self-imposed term mean? *Dalits* literally means "the crushed ones," "those trodden underfoot." These people are forced to live at the edges of towns if not in the bush. They are not permitted to use the same wells as those belonging to a caste but must frequently travel long distances on foot to reach the nearest water source. They are frequently disenfranchised. When Dalit women are raped, the cases are seldom solved. The same is true when Dalits are murdered. Local police officials and public authorities are staffed by members of higher castes, whose attitude ("They are just Dalits") often means that the criminals responsible are not prosecuted.

---

[23]There are actually a number of systems overlying one another (the Jati system, the Varna system, and others). See Axel Michaels, *Hinduism: Past and Present* (Princeton, NJ: Princeton University Press, 2003). See also Jürgen Stein, *Christentum und Kastenwesen: Zum Verhältnis von Religion und Gesellschaft in Indien* (Frankfurt: Verlag O. Lembeck, 2002).

[24]Quoted in Nirmal, "Towards a Christian Dalit Theology," 27. There are currently around two hundred million Dalits in India.

Among the Dalits, there are disproportionately high levels of poverty, illiteracy, illness, and unemployment.

Now the great majority (around 80 percent) of the members of Christian congregations in India are either members of the lower castes or Dalits. There is therefore a need for a Dalit theology. Does one exist? And what would constitute a Dalit theology? In contrast to other contextual theologies, Dalit theology was only developed in the 1990s. The reason is simple: people who have been taught all their lives that they are "nothing" internalize their feelings of inferiority. They themselves come to believe that they are worthless. As a result, they are unable to raise their voices, because they have no voices. *They must first discover their own value before they can muster the courage to speak out against injustice.* At any rate, Dalit theology is no academic pursuit. Rather, it is immediately concerned with understanding the biblical texts; even *handling* the sacred texts is already of great significance for the Dalits in and of itself. Why?

In the Hindu traditions, Dalits are not permitted to set foot in temples, and they are also forbidden to read sacred texts of the Hindu traditions. They are excluded at every level of religion, society, culture, and the economy. Small wonder, then, that in this case the contextualization of the gospel—and of the theology of the cross—cannot be taken to mean understanding the religiocultural (Hindu) milieu as a con-text, i.e., as a "with-text." Instead, it is just the opposite: in this case, contextualization means deculturation, anticulturation, and thus dissent.

JESUS AS A MASTER OF MEDITATION, OR AS A DALIT?
ARVIND NIRMAL

One of the few Dalit theologians to date is Arvind P. Nirmal (1936–1995), who interpreted Jesus as a Dalit. In this case, Jesus is not interpreted within the context of Hindu conceptions. Instead, he is seen from the perspective of the biblical text as critical of that context. The biblical text is read as an answer to the affliction of the Dalits, as an answer to that which was taken from them, which is being kept from them, to the status allocated to them: the untouchables. Some Indian theologians understand Jesus in a way that is analogous to Hindu conceptions of divine incarnation, i.e., as an avatar, similar to the god Vishnu and his ten incarnations, such as the popular god

Krishna. In contrast, Dalit theologians categorically reject such an understanding. To Dalits, indigenization within the religiocultural context of the Hindu traditions is unthinkable.

Jesus is a Dalit—what does that mean?[25] How is the Bible—and the New Testament in particular—read from this perspective? A few observations: Dalits believe that just as Israel had been oppressed by Egypt, Dalits are oppressed by the Hindu culture. Yet God's election applies to both (to Israel as well as to the Dalits). This means that all Hindu values must be reassessed, for in the Hindu context, Dalits are viewed as being farthest removed from the divine, since they are ritually impure. Yet according to the message of the Bible, God—the one God—is closest to the Dalits and they to him, for God has revealed himself to human beings as a human being, even to the point of his shameful death on the cross. This approach of lowliness is already found at the beginning of the Gospels. In terms of the New Testament, Jesus was indeed a Jew but at the same time also a Dalit, for his ancestry includes untouchables such as prostitutes (the prostitute Rahab; see also Tamar). He follows his destiny in order to give justice to the untouchables (Lk 4), which will become evident particularly at the cleansing of the temple. Here Jesus in his holy wrath makes room for non-Jews in the temple; he gives to those who had previously been denied access a place to belong. They belong in the temple; they have the right to read the Holy Scriptures and to participate in ritual worship. This clearly reflects the situation of the Indian Dalits: God on the side of the untouchables, access to the temple, access to the Holy Scriptures and God's election. Jesus of Nazareth suffers death on the cross as a Dalit; after all, he is crucified *outside the gate*, outside the holy city of Jerusalem.

It needs to be noted at this point that for Dalit women, arguably the most popular passage of the New Testament is the story of Jesus and the Samaritan woman (Jn 4). No story corresponds as closely to the reality of the life of Dalit women as does this one. In Jesus Christ, God himself encounters a woman, a foreign woman, a despised woman, a suffering woman, for she— like many Dalit women—must walk a long way on a daily basis in order to fetch water from a distant well. Jesus addresses *her*, the disenfranchised

---

[25]For the following discussion, see ibid., 27-40.

woman, of his own volition, he has a conversation with *her*, he promises *her* the water of life, and *she* becomes a witness of faith.

But let us return to Nirmal. For Nirmal, the theology of the cross serves to confirm the basic approach of the Son of God: he enters the state of low-liness in order to live out the revaluation of the devalued. From this per-spective, his death on the cross takes on a particular significance, for it con-firms what Christians confess about this one God: he really does come into the world of human beings, into the world of the untouchables, whom he proceeds to touch (the lepers, the sick, the possessed, women), whom he visits in their state of exclusion, and together with whom he—and this needs to be heard with Indian ears—*eats*! Finally, he dies on the cross, which clearly distinguishes him from every conception of Hindu gods, who might well appear on earth in the form of avatars but are able to cast off this pro-jection of physicality at any time, because they as gods are not bound by the limitations of human existence (physicality) in the least. Jesus simply is *no* avatar. Rather, he is the one God in the midst of human beings. *Here the theology of the cross becomes anticulturational; it is contextual but not incul-turational; it is normative in the sense of prophetic theology* that prohibits what may *not* be. The caste system and its legitimization on the basis of re-ligious conceptions must come to an end. The conceptions of ritual purity on which it is based must be categorically rejected, for Dalits will never find a home in this culture of oppression.

We must add the critical appraisal that Nirmal's interpretation of the cleansing of the temple does not actually solve the problem, since it continues to presuppose the caste system, which, according to the New Testament, is to be discontinued entirely. That being said, Dalits do not have the luxury of such theological and conceptual rigor (yet), for they are still struggling against the very real oppressive caste system, even though—and this needs to be alluded to at this point—among Dalits, too, a consciousness of caste continues to be in effect, with the result that it is not unknown for more highly placed Dalits to assume a supercilious and aloof attitude towards lower-placed Dalits. And many Indian churches continue to reflect the caste system, which means that the progress toward a just society will be very gradual.

With regard to Christian ashrams, all of this means that Nirmal and others categorically reject the use of elements derived from the Hindu traditions, characterized as they are by Brahman influences. Indian Roman Catholic theologian Antony Kalliath makes the following critical statement:

> In the past the "inculturation theologies" in their conversance with *Brahmanic* religions have forgotten both the religiousness of India's poor and the struggles of the poor. In the history of the Church in India, the profile of Christ was either a *"Gnostic"* Christ, a "colonial Christ," or a *"Brahmanic* Christ." From the nineteenth century, Christ was presented in the frame of fulfillment theology. In the 1960s, monks and mystics propagated an *ash-ramite* Christ. Later, in the 1970s, a universal Christ was the theme of inculturationists. The focus of inculturation was on a personal and interior metacosmic liberation. Now the promise of inculturation resides in the struggles of the oppressed and in their mass culture and religiosity centered around a *"Dalit* Christ." This promise holds the hope for a process that turns the *Church in India* to a *Church of India.* Only by embracing a perspective and an approach of a liberative inculturation can the church overcome its current "credibility-crisis." If the church wants to contain the external threat of rising religious fundamentalism and to triumph over the internal threat of "mission crisis" it has to make an *irrevocable covenant* with the poor, only through whose medium the Gospel genuinely can be inculturated. The *Church in India* can thus be faithful to Jesus Christ and in the process can become the *Church of India,* which is the only acceptable form of church in the unfolding millennium to one billion Indians.[26]

This clearly shows once again that "culture" is never neutral but that by resorting to religiocultural symbolizations, the inculturation of the gospel is always associated with either the exercise or the criticism of power in society. Even though the intent of displaying derived elements in Christian ashrams is to engage in dialogue with the Hindu traditions, it places the ashrams in a difficult position. On the one hand, they meet with rejection from Hindu activists, who claim to play the defining role in Indian society, and on the other, they are rejected by Christian Dalits, who see in them a Christian spirit of compromise that they cannot tolerate for the sake of the *liberating* power of the gospel.

---

[26]Antony Kalliath, "A Call to Liberative Praxis of the Gospel: A Discourse on Inculturation in India with Special Reference to the Catholic Church," in Lalsangkima Pachuau, ed., *Ecumenical Missiology: Contemporary Trends, Issues, and Themes* (Bangalore: United Theological College, 2002), 204-36 (quotation drawn verbatim from 231).

Having made these remarks, we now take leave from India. Yet again it has become clear that in order to achieve intercultural and interreligious understanding, a twofold approach is necessary: first, that of cultural semiotics, and second, that of discourse theory. We will need to pursue this line of thought. The examples from both the macro and micro levels and their mutual interdependency have highlighted the tension with which the topic of inculturation is fraught. Having discussed the meaning of the concept of understanding, and having expounded on the concepts of foreignness and inculturation as symbolizations in the struggle of interpretations, we now turn to the concept of culture itself. We had already pointed out that the talk about *understanding other cultures* is contingent in part on the definition of the concept of understanding. It will now be shown that the understanding of other cultures is just as dependent on the operative definition of culture.

7

On Scientific Discourses and Power

What Is Culture?

Researchers from the fields of ethnology, religious studies, and sociology have provided a plethora of definitions for the term *culture*.[1] The anthropologist Arnold Gehlen (1904–1976), for instance, defines human beings as "deficient beings" because they negotiate life not merely by following their instincts any longer but by resorting to structures that they themselves have created. Were we to accept Gehlen's definition, then culture would encompass for us everything that human beings have created as a kind of "second environment." Then, to use Wolfgang Rudolph's definition, culture would include "every material and non-material element of human existence which is not found in nature but was purposefully constructed by human beings using 'innovations.' Accordingly, 'culture' may be defined as 'the totality of all the products of innovations.'"[2] A plurality of cultures exists worldwide, and their existence in the past and in the present begs the question as to whether the cultures, despite the plurality, are predicated on certain common principles or, conversely, how the differences between them may be explained.

The concept of culture also plays a deciding role when it comes to determining the relationship between Christian traditions and other cultures. This subject matter is discussed using terms such as *accommodation, indigenization, inculturation, contextualization,* or *transculturation*. In many publications on this topic, the problem is that the concept of culture is

[1]For an excellent overview of the various concepts of culture, see Karl-Heinz Kohl, "Ethnologische Theorien," in *Ethnologie—die Wissenschaft vom kulturell Fremden: Eine Einführung* (Munich: C. H. Beck, 1993), 129-66.

[2]Wolfgang Rudolph, quoted in Kohl, *Ethnologie*, 131.

simply presupposed, not precisely defined. As a result, any knowledge gains are severely limited, since despite the introduction of new categories, the metaphors for the various concepts and models of thought often remain the same. At the same time, the explanatory potential of these metaphors is rather inadequate. So it might be helpful to proceed by presenting here a series of current conceptions of culture in order to analyze their theological application or, in a more general sense, the elective affinities between individual conceptions and specific theological models. Examples are provided for each concept of culture from current issues in the area of mission theology in order to demonstrate the relevance of various concepts of culture for the modes of practical interaction that have been implemented in the history of Christianity.

THE DIFFUSIONIST CONCEPT OF CULTURE: A COMMON ORIGIN?

A logical explanation for the similarity between various cultures may be provided by hypothesizing the existence of an older culture of common origin from which various elements diffused. Many tribal myths include stories about an ancient community of humans that was destroyed. In the Bible, for example, the plurality of the peoples is traced back to an event during which God responded to the project of the human beings to construct a tower by confusing their language (Gen 11). A number of attempts were made during the nineteenth and early twentieth centuries to prove the historicity of an ancient human culture. G. Elliott Smith, for instance, identified the Egyptian civilization as an ancient culture. In contrast, proponents of the cultural fields model (*Kulturkreistheorie*) gathered various human artifacts characteristic for a particular area that were seen as an expression of the culture that had lived there. They then analyzed the distribution of such artifacts in an attempt to track the diffusion of cultural elements. Had there perhaps been a single ancient megalithic culture, the diffusion of which might explain the presence of megalithic cultures in various parts of the world?

In the area of religion, Catholic priest Wilhelm Schmidt (1868–1954) hypothesized the existence of a primitive monotheism.[3] Father Schmidt belonged to the Roman Catholic order of the Societas Verbum Divinum (SVD).

---

[3]For his comprehensive work, see Wilhelm Schmidt, *Der Ursprung der Gottesidee*, 12 vols. (Münster: Aschendorff, 1926–1955).

His model of cultural fields (*Kulturkreislehre*)[4] is the basis for a diffusionist approach, according to which there were three primitive cultures (a very speculative hypothesis from a modern perspective): a patriarchal hunter culture, a matriarchal agriculturalist culture, and a patriarchal-nomadic pastoralist culture.[5] Now present-day cultures—and this is an important implication of this approach—are derivatives of the primitive cultures, yet they constitute inferior hybridizations by comparison. The hermeneutics on which this approach is based may be distilled from the following very expressive statement:

> The study of ethnology is not content merely to present a description of the current beliefs and customs of the peoples, nor is it satisfied with studying their outward characteristics, weapons, instruments, clothing, shelters, *occupations*, and industrial arts. Rather, all of this falls under the domain of ethnography, just as the task of geography is to describe the present-day form of the earth, while it falls to the study of geology to penetrate into the inner core of the earth and to attempt to research its history and its development over hundreds, even millions of years. In the same way, the study of ethnology concerns itself with tracing the *history* of not only empires and peoples, but of *entire cultures* and of *culture* as a whole, all the way back to their origins. It does so by means of comprehensive comparisons carried out according to the historical-objective method. One of the most important outcomes of this in-depth research is the recognition that civilization (seen as the product of the human spirit) does not consist so much in the accumulation of tangible goods and progress, as it does in the edification and elevation of the soul itself. Another outcome which completes the first and defines it more precisely is the insight that this civilizing refinement of the soul is not merely the product of the few years of a single life, but rather the far more complex product of inward and outward accomplishments over the course of centuries and perhaps even millennia.[6]

---

[4]Stefan Dietrich has pointed out that the primary audience for whom this model was intended must be identified as the European public, since Schmidt formulated his theory as a scientific and apologetic discipline in opposition to the theories of evolution, for one thing, and to disprove the notion that Catholics are unable to work scientifically, for another. See Stefan Dietrich, "Mission, Local Culture and the 'Catholic Ethnology' of Pater Schmidt," *Journal of the Anthropological Society of Oxford* 23, no. 2 (1992): 111-25, and specifically 113-15.

[5]See Wilhelm Schmidt, "Die Bedeutung der Ethnologie und Religionskunde für Missionstheorie und Missionspraxis," *Zeitschrift für Missionswissenschaft* 18 (1928): 117-31.

[6]Ibid., 122.

According to this statement, Schmidt proceeds on the assumption that (1) each of the cultures derives from an ancient culture and that (2) the nature of a *present-day culture* (for instance, of a Bantu nation in Africa) cannot be appreciated based on a superficial examination of its cultural forms and artifacts (such as tools or behaviors) but that it is necessary to *compare the cultures* in order to expose the hidden, original—and in this sense *pure*—cultures that lie beneath the surface.[7] (3) According to Schmidt, the true nature of a present-day culture thus does not consist in and of itself but rather in and of the ancient culture on which it is based, which is still barely visible and from which it originally derives. Here Father Schmidt adopts a Platonic approach, for the visible manifestations (in this instance, the cultures) are based on pure and timeless forms (like Platonic ideas; in this instance, the ancient cultures).[8] The true nature of things (in this instance, the cultures) becomes apparent when one ignores the outward

---

[7]Schmidt says the following about Hamitic cultures in Africa that frequently occur in an impure and hybridized state: "Elsewhere, [the Hamitic cultures] still live in their original homelands (such as the Gallas [a reference to the Oromo people in Ethiopia] and many others) and have maintained all the natural energy [*sic*!] and purity of their religion and the family [!]." Ibid., 125.

[8]In Plato's thought, that which is outwardly visible is actually just an appearance that bedazzles and misleads the physical eye. The aim is to look past the appearance, not to be led astray by the things that charm the physical eye, but to use the *spiritual eye* to discover the inward truth. In contrast, the *hermeneutics of the physiognomists of the sixteenth and seventeenth centuries* proceeds on the assumption that while there is a significant difference between what is outward and what is inward, the outward form of things makes it possible to deduce the inward form with certainty. When it comes to medicinal herbs, for instance, Oswald Crollius states in his 1609 treatise "Von den innerlichen Signaturen oder Zeichen aller Dinge . . ." that one should aim to "recognize the herbs' hidden beneficial properties by examining their outward form." Yet even in this instance, that which is inward is considered superior to that which is outward; thus Crollius asserts that "the invisible and inward (qualities) are always nobler, more sublime, and more efficacious than the outward, visible ones, which are not as perfect as the inward ones, and in fact inferior to them."

Thus in this instance, that which is outward is not seen as a distortion of that which is inward, as Plato would have it, but rather as a revelation of it. The focus is not on the inward eye as an organ of perception (as in Plato's case) but on the physical eye. The aim is not to be intuitive but to observe. That being said, however, what the two positions have in common is that they both presuppose a difference between that which is outward and that which is inward, whether it be a difference in kind (Plato) or in degree (the physiognomists). Also, both positions presuppose a definitive sense or meaning. The correlation between outer and inner thus takes on a reliable form. In the nineteenth century, this reliability would come to be questioned more and more. See Aleida Assmann, "Zeichen—Allegorie—Symbol," in Jan Assmann, ed., *Die Erfindung des inneren Menschen. Studien zur religiösen Anthropologie* (Gütersloh, Germany: Gütersloher Verlagshaus, 1993), 28-50; for the quotations from Crollius, see ibid., 36-37. For an English translation of Crollius's book, see *A Treatise of Oswaldus Crollius of Signatures of Internal Things; or, a True and Lively Anatomy of the Greater and Lesser World*, trans. Johann Hartmann (London: Starkey, 1669).

appearances and gets to the bottom of things instead (depth hermeneutics: the true nature lies on the inside).[9]

From this perspective—according to Father Schmidt's model of cultural fields—(4) missionaries are able to understand cultures even *before they actually encounter them*, since the results of ethnological research enable "the missionary to comprehend each nation's unique character which it developed over the course of independent development described above and which it never lost entirely even during the subsequent period of hybridization."[10] This means that (5) compared to their former state, present-day cultures are inferior, hybridized products of original cultures. They are therefore in need of refinement by means of the edification of the soul and missionaries intervening in culture and religion. The prescribed solution therefore is a Christian (or more specifically, Roman Catholic) reorganization of the cultures, which would lead them to the true knowledge and worship of God, along with the corresponding social forms (monogamy, family, etc.).[11]

Besides that, Schmidt characterizes the cultures, since he claims to be able to identify certain timeless characteristics within them. For instance, he attests that the so-called Hamitic peoples are particularly suited for integration into hierarchical structures.[12] Other Europeans also adapted this view. Small wonder then that this qualification led colonial administrations to look for Hamitic peoples in their territories who would cooperate well with them (i.e., by using these ethnic groups, they would be able to exercise indirect rule)—or so it was hoped. This development led to conflicts, such

---

[9]Thus Dietrich is correct when he critically concludes that Schmidt sees present-day cultures in a certain sense as products of decay that make no sense in and of themselves but that only make sense when one is able to trace their development back to the ancient cultures in question. Dietrich, "Mission, Local Culture," 117.

[10]Schmidt, "Die Bedeutung der Ethnologie," 130.

[11]Dietrich, "Mission, Local Culture," 115.

[12]Regarding the problem of hierarchy and obedience, Fr. Schmidt writes that this is an area of particular difficulty for some ethnic groups. But in some peoples "there is an element present that is able to give orders and commands: The Hamitic peoples. They have borne witness to this ability by the historic circumstance that almost everywhere in Africa where a higher level of civilization is present, especially in the larger empires with a comprehensive administrative hierarchy, there are Hamitic tribes which have supplied the dynasties, the aristocrats, and the leading classes. They were and in many cases continue to be nomadic herdsmen, and ethnological research shows us that the capabilities which we mentioned were unique to them throughout the entire history of human culture." Schmidt, "Die Bedeutung der Ethnologie," 125.

as the one in Rwanda and Burundi, as will be demonstrated.[13] Let us summarize: For diffusionist thinkers, their conceptions of culture lead them to view the current configuration of a given culture as secondary to the ancient culture that they believe to be at work in the background. While present-day cultures are seen as inferior, "hybridized cultures," the corresponding ancient cultures are seen to embody the character of purity, wholeness, and, constancy. This constitutes an extremely essentialist concept of culture.

Interestingly, we may find elements of such a diffusionist view of culture and religion in various models right up until very recently. An example: During the phase of decolonization (especially in the 1960s and early 1970s), the criticism that African scholars expressed was intended to defend African religion(s) from denigration by Westerners. Particularly effective in this regard were the works of E. Bolaji Idowu (1913–1993), who spoke of African religions as a "diffused monotheism" in his 1973 book, *African Traditional Religion: A Definition*.[14] His choice of words indicates a diffusionist understanding of culture and religion, which brings to mind Father Wilhelm Schmidt's thesis of a primitive monotheism. At approximately the same time, a similar position was taken by Kenyan theologian and scholar of religious studies John Mbiti (b. 1931) in his books *Concepts of God in Africa* (1970) and *African Religions and Philosophy* (1969).[15] Ironically, this position adopts the presuppositions of Western authors, namely the particular appreciation for monotheistic concepts, while the claim is made that these have always comprised the nature of African religions. The claim to essential uniformity makes it possible for the African religions to compete as a more or less uniform configuration with Christianity, which is perceived as being uniform to the same extent. As a result, however—one may critically remark—African religions in their particularity were not sufficiently treated

---

[13]See chapter eight in this volume, under the heading, "Colonial Indirect Rule and Ethnic Identity: The Example of the Fulani." For earlier examples of diffusionist thought, see Bartolomé de Las Casas and Durán (see chapter sixteen in this volume, under the heading, "Theological Rationales for International Human Rights Issues").

[14]E. Bolaji Idowu, *African Traditional Religion: A Definition* (London: SCM Press, 1973).

[15]John Mbiti, *Concepts of God in Africa* (London: SPCK, 1970). In *African Religions and Philosophy* (Nairobi: Heinemann, 1969), 30, Mbiti says, "I maintain that African soil is rich enough to have germinated its own original religious perception. It is remarkable that in spite of great distances separating the peoples of one region from those of another, there are sufficient elements of belief which make it possible for us to discuss African concepts of God as a unity and on a continental scale."

with dignity any longer (even though Mbiti naturally proceeds on the basis of a plurality of different African religions, to which he nevertheless ascribes an essentially common essence), but rather pressed into the framework of an apologetic discourse.[16]

THE FUNCTIONALIST CONCEPT OF CULTURE:
SIMILAR STRUCTURES?

Functionalist theories of culture do not ascribe the similarity and analogousness between cultures to a common origin but to the analogous function that cultures serve in general. As a result, it is possible for cultures to develop totally independently in various areas of the world and yet display certain similarities, since their development is contingent on the demands of human existence. After Emile Durkheim's (1858–1917) efforts laid the groundwork, it was Bronislaw Malinowski (1884–1942) and Alfred R. Radcliffe-Brown (1881–1955)[17] in particular who contributed to the wide appeal of this approach.[18] Malinowski's theory proposed that culture serves to satisfy the needs of human beings and that it therefore reflects natural challenges.[19] His goal was to be able to ascribe meaning to the apparently so abstruse rituals and customs of traditional peoples and to avoid labeling them as irrational, childish, or even idiotic, the way other Europeans still

---

[16]Rosalind Shaw infers (and rightly so), "Parrinder, Idowu and Mbiti thereby created an authorized version of African religions as 'African Traditional Religion' which is still strongly hegemonic." Rosalind Shaw, "The Invention of 'African Traditional Religion,'" *Religion* 20, no. 4 (1990): 339-53, quotation drawn from 345.

[17]According to Malinowski, the ultimate purpose of cultural institutions is their function. This approach was later radicalized by proponents of the structuralist approach, represented in the field of ethnology by Claude Lévi-Strauss (1908–2009) in particular. He searched the cultures for certain underlying codes. Lévi-Strauss's concept of structure was even more abstract than that of Radcliffe-Brown. Kohl comments, "For Lévi-Strauss, social relationships merely comprise the building blocks for the construction of models, which in turn reveal the social structure. And the social structure again serves as the basis for the empirically verifiable social relationships on a subconscious level, just as do the rules of grammar for the actual speech act." Kohl, *Ethnologie*, 142-43.

[18]Bronislaw Malinowski, "A Scientific Theory of Culture," in *A Scientific Theory of Culture* (1944; repr., Chapel Hill: University of North Carolina Press, 1977), 1-144.

[19]A similar argument had been presented earlier by Henry Morgan (1818–1881). See also Marshall David Sahlins, *Culture and Practical Reason* (Chicago: University of Chicago Press, 1976). For Morgan, "meaning" ultimately derives from nature itself, for language is used to demarcate the differences people perceive. Language thus symbolically represents the reality of the world, whereby "symbolically" is to be understood only in the sense of another form; it portrays nature, so to speak (see ibid., 95).

frequently did during his time. No matter what impression a traditional society might make on a Western observer, no matter how "savage" and incomprehensible the rituals might appear, they are neither "irrational" nor "childish," as many in the nineteenth century continued to believe; rather, Malinowski claimed that there is a very unique logic inherent within them. What provided him with the key was the hypothesis that these customs *served some material benefit*. The *ethnologist carrying out the analysis* may come to understand the meaning behind these rituals and cultural expressions by examining the functions allocated to them, of which the indigenous people are perhaps (or possibly even very often) not even aware themselves. But this means that in so doing, the ethnologist comes to understand them better than they do themselves.[20]

Malinowski provides the following definition:

> Culture is an integral composed of partly autonomous, partly coordinated institutions. It is integrated on a series of principles such as the community of blood through procreation; the contiguity in space related to cooperation; the specialization in activities; and last but not least, the use of power in political organization. Each culture owes its completeness and self-sufficiency to the fact that it satisfies the whole range of basic, instrumental and integrative needs.[21]

For Malinowski, culture is a system created by human beings that surrounds them like a kind of "secondary environment" and allows them to satisfy their needs (nutrition, procreation, etc.).[22] This secondary environment becomes *comprehensible* when analyzed from the perspective of what Malinowski calls the basic needs of human beings. These are then met by the corresponding cultural responses.

---

[20]In the process, the personal interpretations provided by the indigenous people are critically appraised, in order to determine and expound on the underlying nature of the function that they serve. Malinowski lists certain basic needs occasioned by, among others, metabolism, procreation, physical comfort, security, movement, growth, and health, to which the following cultural responses correspond: the provision of nutrition, kinship, shelter, protection, activities, education, and hygiene. All of these cultural reactions now manifest themselves in specific forms, patterns of human society, communal rituals, implements, spatial perceptions, conceptions of time, etc. For this reason, people sometimes describe this as a functionalist concept of culture.

[21]Malinowski, "Scientific Theory of Culture," 40.

[22]Bronislaw Malinowski, *Eine wissenschaftliche Theorie der Kultur: Und andere Aufsätze* (Frankfurt: Suhrkamp, 1975), 75.

This approach ascribes a certain rationality to cultures. *Yet it must be observed—and this is important—that Malinowski did not induce this rationality from the views of members of any ethnic group and that he therefore did not seek to describe a structure separate from himself (as the observer). Rather, he was speaking from a quasi-etic perspective, attributing functionality and usefulness to certain cultural customs* and thereby becoming an outside interpreter himself, one who truly understood, one who provided explanations from the outside.[23] This begs the question whether Malinowski did justice to his own demand that indigenous people should be portrayed from their own perspective; after all, here he was introducing utilitarian considerations as a criterion, which might be completely meaningless from the perspective of indigenous people. And conversely, that which was and is very meaningful for indigenous people might become indiscernible from the perspective of functionalism, since the functionalist observer would not even be interested in it (if it lacked an observable or presumable function). American ethnologist Marshall Sahlins is correct when he offers the following criticism:

> Utilitarian functionalism is a functional blindness to the content and internal relations of the cultural object. The content is appreciated only for its instrumental effect, and its internal consistency is thus mystified as its external utility. . . . But a theory ought to be judged as much by the ignorance it demands as by the "knowledge" it affords. There is an enormous disparity between the richness and complexity of cultural phenomena such as the Intichiuma and the anthropologist's simple notions of their economic virtues.[24]

Hermeneutically, what emerges from this concept of culture is that the comparability of cultural configurations is ascribed to the analogousness of the needs that they meet and thus to their functional similarity. Marshall Sahlins has pointed out (and rightly so) that this constitutes a reductionist concept of culture. The work of Lutheran missionary Bruno Gutmann comprises a theological variant to it. Gutmann viewed cultures (and certain religious institutions) as God-given structural orders that need to be maintained.[25]

---

[23]Sahlins presents his similar criticism in Marshall David Sahlins, *Kultur und praktische Vernunft* (Frankfurt: Suhrkamp, 1981), 112.
[24]Sahlins, *Culture and Practical Reason*, 76.
[25]See the discussion on Gutmann in this volume in chapter nineteen.

THE EVOLUTIONARY CONCEPT OF CULTURE:
A UNIVERSAL PROCESS?

Evolutionism is one of the most significant schools of thought of the nineteenth century. History is viewed as a process of continual spiritual improvement. Philosopher Georg Friedrich Wilhelm Hegel (1770–1831) interpreted the history of humanity as a process in which the world spirit (*Weltgeist*) indwelling the world rises up through the medium of the various cultures and religions from an initial unconsciousness to his perfected consciousness as an "absolute spirit." Similarly, Auguste Comte (1798–1857) saw the history of humanity as progressing according to his so-called law of three stages. It states that the initial magical stage leads to the (higher) religious stage, to be succeeded in turn by the third stage, that of the scientific knowledge of the world. In each case, the succeeding stage outpaces the former. James George Frazer (1854–1941) argued along the same lines. The entire course of the history of cultures is assessed using as criterion that culture considered to have achieved the highest stage of development. In the nineteenth century, many scholars on both sides of the Atlantic did not doubt that the only contender at the time was the European-American culture. This theory was proposed in the guise of ethnology, for instance, by Lewis Henry Morgan (1818–1881) in his 1877 work *Ancient Society*.[26] Morgan distinguished between three stages of culture, namely savagery, barbarism, and civilization; in his view, the transition from one to the other was made possible in each case by a key innovation.[27] Thus history could be interpreted according to evolutionary regularities.

The evolutionary understanding of culture had a widespread theological impact within the movement of cultural Protestantism, which proceeded on the basis of a religiocultural evolution of humanity, assuming that Western Protestantism comprised the consummation of this evolutionary development. As was observed in the approach of Ernst Troeltsch, here too the spiritual underpinnings of the scientific, technical-industrial, and ethically superior Western civilization were located in the fundamental convictions of Protestant Christianity. The individuality of particular cultures was

---

[26]Lewis Henry Morgan, *Ancient Society: Or, Researches in the Line of Human Progress from Savagery Through Barbarism to Civilization* (London: Macmillan, 1877).
[27]Kohl, *Ethnologie*, 151-52.

plotted as a point in the greater continuum of the course of human history. At the same time, a value was assigned to each culture. Only *that culture seen as having reached the highest stage of development*—i.e., a constituent culture—could serve as the criterion of culture in the sense of a progressive civilization, not, as in Gutmann's case, a function of cultural institutions that is at odds with the process of technological and scientific development.

This model of thought soon encountered criticism. Friedrich Nietzsche, for instance, noted in his 1873 treatise "Vom Nutzen und Nachteil der Historie für das Leben" that

> history understood in this Hegelian fashion has been mockingly called God's sojourn on earth, though the god referred to has been created only by history. This god, however, became transparent and comprehensible to himself within the Hegelian craniums and has already ascended all the dialectically possible steps of his evolution up to this self-revelation: so that for Hegel the climax and terminus of the world-process coincided with his own existence in Berlin. Indeed, he ought to have said that everything that came after him was properly to be considered merely as a musical coda to the world-historical rondo or, even more properly, as superfluous. He did not say it: instead he implanted into the generation thoroughly leavened by him that admiration for the "power of history" which in practice transforms every moment into a naked admiration for success and leads to an idolatry of the factual: which idolatry is now generally described by the very mythological yet quite idiomatic expression "to accommodate oneself to the facts." But he who has once learned to bend his back and bow his head before the "power of history" at last nods "Yes" like a Chinese mechanical doll to every power, whether it be a government or public opinion or a numerical majority, and moves his limbs to the precise rhythm at which any "power" whatever pulls the strings.[28]

Those who favor an evolutionary interpretation of history and cultures must face the question whether the actual implementation of cultural models takes place due to the goodness of a value or simply due to the power of weapons. Is the degree of technological advancement, scientific progress, and mastery of the world in fact an appropriate criterion to measure the

---

[28]Cited from the English translation: Friedrich Nietzsche, "On the Uses and Disadvantages of History for Life," in *Untimely Meditations*, trans. R. J. Hollingdale, ed. Daniel Breazeale, Cambridge Texts in the History of Philosophy, 2nd ed. (1997; repr., Cambridge: Cambridge University Press, 1999), 104-5.

goodness of a culture? While nineteenth-century Europe might well have patted itself on the back in this regard, these hypotheses were thoroughly discredited in the twentieth century by the atrocities of the two world wars. In addition, this view of history was indeed politically exploitable—after all, it served to warrant Europe's bid for hegemony. From this perspective, religion-historical typologies such as the triad magic-religion-science are by no means harmless, for once the claim was made that indigenous people had no form of true religion at all, these interpretive formulas were used to deny them certain rights (such as land ownership) and to promote the colonial appropriation of their lands.[29]

THE RELATIVISTIC CONCEPT OF CULTURE: SEPARATE ENTITIES?

It has been shown that diffusionism answers the question as to the similarity or an analogousness of cultures by hypothesizing a common culture of origin. Functionalism does so by pointing to the similar functions that social institutions are created to carry out. Evolutionism answers the question by focusing on the common evolutionary processes that cultures follow. In contrast, relativistic approaches in the area of cultural theory do not ask this question at all. Instead, each culture is initially considered as a closed unit, as an individual entity whose particular characteristics may be explained using a common leitmotif. Approaches of this nature may be found especially among American proponents of *cultural anthropology*. Its founder is considered to be German-born anthropologist Franz Boas (1858–1942), who was installed in 1899 as a professor of anthropology at Columbia University. He had a large number of students, the most significant of which include Alfred Kroeber (1876–1960),[30] Melville Herskovits (1895–1963), Ruth Benedict (1887–1948), and Margaret Mead (1901–1978).[31] Ruth Benedict in particular highlights the uniqueness of every single culture—people are born into a culture and are thus formed by the customs, values, behaviors,

---

[29]David Chidester, "Anchoring Religion in the World: A Southern African History of Comparative Religion," *Religion* 26 (1996): 141-60, especially 142-44, 146. Later interpretations downgrade tribal religions to the immature level of the childhood of humanity (150).

[30]Alfred L. Kroeber and Clyde Kluckhohn, *Culture: A Critical Review of Concepts and Definitions*, Papers of the Peabody Museum of American Archaeology and Ethnology 47 (Cambridge, MA: The Museum, 1952).

[31]See Josef Franz Thiel, *Grundbegriffe der Ethnologie*, 4th ed. (Berlin: Reimer, 1983), 32ff.

paradigms of perception, etc., prevalent within that culture.[32] In this way, people are molded by their particular cultures. Methodologically speaking, this means in turn that every culture can only be understood and described in its actual sense within the medium of the terminology it has produced. Understanding cultures from the inside out implies that in terms of ethics, it is illegitimate to apply a benchmark to assess them from the outside, which in turn leads to a relativism of cultural values: each culture may only be understood on its own terms, and no culture may force another to adopt its own value systems on the pretext of superiority. However, if it is only legitimate to assess values on a culturally intrinsic basis, then all forms of universalistic value systems must be rejected.

Naturally, culturally relativistic approaches proceed on the assumption that cultures must satisfy certain basic human needs; at the same time, they do not focus on what is common but on what is unique. This also has political implications. Thus, for instance, Melville Herskovits played a paramount role in the drawing up of a draft declaration submitted by the American Anthropological Association in 1947 to the human rights commission of the United Nations. It demands that special consideration be granted to various cultures over against every form of universalistic ideology.

Culturally relativistic approaches show a certain affinity to the organological concept of nation (*Volksbegriff*) of Johann Gottfried Herder (1744–1803), on the one hand, and to that of Romanticism, on the other, for adherents of this current of thought also spoke of the inalienable individuality of various cultures and nations.[33] Here it must be noted that Herder's concept of culture was directed toward the *equality* of the most diverse cultures as opposed to the understanding of culture typical to Enlightenment philosophy, which was as elitist as it was Eurocentric.[34] As a result of Herder's influence, an essentialist concept of peoples and culture was in vogue in the

---

[32]See Ruth Benedict, *Patterns of Culture* (New York: Penguin Books, 1934).

[33]For more on Herder's concept of culture, see Wolfgang Müller-Funk, *Kulturtheorie: Einführung in Schlüsseltexte der Kulturwissenschaften* (Tübingen: Francke, 2006), 77-92.

[34]According to Herder, the cultures of ethnic groups in the Pacific or in Africa are just as valuable as the cultures of Europe. Herder's concept of culture, when compared with the thought of his time, reveals an emancipatory potential, for it categorically denounces a homogenizing, collective view of human history. See Herder's 1774 (polemical) paper, "Auch eine Philosophie der Geschichte zur Bildung der Menschheit." Johann Gottfried Herder, *Auch eine Philosophie der Geschichte zur Bildung der Menschheit* (1774; repr., Frankfurt: Suhrkamp, 1967).

nineteenth and into the twentieth century, which viewed the culture of a people as an expression of the "national spirit" (*Volksgeist*) or "nature" (*Wesen*) inherent to the people. Yet this view also posed a danger. When this essentialism was fused with the concept of race during and after the last third of the nineteenth century, it made it possible to interpret the cultural peculiarities of peoples in a pseudo-scientific manner as an expression of their biological-racial dispositions. This was a line of thought on which the National Socialists picked up and that they developed into a comprehensive ideology of race—with terrible consequences.

For a long time, only the notion of the individuality of peoples and cultures met with acceptance in the field of theology. Thus one may also understand the work of Bruno Gutmann as a merging of an organological concept of peoples and culture and a functionalist concept of culture. The hermeneutical difficulty of the relativistic approach consists in the fact that according to its presuppositions, it is not possible adequately to understand a culture from the outside. If each culture constitutes a quasi-independent universe of meaning, then each of these may only be understood from the inside—which is inherently impossible for an outside observer to accomplish. For no observer is able to shed the assumptions, expectations, and paradigms of thought inherent within her own culture. Does this approach not therefore imply that despite or precisely because of the emphasis on carrying out studies of individual, bounded peoples and cultures, it becomes impossible to formulate a theory of culture? And does this not undermine the legitimacy of a distinct field of science?

THE SEMIOTIC CONCEPT OF CULTURE: CULTURE AS A TEXT?

American anthropologist Clifford Geertz claims that it is a cardinal error to believe that culture is something present within people, in mental constructs, or in other constructs such as regularities in the area of symbol formation or the like.[35] He therefore protests against concepts of culture that describe culture as a "map," "sieve," or "matrix." According to Geertz, if one were to understand culture as an ensemble of symbols and one's task as isolating its elements in order to explain the relationship between the individual symbols,

---

[35]Clifford Geertz, "Thick Description: Toward an Interpretive Theory of Culture," in *The Interpretation of Cultures* (1973; repr., New York: Basic Books, 2000), 3-32.

and if one then were to interpret these symbols as aspects of a compre-hensive system, then one would run the risk of "locking cultural analysis away from its proper object, the informal logic of everyday life."[36] In contrast, Geertz considers culture to be something "public." Culture is not a reflection or expression of "something" located in the depths of human thought; rather, culture only "exists" to the extent that it is public—and thus observable, mediated, and interpersonal. Geertz attempts to explain this using a Beethoven quartet as an illustration. The Beethoven quartet is not expressed by or coterminous with the score, the properties of the instruments, or the abilities of the musicians; rather, it comes into being during the perfor-mance. For Geertz, "culture is public because meaning is."[37]

All symbolical expressions of culture are only accessible and interpre-table in the public domain. Geertz is thus a proponent of a semiotic concept of culture: "Believing, with Max Weber, that man is an animal suspended in webs of significance he himself has spun, I take culture to be those webs."[38] Cultures—when understood in the sense of symbol systems—only become accessible "by inspecting events, not by arranging abstract entities into unified paradigms."[39] While cultural actors act in ways influenced by the interpretive paradigms in which they live, these do not determine the be-havior of the actors. According to Geertz, events might therefore have transpired very differently to the way in which they were recorded in the ethnographic description. Geertz critically distances himself from behav-iorist, cognitivist, and structuralist approaches when he says, "nothing has done more, I think, to discredit cultural analysis than the construction of impeccable depictions of formal order in whose actual existence nobody can quite believe."[40]

Geertz's concern is that it is not legitimate to describe the events that take place in a particular culture in and of themselves; rather, one may only de-scribe them by seeking to understand the *interpretations provided by those*

---

[36]Ibid., 17.
[37]Ibid., 12. "As interworked systems of construable signs . . . , culture is not a power, something to which social events, behaviors, institutions, or processes can be causally attributed; it is a context, something within which they can be intelligibly—that is, thickly—described" (14).
[38]Ibid., 5.
[39]Ibid., 17.
[40]Ibid., 18.

personally involved in the events. These personal interpretations—the "indigenous theories" and allocations of meaning—are the proper object of interpretation, which can only succeed, however, if they are gauged within the entire spectrum of interpretive contexts. After all, seeing culture as a text means seeing it as a web of meaning that may be described as an interpenetration of various dimensions such as the social dimension, the aesthetic dimension, the economic, etc. An event may have various meanings and levels of meaning. From a methodological perspective, the aim therefore is to understand the object under observation as best as possible from within the semantic setting that the members of the culture in question themselves use. In this way, superficial terms of analysis are avoided whenever possible.

Accordingly, the work of ethnology is to describe events and to interpret associations, whereby the approach to these events and interpretations is provided by informants from the culture in question. What then is the result of "ethnological analysis"? Geertz dislikes answers like "the conceptual manipulation of discovered facts" or "a logical reconstruction of a mere reality," for a science that claims to uncover the "universal properties of the human mind" is pretending to describe something that does not exist.[41] Ethnographic analyses therefore do not seek to "discover" something that exists in and of itself, as it were; rather, the concern is a far more humble and at the same time more ambitious one: "Cultural analysis is (or should be) guessing at meanings, assessing the guesses, and drawing explanatory conclusions from the better guesses, not discovering the *Continent of Meaning* and mapping out its bodiless landscape."[42] The proper objects to be described are therefore events, actions, statements, and other things, whereby the notion must be rejected that behind them is a definitive structure, a bounded whole.[43] For the most part, assertions made about such structures are formulated on the basis of generalizations. "The notion that one can find the essence of national societies, civilizations, great religions, or whatever

---

[41]Ibid., 20.

[42]Ibid., 20.

[43]"So, there are three characteristics of ethnographic description: it is interpretive; what it is interpretive of is the flow of social discourse; and the interpreting involved consists in trying to rescue the 'said' of such discourse from its perishing occasions and fix it in perusable terms. . . . But there is, in addition, a fourth characteristic of such description, at least as I practice it: it is microscopic." Ibid., 20-21.

summed up and simplified in so-called 'typical' small towns and villages is palpable nonsense."[44]

As far as the theory is concerned, according to Geertz cultural theory is "not its own master"; it continues to be unseverable from the thick description of the events, actions, and interpretations of the actors.[45] This means that grandiose flights of abstraction are out of the question. A second limitation follows from the first; namely, that a cultural theory cannot predict anything. For wherever generalizations are impossible, any predictability based on them is also impossible. Accordingly, in an interpretive science, theory aids in distinguishing "between setting down the meaning particular social actions have for the actors whose actions they are, and stating, as explicitly as we can manage, what the knowledge thus attained demonstrates about the society in which it is found and, beyond that, about social life as such."[46] According to Geertz, culture is "intrinsically incomplete," which will not come as a surprise after what has been said thus far. The more impressive the assertions that are made in the field of ethnography, the more contestable they are. That being said, it is possible to try to avoid this dilemma, as the author humorously puts it:

> There are a number of ways to escape this—turning culture into folklore and collecting it, turning it into traits and counting it, turning it into institutions and classifying it, turning it into structures and toying with it. But they *are* escapes. The fact is that to commit oneself to a semiotic concept of culture and an interpretive approach to the study of it is to commit oneself to a view of ethnographic assertion as . . . "essentially contestable." Anthropology, or at least interpretive anthropology, is a science whose progress is marked less by a perfection of consensus than by a refinement of debate. What gets better is the precision with which we vex each other.[47]

Geertz uses the term *text* in the sense of "webs," whereby cultural forms of expression such as gestures of courtesy, rituals, or feasts may be read as texts to the same extent as clothing, architecture, works of art, codes of conduct, and others. Just as a written text may be interpreted in many different ways

---

[44]Ibid., 22.
[45]Ibid., 25.
[46]Ibid., 27.
[47]Ibid., 29.

because it has more than one meaning, so also may cultural forms of expression be read as texts reflecting the multitude of allocations of meaning *mediated within the society*. First, therefore, social interactions are interpreted as signs, whereby, second, the signs may have different meanings depending on the particular circumstances. Thus a sign such as a spoken expression may be modified by an additional sign such as the speaker's change in voice to connote, say, a joke, and may be interpreted by the hearers as such. However, it is also important to note, third, that people's actions may have consequences that they themselves did not intend. People are therefore not "in control of the situation" when they interact socially. The meaning content that they communicate may be interpreted in many different ways beyond their control.

The advantages of this concept of culture are self-evident: it is possible to interpret cultures in a more holistic manner than is possible when limited to the aspect of functionality. In addition, truly everything may be read as a text, whatever it may be, as soon as a community allocates meaning to it. As a result, an important consequence arises as far as the topic of intercultural theology is concerned: *semiotic holism*—that is to say, theology is not merely deposited in written texts or doctrinal formulae but is also expressed in ethics, etiquette, social structures, ways of relating, and associations of meaning, all of which may differ from one cultural context to the other. Seen from this perspective, it is at least questionable whether there is such a thing as a universal "core" of the message that may be translated. Yet the semiotic concept of culture has also met with criticism:

(1) *Interpretive sovereignty*: What determines the manner in which the interpretation is conducted? Is it the subjectivity of the author, or does the author actually engage in dialogue with the people whose culture he is attempting to describe? Is he the high and mighty interpreter in the background who understands their culture better than they do themselves? It was Vincent Crapanzano in particular who expressed this criticism.[48] (2) Is *culture once again being seen as a unit here*? Is it not possible for culture to be interpreted in endlessly different ways? And if yes, who vouches for the

[48]Vincent Crapanzano, "Das Dilemma des Hermes: Die verschleierte Unterwanderung der ethnographischen Beschreibung," in D. Bachmann-Medick, ed., *Kultur als Text. Die anthropologische Wende in der Literaturwissenschaft* (Frankfurt/M.: Fischer Verlag, 1996), 161-93.

uniformity of feelings and attitudes among the members of a culture? (3) Is the *reading* that is taking place here *apolitical*? Is the metaphor of "culture as a text" not dangerous in the sense that it suggests it is possible to read from a detached perspective, whereas understanding always constitutes a part of the social act, one shaped by special interests and determined by constellations of power? (4) Which is the operative *concept of text*? Is culture as a text not subject to different *conditions of manufacture* than a written text, than a recorded text, which generally only has one author? Furthermore, should the *culture in which texts are received* (such as the liturgical use of repetition) not also be taken into account as far as meaning is concerned? Does cultural interaction not present *totally different dimensions of corporality*, of staging, of the meaningfulness of smell and taste, than does a written and thus disembodied text? Is there not a narrative structure inherent within each text that produces effects of its own?

THE DISCOURSE-THEORETICAL CONCEPT OF CULTURE: CULTURE AS A FIELD OF DISCOURSE?

Discourse theoretical models of culture represent yet another approach. In this approach, culture is essentially no longer viewed as a unit (as is still the case in semiotic theories of culture) but rather *as a complex field of action, characterized by tension, i.e., as a field of discourse.* This alerts us to the circumstance that there are dividing lines not merely between cultures as a whole but also within each individual culture, since cultures are not homogenous within themselves; rather, processes of negotiation are constantly taking place within them between various intracultural actors. One of the spiritual fathers of discourse theory was French philosopher Michel Foucault (1926–1984). According to Foucault, the aim is to investigate the conditions within which knowledge or experience is possible, i.e., the conditions that predicate the gaining of knowledge and experience. Foucault asks, What are "the prerequisites for the making of statements, the laws of their coexistence with each other, and the specific form of their way of being?"[49] Thus, what constitutes an object of discourse? Let us take as an example the current European debates about the use of headscarves by Muslims. What

---

[49]Michel Foucault, *Archäologie des Wissens* (Frankfurt: Suhrkamp, 1981), 184. For an English translation of the French original, see *The Archaeology of Knowledge* (London: Routledge, 1989).

are the different forms in which people take positions on the issue? Examples might be comments on news reports and talkshows, legal regulations (such as with regard to public spaces), etc. What are the concepts that lend a certain weight to certain assertions? In this instance one might mention, say, the unverbalized presupposition of the religious neutrality of the state. Furthermore, the analysis needs to take into consideration who selects which strategy from which position in order to take a certain line of argument in the discourse.

Since the 1980s especially, scholars from the area of postcolonial studies have made important contributions to this research perspective, particularly scholars from an immigrant background now living in Western societies.[50] These people were frequently not viewed as locals in their countries of residence, e.g., as Britons in Great Britain, nor was this the case in their country of origin (e.g., as Pakistanis in Pakistan); rather, they found themselves located in a "third space." Westerners tended to classify people according to binary pairs as either insiders or outsiders, locals or foreigners, with the result that "normal people" were seen to comprise the center and other cultures the periphery. In contrast, these authors insist that each of these representations essentially formed part of a discourse of alterity, which—either consciously or unconsciously—served to prop up the West's monopolization of the agenda and indeed Western hegemonic power.

Accordingly, the emphasis was placed not on what people in any given culture have in common but on what sets them apart. As a result, intercultural encounters could not be neatly classified in terms of subject-object constellations, since this would only have served to perpetuate the West's self-portrayal as the only or principal actor in each case. Also, many individual studies demonstrated that this self-portrayal was false, since local populations functioned as actors during intercultural interactions in various ways. The following example serves as an illustration.

The majority of immigrants living in the London neighborhood of Southall identify themselves as "Asians" (as opposed to the British majority society). Yet this "identity" is only one among many, for the residents go on

---

[50]Werner Schiffauer, "Der cultural turn in der Ethnologie und der Kulturanthropologie," in Friedrich Jäger, *Handbuch der Kulturwissenschaften* (Stuttgart, Germany: J. B. Metzler, 2004), 2:502-17, especially 507.

to use a wide variety of additional identity markers to distinguish themselves from one another as, say, Sikhs, Hindus, Muslims, or Afro-Caribbeans.
For example, Hindus frequently view *Hindu culture* as an overarching one
that also includes the (traditionally majority lower-caste) Sikhs. At the same
time, this inclusivity also constitutes a claim to power, against which the
Sikhs defend themselves. The Muslims perceive themselves as *a community
of Muslims*, i.e., as bracketed together not by culture but by religion, albeit a
religion composed of many different cultural communities (Muslims from
Pakistan, India, Malaysia, Arabic countries, etc.). Conversely, the Afro-
Caribbeans, emerging from a long history of enslavement, see themselves
faced with the need *to begin to identify (create) a common culture.*[51] Thus we
find here very different approaches as to the relationship between what is
commonly designated as culture, community, and religion.

But that is not all. We find further distinctions *even within these configurations*; for instance, independent, separate communities formed within
what was commonly viewed as the Sikh culture. So in this instance, competition between various castes plays an important role.[52] Thus the "identity"
of social groups is continually being redefined; rival claims to power between the groups are at the heart of the issue, and this is the reason for the
multiple assignations of identity, at least according to culture, religion, and
community, e.g., a Sikh identifying herself *as Asian on a cultural level* over
against the British majority society, *as belonging to the Sikh religion* over
against the claim by Hindus that her cultural identity is Hindu, and *as a
member of the Jat caste* within the Sikh community over against another

---

[51]Gerd Baumann, "Ethnische Identität als duale diskursive Konstruktion: Dominante und demotische Identitätsdiskurse in einer multiethnischen Vorstadt von London," in Aleida Assmann
and Heidrun Friese, eds., *Identitäten*, vol. 3 of *Erinnerung, Geschichte, Identität*, 2nd ed. (Frankfurt: Suhrkamp, 1999), 288-313, specifically 299-300.

[52]At issue is a dispute regarding caste status between Sikhs from the Jat caste (farmers), who had
immigrated in the 1950s and 1960s from India, and Sikhs from artisan castes who had immigrated in the 1970s from East Africa (where they had lived for three generations). When the
former claimed that the Jat caste was superior, the latter responded by *forming their own communities*, arguing for the higher status of their own caste on the basis of a higher level of education and greater economic power, and by resorting to new (and, in part, newly invented) traditions. According to these, their own past in India was not that of landless serfs serving the
landowning Jat caste, but rather that of a patronage "of artisans who were actually superior to
the landowning, yet poorly qualified Jat." They pointed out the high level of social mobility in
East Africa, that they had servants there, and the like. See Baumann, "Ethnische Identität," 301.

caste's claim to superiority.[53] From this perspective, the subject matter of intercultural theology appears in a new light, for it concerns the event of the inculturation of the gospel as a process of negotiation in which issues of power and status play an important role, as do such questions as who defines Christian identity, which position someone takes in the field of social institutions and interactions, and many others besides.[54]

CONCEPTS OF CULTURE AND AN INTERCULTURAL HERMENEUTICS

The deliberations above have shown how vital the preconception of culture is for the issue of intercultural understanding. Both aspects are mutually interdependent. The debate in the area of mission studies surrounding the topic of inculturation also highlights variations of such concepts of culture, although little attention is given to the complexity of the issue. Now for quite some time, calls have been made for mission studies to be understood as a hermeneutical discipline.[55] Theo Sundermeier made an important contribution in this regard in the form of a hermeneutics of foreignness.[56] Sundermeier points out (and rightly so) that such topics as the perception of medicine and healing,[57] of art,[58] and of ritual performances (such as at festivals[59]) are of particular importance for intercultural understanding.

We will now pick up on this line of thought and extend it. In the following section we will do so by beginning to examine from the perspective of cultural semiotics other forms of expression such as spatial paradigms, systems of time, clothing, and other factors that play a role in intercultural exchanges,

---

[53]Ibid., 306ff.

[54]For more recent debates in the area of cultural studies, see the discussion under "postcolonial turn" in chapter twenty-three.

[55]Theo Sundermeier, *Den Fremden verstehen* (Göttingen: Vandenhoeck, 1996).

[56]For contributions from other disciplines, such as philosophy and German studies, see for instance Bernhard Waldenfels, *Der Stachel des Fremden* (Frankfurt: Suhrkamp, 1990); Ram Adhar Mall, *Philosophie im Vergleich der Kulturen* (Darmstadt, Germany: Wissenschaftliche Buchgesellschaft, 1995).

[57]For example, see Thomas Lux, "Zur Rezeption des Fremden in der Medizin: Der Begriff Malaria bei einem Beniner Krankenpfleger," in Theo Sundermeier, ed., *Den Fremden wahrnehmen: Bausteine einer Xenologie* (Gütersloh, Germany: Gütersloher Verlagshaus, 1992), 76-98.

[58]Theo Sundermeier, "Die Daseinserhellung durch Kunst übersteigt immer die des Wortes," in *Jahrbuch Mission 1990* (Hamburg: Evangelisches Missionswerk in Deutschland, 1990), 29-41; Sundermeier, *Christliche Kunst weltweit: Eine Einführung* (Frankfurt: Otto Lembeck, 2007).

[59]Jan Assmann and Theo Sundermeier, *Das Fest und das Heilige* (Gütersloh, Germany: Gütersloher Verlagshaus, 1991).

attempting to determine their semantic content for various actors. We will also need to address from the perspective of discourse theory the issue of perceptions of indigeneity and ascriptions of foreignness as well as the exercise of power that they manifest. We will present a number of examples and then incorporate both perspectives into an integral concept of culture.

8
· ·

Cultural Semiotics, Discourse Theory, and Intercultural Hermeneutics

Now, how may elements of cultural semiotics on the one hand and of discourse theory on the other be utilized for the construction of an intercultural hermeneutics? The following examples will serve to illustrate a number of aspects of a semiotic concept of culture and also of a discourse-theoretical concept of culture. We will use the example of the Ewe to consider how the "Christian" model of life created new social and interpretive paradigms. We will then address the discourse-theoretical question: Just how does "ethnic identity"—again using the example of the Ewe—come about? In this regard, the discourse-theoretical approach assumes that an ethnic identity does not exist as such, but rather that such an identity comes into being as a result of complex discourse formations and is subject to constant change. Ascriptions of indigeneity and foreignness play an important role in this regard. This will be demonstrated in what follows using the topic of language and the politics of language as well as the topic of ascriptions of foreignness and *indirect rule*. Beyond that we will investigate in what form of cultural memory these ascriptions are consolidated. This will segue into insights from the field of cultural semiotics arising from the work of Jan and Aleida Assmann.

"Clothes Make the Man": The Issue of Clothing from the Perspective of Cultural Semiotics

Let us begin with some observations from the discipline of cultural semiotics. Kirsten Rüther has shown that the Lutheran missionaries of the Berlin and Hermannsburg Mission Societies initially viewed the dress habits of

newly converted indigenous people rather nonchalantly.[1] In the early phase
of these missionary efforts (ca. 1860–1870), the missionaries were still very
interested in the African manner of dress and in the materials used (leather,
raffia, etc.). Even so, they were favorably disposed when converts attempted
to adopt similar dress to that of the Europeans, since the missionaries viewed
this as a general sign of their inner disposition—i.e., that the converts were
taking their new Christian faith very seriously and setting themselves apart
from their traditional context of origin accordingly. However, as the years
went on, the missionaries' attitudes and interpretation of dress styles
changed considerably. During the 1870s, the missionaries integrated themselves into the society of the Boer settlers more and more, and in the process
the adoption of European dress styles by indigenous Christians came to be
viewed as *evidence of their intent to put themselves on the same social level as
the whites.* This was seen in turn as an illegitimate transgression of limits and
as endangering the missionaries' own position of power. In consequence,
the missionaries repeatedly tried to prohibit blacks from dressing like whites,
using such means as rules for life on the mission stations. Since 1891 and 1895
respectively, Hermannsburg and Berlin missionaries introduced rules of
dress (*Kleiderstaat*) on all their stations in southern Africa, according to
which offenses resulted in ecclesiastical punishments such as exclusion from
Holy Communion, being denied the right to marry, and the like.[2]

While during the 1860s the dress styles of indigenous people were still
rather eclectic due to the limited availability of European clothing (one
carried an umbrella, another wore a pair of shoes or a shirt, whatever he
happened to have, and wore it with pride), and while during the 1870s, when
the availability of European clothing improved, dress styles were still eclectic,
during the 1880s and afterward European clothing became downright fash-
ionable, even according to European standards—especially in the cities—
although it must be noted that from this time forward indigenous people
preferred British clothing to that of the Germans and Boers. This raised the

---

[1]See Kirsten Rüther, "Heated Debates over Crinolines: European Clothing on Nineteenth-Century
Lutheran Mission Stations in the Transvaal," *Journal of Southern African Studies* 28 (2002): 359-
78; for a summary, see especially 365-68. See also Rüther, *The Power Beyond: Mission Strategies,
African Conversion and the Development of a Christian Culture in the Transvaal* (Münster: LIT
Verlag, 2002).
[2]Rüther, "Heated Debates," 375.

very practical (but actually mission-theological) question: How precisely should African Christians live—e.g., in terms of clothing? Should they continue to adopt African dress? Should they wear mixed fashions or totally European dress styles? African items of clothing continued to be used especially among women in rural areas and in those political-social constructs in which blacks continued to be in charge for a long time (such as among the Pedi). In contrast, wherever and to the extent that colonial power was exercised, there was a greater tendency for people to adapt to European dress habits.

Thus during the early transition phase, *indigenous people demonstrated tremendous uncertainty* especially in their perception of *the social status expressed by means of dress habits.* This shows once again that the processes of transformation went hand-in-hand with multifaceted processes of negotiation within the black indigenous population. For example, one indigenous chief stopped attending worship services because he lacked European clothing. When he mentioned to a missionary that he was unable to attend because of his clothing, the missionary replied that before God all people are equal. Obviously, the missionary did not understand the chief's underlying motives. This particular congregation had adopted the practice that Christians who had come into the possession of items of European clothing— regardless of the source (a gift, for instance)—*sat all the way in front,* whereas those wearing traditional African clothing *sat all the way at the back.* Thus the possession of clothing represented the social hierarchy of the Christian congregation, and for this reason the chief would have incurred shame if he had had to sit *at the very back* in the Christian congregation because of his *traditional high rank.* Only after he had purchased corresponding items of clothing did he attend worship services again, which—we may conclude— brought his social role in the indigenous hierarchy into line with that in the Christian community, at least in his perspective.[3]

From the perspective of cultural semiotics, these examples demonstrate the significance of clothing as a means to portray social distinctions and societal hierarchies. Clothing is therefore never just a matter of "outward formalities" but rather a multifaceted, meaningful event. Even Great Britain

---

[3]Ibid., 365.

as a colonial power understood the significance of clothing as a means of distinction and as an instrument to raise the morale of British colonial troops and colonial administrations abroad, and for this reason uniformity was prescribed to the greatest extent possible.[4] Wearing European clothing meant that indigenous Christians occupied a multidimensional position in society; it marked their distance from the traditional culture of origin and their proximity to modern life and the European culture, which in turn emphasized their elevated social status over against the older hierarchies. The blacks were looking to the whites, and the analogousness of the clothing indicated—albeit implicitly—that the blacks occupied the same legal status as the whites. This was a sign, and as we have seen, the whites clearly saw it as such—and reacted accordingly.

The example demonstrates that clothing as a sign system was and continues to be dependent on various contexts, of which we might mention the following factors (which by no means constitute an exhaustive list). To begin with, the power-powerlessness factor is paramount: as long as the missionaries were dependent on blacks, clothing was for them a *religious symbol* of distinction (of "true conversion"). But in the later colonial context, when the relationship of power had become inverted, clothing came to be understood as a *social sign* ("the pretense to a social status equal to that of the whites"). In addition, we might mention the lack or supply of goods (in this instance, textile goods), the new configuration of social-hierarchical standings, and many others besides.

THE COMMUNICATION OF SPACE (PROXEMICS): LIFE ON THE MISSION STATIONS AS A SIGN SYSTEM

Often, missionaries were formally invited to settle in the territory of a particular tribe.[5] In these cases, it was usually the local chiefs who allocated the

---

[4]See Helen Callaway, "Dressing for Dinner in the Bush: Rituals of Self-Definition and British Imperial Authority," in Ruth Barnes and Joanne Bubolz Eicher, eds., *Dress and Gender: Making and Meaning* (Oxford: Berg, 1993), 232-47.

[5]Peel uses the example of the missionaries of the Church Missionary Society in the nineteenth century who worked among the Yoruba (in what is today Nigeria) to point out that such invitations were extended for a number of different reasons; one example was that the chiefs wanted to share in the—obviously visible—power of the whites. See John D. Y. Peel, *Religious Encounter and the Making of the Yoruba* (Bloomington: Indiana University Press, 2003), 124: "They wanted not only allies and technology, but also access to the hidden sources of the white man's power."

land for mission stations to the missionaries. The land in question was not infrequently located on hills that had been used as burial places for those who had fallen in battle and that were therefore considered unsuitable for settlement from the perspective of the locals, since they feared the presence of evil spirits. The missionaries would accept these sites (frequently without being aware of their significance for the indigenous people) and construct their mission stations on them.[6] The indigenous people considered the success of these forms of settlements (i.e., the survival of the missionaries) to be significant since the missionaries remained unharmed, which was attributed to the power of the God whom they proclaimed. Even *the construction of a station as such* was considered by the indigenous people *to be a sign*: the strong God of the missionaries was protecting them from evil ancestors or from the spirits of a particular place (a former burial site)—or at least, that is how it was read. Frequently, the missionaries remained unaware of this reading. The special separation may be seen to constitute a second level of meaning: such a mission settlement spatially manifested the demarcation between the traditional religion and the Christian one since the settlement in terms of its entire materiality was distinct from the surrounding towns and settlements: the houses were built differently, rectangularly, according to European prototypes; the clothing of the residents (the missionaries and Christian converts) was new and different; the ordering of time as far as the daily routine was concerned was different, and also as far as the ordering of the days was concerned (the institution of new days of rest, such as Sunday rest); a different type of family order was instituted (polygamy was forbidden), as were very different social paradigms, as opposed to the towns of origin; and many others.

The materiality of everyday life on a station like that was in itself a comprehensive sign system, even if most missionaries did not intend it to be such, since they considered the life they modeled to be for the most part "normal" and "Christian." Let us analyze some of these aspects: There was a great deal of

---

This also gave them an interest in the specific character of missionaries as European *priests*: men who professed expertise in the world of 'spirit' or the hidden sources of power (*awo*) and so were comparable with the religious specialists that they already knew, such as diviners and Muslim *alufa*."

[6]For what follows, see Birgit Meyer, "Christian Mind and Worldly Matters: Religion and Materiality in Nineteenth-Century Gold Coast," *Journal of Material Culture* 2, no. 3 (1997): 311-37.

work to be done on the mission stations, and the salaries enabled construction workers, artisans, and teachers to achieve a greater level of independence from the extended family, greater mobility, and thereby the opportunity to relocate. Compared to the traditional towns, these groups were social climbers. By substituting the model of the nuclear family for that of the extended family, the separate house of the nuclear family for the men's huts and women's huts in a large kraal, and the model of men working while the women remained at home for that of the traditional society, obviously different emphases were made. Not only that, but new social relationships were created, as well as new models of spatial planning, body perception, role allocation, work routines, organizing space and time, and even new anthropological models. After all, the conception of a human being in the traditional religious configurations of the Ewe was a rather more open one in the sense that it was believed that each person was influenced by a spiritual being. The missionaries strongly opposed this notion and in so doing insisted that both the self and the environment are controllable.

Let us note: the task of intercultural theology is to apply the hermeneutics of cultural semiotics in order to make "visible" those sign systems that would otherwise go unnoticed by normal observers. Beyond that, intercultural theology endeavors to discover new ascriptions of semantic content in religiocultural transformation processes. Such new ascriptions are—and this is an important discovery—often athematic, unplanned, intuitive, and associative. Now, from a hermeneutical perspective this observation does not suffice; it is also important to factor in an insight contributed by the discourse-theoretical perspective, namely that new ascriptions are often made as conscious identity constructs. The following two examples will serve to illustrate this principle.

Ethnic Identity as a Construct and Language Issue: The Example of the Ewe

With regard to the Ewe, Birgit Meyer points out that the work of the North German Mission Society (*Norddeutsche Missionsgesellschaft*) contributed significantly to the construction of the ethnic identity of "the" Ewe. This "identity" did not exist as such prior to their arrival of the missionaries; rather, it was formed as a new construct as a result of interactions between them and the indigenous people.[7] At the risk of oversimplifying the issue, we might name the following aspects as being of particular significance: (1) The *historical background*: In the year 1847, the missionaries entered the territory of what is today southeastern Ghana and southern Togo. A number of smaller ethnic groups lived independently from one another in this area; linguistically, however, they belonged to the same family of language. (2) The *interpretive paradigms of the German missionaries*: The missionaries were influenced by the views of mission society director Franz Michael Zahn (1833–1900), a prominent figure of the German history of mission. He served as the director of the North German Mission Society from 1862 to 1900.

(a) Under the influence of Johann Gottfried Herder, Zahn became a proponent of the idea that an individual *Volksgeist* ("spirit of the people" or "national spirit") is inherent to each people. This national spirit manifests itself in the specific culture and particularly in the specific *language* of a people. The important role assigned to a culture's language may be understood as a reaction to the political situation of the German territories: during the time of German Romanticism (and afterward), language was considered an especially important deciding factor in terms of cultural unity for the reason that there was no German state that embodied the German nation, and thus language was the only remaining unifying factor that represented the cohesion of the diverse political entities that made up the German lands.

(b) Yet whereas Herder viewed the peoples as independent cultural units occupying the same level, Zahn believed that the existence of all peoples was originally based on their relationship to God but that the tower of Babel and its consequences, namely the confusion of language and the dispersal of humanity, ruined this relationship. According to Zahn, the peoples distanced themselves from God, and this manifested itself not only in the *corruption of their relationship with God*[8] but in consequence also in the *fragmentation of the peoples* and in a certain *degeneration of their language*. In the past, as now, the task of

---

[7]The following discussion will serve to summarize a number of Birgit Meyer's main points in a systematic manner. See Birgit Meyer, "Christianity and the Ewe Nation: German Pietist Missionaries, Ewe Converts and the Politics of Culture," in Artur Bogner, Bernd Holtwick and Hartmann Tyrell, eds., *Weltmission und religiöse Organisationen* (Würzburg, Germany: Ergon Verlag, 2004), 541–69.

[8]Franz Michael Zahn, "Die Muttersprache in der Mission," *Allgemeine Missions-Zeitschrift* (1895): 337–60. See also Werner Ustorf, *Die Missionsmethode Franz Michael Zahns und der Aufbau kirchlicher Strukturen in Westafrika (1862–1900)* (Erlangen, Germany: Verlag der Ev.-Luth. Mission, 1989).

mission is to "introduce the pagan peoples to the proper use of their own language." In other words, *by virtue of their education and knowledge of God, the Christian missionaries can and must provide outside help to the peoples to meet them in their state of religious, cultural, and linguistic alienation and lead them back to their own origins—which the missionaries must identify.*[9] Zahn's pointed comment refers, "The more homogenous the people are, and the more sophisticated their culture is as a result, the less divided they will be linguistically."[10]

The implications of the understanding of culture and language are extensive. Despite the existing plurality of people groups, kinship groups, and clan groups, of languages and dialects, of fractions and frictions, the missionaries should remain undeterred, for they know ahead of time (on the basis of a certain reading of biblical proof texts as well as of their own cultural character, which they have not necessarily thought through) that the following holds true: (1) Contrary to the bewildering plurality they might find on the ground, there *is* (or there *was* once) in each case *one* people, a *single unit with clearly defined boundaries* and a *uniform* language, whereas dialects are considered to be deviant mutations. (2) The current form of the culture and language *has deviated and deteriorated from the original, divinely determined form*. (3) Accordingly, the goal of the missionary efforts is first to overcome the fragmentation, second to standardize the language, third to seek out the protolanguage (which undoubtedly existed) to this end, fourth to raise the linguistic standard of this protolanguage in order to enable its revival, and fifth to serve as an appropriate vehicle to express the Christian teaching about God. This understanding of culture is thus both a diffusionist and an essentialist one. At the same time, the logical inconsistencies of the idea are unmistakable, since it is assumed that there will be only one single human language in the end. Therefore, the aim is not to understand cultural configurations in and of themselves but rather to subject them to a certain predetermined interpretive paradigm that centers on one single vision for the future (one people, one language, one culture, one belief in God)—in spite of all imponderabilities, detours, and setbacks.

---

[9]Zahn therefore considers the contemporary contribution by African cultures to the glorification of God to be negligible and only expects them to become significant in future—i.e., after they have been become sufficiently sophisticated. Zahn, "Die Muttersprache," 351.

[10]Ibid., 341.

(c) Zahn concluded that one of the important tasks of the missionaries was to study indigenous languages on site. Another was to "elevate" and "purify" the languages of the peoples so that the pure national spirit could come into its own along with the Christian faith. *Thus for Zahn, ennoblement is not coterminous with a cultural convergence with European culture; rather, ennoblement means the restoration of the original national spirit in an original (Christian) relationship with God and the restored unity of the people as a whole.* Ennoblement means to lead the people back to their own cultural roots and thus to lead them to a point at which all peoples with their own respective cultures and unique characteristics are considered equal. Practically speaking, ennoblement means to trace the steps back from the state of fragmentation into various dialects (seen as inferior) to the unity of the—allegedly—original language. After all, it was assumed that there had been *only one language.* This clearly demonstrates the influence of Herder's organologically unifying "peoples concept." Ennoblement is the reversal of fragmentation into people groups and the restoration of the one people; it is the return from a state of being separated from God to the worship of the triune God by means of the divine Word. If possible, every indigenous Christian should be able to read this Word in the written form of "the Bible" in his "mother tongue," which yet again serves to underline the principle that writtenness takes precedence over orality.

(3) *Missionary work and "ethnogenesis"*: Let us follow the course of events as it unfolded. In light of our context, we will concentrate deliberately only on the language issue as we do so: (a) The missionaries of the North German Mission Society learned indigenous languages/dialects and conducted research into *what they believed to be the most original and the purest manifestation* of "the" Ewe language, which they claimed to find in the Anlo dialect of a group of coastal inhabitants.[11] (b) By means of dictionaries, grammars, and Bible translations, this dialect was standardized as "the" Ewe language. At the same time, attempts were made geographically to localize "the Ewe people" and in so doing to define them. This constitutes an objectification that, as Meyer states, may be viewed purely as a construct of the missionaries,

---

[11]Meanwhile, this was nothing more than an assertion. It is remarkable that this happened to be the dialect spoken in the area in which the mission station of the missionaries in question was situated.

for up until that point in time there had never been such an entity as a single Ewe people.[12]

(c) Since the mission society maintained schools, those indigenous people who spoke other dialects or even languages—from the interior, say— first had to learn the Ewe language used by the missionaries (which had up until then been only one regional language among many). In this way, the basic assumptions that the German missionaries brought with them led to the establishment of what they had posited—thanks to an infrastructure defined by language and by the promulgation of the language through the education system.[13] If the missionaries had begun their work farther north,

---

[12]Meyer, "Christianity and the Ewe Nation," 550. At this point one should also take the pragmatic aspects of the issue into consideration: it was simply a matter of capacity—the missionaries were unable and unwilling to translate the Bible into every single dialect. Yet consideration was also given to a theological factor, namely the unity of the nascent church across linguistic boundaries. Many affiliated with the mission clearly anticipated that translating the Bible into a number of languages would cause the nascent church to be fragmented by "tribalization," which in turn posed the danger that the church might split along ethnic lines. Such schisms were indeed known to have taken place. Both aspects feature in a 1907 text by Berlin mission inspector Karl Axenfeld, who was commenting on the many ethnicities in the area to the north of Lake Nyasa: "It must be clarified at the outset that it would be impossible to treat all six or seven linguistic areas of our Nyasa mission the same. That would mean seven forms of printed literature, seven seminaries, seven groups of missionaries, i.e. an enormous overhead of means and personnel, which—and this would be the worst part of all—would destroy the unity of the nascent church. . . . I cannot concede that the mission is obligated to preserve the languages of hundreds of smaller African tribes by means of printed literature." Quoted in Thorsten Altena, *"Ein Häuflein Christen mitten in der Heidenwelt des dunklen Erdteils": Zum Selbst- und Fremdverständnis protestantischer Missionare im kolonialen Afrika 1884-1918* (Münster: Waxmann, 2003), 98-190, specifically 140-41. In practice, this meant that the larger language groups received preferential treatment from the mission societies (which sometimes led to the suppression of smaller language groups). Conversely, the status of some languages as the lingua franca of a certain area (e.g., Kiswahili in East Africa or Sango in West Africa) was officially recognized. This meant, however, that the organological principle that "the essence of a people is expressed in its language" was effectively abandoned—for pragmatic reasons.

[13]See Arthur J. Knoll, "Die Norddeutsche Missionsgesellschaft in Togo 1890-1914," in Klaus J. Bade, ed., *Imperialismus und Kolonialmission* (Wiesbaden, Germany: Steiner, 1982), 165-88. The North German Mission Society had begun to maintain schools long before Germany took over the territory as a colony. At the turn of the century there were three types of schools in Togo: (1) elementary schools, (2) high schools, and (3) trade schools. The statistics reflect the significance of the mission societies: in the year 1911, of the total of 324 schools, 315 were elementary schools. Meanwhile, the colonial government attempted to prevent the formation of an indigenous elite. For this reason, the education of indigenous people was carried out almost exclusively by representatives of the Bremen Mission Society and by Steyler missionaries. Of the 315 elementary schools, 166 were maintained by the Roman Catholic missionaries of the Steyler order, the Society of the Divine Word (*Societas Verbum Dei*); 141 by the North German Mission Society; six by the Wesleyans; and only two by the government. In the year 1911, there were 319 mission schools in the country and only five government schools.

then a different language might well have become "the" language of "the" Ewe. The "Ewe people" construct is thus an accident of history, yet it became more and more of a reality as a construct as it was reinforced by the institutions of the education system and the church (and later the colonial administration). At any rate, the German colonial administration adopted this language in the year 1912.[14]

The results of the research that the missionaries carried out in the fields of ethnology, history, and geography were taught in the schools. The idea was that this would substantially contribute to the development of a national Ewe consciousness.[15] Conversely, bringing together indigenous people from all manner of kinship groups, clans, and tribes in the Protestant Ewe church in a single religious context and using a homogeneous language had a unifying effect on them. Whereas previously, kinship relations had been associated with the various local cults, a disassociation now took place in that regard, which led to a social restructuring and to a communitization that rose above clan divisions (however, in light of ecclesiastical structures, this begs the question whether and to what extent clan structures now asserted themselves in a new way). *Birgit Meyer points out that the consolidation of this "Ewe nation" reflects the view of German Romanticism, which had been strongly impacted by the pietistic movement, for here "nation" was not understood in terms of a political system but rather as a linguistic-cultural unit. Conversely, the idea of an "Ewe" nation may have been an attractive one for the indigenous people in the region; on the one hand, it was an expression of participation in modernity (even though this term was not used as such), and on the other, it offered the proposition of a counterweight over against other, more centralized ethnic groups such as the Asante.*[16]

This example clearly shows that various factors played a role in the intercultural interactions: in terms of the missionaries, their own social, geographic, and political origins need to be considered (i.e., urban or rural, or the political situation at the time), as well as their theological position (i.e., theological anthropology). In terms of the indigenous people, their social

---

[14]This Ewe is still in use as a literary language today, while in everyday life people switch between various dialects. See Meyer, "Christianity and the Ewe Nation," 551.

[15]Ibid., 554.

[16]Ibid., 555.

status plays a role, as well as their interest in benefiting from the products and abilities of the whites; consideration needs also to be given to the political circumstances in the area (the initial dependency of the missionaries, invitations issued by local chiefs) as well as to the processes of exchange and configuration in various areas. It must be recognized that the mission stations constituted new and clearly demarcated settlements that stood out from their surroundings because of their new social forms (nuclear family), new forms of production (skilled crafts and trades, distribution, monetary exchange), new forms of time (new festivals, a new weekly rhythm, Sundays), new artifacts (clothing), and new role patterns (men work, women are restricted to the home). *In summary, a cultural semiotics of transformative processes is needed to reconstruct these events and their significance for various role players, such as the important issue of clothing. Clothing can serve as a means of distinction, as a means to demarcate actual or aspired-for positions within hierarchical structures, as a sign of belonging to the new movement or of wishing to do so. Clothing oneself may be viewed as a creative process of selection, adaptation, transformation, and configuration of previously distinct artifacts. Aspects of uncertainty and contingency need also to be factored in when considering this issue, as well as the ascription of meaning and shifts of meaning on the part of various actors.*

Colonial Indirect Rule and Ethnic Identity: The Example of the Fulani

Authors such as Birgit Meyer, John David Yeadon Peel,[17] or Frank Salamone have pointed out that certain ethnic identities only came about because of the colonial situation in the first place.[18] The topic of rule in the sense of *indirect rule* often plays a specific role in this regard, since in many instances British colonial rule attempted to harness local systems of rule for the benefit of its own sovereignty. At the beginning of the twentieth century (1931),

---

[17]See his excellent study: John David Yeadon Peel, *Religious Encounter and the Making of the Yoruba* (Bloomington: Indiana University Press, 2003). See also his previous work: "The Cultural Work of Yoruba Ethnogenesis," in Elizabeth Tonkin, Malcolm Chapman and Maryon McDonald, eds., *History and Ethnicity* (London: Routledge, 1989), 198-215.

[18]Frank A. Salamone, "Colonialism and the Emergence of Fulani Identity," *Journal of Asian and African Studies* 20 (1985): 193-202. See also "Indirect Rule and the Reinterpretation of Tradition," *African Studies Review* 23 (1980): 1-14.

British (and European) personnel in northern Nigeria numbered only 1,825 persons over against the 11.5 million members of the indigenous population—an infinitesimally small minority. British sovereignty therefore relied heavily on regional authorities. The Hausa-Fulani, believed by the British colonial administration to be of Hamitic descent,[19] were seen as natural allies. As Muslims, they seemed more closely related to the Europeans than the local population, whose religion was considered pagan.[20]

It comes as no surprise that the small ruling class of the Hausa-Fulani came to identify themselves by this appellation that had been given to them by others, adopting first the label "Fulani," second the view that they constituted a "single" ethnicity, third the claim to Hamitic descent, and finally the emphasis on their religious identity as Muslims. In this way, the Hausa-Fulani shored up the power the British afforded them. The appellation ascribed to them by others became one that they ascribed to themselves, and in the context of heterogeneous ethnic constellations, ethnic lines of demarcation were drawn on the basis of religious identity markers.

This pattern was repeated in many parts of Africa subjected to British colonial rule and elsewhere, such as in the Belgian colonial territories.[21] Meanwhile, Christian missionaries did not always share the view of the British colonial administration, with the result that colonial authorities attempted to curtail the influence of the mission societies. It stands to reason that this had a paramount influence on the running of the schools.[22] In this regard, the presuppositions of the British led to very tangible consequences. One particular area in which this was the case was that of relationships between Christians and Muslims.[23] The colonial authorities

---

[19] According to Genesis 9:18 the sons of Noah were Shem, Ham, and Japheth. Among the descendants of Ham (see the narrative in Gen 10:6-20), it is particularly Nimrod who stands out, a man said to have been a "mighty hunter" (Gen 10:8). The interpretive paradigm of "Hamitic descent" was applied in various forms in various parts of Africa to define intercultural relationships (and especially lines of demarcation).

[20] Salamone, "Colonialism," 196.

[21] For an example, see the formation of the "ethnicity" of the Hutus and the Tutsis and its development in the context of Belgian colonial history. Karl-Heinz Kohl, "Ethnizität und Tradition aus ethnologischer Sicht," in Aleida Assmann and Heidrun Friese, eds., *Identitäten*, vol. 3 of *Erinnerung, Geschichte, Identität*, 2nd ed. (Frankfurt: Suhrkamp, 1999), 269-87.

[22] Salamone, "Colonialism," 198.

[23] "It appears clear, then, that the Fulani, or 'Hausa-Fulani' as the British began to refer to the ruling elite of the old Hausa emirates, had to redefine their identity in light of the new political situation that the British conquest brought to Northern Nigeria as a whole. Their very use of

positively expected tensions to erupt between Muslims and Christian mission societies, which had the beneficial side effect—as far as they were concerned—of enabling them to keep the rival interpretive power of the missionaries out of certain areas. The Hausa-Fulani emirs also played this role to a certain extent, which shored up their power base. Conversely, this denied them access to Western education, which might have given them power in a different way.[24] The Islamic presence in this region thus came to serve as an obstacle that barred access to the school system; it played this role as a result of the specific situation, not because the Islamic religion was somehow inclined "that way."[25]

Thus far, we have discussed similar patterns—i.e., the construction of new self-designations by partially, tactically, or unconsciously adopting appellations ascribed by others and the institutional consequences that arise as a result—that we found in various examples, such as the caste system in India, the identity of the Ewe or that of the Fulani. Similar observations have been made in other cultural contexts, such as that of nineteenth-century Japan.[26] *Cultural transformations are therefore processes in which identity may be positively "constructed" in a goal-directed fashion. The aspect of power and the exercise of power as well as its justification thus take on a considerable significance.*

EUROPEAN ASSERTIONS OF IDENTITY: THE EXAMPLE OF COLONIAL EXHIBITIONS

Aleida Assmann (b. 1947) distinguishes between two dimensions of culture, which she calls "lifeworld" and "monument." She associates the *lifeworld* aspect of culture with everyday language, i.e., with the proximal aspects of culture presented in the immediate surroundings in which the communicating community lives. In contrast, she defines the *monument* aspect of

---

religious and traditional criteria as a marking device . . . is best understood as a response to their negotiations with the British and a means toward establishing themselves as 'natural rulers' in the colonial evolutionary ideology." Ibid., 198.

[24]Salamone emphasizes that according to British colonial ideology, the authorities expected not only a dichotomy between Islam and Christianity, but also—from an evolutionary perspective—an essential fusion to take place between Western education and Christian religion. Ibid.

[25]In light of the platitudes frequently expressed in this regard, this cannot be emphasized enough.

[26]Shingo Shimada and Jürgen Straub, "Relationale Hermeneutik im Kontext interkulturellen Verstehens: Probleme universalistischer Begriffsbildung in den Sozial- und Kulturwissenschaften— erörtert am Beispiel 'Religion,'" *Deutsche Zeitschrift für Philosophie* 47, no. 3 (1999): 449-77.

culture as the symbolic language of the unique, the ceremonial, the distant, the permanent, and the fixed. Lifeworld occurs and is not oriented toward an observer; it is just a given, whereas, in general, monument is conceptualized with an observer in mind.[27] Cultural artifacts such as buildings, statues, or texts were intended to maintain communication over long periods of time. They do not depend on immediacy but rather on distance, on prominence, on magnitude, and on costliness. It is only when both dimensions occur together, Assmann claims, that one may speak of culture. In regard to the colonial era, one may consider the colonial exhibitions, which were held over a period of about one hundred years along the lines of monument. They served to portray, strengthen, and perpetuate the European self-conception.

Hans-Jürgen Lüsebrink is correct when he points out the significance of the colonial media for the construction of identity.[28] He identifies the colonial exhibitions as a particularly effective example. These were held for about a century in a number of European countries such as France (the Expositions Coloniales in Paris), Great Britain (London), Germany (the Völkerschauen in Berlin), and Belgium (at Tervuren in the vicinity of Brussels).[29] Such exhibitions may be understood along the lines of stage productions: foreign peoples are presented from a colonial perspective in European countries. At least five aspects are of particular interest in this regard. First, these exhibitions exploited *the exotic foreignness of other peoples* and used it as a means to draw a mass audience. Second, however, they did not portray the colonial peoples in what may be considered as their traditional aspect but rather *in terms of their "being civilized" by the colonial power in question*. Third, this served *to establish the colonial ideology of the civilizing mission of Europe or of a specific nation* by pointing out one's own civilizatory achievements among the "savages," such as the construction of schools, streets, new forms of agriculture (e.g., plantations), crafts, trade, and others. This colonial ideology was characterized by the evolutionary

---

[27]Aleida Assmann, "Kultur als Lebenswelt und Monument," in Aleida Assmann and Dietrich Harth, eds., *Kultur als Lebenswelt und Monument* (Frankfurt: Fischer Taschenbuch Verlag, 1991), 11-25, especially 11-14.

[28]Hans-Jürgen Lüsebrink, "Geschichtskultur im (post-)kolonialen Kontext: Zur Genese nationaler Identifikationsfiguren im frankophonen Westafrika," in Assmann et al., *Identitäten*, 401-26.

[29]See also Stefan Goldmann, "Wilde in Europa: Aspekte und Orte ihrer Zuschaustellung," in Thomas Theye, ed., *Wir und die Wilden* (Reinbek bei Hamburg, Germany: Rowohlt, 1985), 243-69.

thought predominating in the nineteenth century, according to which the story of humanity is experiencing a constant upward trend in terms of civilization and culture, with the European civilization and culture in the vanguard.

Fourth, they served *to demonstrate the greatness of one's own nation*, e.g., that of France especially after the humiliation of the defeat by Germany in the year 1870; it was pointed out that France was not just a regional power but in fact a global empire with a population of one hundred million and an area of about 4.2 million square miles. Fifth, *this portrayal took place in the context of territorial entities, manifested for instance in the sections of the exhibits*, that suggested a kind of common bond. In other words, the existence of something like national entities was being postulated. They represented a concurrence of exoticism, self-justification of the colonial occupation of territory, and the definition of what would later become national areas by the creation of borders, etc. In so doing, the European image of Africa was permanently influenced, since these exhibits were mass events with a great impact, as the example of the 1931 exhibition in Paris shows—it was visited by about forty million people. Some other exhibitions in the previous decades had also been visited by from thirty to forty million people.[30]

The exhibitions and other media of the colonial discourse, such as journals, scientific publications, or memorials, disseminated the geographic and cultural ascriptions of Western provenience. From the beginning of the twentieth century onwards, they were met by an anticolonial oppositional discourse on the part of African intellectuals, who nevertheless continued to draw on these same ascriptions. Thus Ivorian black author Bernard Dadié placed indigenous heroic figures like Queen Aura Pokou or resistance fighter Amadou Bamba alongside and on the same level as the heroic figures of the colonial powers like Vercingetorix, Joan of Arc, and Binger. The hypothesis: It is not only you Europeans who have heroes; so do we Africans. As a consequence of this oppositional discourse, after the gaining of independence—in this case that of the Ivory Coast—these heroes, who had originally been recognized over an undefined area in Africa (a region), were now appropriated, as it were, for a specific nation—in this case, the Ivory

---

[30]Lüsebrink, "Geschichtskultur," 404-7.

Coast. They were "nationalized" and stylized by means of memorials, postage stamps, and especially by means of curricular contents in schools and universities as the foundation of one's own national identity.[31] That means *that which had been overlooked or folklorized in the French colonial literature now came to occupy the center of attention.* The colonial discourse (Europe's self-portrayal and the portrayal of its heroes) had invoked an oppositional discourse: African intellectuals searched for, located, and propagated Africa's heroic figures. In so doing, these heroes were also put on pedestals and pressed into service as "icons" of a national consciousness. It was up to the next generation of African intellectuals, especially that of the 1970s and 1980s, to deconstruct these "African" relics of the colonial constellations once again. They did so by pointing out that at times these "African heroic figures" had been employed in a brutal manner over against local ethnicities, so that they could not very well be used to stylize allegedly African values.[32]

Thus what first comes across as contributing to identity formation is actually a result of the colonial culture itself, one that defies the customary polarity between active colonizers and accommodating colonial objects: first, colonial techniques of identity formation were adopted; second, the subject matter was reinterpreted; third, it was used against the colonizers; and fourth, it is the colonial culture (schools, print media, memorials, the press, etc.) that provided and continues to provide the institutional framework for this kind of identity formation.

Intercultural Hermeneutics from the Perspective of Discourse Theory and Cultural Semiotics

After our discussion thus far, we can provide the following (by no means exhaustive) summary in view of postcolonial research from a discourse-theoretical perspective: (1) *The colonizers' etic ascriptions of others define the colonial discourse; at the same time, these ascriptions may often be seen as projections of the colonizers' own inward state of being.* In other words, the colonizers describe other cultures from their own perspective; in the process, these descriptions often reveal more about the colonial actors, i.e., about their appetites, wishes, and fears, than about the other cultures that they

---

[31]Ibid., 417ff.
[32]Ibid., 423.

allegedly describe. (2) Such etic ascriptions are usually employed—consciously or unconsciously—*to prove one's own cultural superiority*. (3) This proof of one's own cultural superiority can then be used *to justify the colonial appropriation of territory*. (4) As colonial expansion takes place, *the "knowledge" that has been acquired* and that, as we said, may be understood as a projection *is applied and put to use in various ways*. For one thing, it is used *as a basis for mentality formation in the form of publications, media, training courses, the colonial press, and others*. For another, it comes to function *as a paramount factor in the colonial administration*, which may affect such aspects as *the transfer of rights to indigenous elites*, the *implementation of systems of law, and the like*. (5) *The social makeup of ethnicities often changed as a result of and in accordance with these institutionalizations*. One example of this is the merging of ethnicities that previously did not consider themselves to be mutually related. Another is the fortification of the power bases of chiefs by the colonial administration, which led to the establishment of a new kind of chieftaincy, one that did not exist before. There simply had been no precedent within the traditional configurations of the ethnicities in question in terms of the scope of authority and the extent of power. (6) It is thus legitimate to assert that *undoubtedly, such projections (images created of other cultures) created new realities* (cultural reconfigurations that took place under the influence of the colonial apparatus and—in a more general sense—of the colonial situation). (7) As far as the original cultural identity of each respective ethnicity is concerned, because of the lack of primary documentation in many areas, it is impossible to apply ethnological research methods to document the tribal traditions, hierarchical relationships, ethnic alliances, etc., the way they are presumed to have existed in the precolonial era. There is little need to mention that the precolonial circumstances were themselves contingent on historical developments and, that as it was, the *ethnic cultures were constantly "in a state of flux."* (8) This finding in turn implies that whenever an "original African culture" is posited or sincerely suggested, such talk often also represents a projection motivated by special interests (keyword: *African renaissance*). (9) The analysis of colonial constellations has shown that *indigenous populations were often very interested in the new technology of the whites*, which gave rise, for instance, to white missionaries being invited by chiefs to establish stations in tribal territory. In addition, there are frequently individuals and social groups present within ethnicities who seek to elevate their own social status by means of contact with whites and by adopting elements (technology, clothing, etc.) that had hitherto been culturally foreign to them. (10) In these complex constellations, *indigenous people must therefore also be considered as actors and in fact to the same extent as the whites were (in the case of the colonial period).* Even in those instances where the colonial administration exercised total control, it can be shown that the indigenous population responded to varying degrees by adapting, reinterpreting, or resisting the outside influences.

The examples have shown that when it comes to the analysis of intercultural and interreligious processes, two hermeneutical approaches are indispensable. The first is the cultural-semiotic approach, which is helpful for determining those cultural aspects that are taken for granted and of which the actors are thus frequently unaware. The second is the discourse-theoretical approach, which is helpful in the analysis of stylizing etic and emic ascriptions. These two approaches may be integrated into the concept of culture presented by Aleida Assmann by correlating her aspect of culture as lifeworld with the cultural-semiotic approach and her aspect of culture as monument with the discourse-theoretical approach. In the unconscious self-evidence of everyday performances, cultural patterns are indeed "proximal" to people; they are not directed at an addressee, nor characterized by distance, nor do they take on a heightened meaning. This is true for the performance of linguistic communication, for unconscious behaviors like etiquette, for certain everyday habits, for things taken for granted in relations between the sexes, for basic performances such as greeting, celebrating, working, and sensing shame, or aesthetic feelings such as longing or loathing. *A hermeneutics of cultural semiotics seeks to identify those cultural patterns that members of a certain culture perceive as signs (such as signs of decorum, or as signs of a good character, etc.) and to interpret them.* In this regard, the sense of cohesiveness of a given cultural group is expressed through the things it takes for granted, through the psychological relief afforded by familiarity, through what does not need to be vocalized, through what is known and trusted—in short, through what the group associates with "being at home."

As important as this dimension of culture is, the other dimension is just as important—the one that Aleida Assmann designates as *monument*. Monument includes human artifacts constructed to endure, such as buildings with a unique significance (such as temples or palaces), which attract attention by means of distance (e.g., grandness, durable building material, special location in a city or in the countryside) with respect to their addressees (both inside one's own social group and over against outsiders) and that are intended to communicate certain messages. But it also includes memorials, writing (such as texts inscribed in steles), markers of possession, and such things as festivals and ceremonies that serve to impart temporal rhythms. Monuments are directed toward addressees in that they stylize what is particular to one's own culture and thus serve to delineate between insiders and outsiders. Thus cultural monuments as a medium are used to assert power, for instance to define one's own identity, as we have seen in the example of the colonial exhibitions.

Intercultural hermeneutics is thus tasked with analyzing stylizations of power. This applies especially to a specific aspect of cultural action: namely, the stylization of one's own culture as that which is taken for granted, as the superior culture that is normal and not to be questioned. In this regard, time itself is used to justify and defend one's own culture. Such stylizations frequently intend to create the impression that the cultural ascriptions in play have always been the way they are now. This was seen, for example, in the Indian stylizations of the god Ram, who the Hindu activists claim always to have been the one unifying god of India—which was manifestly not the case historically.

This leads us to redefine what an intercultural hermeneutics is: from a cultural-semiotic perspective, it is the attempt to decode other, foreign cultures using the medium of their own conceptions and terminology, i.e., to identify that meaning, those referential connections, and that relevance that things have for people from the culture in question.[33] *This attempt must, however, be augmented by the discourse-theoretical perspective, since it is necessary critically*

---

[33]The hermeneutics presented by Theo Sundermeier is very appealing in the way it demonstrates the steps and aspects that need to be considered for the process of understanding; however, in my opinion, he does not adequately cover the discourse-theoretical perspective. See Theo Sundermeier, *Den Fremden verstehen* (Göttingen: Vandenhoeck, 1996).

to analyze the pan-cultural desire to portray certain cultural configurations as self-evident. I consider such a new intercultural hermeneutics significantly to surpass older approaches to hermeneutics, which tended to be oriented more toward understanding texts or more toward appreciating what others consider to be meaningful, etc.

In the following chapters we will frequently need to refer back to this understanding of intercultural hermeneutics. The aim will be to analyze the scope of certain proposed intercultural theologies in terms of how these may be understood from the perspective of local sign systems, on the one hand, and to what extent they remain inseparable from their discourse location, on the other.

In conclusion, we need to emphasize once more that cultures are to a certain extent delimitable spheres containing those things taken for granted within one's own lifeworld; yet at the same time, they are conceptual formations of social cohesion oriented toward certain publicly communicated identity markers.

PART III

On the Plurality of Contextual Theologies

The Example of Africa

The development of autonomous theologies in Africa, Asia, Latin America, and other parts of the world is a relatively new phenomenon. Even though initial efforts toward an Indian theology were made as early as the nineteenth century, one may only speak of Asian and African theologies to any appreciable extent from the 1960s onwards. As far as Protestant churches are concerned, this probably has to do with the era of decolonization, which made the appointment of indigenous church leadership possible and also allowed new emphases to be made in the area of theological education. That being said, the influence of Western theologies still dominated the scene for decades and continues to do so to this day in some areas. As far as the Roman Catholic Church is concerned, the Second Vatican Council (1962–1965) provided the decisive impetus for autonomous local theologies by allowing the mass to be celebrated not just in Latin, as had been the case previously, but also in local languages, and fundamentally by granting the freedom for the development of cultural distinctiveness on a local level.

9

Contextual Theologies Worldwide

Some Preliminary Remarks

The Ecumenical Association of Third World Theologians (EATWOT) was founded in 1976 in Dar es Salaam as an international platform for contextual theologies.[1] The goal of this *informal association* of theologians was to allow theologians with a non-Western background to make their voices heard on an international level. All twenty-three participants of the meeting in Dar es Salaam hailed from countries in the so-called Third World. They (initially) concentrated on promoting a Christian South-South dialogue and therefore decided *to exclude Europeans and North Americans as participants at future conventions.*

CONTEXTUAL (ACADEMIC) THEOLOGIES AND EATWOT

Methodologically speaking, those attending the founding conference of EATWOT agreed that, to begin with, an active engagement is necessary to pursue theology, followed by reflection, which in turn provides the basis for further engagement. This addressed a key concern of the proponents of the emerging Latin American liberation theology. Accordingly, as far as the Latin American theologians were concerned, the pursuit of theology was located in the struggle for justice and against oppression or at least—formulated more generally—in engagement, according to the broad consensus. The structuring and organization of the content, however, proved to be highly controversial. For example, many Latin American liberation theologians

---

[1]Arnulf Camps, "Die ökumenische Vereinigung von Dritte-Welt-Theologen (EATWOT)," in Giancarlo Collet, ed., *Theologien der Dritten Welt: EATWOT als Herausforderung westlicher Theologie und Kirche* (Immensee, Switzerland: Neue Zeitschrift für Missionswissenschaft, 1990), 183-200, specifically 184. See also EATWOT, *Von Gott reden im Kontext der Armut.*

considered elements of Marxist theory indispensable for the analysis of societal praxis. In response, Asian and African representatives insisted that
folk-religious traditions could provide the substrate on which liberation efforts could take root and that these traditions should not just be seen as
obstacles to the liberation movement, which was the view of the majority of
Latin American liberation theologians at the time.[2]

The three next EATWOT conferences after the one in Dar es Salaam
(1976) took place in 1977 in Accra (Ghana), in 1979 in Colombo (Sri Lanka),
and in 1980 in São Paulo (Brazil). They clearly showed the fault lines between theologians from various contexts. For instance, the Latin American
liberation theologians perceived the US-American "black theology of liberation" as "American" and "bourgeois"; in their opinion, it paid too little
attention to the class conflict. Conversely, against the background of the race
issue in the United States, James H. Cone's (b. 1938) "black theology" portrayed the Latin American liberation theologians as "European" and "white."
After the São Paulo conference (1980), Cone turned his back on EATWOT,
accusing the Latin American liberation theologians of denying and turning
a blind eye to the prevalence of racism in their own countries.[3] As far as the
African sphere was concerned, tensions between political theologies and
theologies of inculturation made themselves felt. These were represented by
proponents of the black theology of South Africa in the context of the
apartheid struggle, on the one hand, and by proponents of the so-called
African theologies in the context of inculturation efforts, on the other. In
addition, the question was debated to what extent the gospel was permitted
to have political implications. At additional conferences such diverse issues
as good governance, nation building, reconciliation, ecology, and women's
issues were debated.[4]

---

[2]Camps, "Die ökumenische Vereinigung," 185.
[3]Ibid., 186-87.
[4]The following conferences need to be mentioned in this regard: New Delhi (1981); Geneva
(1983); the second general assembly in Oaxtepec, Mexico (1986); the third general assembly in
Nairobi (1992); the women's assembly of EATWOT in San José, Costa Rica (1994); the Asian
Theological Conference of EATWOT in Yogyakarta, Indonesia (1995); the fourth general assembly in Tagaytay, the Philippines (1996); the fifth general assembly in Quito, Ecuador (2001);
and the sixth general assembly in Johannesburg, South Africa (2006). See the homepage of
EATWOT, www.eatwot.net (accessed March 13, 2015).

Contextual Theologies in Asia

Klaus Hock questions the rubrication of "Asian theologies," and rightly so, since the contexts of the various Asian countries are so different that one is hard put to find a single common denominator for them. Besides, geographically speaking, it is almost impossible to delimit the term.[5] Hock's objection is credible, and we therefore content ourselves with speaking only of contextual theologies in Asia. Besides the wide variety of cultures in the various countries, the historical framework also varies tremendously, for the history of colonization in particular proceeded in very different ways and in a very checkered manner in many places. The Philippines, for instance, had been part of the Spanish colonial empire for centuries, with the result that about 90 percent of the population is Catholic today, while in India Europeans were also present over a long period, but for much of that time only in the coastal areas. It was only in 1856 that Great Britain succeeded in subjugating the entire Indian subcontinent. Currently, approximately 2.4 percent of the Indian population is Christian; even so, the number of Christians still comes to about twenty-nine million, since the entire population consists of about 1.2 billion people. This percentage has remained virtually unchanged for a long time.

In other countries such as South Korea the percentage of Christians in the entire population has dramatically increased. Whereas Christians hardly accounted for more than 1 or 2 percent in the year 1900, currently about 33 percent of South Koreans belong to Christian churches. Things are very different in Japan, where from 1900 to 2000 the percentage of Christians remained fairly stable at around 1 percent of the population, and it continues to do so today. By way of contrast, the Christian influence is disproportionately high in the education sector. All Western missionaries were expelled from China in 1949. Since then, strong growth has been recorded, especially since the 1970s. In Indonesia, it is estimated that about 10 percent of the population are Christian, whereas the number is much lower in many other countries such as Burma, Thailand, Vietnam, or Laos. In summary, the *cultural contexts* in these countries are very diverse; at the same time, the *socioeconomic contexts* in various countries and over certain

---

[5]Klaus Hock, *Einführung in die Interkulturelle Theologie* (Darmstadt: Wissenschaftliche Buchgesellschaft, 2010), 71-72.

periods of time feature certain similarities as far as their global economic development is concerned.

In these and in other parts of the world one may distinguish between two basic types of theologies: those emphasizing the religiocultural domain and those underscoring socioeconomic and sociopolitical themes. Frequently, these two areas, which are theoretically distinct, in reality overlap and interpermeate each other. Let us proceed to highlight some important names and themes. In a search for big-name contextual theologians among the churches associated with the World Council of Churches a considerable list is easily to be found. For Sri Lanka, one could mention Aloysius Pieris (b. 1934) on the Roman Catholic and Lynn A. de Silva (1919–1982) on the Protestant side. These two rendered outstanding service to the Christian-Buddhist dialog. Indian theologians also come to mind, such as Vengal Chakkarai (1880–1958), M. M. Thomas (1916–1996), or Stanley Samartha (1920–2001).[6] For Taiwan, one could name Choan-Seng Song (b. 1929), with his "third-eye theology."[7] For Japan, one could point to Kazoh Kitamori (1916–1998), with his "theology of the pain of God."[8] Another famous Japanese theologian was Katsumi Takizawa (1909–1984), who formulated his theology in the process of intensive dialogue with Buddhist traditions and spoke of Christ as the Immanuel, as the "God with us," doing so in a manner that forged links to Buddhist conceptions. Yet another was Kosuke Koyama (1929–2009), who pointed out in his "water buffalo theology" that it is necessary to pursue theology in simple ways that people can understand, for they spend most of their lives in the fields—like water buffalo—and so it is necessary to focus on their problems and to speak their language.

What many of these models have in common is that they trace what God did in the cultures and religions of their countries before the Christian missionaries arrived. The intent is thus to pay tribute to these traditions and

---

[6]These three names are representative of many others. The following highly recommendable reference work, edited by John England and others, lists around one hundred theologians from India alone who are *well-known* both nationally and internationally: John England et al., eds., *Asian Christian Theologies: A Research Guide to Authors, Movements, Sources*, 3 vols. (Maryknoll, NY: Orbis Books, 2002–2004).

[7]Choan-Seng Song, *Third-Eye Theology: Theology in Formation in Asian Settings* (Maryknoll, NY: Orbis Books, 1979).

[8]The work was published in 1946. Kitamori's theological reflections also captured the attention of European theologians such as Jürgen Moltmann.

simultaneously to interpret socioeconomic and political constellations. Thus the Korean *minjung* theology inquired after the simple people. The gospel is intended in the first instance for the simple people, as New Testament scholar Ahn Byung-Mu (1922–1996) demonstrated by comparing the term for the simple people (the Korean word *min* = people; *jung* = the masses) with the Greek term *ochlos* as used in the Gospel of Mark. Other theologians were thinking along the same lines, such as Kim Yong-Bock (b. 1938). They believed that it was particularly in the suffering of the people—designated in Korean by the word *han*—that God had been present in a certain manner in Korea before the advent of Christianity. The liberation-theological *minjung* theology was particularly influential during the time of President Park Chung-Hee (1961–1979), whose program of modernization was accompanied by widespread political repression, abductions, torture, and murder.

Those few highlights will suffice for the present. The question arises of what the actual object of investigation is to be when it comes to contextual theologies. Klaus Hock states that in Asian theologies, the "cosmic significance of Christ plays a preeminent role."[9] This is an accurate assessment, and Hock is also correct in immediately delimiting his verdict in light of the tremendous variance between the cultural contexts in question. The following statement seems to me to be of particular significance as far as Hock's understanding of intercultural theology is concerned:

> It is nevertheless remarkable that Asian theologies are not characterized by denominational differences, but by other diverse and contextually contingent factors such as cultural, socio-economic, political, and other aspects. One exception to this rule is conventional theologies such as those imported by the mission societies—and it goes without saying that these are also represented at institutions of theological education. Another is evangelical theologies, to which no further attention will be devoted here. The reason is that they continue to operate with a traditional adaptive paradigm based on the model of the cultural investiture of the unchanging Gospel—a paradigm that is actually the opposite to that of the various contextual Asian theologies.[10]

One of Hock's main criteria seems to be that contextual theologies are formulated to express something new, to secure liberation from Western

---

[9]If Hock spurns this term, why then does he use it himself?
[10]Both citations are drawn from Hock, *Einführung*, 83.

theologies, and to explore new directions. So far, so good. Yet the question arises: Are the "conventional" theologies in these countries really all that conventional? And are evangelical theologies—whatever they may be—in actual fact all that resistant to innovation or contextualization (as those who hold to them often believe)?[11] Should the question not be asked: *What exactly are these theologies?* In what forms do they manifest themselves? Of course, conservative and evangelical theologians in various parts of the world might condemn some theological approaches as "syncretistic" because of their contextualization. But is it not possible for innovations to take place along with the orthodoxy they consciously seek and present to the outside world? Furthermore, should such forms not be of interest to the subject of intercultural theology precisely in those cases? The question is, in which diverse manifestations are global discourses (such as that of the evangelical movement) adopted on a local basis? In addition, there are overlaps between the Pentecostal movement on the one hand and the evangelical movement on the other. In short, it pays to factor in these movements to a greater degree.

Let us consider an example. The Yoido Full Gospel Church in South Korea is well known internationally. It is said currently to consist of about

---

[11]To give just one example: Terence Ranger highlights the work of V. Neckebrouck on the conversion of the Kikuyu in the early phase of the Christian mission period. It seemed as if the Kikuyu *had turned their backs on their past completely* and had ascribed fully to the culture and religion of the colonial power. Did this truly constitute something radically new, an alienation from their former culture? Ranger answers no. He claims that there was actually a remarkable continuity beneath the surface, since similar instances of reorientation had manifestly taken place before the arrival of the whites. For example, it was possible for a Kikuyu (the Kikuyu were cultivators) to become a Maasai (the Maasai were pastoralists), and vice versa. This adoption of a new economic system (that of the other people) went hand in hand with the adoption of religious customs and a new lifestyle. The change was publicly recognized by a ritual called *guciaruo*. It is therefore possible that the conversion of a Kikuyu to another economic system (related to the colonial presence), as well as the adoption of another religio-ritual tradition and lifestyle, was far more *contextual* than it first appeared to be. See Terence Ranger, "The Local and the Global in Southern African Religious History," in Robert W. Hefner, *Conversion to Christianity* (Berkeley: University of California Press, 1993), 65-98, specifically 66-67. Interestingly, the rejection of "adaptation" on the part of, say, "evangelical" missionaries, on the one hand, and the Kikuyu individuals in this example, on the other, may be seen as *doubly contextual*. In the case of the missionaries, it may be seen as contextual in terms of their context of origin (such as the United States—see chapter twenty-one under the heading, "Inculturation in the Matrix of Several Determining Factors," key word: the "political-subjective" concept of the nation), which takes the congregation as a reference more so than it does the culture. In the case of the Kikuyu, it may be seen as contextual in terms of *the maintenance of a(n already conventional) mode of transition* that demands a radical reorientation in terms of economic, ritual, and practical aspect.

seven hundred thousand members.[12] It was founded in the year 1958 by Pastor David Yonggi Cho (b. 1936). The designation "Full Gospel" connotes the holism of the gospel, including health and well-being. The Yoido Full Gospel Church is based on the theological principles of its founder, such as the doctrine of the "fivefold Gospel"[13] and the "threefold blessing." The text 3 John 2 is of paramount importance in this regard: "Dear friend, I pray that you may enjoy good health and that all may go well with you, even as your soul is getting along well" (NIV). It is claimed that this passage refers (1) to the *spiritual blessing*, i.e., the gift of eternal life; and (2) to the *environmental blessing* as well as (3) *the physical blessing of health*.[14] Interestingly, Cho expands on the latter with a fourfold interpretation of the blood of Jesus. He first draws attention to the *blood of Gethsemane*, where according to Luke 22:44 the sweat of Jesus fell to the ground like drops of blood. This, he says, is the blood of the obedience of Jesus, the blood that also atones for human disobedience. Then he speaks of the blood that was shed when *Jesus was flogged* in Herod's palace. This includes the promise of the healing of sickness: "He took our illnesses and bore our diseases" (Mt 8:17). The blood that is shed when the *crown of thorns* is placed on Jesus' head in the courtyard of Pilate is the third type. It cancels out the curse of the ground from the fall into sin, namely "thorns and thistles it shall bring forth for you," thereby bringing about the blessing of well-being in every aspect (Gal 3:13-14). Finally, the fourth kind of blood is that which Jesus sheds on the cross. Cho interprets the statement "it is finished" (Jn 19:30) to mean that the blood of the Abandoned One has saved the abandoned ones, that this blood saves the soul from the eternal fire. In this way, the fourfold shedding of blood taken as a whole brings about salvation by supplying people with the *power of the obedience of Jesus*, by making it possible for *physical illnesses to be healed*, by *breaking the curse of the ground*, and finally by procuring *salvation for the soul*.

---

[12]In view of the tendency of some churches to pad their membership numbers, such information is generally to be treated with caution. That being said, the members of the Yoido Full Gospel Church undoubtedly number in the hundreds of thousands.

[13]This comprises (1) the gospel of regeneration, (2) the gospel of the fullness of the Holy Spirit, (3) the gospel of the gift of divine healing, (4) the gospel of the gift of blessing, and (5) the gospel of the kingdom of God and the second coming of Christ. This understanding of the gospel is then detailed and applied to daily life by the doctrine of the threefold blessing.

[14]See David Yonggi Cho, *A Bible Study for New Christians* (Seoul: Seoul Logos, 1997), 47-66.

I will break off at this point. Cho's theological doctrine is indubitably based on a form of Biblicism that will seem very foreign to theologians in this part of the world. Yet it is remarkable—no matter what one may think of Cho's statements from an exegetical perspective—how he attempts to develop a "holistic" gospel on a biblical basis and to provide it with a christocentric focus. His approach elicits several *reciprocal questions*: First, it must be asked, where are the elements of this theological approach drawn from? Which role does the subject of blood play in Korean contexts? Which kind of blood theology could Cho have adopted from American missionaries, notwithstanding his claim to have received his theological insights through the working of the Holy Spirit? How does Cho adapt theological models of doctrine from other contexts, and how does he implement them practically in healing services? How much of what he teaches has been adopted from shamanistic traditions, and how were traditional elements reinterpreted? In short, (1) the task of intercultural theology is to remain hermeneutically sensitive even (and especially) over against those forms of expression of Christian life and Christian doctrine in a given context which an observer might consider to be offensive. In terms of our example, it is not helpful immediately to respond with the stereotypic objection that of course "conventional" and/or "evangelical" theologies are not truly contextual. (2) The question is not only which new theological ideas are being developed in the orbit of academic contextual theologies; rather, we must also ask which of these theologies actually *arrive* at the much-vaunted grassroots level. How do academic approaches become usable in the everyday life experiences of Christians in Asia? Do these approaches in actual fact reflect how people experience life? When we ask these questions, we must clarify that of course contextual theologies, just like all theologies, are not only to be evaluated pragmatically, i.e., in terms of their practical value for the masses. Nevertheless, it must be permissible to ask in which form theologies become relevant for people. From my observations I would hazard the suspicion that they are not so much academic theologies as they are ritual and other innovations.

Contextual Theologies in Latin America

In the late 1960s and early 1970s, it was especially the Latin American *liberation theology* that became internationally known as a contextual

theology.[15] As early as 1968, during the second general assembly of the Conference of Latin American Bishops in Puebla, Gustavo Gutiérrez (b. 1928)
presented his thoughts on this matter, which he summarized in his 1971
publication *Teología de la Liberación*.[16] Briefly stated, Gutiérrez's concern is
that theology can only be developed when the praxis serves as its hermeneutical locus.[17] This locus is the struggle alongside the poor and oppressed;
so instead of forming alliances with the powerful, the way the state churches
typically do, the church should turn back and become a "church of the
poor."[18] Another classic of Latin American liberation theology is the book
Jesus Cristo Libertador by Brazilian Franciscan Leonardo Boff (b. 1938),
which was also published in 1971.[19] This liberation movement took many
shapes and forms in Christian grassroots communities. Liberation theologians demanded that theologians should continually alternate between
living with the poor and returning to the institutions of education to reflect on the experience in their teaching.[20] A catch phrase from this time
stated, "Orthopraxy, not orthodoxy."[21] Other important names are Ruben

---

[15]For an overview, see Ignacio Ellacuría and Jon Sobrino, eds., *Mysterium Liberationis: Grundbegriffe der Theologie der Befreiung*, 2 vols. (Lucerne, Switzerland: Exodus, 1995–1996). For the
Spanish original, see *Mysterium Liberationis: Conceptos fundamentales de la Teología de la Liberación* (Madrid: Editorial Trotta, 1990). For an English translation, see *Mysterium Liberationis:
Fundamental Concepts of Liberation Theology* (Maryknoll, NY: Orbis Books, 1993). For the
historical aspect, see Roberto Oliveros, "History of the Theology of Liberation," in Ellacuría
and Sobrino, *Mysterium*, 1:3-32. See also the helpful selection of pertinent literature up to the
early 1990s in the bibliography in the German edition of Ellacuría and Sobrino, *Mysterium*,
2:1281-91.

[16]For a German translation, see Gustavo Gutiérrez, *Theologie der Befreiung*, trans. Horst Goldstein,
8th ed. (Munich: Kaiser). For an English translation, see *A Theology of Liberation: History, Politics,
and Salvation*, trans. Caridad Inda and John Eagleson (Maryknoll, NY: Orbis Books, 1973).

[17]It must be observed that an exchange of ideas took place between Latin American and European
theology from an early stage, since a number of the liberation theologians received their doctor-
ates in Europe. Liberation theology received strong support early on from such European Catholic theologians as Yves Congar, Edward Schillebeeckx, and Johann Baptist Metz, or from Protestant theologians such as Jürgen Moltmann and Dorothee Sölle.

[18]The conference of bishops initially proceeded to pursue a reform course on the basis of liberation-
theological principles, trying to make use of the freedom in organizing the church granted by
Vatican II. Later, at the third general assembly of the Conference of Latin American Bishops
held in Medellin in 1979, the subject of the poor received considerable attention.

[19]For an English translation, see Leonardo Boff, *Jesus Christ Liberator: A Critical Christology for
Our Time* (Maryknoll, NY: Orbis Books, 1978).

[20]It is quite obvious that in so doing they were orienting themselves according to Gramsci's concept of an "organic intellectual." As far as the methodology is concerned, see Clodovis Boff,
"Epistemology and Method," in Ellacuría and Sobrino, *Mysterium*, 1:57-84.

[21]A compendium of principles from the early period is found in Leonardo Boff and Clodovis Boff,

Alves (1933–2014) and Hugo Assmann (1933–2008) from Brazil; Jon Sobrino (b. 1938), a native Spaniard living in El Salvador since 1958; and José Miguez Bonino (1924–2012) from Argentina.[22] Elsa Tamez (b. 1950) serves as an example of a prominent female liberation theologian.

Looking back, we may divide the history of Christianity in this continent as follows: (a) from the discovery of America until the beginning of the nineteenth century; (b) from the early nineteenth century to the beginning of the 1950s; (c) from 1960 to the present—liberation theologies in the phases of inception, consolidation, and diversification. Liberation theologians energetically champion the rights of the oppressed, and for this reason a number of them had to give way to political pressure and animosity. For instance, Hugo Assmann and José Comblin (1923–2011) had to leave first Brazil and then Chile; Enrique Dussel (b. 1934) had to leave Argentina; and Franz Josef Hinkelammert (b. 1931) was forced to leave Chile. In addition, a whole series of liberation theologians were targeted by death squads; for instance, Antonio Pereira Neto was murdered in 1969 in Brazil, and Archbishop Oscar Romero (1917–1980) was shot to death during a worship service at the altar. In 1989, six Jesuits, their housekeeper, and her daughter were killed. Among these liberation theology–minded Jesuits was Ignacio Ellacuría (1930–1989). These assassinations by the military regime, which lasted for over twenty years, led liberation theologians to reformulate a theology of martyrdom. Such a theology was formulated most impressively by Jon Sobrino, a man who escaped the last-mentioned massacre and a close friend of Ellacuría.[23]

Whereas initially Latin American liberation theology was oriented predominantly toward politics, the value of other themes was soon discovered as well

---

Wie treibt man Theologie der Befreiung?, trans. Michael Lauble (Düsseldorf, Germany: Patmos Verlag, 1986).

[22]As it was, the Vatican accused the proponents of liberation theology of uncritically adopting a Marxist analysis of society, replacing redemption through Christ with an intramundane liberation, and of a revisionist interpretation of biblical texts in general. This criticism was based particularly—but not only—on the book *Church, Charism and Power: Liberation Theology and the Institutional Church* by Leonardo Boff. See "Instruktion der Kongregation für die Glaubenslehre über einige Aspekte der 'Theologie der Befreiung' vom 6. August 1984," *Veröffentlichungen des Apostolischen Stuhls* 57 (Bonn), no. 1. From 1985 onward, a sentence of "obedient silence" was imposed on Leonardo Boff. Even though the Vatican moderated its position in 1986, on the whole its critical attitude toward liberation theology remained in place.

[23]See Enrique Dussel, "Chronologische Darstellung der Entstehung und Entwicklung der Theologie der Befreiung in Lateinamerika (1959–1989)," in Riolando Azzi et al., *Theologiegeschichte der Dritten Welt* (Munich, Germany: Chr. Kaiser, 1993), 268-364, and specifically 315-16.

(though not in opposition to it), such as the meaning of a spirituality of liberation, gender issues, the issue of indigenous Indian cultures, and ecology—to name just a few. From the 1960s onward, its basic principles (God's "option for the poor") received more and more of a hearing from the Conference of Latin American Bishops. From the late 1970s onward, however, a gradual polarization took place between those bishops who were closer to the grassroots communities and those who tended to orient themselves toward the theological leadership asserted by the Vatican and dissociated themselves from many aspects of liberation theology. Yet since the end of the military dictatorships, many of the concerns of liberation theology remain as acute today as they ever did. In fact, they have been augmented by the need for a service of *reconciliation* in societies traumatized for decades by abductions, torture, and murder.[24]

Besides liberation-theological initiatives, mention must be made of Latin America's rapidly growing Pentecostal movement (in the form of, say, classic Pentecostal churches, neo-Pentecostal churches and movements, and transnational Pentecostal churches).[25] Conversely, we must take into account the wealth of diversity subsumed under this (vague) umbrella term in terms of congregations, churches, and movements.[26] In addition, we must also point out that the so-called evangelical movement encompasses a wide spectrum of positions, such as socially concerned evangelicals like René Padilla (b. 1932) or Orlando Costas (1942–1987).

CONTEXTUAL THEOLOGIES IN AFRICA

The circumstances of Christian churches in various parts of sub-Saharan Africa are as diverse as each individual nation. Given our framework, it is impossible to come even close to documenting the history of Christianity in this part of the world.[27] Therefore, in what follows, our aim will be merely

---

[24]See especially the work of Robert Schreiter, *The Ministry of Reconciliation: Spirituality and Strategies*, 6th ed. (Maryknoll, NY: Orbis Books, 2004).
[25]Timothy J. Steigenga and Edward L. Cleary, eds., *Conversion of a Continent: Contemporary Religious Change in Latin America* (New Brunswick, NJ: Rutgers University Press, 2007).
[26]Michael Bergunder, "Zur Einführung—Pfingstbewegung in Lateinamerika: Soziologische Theorien und theologische Debatten," in *Pfingstbewegung und Basisgemeinden in Lateinamerika: Die Rezeption befreiungstheologischer Konzepte durch die pfingstliche Theologie*, Weltmission heute 39 (Hamburg: EMW, 2000), 7-42, 138-42.
[27]See Klaus Hock, *Das Christentum in Afrika und im Nahen Osten* (Leipzig: Evangelische Verlagsanstalt, 2005).

to highlight some of the major developments. Our focus will be on sub-Saharan Africa. We must make a point of clearly stating that of course the New Testament records the beginning of the presence of Christianity in Africa (one need only think of Simon of Cyrene, who carries the cross of Christ for a time, Mt 27:32). Christianity spread very quickly to the area of North Africa and also, for instance, to Ethiopia, where a Christian kingdom existed from about 330 to 1974. It is necessary to mention these circumstances in light of the widespread preconception that Christianity came to Africa as the Western religion of the colonial overlords—which, as it stands, would constitute an inaccurate abridgement of the truth.

10

The Development of Contextual Theologies in Africa

An Overview

Presumably, Christianity has only been present in sub-Saharan Africa since the fifteenth century. From the perspective of the history of religion it is therefore still rather a recent phenomenon.[1] Since the beginning of the nineteenth century, congregations and churches came into being in many places as a result of the work of European and North American Protestant and Catholic mission societies. Whereas between 1 and 2 percent of the sub-Saharan population was Christian around the year 1800, by 1900 this percentage had increased to about 10 percent. And the twentieth century has marked one of the greatest religious changes the world has ever seen. The percentage of Christians in the overall population increased from 10 percent to over 50 percent, and in some countries (like Rwanda and Burundi) to as much as 60 to 90 percent. At the same time, rapid societal and cultural change took place in many countries.[2] It is perfectly obvious that all of this had to be managed theologically, ethically, and above all ritually. In order to get a general idea of the current state of Christianity in sub-Saharan Africa, we must begin by gaining an appreciation of the most important Christian traditions and their numerical representation. Nigeria

---

[1]Naturally, we should include at this point a discussion about the early presence of Christians in sub-Saharan Africa, such as during the time of the Portuguese presence from the fifteenth to the eighteenth centuries. One might mention the baptism of chief Nzinga Nkuwu in 1491 in modern-day Congo and many other things besides. For an initial overview, see Adrian Hastings, *Religion in Geschichte und Gegenwart*, 4th ed., s.v. "Afrika. III. Christentumsgeschichte."

[2]Patrick Johnstone, *Gebet für die Welt: Handbuch: Umfassende Informationen zu über 200 Ländern* (Holzgerlingen, Germany: Hänssler, 2003), 67.

may serve as our example in this case, although we need to add that our sole intention is to provide a basic representation of numerically significant forms of Christianity in sub-Saharan Africa. It goes without saying that the quantitative size of the various churches and forms of Christianity varies from country to country and that the orientations and contexts are also tremendously diverse.

The Example of Nigeria: Mission Churches, AICs, the Pentecostal Movement

In what follows, the term *mission churches* is used to designate those churches that came into being as a result of the work of Western missionaries and that remain affiliated with the founding mission societies or "mother churches," as the case may be. Nigeria serves as a case in point. The population of the West African country of Nigeria is currently estimated at 140 million people. Of those, about 52 percent are Christian, around 41 percent Muslim, and 6 percent or so continue to belong to various forms of tribal religions. In simplified terms, one might say that around 25 percent of Christians belong to the Roman Catholic Church, around 20 percent to the Anglican Church, and around 25 percent to various Protestant denominations, of which there are approximately 523 at the present time.[3] Most of these churches grew out of mission work and may therefore be designated as "mission churches." The other 30 percent are composed of African Independent Churches or African Initiated Churches (AICs), which we shall discuss at a later stage. We will initially focus on those churches that came into being as a result of the work of missionaries (i.e., Protestant, Anglican, and Roman Catholic churches).[4]

(1) These churches were *founded* by Western mission societies that continued to dominate, if not actually administrate them, even into the 1960s. Many of these mission churches struggled and continue to struggle with the problem of simultaneously belonging to the Christian religion and African

---

[3]These include Methodist churches, Baptist churches, Reformed churches, Lutheran churches, churches of the Moravian Brethren, Presbyterian churches, and others.

[4]Of course the classification presented above is painted with a broad brush, since on the one hand, the mission churches have more of an "African" character than might first seem to be the case, and on the other, the African Initiated Churches cannot simply be labeled "authentically African," as such a designation would hinge on an essentialist and overly static understanding of culture. For the research debate, see Birgit Meyer, "Christianity in Africa: From African Independent Churches to Pentecostal-Charismatic Churches," *Annual Review of Anthropology* 33 (2004): 447-74.

culture. The reason is that both the ecclesiastical customs (the structure of worship services, the hymnody, the liturgical instruments, the sacramental life, and the ethics) and the theological doctrine often continue to be defined by the European and/or North American heritage and traditions. Conversely, these traditions constitute an important aspect of the mission church's own identity, even though this varies from church to church. In addition, membership in international Christian organizations also plays a significant role. This membership is just as evident in the case of the one global Roman Catholic Church as it is in that of the one Anglican Church family, since every national Anglican Church is derived from the apostolic succession of the archbishop of Canterbury. For the Lutheran churches, membership in the Lutheran World Federation plays an important role, as does membership in the World Communion of Reformed Churches for the Reformed counterparts. Similar international federations exist in the case of other denominations. The role they play varies from supplying finances for church projects in the areas of mercy work, development-based initiatives, missionary initiatives, and education to making contributions in terms of scholarships, international education, the discussion of fundamental theological issues, public relations, and many others.

(2) In addition to these mission churches, there is a wide variety of so-called African Initiated Churches (AICs). These are churches that were founded in Africa by African founder figures—prophets, apostles, and faith healers, both male and female.[5] In Nigeria, these churches make up about 30 percent of the total.[6] We must clarify at this point that the term *African Independent Churches* reflects the perspective of the mission churches, since

---

[5]Here is a small selection of AICs *from Nigeria* who are members of the Organization of African Instituted Churches (for more on the OAIC, see chapter twenty-four under the heading "African Initiated Churches and the Search for Ecumenical Partnerships"): Aladura Apostolic Church; Aladura Church of God International; Blessed New Jerusalem Church of Nigeria; Celestial Church of Christ; Christ Apostolic Mission Church; Christ Army Church of Nigeria; Christ Church of Light; Christ the Lamb Sabbath Galilee International; Christ the Saviour Church Aladura; Messiah Gospel of Cherubin and Seraphim; Mission of True Sabbath of Nigeria; New Eden Light of Jesus Christ; New Temple Spiritual Church of Nigeria; Sacred Cherubim and Seraphim Church; Spiritual Healing Temple of God; Trinity Council Church; True Covenant of God Sabbath Mission; United Spiritual Church of Nigeria; Universal Praying Band; and Wonderful Power of Christ Church. In addition to these, there is also a whole range of other AICs. See World Council of Churches, "WCC Member Churches," www.oikoumene.org/en/member -churches/list?set_language=en (accessed March 19, 2015).

[6]Johnstone, *Gebet für die Welt*, 707.

when one asks, "Independent from whom?" the answer is that these African churches declared their independence from the mission churches, i.e., they broke away from them. This is the case for a great many churches in southern Africa but only for a few in West Africa. Yet there are also a large number of churches that came into being on their own without any ties to the mission churches, and for this reason the term *African Initiated Churches* has come into use. From 1960 to 1980, very many such churches were founded in Nigeria. The transition from churches in which African cultural elements play a significant role to those with a strong international orientation is a fluent one. The boundaries between the African Initiated *Churches*[7] and the global Pentecostal movement[8] are equally fuzzy. Their classification generally depends on the eye of the beholder. Unfortunately, we cannot elaborate on that at this point. It is important to recognize that many parts of the African (just as, say, the Indian)[9] Pentecostal movement do not consist of churches founded by North Americans; rather, they were founded as local, regional, and thus indigenous initiatives. To relapse into the perception paradigms of the nineteenth century (as if to say, "everything that is Christian comes from the West") is disingenuous and simply does not reflect the reality.[10]

In these churches the theme of "inculturation" or "contextualization" is irrelevant, since they present themselves as essentially "African" as it is. From an analytical perspective one might say that the respective founder figures intuitively contextualized the Christian message, which is evident in the specific forms of piety, ritual practices, and theological paradigms of these

---

[7]For an introduction, see Ogbu Kalu, *African Pentecostalism: An Introduction* (Oxford: Oxford University Press, 2008); Afeosemime Adogame, Roswith Gerloff, and Klaus Hock, eds., *Christianity in Africa and the African Diaspora: The Appropriation of a Scattered Heritage* (London: Continuum, 2011). See also Allan Anderson, "The Newer Pentecostal and Charismatic Churches: The Shape of Future Christianity in Africa?," *Pneuma* 24 (2002): 167-84.

[8]Stanley M. Burgess and Ed M. van der Maas, eds., *The New International Dictionary of Pentecostal and Charismatic Movements* (Grand Rapids: Zondervan, 2002); Allan Anderson et al., eds., *Studying Global Pentecostalism: Theories and Methods* (Berkeley: University of California Press, 2010).

[9]See Michael Bergunder, *Die südindische Pfingstbewegung im 20. Jahrhundert* (Frankfurt: Peter Lang, 1998).

[10]The recurrence of such paradigms demonstrates either a complete lack of knowledge of the circumstances on the ground (for instance, when Western media constantly make it seem as if some US-American fundamentalists are responsible for everything that happens in Christianity outside Europe) or delusions of grandeur on the part of missionaries (i.e., when people associated with Western mission organizations continue to believe that they are indispensable for the running of Christianity on a global level).

churches.[11] The diversity among these churches is immense; it is estimated that Nigeria alone is home to about 4,200 different kinds. It is estimated that there are currently about 15,000 different AICs in sub-Saharan Africa as a whole. These churches vary in size from a few dozen to several million people. Historically, one may distinguish between various revival movements in Nigeria and large churches that developed out of each of these. For example, in Nigeria the Aladura churches developed out of revivals by Africans among Africans from the 1920s onward, the Christ Apostolic Church at the beginning of the 1940s and the Church of God Mission International in the 1970s. Some of these churches have more than a million members today.

BETWEEN INCULTURATION AND JESUS SUPER POWER: THE EXAMPLE OF ALADURA

Aladura is a designation that applies to a number of churches. The designation is derived from the Yoruba term *al adua*, which means something like "the owners of the prayer."[12] This identifies the congregations and churches as belonging to those in whom prayer and the healing associated with prayer play an extremely important role. The larger churches include the Church of the Lord Aladura (CLA), with about 1.3 million followers currently;[13] the Christ Apostolic Church (CAC), with about two million followers today; and the Celestial Church of Christ (CCC) and the Cherubim and Seraphim (C&S) church, with about eight hundred thousand followers each. Some of these churches came into being when African founding figures broke away from mission churches (in the case of the CAC, the CLA, and the C&S); others were founded independently by indigenous charismatic leaders (such as the CCC).[14] Now, what distinguishes these churches from one another?

The CCC considers itself to be the "celestial church" of Revelation 4, which carries out and reenacts on earth the worship service continually taking place in heaven. Both this church and the C&S have liturgical worship services. The congregation members wear white cassocks. The CCC venerates angels, especially the archangel Michael, who is seen as the bearer of

---

[11]See the discussion in chapter twenty.
[12]Afeosemime Adogame, *Religion in Geschichte und Gegenwart*, 4th ed., s.v. "Aladura."
[13]Johnstone, *Gebet für die Welt*, 707.
[14]Adogame, "Aladura."

the Holy Spirit. This example shows that several AICs have unique theological doctrines. Hymns and the sermon occupy important positions in the worship service, as do ritualized movements, holy water, incense, and kneeling during prayers.[15] The hierarchy of this church is elaborately structured into about twenty ranks. Dietary laws are observed.[16] Prophets and prophetesses are important in terms of the prophecies and guidance they provide and the healings and exorcisms they perform.

The C&S church, which suffered repeated schisms and is thus very diverse, came into being in 1925 when a seventeen-year-old Nigerian woman by the name of Abiodun Akinsowon experienced an angelic vision in which she was commissioned to found a Christian community. Together with preacher Moses Orimolade Tunolase[17] she initially founded a prayer group within a mission congregation of the Anglican Church Missionary Society. They traveled throughout western Nigeria, engaging in missionary proclamation and performing exorcisms. After they initially founded the Cherubim and Seraphim Society within the mission congregation, they left it in 1926 and founded an independent church. In this church too angels play an important role as protectors and guides. The worship service as a whole is derived from the Anglican liturgy, although the ecstatic visions of prophets and prophetesses also play a significant role. The service of active prayer for healing and exorcism is very popular both inside and outside the church. The C&S considers most traditional cults to fall under the power of Satan, though not all. It is granted that some cults serve the one God without being aware of it.

To understand the historical background of the CAC and that of the other Aladura church bodies, one must bear in mind the great flu epidemic of 1918, which resulted in millions of deaths. During this time, prayer groups were formed within the mission churches in Nigeria in order to respond to the epidemic with prayers for healing. Meanwhile, this led to conflicts with some church leaders, such as those of the Anglican and Methodist mission churches. Some of the prayer circles then contacted (by letter) the Faith

---

[15]Worship services are held on Wednesdays (the mercy day), Fridays (the power day), and Sundays, although Thursdays are also considered to be holy.

[16]For instance, it is forbidden to consume kola nuts, since these are reserved for ritual usage in the Yoruba religion (and in other tribal religions). Pork, tobacco, and alcohol are also prohibited.

[17]He had been the one to wake her from a lengthy trance.

Tabernacle, a Pentecostal organization in the United States. A favorable response soon led to the founding of a denomination of this same Faith Tabernacle in Nigeria. When in 1930 a major revival took place in Nigeria at which thousands of people were healed and converted to Christianity, the Nigerian Faith Tabernacle experienced significant growth. In 1931 it associated itself with the Apostolic Church of England, yet severed the ties again after some time. An internal schism in 1942 resulted in the founding of the Christ Apostolic Church, a church body with a Pentecostal orientation.

In the 1980s this church body had more than a million members. The Christ Apostolic Church currently maintains its own university in Ikeji Arakeji (JABU) as well as a theological faculty in Ile Ife (Nigeria) and many other schools and institutions besides. As in all Aladura church bodies, prayer plays a preeminent role, as do faith healing, prophecies, exorcisms, and the practice of fasting. That being said, in this instance the congregation members do not wear white cassocks during the worship services. Just like the other Aladura churches, this church body also has a strongly hierarchical structure— its leadership is composed of a threefold group of apostles, prophets, and evangelists, while pastors, deacons, and deaconesses constitute a lower level. The church body considers itself to belong to the global Pentecostal movement. The following example demonstrates that both the AICs and the Pentecostal churches of the 1980s should be seen as *transnational networks*.[18]

TRANSNATIONAL NETWORKS: THE EXAMPLE OF THE CHURCH OF GOD MISSION INTERNATIONAL

The Redeemed Christian Church of God[19] and the Church of God Mission International (the latter founded by Benson Idahosa) are among the very influential neo-Pentecostal churches in Nigeria and West Africa in general.[20] This shows that certain AICs function as global institutions, i.e., as transnational church bodies. In so doing they serve as bridges between locality

---

[18]Matthews A. Ojo, "Transnational Religious Networks and Indigenous Pentecostal Missionary Enterprises in the West African Coastal Region," in Adogame, Gerloff and Hock, *Christianity in Africa*, 167-79.
[19]For more on this church, see the last two sections of chapter twenty.
[20]Klaus Hock, "'Jesus-Power—Super-Power!' Annäherungen an die Schnittstellen zwischen christlichem Fundamentalismus und Neuen Religiösen Bewegungen in Afrika," *Zeitschrift für Missionswissenschaft* 21 (1995): 134-50.

and globality; this function also characterizes their identity and praxis.[21] Yet the same is also true for other church bodies worldwide that are seen to belong to the Pentecostal movement. The Brazilian Universal Church of the Kingdom of God, for instance, has daughter congregations in the most diverse countries, as many as four hundred or so in southern Africa alone.[22] Here too, even the name shows the transnational orientation: *Universal Church of the Kingdom of God.* Yet let us return to the African example of the Church of God Mission International and its founder, Benson Idahosa. Born in 1938 and growing up in a traditional Edo family, Idahosa was a sickly child.[23] As a young adult, he was converted by a Pentecostal Igbo pastor. Following his conversion, he founded a storefront church in Benin. This church grew quickly as a result of miraculous healings performed by Idahosa and some evangelistic campaigns. In 1971, he studied for a few months at Gordon Lindsay's Christ for the Nations Institute in Dallas, Texas. An American missionary in Benin had facilitated the contact. After his return, the rapid growth of Idahosa's Church of God Mission continued. Within a few years it had become a large international organization running Bible schools, holding mass revival meetings, and featuring televangelists in various countries.

Even though the so-called prosperity gospel is preached in the Church of God Mission International, according to which God's work is characterized by granting wealth to the faithful, the Church of God Mission is nevertheless an independent African phenomenon and should not be seen as a subsidiary of Western Pentecostal churches. Any funds donated to the church are used for welfare programs, development programs, and education initiatives, which constitute a holistic approach when compared to the exclusive focus on the salvation of souls. The educational institutions founded by the church have had an especially strong impact on the transnational level. Matthews A. Ojo points out that the All Nations Christ Bible

---

[21]See Anna D. Quaas, *Transnationale Pfingstkirchen: Christ Apostolic Church und Redeemed Christian Church of God* (Frankfurt: Lembeck, 2011).

[22]Paul Freston, "The Universal Church of the Kingdom of God: A Brazilian Church Finds Success in South Africa," *Journal of Religion in Africa* 35 (2005): 33-65.

[23]It is interesting to observe that it is said that very many of those who would later become prophets and prophetesses were ill as children. This might be due to the high prevalence of childhood illnesses in African countries due to the poor medicinal care, but it might also be that this is a standing topos of the lives of prophets and prophetesses.

Institute (ANCBI) in Benin City counts among the graduates of its courses people from the most diverse West African countries, a number of whom went on to found their own churches after returning to their home countries, such as Duncan Williams, who founded the Christian Action Faith Ministries International in Ghana (1979), or Charles Agyem-Asare, who founded the World Miracle Bible Church (1986), also in Ghana, which is currently one of the largest Pentecostal churches in the country.[24] Another institution that was and is just as influential is the International Bible Training Centre, established in 1980 by William F. Kumuyi, the founder of the Deeper Life Bible Church.[25]

Other networks within Africa operate via daughter congregations of especially Nigerian Pentecostal churches located in other African countries via the education of Christians from other countries in Nigerian educational institutions; via evangelists from Nigeria, Ghana, and other countries who travel about in foreign countries as missionaries; via media such as CDs, video and audio cassettes, television stations, and the Internet; and via large international conferences.[26] This presents a wide field for mission studies research, especially since in addition to the immediate activities of Pentecostal churches and AICs, a number of mission organizations have also been founded, such as Calvary Ministries or the Christian Missionary Foundation.

A similar example is that of the Deeper Life Bible Church, founded by William Kumuyi (b. 1941) in the year 1982. He is a former Anglican who had a conversion experience in 1964 under the influence of the Apostolic Faith Church.[27] A few years later, he left the Apostolic Faith Church.[28] Currently the Deeper Life Bible Church is estimated to have several million

---

[24]Ojo, "Transnational Religious Networks," 171ff. For a discussion of the founding of other churches, see ibid.

[25]See Cephas N. Omenyo, "African Pentecostalism and Theological Education," in Dietrich Werner et al., eds., *Handbook of Theological Education in World Christianity: Theological Perspectives—Regional Surveys—Ecumenical Trends* (Oxford: Regnum Books International, 2010), 742-49, and especially 745. For more on Kumuyi, see below.

[26]Ojo, "Transnational Religious Networks," 170-73.

[27]For more on Kumuyi's person, see Matthews A. Ojo, "Deeper Life Christian Ministry: A Case Study of the Charismatic Movements in Western Nigeria," *Journal of Religion in Africa* 18 (1988): 141-62, especially 144ff.

[28]Afeosemime U. Adogame, *The New International Dictionary*, s.v. "Deeper Christian Life Mission (International)." Kumuyi previously served as a mathematics lecturer at the University of Lagos.

members (around one million in Nigeria alone).[29] It has branches not only in various West African countries but also in Europe and elsewhere. In contrast to the Church of God Mission International, members of the Deeper Life Bible Church are forbidden from watching TV. Since the 1980s, the emphasis has shifted from evangelization to healing. The church emphasizes the need to be born again, a rigid ethics, a literal reading of Holy Scripture, the atoning sacrifice of Christ, the proclamation of the end times, an exclusivist understanding of the church, and spiritual gifts. Also, in this church body the correlation between the prosperity gospel and social services is taken for granted.[30]

CONTEXTUAL THEOLOGIES: MALE AND FEMALE VOICES

The cultural patterns prevalent in the various sub-Saharan countries display certain similarities, although it must be added that this does not mean that they are exactly alike; rather, there are some significant differences between them.[31] For this reason, the contextualization of the Christian faith is a controversial subject that continues to be contested first between proponents of inculturation theologies and proponents of liberation theologies, second in the area of the traditions favored by the mission churches and those favored by the AICs (naturally and especially also within these churches and movements),[32] and third in theologies developed by men and those developed as African women's liberation theologies by women. The inception of autonomous theologies dates back to the 1960s. Yet it is almost impossible to survey all of the burgeoning literature on various approaches toward African theology today.[33] However,

---

[29]Johnstone, *Gebet für die Welt*, 707.
[30]Hock, "'Jesus-Power—Super-Power!,'" 141.
[31]For an overview, see Edward Geoffrey Parrinder, *African Traditional Religion*, 2nd ed. (London: SPCK, 1962); John Mbiti, *African Religions & Philosophy* (New York: Praeger, 1969); Theo Sundermeier, *The Individual and Community in African Traditional Religions*, Beiträge zur Missionswissenschaft/Interkulturellen Theologie 6 (Münster: LIT, 1998).
[32]For a discussion of gender issues in Pentecostal churches, designated here as New Generation Churches, see the empirical research presented in Bolaji O. Bateye, "Paradigmatic Shifts: Reconstruction of Female Leadership Roles in the New Generation Churches in South-Western Nigeria," in Adogame, Gerloff and Hock, *Christianity in Africa*, 113-25.
[33]For an overview, see John Parratt, *Theologiegeschichte der Dritten Welt: Afrika* (Munich: Chr. Kaiser, 1991); and Heribert Rücker, "'Afrikanische Theologie': Charles Nyamiti, Tansania," in Hans Waldenfels, ed., *Theologen der Dritten Welt: Elf biographische Skizzen aus Afrika, Asien und Lateinamerika* (Munich: Beck, 1982), 54-70.

articles in anthologies may provide a good impression of the basic theological ideas.[34] Meanwhile, a number of African theologians have published their work in monographs that have gained international renown. On the Roman Catholic side, one might mention Bénézet Bujo (b. 1940)[35] from Zaire, Oscar Bimwenyi-Kweshi (b. 1939),[36] Francois Kabasélé (b. 1948) from Zaire, Bishop Titianma Anselme Sanon (b. 1937) from Burkina Faso, Charles Nyamiti (b. 1931)[37] from Tanzania, and Fabien Eboussi Boulaga (b. 1934)[38] from Cameroon. On the Anglican side, one might mention Kenyan John Mbiti (b. 1931) and Ghanaian John Pobee (b. 1937).[39] Representatives from the Protestant side include Kwesi Dickson (1929–2005),[40] Methodist Gabriel M. Setiloane (b. 1925)[41] from South Africa, Methodist Gwinyai H. Muzorewa (b. 1925) from Zimbabwe, and Presbyterian Kwame Bediako (1945–2008) from Ghana.[42] Prominent representatives of the younger generation include Kenyan Jesse Ndwiga Kanyua Mugambi (b. 1947) and South African Tinyiko Sam Maluleke (b. 1961).

An observant reader might have noticed that the names we just listed are all men's names. Even the 1987 compendium *A Reader in African Christian*

---

[34]Yvette Aklé et al., eds., *Der schwarze Christus: Wege afrikanischer Christologie*, trans. Ursula Faymonville (Freiburg im Breisgau, Germany: Herder, 1989); Kofi Appiah-Kubi et al., eds., *African Theology en Route: Papers from the Pan-African Conference of Third World Theologians, December 17-23, 1977* (Maryknoll, NY: Orbis Books, 1979); John S. Pobee, ed., *Exploring Afro-Christology* (Frankfurt: P. Lang, 1992); and Robert Schreiter, ed., *Faces of Jesus in Africa* (Maryknoll, NY: Orbis Books, 1991).

[35]Bénézet Bujo, *African Theology in Its Social Context* (Maryknoll, NY: Orbis Books, 1992).

[36]Oscar Bimwenyi-Kweshi, *Alle Dinge erzählen von Gott: Grundlegung afrikanischer Theologie* (Freiburg im Breisgau, Germany: Herder, 1982).

[37]Charles Nyamiti, *Christ as Our Ancestor: Christology from an African Perspective* (Gweru, Zimbabwe: Mambo Press, 1984); Nyamiti, "African Christologies Today," in J. N. Kanyua Mugambi et al., eds., *Jesus in African Christianity: Experimentation and Diversity in African Christology* (Nairobi: Initiatives, 1989), 17-39; Nyamiti, "African Christologies Today," in Schreiter, *Faces of Jesus in Africa*, 3-23.

[38]Fabien Eboussi Boulaga, *Christianity Without Fetishes: An African Critique and Recapture of Christianity* (Maryknoll, NY: Orbis Books, 1984). For the French original, see *Christianisme sans Fétiche: Révélation et Domination* (Paris: Présence Africaine, 1981).

[39]John S. Pobee, *Toward an African Theology* (Nashville: Abingdon, 1979).

[40]Kwesi Dickson, *Theology in Africa* (Maryknoll, NY: Orbis Books, 1984).

[41]Gabriel M. Setiloane, *Der Gott meiner Väter und mein Gott: Afrikanische Theologie im Kontext der Apartheid* (Wuppertal, Germany: Peter Hammer, 1988).

[42]Kwame Bediako, *Christianity in Africa: The Renewal of a Non-Western Religion* (Edinburgh: Edinburgh University Press, 1995). For more on his person and work, see Andrew F. Walls, "Kwame Bediako: 1945 to 2008; Presbyterian; Ghana," and "Dictionary of African Christian Biography," Center for Global Christianity and Mission at Boston University School of Theology, www.dacb.org/stories/ghana/bediako_kwame.html (accessed March 21, 2015).

Theology, edited by John Parratt, lists only men.[43] To be sure, women's voices have only come to the fore since the 1980s. Ghanaian woman theologian Mercy Amba Oduyoye (b. 1934) describes a theology created only by men as a "one-winged theology," i.e., as a theology that cannot fly because it has only one wing, as something to be avoided at all costs. Instead, one should develop a "two-winged theology," i.e., a theology with two wings, whose second wing represents women's concerns.[44] In short, the criticism voiced by African women theologians states that a theology of inculturation may not uncritically orient itself toward a given culture, which is often the case with inculturation theologies developed by men. No culture is positive in and of itself; rather, many cultures and religions include traditions that either directly lead to the oppression of women, contribute to it, or at the very least tolerate it. Thus African women theologians attempt on the one hand to honor African cultures in order to counteract cultural alienation, yet on the other hand they have to adopt a critical stance over against those traditional elements that lead to the oppression of women.

Meanwhile, the issue of women's rights does not only include aspects of the dignity of women or their quality of life; rather, it is first and foremost an issue of developmental policies, since—to cite just one example—in many countries, as much as 90 percent of the work is performed by women.[45] The All Africa Conference of Churches (AACC), a conference held in 1980 in Ibadan (Nigeria), is seen as a monumental turning point toward a more public perception of a liberation theology by and for women in Africa. The theme of this conference was "Women Theologians—Partners in the Community of Women and Men and Church and Society." Three years later, the Women's Commission of the EATWOT was founded. Subsequently, continental conferences were held for both the French- and English-speaking parts of Africa. Then in 1989 the Circle of Concerned African Women Theologians was convened for the first time. Its goal is to conduct analyses to determine the view of women in African traditions.[46] The list of the most

---

[43]John Parratt, ed., *A Reader in African Christian Theology* (London: SPCK, 1987).
[44]Mercy Amba Oduyoye, *Hearing and Knowing: Theological Reflections on Christianity in Africa* (Maryknoll, NY: Orbis Books, 1986).
[45]Doris Strahm, *Vom Rand in die Mitte: Christologie aus der Sicht von Frauen in Asien, Afrika und Lateinamerika*, 2nd ed. (Lucerne, Switzerland: Edition Exodus, 1997), 158-59.
[46]See for instance the mission statement of the CAWT, www.thecirclecawt.org/index.html (ac-

prominent African women theologians includes Ghanaian Methodist Mercy Amba Oduyoye (b. 1934), currently probably the most well-known African woman theologian; as well as Cameroonian Baptist Louise Tappa,[47] an ordained minister and systematician;[48] Cameroonian Thérèse Souga,[49] who belongs to a Catholic order; Isabel Apawo Phiri from Botswana; Musa W. Dube (b. 1964), who is also from Botswana; Kenyan Anne Nasimiyu-Wasike,[50] also belonging to a Catholic order; Kenyan Catholic woman theologian Teresa M. Hinga (b. 1940);[51] and Nigerian Teresa Okure (b. 1941).[52]

In what follows, we will consider some examples of both African theologies and African women's theologies. Here Christ is presented as an ancestor, a healer, a chief, a master of initiation, a friend of women, an anointed one, or as the man who first modeled "mothering." It will be demonstrated that these contextual theologies do not only feature a range of different emphases as far as their content is concerned, but that they also vary in form depending on their authors and the interests that determine the conceptions on a conscious or unconscious level.

---

cessed September 12, 2011). Currently, about six hundred women belong to the organization. Conventions have been held, projects have been promoted, and about one hundred books have been published, although it must be added that it is difficult to introduce these into the curricula of various educational institutions, as woman theologian Isabel Apawo Phiri from Botswana states. See James Amanze, "History and Major Goals of Regional Associations of Theological Schools in Africa," in Werner et al., *Handbook of Theological Education*, 346-67; for more on the CAWT specifically, see 351-54.

[47]Louise K. Tappa, "Ein Gott nach dem Bild des Mannes," in John Pobee et al., eds., *Komm, lies mit meinen Augen: Biblische und theologische Entdeckungen von Frauen aus der Dritten Welt* (Offenbach, Germany: Burckhardthaus-Laetare-Verlag, 1987), 135-42; Tappa, *Das Christus-Ereignis aus der Sicht afrikanischer Frauen* (Lucerne, Switzerland: Edition Exodus, 1992), 62-69; Tappa, "Woman Doing Theology," *Ministerial Formation* 48 (1990): 29-30.

[48]Strahm, *Vom Rand in die Mitte*, 191ff.

[49]Thérèse Souga, "Das Christusereignis aus der Sicht afrikanischer Frauen—Eine katholische Perspektive," in Regula Strobel, *Leidenschaft und Solidarität: Theologinnen der Dritten Welt ergreifen das Wort* (Lucerne, Switzerland: Edition Exodus, 1992), 51-61.

[50]She belongs to the Little Sisters of St. Francis.

[51]Teresa M. Hinga, "Jesus Christ and the Liberation of Women in Africa," in Mercy Amba Oduyoye and Rachel Angogo Kanyoro, eds., *The Will to Arise: Women, Tradition, and the Church in Africa* (Maryknoll, NY: Orbis Books, 1992), 183-94.

[52]Teresa Okure, "Jesus, der Mann, der in der Art der Frauen wirkte," in *Jahrbuch Mission 1993* (Hamburg: Missionshilfe Verlag, 1993), 53-62; Okure, "The Significance Today of Jesus' Commission to Mary Magdalene (John 20:11-18)," *International Review of Mission* 81 (1992): 177-88; Okure, "Inculturation: Biblical/Theological Bases," in Teresa Okure et al., *32 Articles Evaluating Inculturation of Christianity in Africa*, Spearhead 112-114 (Eldoret, Kenya: AMECEA Gaba Publications, 1990), 55-86.

Evangelical Theologies and Inculturation in Africa

The wide range of concepts that can fall under the description "contextual theologies" is evident when one considers the full ecumenical gamut in its global dimension and not just those forms of contextual theology located within the networks of churches and movements that are associated with the World Council of Churches one way or another. If our description is to be a truly ecumenical one, then we will need to expand our focus to include the large number of evangelical churches, institutions, associations, and movements that are out there. In addition, we would need also to mention those churches that describe themselves as fundamentalist, i.e., those that adopt a separatist position in terms of church politics and that keep aloof from other Christian communions for the sake of the purity of their doctrine and practice (as opposed to the various strands of evangelicalism such as the new evangelicals, the radical evangelicals, etc.).[53]

In my experience, very few publications have attempted to cater for such a wide ecumenical spectrum, i.e., to include those Christian churches and movements that consciously dissociate themselves from others. The result is a questionable limitation of perspective. It is important at least to be informed about these churches and communions, even and especially if one does not agree with their positions. It is impossible to achieve an ecumenical perspective in any other way, since the toleration of what is different, foreign, or offensive is simply part and parcel of an intercultural hermeneutics. It remains an inescapable hermeneutical task. It is not helpful, therefore, to engage in polemical sideswiping or simply to ignore these forms of Christian churches and congregations.[54]

On a methodological note, it is very important that we proceed by clarifying the meaning of the term *evangelical:*[55] this term refers to the way in

---

[53]In 1948 a number of fundamentalist churches joined under the leadership of Carl McIntire to form the International Council of Christian Churches, obviously as a rival association to the WCC. However, the ICCC remained a small association.

[54]John Parratt, for instance, completely disregards in his portrayal not only evangelical missions and churches but also their theology. See Parratt, *Theologiegeschichte.*

[55]The term *evangelical* was used in sixteenth-century England to denote *reformist circles within the church,* but it was soon replaced by the term *Protestant.* In contrast, in eighteenth-century England the word was used to denote a *revivalist movement* that rebelled against the lectures on moralism commonly held at the time that again emphasized the doctrine of justification, the communion of believers, the commitment to a personal savior, and mission. In 1846, a fusion in England resulted in the formation of the Evangelical Alliance. This was *not an association of churches, but rather of active groups within churches.* A new Evangelical Alliance was founded in 1970.

which not only certain theologians see themselves but also those churches and organizations that have joined to form national evangelical alliances.[56] Most of these churches and organizations can be considered to belong to the new evangelicals, a movement that was formed in the 1940s and is characterized by at least the following: a strong emphasis on the authority of the Bible, a personal relationship with Jesus on the part of the believers, a strong community orientation, extensive involvement in missions, and an accentuation of Christology and soteriology (the incarnation, the virgin birth, the physical resurrection of Jesus Christ, his death as substitutionary atonement, the doctrine of justification, and the sinlessness of Jesus).

However, it is difficult to define "evangelical" churches or organizations in sub-Saharan Africa, since many of the African members of the World Council of Churches are characterized by a form of piety that one might designate as "evangelical" in the way it was defined above and as "conservative" from the perspective of the European mainline churches. In contrast, the praxis of many of the African congregations and churches deriving from the evangelical faith missions is characterized just as much by folk-religious views and practices (which give rise to a fear of "syncretism" among evangelical theologians), as is the case in other churches. The boundaries are fluid, as is demonstrated by the African churches and organizations that belong to both the WCC and to evangelical associations.

The institutional platform of evangelical theology in Africa developed within a particular historical situation. In 1961, at its general assembly in New Delhi, the World Council of Churches, which had been founded in 1948, integrated into its structures the International Missionary Council, which had been independent up until that time. The reason for this was the realization that mission is not a special task of the church but an integral part of its very nature. In the wake of decolonization, many countries founded their own national council of churches, which in Africa's case in 1963 proceeded jointly to found the All African Council of Churches with

---

[56]The term *evangelical* can be used both in the sense of the German word *evangelisch*, i.e., to describe certain Protestant churches such as the Evangelical-Lutheran (*Evangelisch*-Lutherische) churches, and in the sense of the German word *evangelikal*, i.e., to denote such movements as the "new evangelicals" or the "national evangelical alliances" that have been founded in many African countries. See Detlef Kapteina, *Afrikanische Evangelikale Theologie*, 2nd ed. (Nuremberg, Germany: VTR, 2001), 25.

an office in Nairobi. In 1966, two large associations of evangelical mission societies in the United States, the Interdenominational Foreign Missions Association (IFMA)[57] and the Evangelical Foreign Missions Association (EFMA),[58] held a consultation in Wheaton, Illinois, at which they dissociated themselves from what they considered to be the too-liberal view of religion prevalent in the WCC milieu. Whereas the African Evangelical Office (AEO) had been founded as early as 1962, the Association of Evangelicals in Africa and Madagascar (AEAM) was founded in 1966 as a continental association of evangelicals, thus at the same time as the AACC.[59] The founding of these associations brought a strongly conservative US-American Protestantism to bear on an international level. From the beginning, the members of the AEAM included African Pentecostal churches, albeit only those that were founded by Pentecostal missions from overseas. This again demonstrates the US-American influence, since the American Pentecostal churches considered themselves to be part of the new evangelicals.[60] The ongoing polarization between the WCC and the evangelicals led to the founding of the Lausanne Committee for World Evangelization as an additional global platform for evangelical concerns besides the World Evangelical Federation.

The evangelical movement is loosely structured into a number of umbrella organizations. These include, for instance, the World Evangelical Fellowship (WEF), the Lausanne Committee for World Evangelization (LCWE), and the International Fellowship of Evangelical Mission Theologians (INFEMIT). In addition to these, there are also associations on a continental level such as the Association of Evangelicals in Africa (AEA), which took this name in 1993,[61] and the African Theological Fraternity (ATF), associated with INFEMIT.[62]

---

[57]Founded in 1917.
[58]This association was founded in 1940. It was later renamed as the Evangelical Fellowship of Mission Agencies.
[59]Kapteina, *Afrikanische Evangelikale Theologie*, 62ff.
[60]Ibid., 35. Many of these American Pentecostal churches were and are also members of the North American Association of Evangelicals (NEA).
[61]The organization in question is the Association of Evangelicals in Africa and Madagascar (AEAM), which was renamed as the AEA in 1993.
[62]Kapteina, *Afrikanische Evangelikale Theologie*, 9.

Table 1. A typology of churches and movements in Sub-Saharan Africa: Nigeria as a case study

National Associations	Continental Associations	Global Associations
-> National Council of Churches	-> All African Council of Churches	
AFRICAN CHURCHES STANDING IN THE TRADITION OF THE MISSION CHURCHES[a]		
(A) Roman Catholic Church		**Vatican, papacy, councils**
	-> Association of Member Episcopal Conferences in Eastern Africa (AMECEA)	Observer status.
	-> Symposium of Episcopal Conferences of Africa and Madagaskar (SECAM)	
		World Council of Churches
(B) Anglican Church		Lambeth Conference (->WCC)
(C) Protestant Churches		
Lutheran churches		Lutheran World Federation (->WCC)
Reformed churches		World Communion of Reformed Churches (->WCC)
Methodist, Presbyterian, Baptist churches et al.		other associations (->WCC)
(D) Evangelical Movement	*Dual memberships in the WCC are possible*	World Evangelical Fellowship (WEF)
		Lausanne Committee for World Evangelization (LCWE)
(E) Fundamentalist Missions / Churches (separatist)		International Council of Christian Churches (ICCC)
(F) Pentecostal Churches from the USA as Mission Churches		
AFRICAN INDEPENDENT CHURCHES / AFRICAN INSTITUTED CHURCHES (AICS)		
(G) African Independent Churches[b]	-> Organization of African Instituted Churches	
(H) African Pentecostal Churches (transnational in part)		

[a] Orthodox Churches are not listed here, since Orthodox mission efforts are still a fairly recent phenomenon.

[b] In 2010 there were around fifteen thousand different African Independent Churches and African Instituted Churches (AICs) on the African continent. Fewer than twenty have joined the WCC to date.

11

African Theologies

Jesus Christ as (Proto-)Ancestor, Master of Initiation, and Healer

The overview above may have indicated the diversity of the various associations of churches in the area of sub-Saharan Africa. These consist of various church bodies originally founded as mission churches, several churches associated with the African Independent Churches or African Initiated Churches, and other churches associated with the Pentecostal movement. It has become clear how difficult it is to attempt any form of categorization, since the everyday reality frequently defies such classification efforts. It is absolutely essential to take cognizance of this complexity in order to form a reasonably realistic appreciation of the various local contexts. Bearing this complexity in mind, we now turn our attention to various strands of contextual theologies, beginning with representatives of the so-called African theology, which emphasizes the cultural frame of reference of African religiosity. We begin with Bénézet Bujo.

JESUS CHRIST AS A (PROTO-)ANCESTOR: BÉNÉZET BUJO

Bénézet Bujo (b. 1940) is a Roman Catholic theologian. He served at one time as a professor in the Catholic faculty at Kinshasa, Zaire. Bujo was awarded a doctorate in moral theology at the University of Würzburg (Germany). He most recently held a position as a theology professor in Switzerland. Bujo fundamentally believes that the ancestors have an influence on the lives of Africans by means of their gestures, their rituals, and their language. The past of the fathers, now present as ancestors, is for him a guarantee of salvation. "The remembering and reenactment of the deeds of ancestors and elders is a memorial-narrative act of salvation designed to secure total community, both before and after death, with all good and benevolent ancestors."[1] The conceptual connection arises from the anthropology of sub-Saharan tribal religions. Let us proceed by providing a brief explanation, beginning with the term *tribal religions*. This term already indicates the ambit of these religious configurations: it normally spans small communities numbering from a few hundred to several thousand members who consider themselves to be affiliated because they share a common progenitor (male or female) or hero, who live in the same area, are economically interdependent, speak the same language, and participate in the same cult.[2] That being said, once the ritual of burial is completed, the deceased are not considered to be "dead" and thus "absent." Rather, once they have passed life on (i.e., once they have procreated and had grandchildren), they are seen as ancestors, as the "living-dead" (Mbiti) who are still present in the vicinity of the hut or the kraal.

The ancestors demand ritual veneration and are able to bestow blessings on the tribe, the clan, or the family, as the case may be. They may grant such blessings as an abundance of children, peace among the members of the tribe, fertility of land and animals, success in business, and the like. According to the tribal religious view, the ancestors are only interested in their own family, and this is also the case for the powers or divinities of a tribal religion—hence the term, since the scope of validity for these religions was limited to the group affiliated by relations (and in many instances continues to be, wherever these religious configurations are present today). The majority of Western missionaries denounced the veneration of ancestors and attempted to replace it with the Christian faith. However, since for tribal religious traditions the

---

[1]This quote and the following discussion are drawn from Bénézet Bujo, *African Theology in Its Social Context* (Maryknoll, NY: Orbis Books, 1992), 78.

[2]It deserves mention that this image of tribal religions is interpreted by some today as the result of the colonial administrative policy of granting special privileges to regionally delimited social formations. Terence Ranger argues that Great Britain as a colonial power fought against African religious configurations that extended transregionally and that, conversely, it promoted the regional limitation of religious configurations so as to control them more effectively. Ranger claims that the "image" of "tribal" religions developed to a significant degree as a result of these processes and that this rigidified into essentialist patterns ("the" tribal religions as regionally delimited configurations). See Terence Ranger, "The Local and the Global in Southern African Religious History," in Robert W. Hefner, *Conversion to Christianity* (Berkeley: University of California Press, 1993), 65-98.

most important value of a successful life consists of its immanence in the here and now, African Christians frequently continued to venerate the ancestors in secret. For many African Christians, the ancestors continue to play a vital role. Often the result was that they came to lead parallel but separate existences, being African in terms of their culture and Christian in terms of their religion. That being said, African Christians frequently kept their practice of ancestor veneration secret. Since the 1980s, African theologians increasingly sought to develop a theology that incorporates the ancestor concept. In this sense, Jesus may be understood as the "archetypal ancestor" or "original ancestor" or even, as Bujo contends, as the "proto-ancestor."

(a) *Jesus Christ as ancestor—a note on methodology.* It is fundamentally important for Bujo that the starting point of African theology is "from below," i.e., from within the conceptual framework of the African mind. This means that the first step would be to read the New Testament with the ancestor concept in mind. In so doing, certain aspects suggest themselves, just as if one were to read the New Testament from the perspective of the theme of initiation. In a second step, however, it becomes clear that the New Testament accords a unique role to Jesus Christ, with the result that it is not legitimate simply to assimilate him into the concept of ancestors that had hitherto served as the heuristic horizon. Jesus Christ is therefore not just one ancestor among many. This means, third, that the New Testament directs the reader back to her prior conception of the ancestors, which is now enriched, corrected, and transcended by the message of the gospel. This also means that it is only possible fully to understand the ancestors from this perspective, i.e., from the perspective of the Christ event. Thus it is not (or no longer) the traditional ancestor concept that defines what the ancestors are and possibly may be according to God's will; rather, the gospel supplies this definition in its truest and most profound sense. In so doing, Jesus Christ emerges as the basis, benchmark, and objective of that ancestor concept. Thus Jesus Christ is no longer merely *the* ancestor or, from a longitudinal prospective, the original ancestor; rather, he is the proto-ancestor, the one who embodies and will continue to embody the basis and objective of the ancestor concept.

(b) *Aspects of an ancestor-Christology in the New Testament.* Bujo attempts to provide a comprehensive definition of a Christology that in all its aspects seeks to portray Jesus as an ancestor. We will content ourselves with highlighting only some of these. First, *Jesus embodies* the principal value of African thought, *the life force*, not only by giving "life . . . to the full" (Jn 10:10) but by being this life force in person (Jn 11:25). Therefore, the following applies: "Jesus Christ is the ultimate embodiment of all the virtues of the ancestors, the realization of the salvation for which they yearned."[3] In his healings and also in, say, the resurrection of Lazarus, Jesus Christ embodies the life force.

> It is within this perspective that Jesus Christ is the Proto-Ancestor for the African. Jesus Christ identified himself with humankind, so that he constitutes their explanation. From now on, Jesus makes his own all the striving of the ancestors after righteousness and all their history, in such a way that these have now become a meeting-place with the God of salvation. Above all, Jesus Christ himself becomes the privileged locus for a full understanding of the ancestors.[4]

Bujo here refers to Hebrews 1:1-2, which speaks of the prophets who preceded Jesus Christ and of the cloud of witnesses. The ancestors are fulfilled in him.

On an *ethical level*, Jesus Christ as the proto-ancestor places special emphasis on the value of human beings, since he came not only to deliver salvation by means of divine revelation but to grant life to the full on all levels of society. That is to say, the coming of the person of Christ is an event that establishes and enables community, as shown by extending hospitality to sojourners and demonstrating care for family members, orphans, and the underprivileged. For Bujo, the values of African ethics are fulfilled in Jesus' Sermon on the Mount. At the same time, however, Jesus transcends these values in their traditional form since he extends the scope above and beyond the communal association of the tribe and the clan to *all people*. This ethics of Jesus Christ criticizes and condemns traditions of tribal chauvinism just as much as those of colonialism and every form of human self-seeking. Life in community is the principal value universalized by Jesus Christ as the proto-ancestor.

---

[3]Bujo, *African Theology*, 81.
[4]Ibid., 83.

The qualities and values of the African ancestor concept are fulfilled in Jesus Christ. In this regard, *a father's last words* to his children play an especially important role. These words are considered to be life giving and normative. In this context, Bujo is able to establish a connection with Jesus' farewell discourses in the Gospel of John (Jn 14–16) and Jesus' parting words in general, which he interprets from an ancestor perspective. In conclusion, as far as death and resurrection are concerned, Jesus is the one who proclaimed the kingdom of God, which was sealed by death and resurrection. The death and resurrection of Jesus highlight the uniqueness of his person. He dies for the sake of the "kingdom message," and therefore his death is of soteriological significance. The resurrection reveals the relationship that existed between Jesus and God, and is simultaneously to be seen as a new creation.

Discussion and Critical Questions

The strength of Bujo's model is that he attempts to apprehend the concept of the ancestors in a constructive manner and to integrate it into Christian doctrine and practice. This is all the more significant because many aspects of Jesus' history contradict the traditional ancestor concept. For instance, according to the traditional ancestor concept, only those who have had children of their own (including at least one son) and grandchildren, i.e., those who have *passed on* life and the life force to others, are able to become ancestors in their own right. Since Jesus of Nazareth died without marrying or fathering children, this is not the case for him. In addition, people only become good ancestors by dying a good death, to wit, after as long a life as possible. But an *evil death*, i.e., an untimely death at a young age, does not bode well, and this is especially true if a person dies as a result of an accident or murder. Yet this is true for Jesus Christ, since he died the death of a political insurgent at a young age—he was murdered. One might adduce a whole series of additional such aspects.

Small wonder, then, that Bujo bases his argument on didactic and symbolic statements such as the incarnation of the Word, the image of the fullness of life, and other aspects such as the practice, the healings, the preaching, and the parting words of Jesus. Conversely, the differences to the traditional setting of African tribal culture can also be seen in a positive light, since they emphasize the incomparable uniqueness of Jesus Christ. In any case, Bujo sees in ancestor Christology a way to relate elements of the African tribal cultures with the Christian faith. Later, we will need to face the issue of whether this approach indeed represents a pan-African Christology. We will do so as we perform the crosscheck of investigating which appellations are used for Christ in African congregations, i.e., on the grassroots level, using the Lutheran churches of Tanzania as an example.

JESUS CHRIST AS A MASTER OF INITIATION: TITIANMA ANSELME SANON

A number of African theologians see Jesus as a master of initiation.[5] In what follows, we will highlight the concept of Titianma Anselme Sanon. Sanon, in Burkina Faso, proceeds on the assumption that human beings assimilate knowledge with their whole body. This was always the case, he believes, in the initiation rites of the tribal religions, since they transmitted corporeal experiences to the initiates. Sanon goes on to claim that it is legitimate for the Christian church to absorb these traditions. In each case, young people were incorporated by age group into the values and traditions of the tribal community by being *secluded* from the community during the initiation phase for a set period, which could last anywhere from a few months to three years. First, a ritual "killing" of the boys was carried out, and then they lived outside of the village in a bush camp. Here they were welded together as a group; they learned the tribe's traditions, the values, the rituals; and they learned a secret language, which they were forbidden to disclose. The camp was led by a master of initiation and some helpers. Reintegration into the community took place using rituals symbolizing a new birth (such as crawling through an underground tunnel, which represented their emergence from the womb), followed by a great feast. Now the young men were ready to receive permission to marry.

Each initiation group had a symbol, a distinctive mark. According to Sanon, the only purpose of this symbol was to induct the initiate into the order to which the symbol itself belonged. The entire initiation is symbolic. "The pedagogy of participating in the initiation thus encompasses three

---

[5]Titianma Anselme Sanon, *Das Evangelium verwurzeln: Glaubenserschließung im Raum afrikanischer Stammesinitiationen* (Freiburg im Breisgau, Germany: Herder, 1985).

things: The ritual that is carried out (or the cult, as the case may be) refers to a cultural order, which in turn is rooted in a founding event that took place in the hoary past of the ancestors."[6] In Sanon's view, the three main symbols are the following: the mask (and its presentation during the dance), the secret language, and the secret itself.[7]

Is it legitimate for the Christian church to adopt these tribal initiation rites and integrate them into its liturgical procedures? Sanon answers in the affirmative, reasoning that there is a distinction among the religion, the cult, and the culture and that the initiation merely comprises a "cultural event." The cult, thus for instance Christian baptism, may take various cultural forms of expression and nevertheless continue to exist in essence. The initiation culture may thus contribute to a new understanding of the Christian faith. According to Sanon, this tradition "is integrated into [God's] plan of salvation by the church."[8] Congruency with New Testament references in this regard is of importance to Sanon. Jesus himself is designated as a "Nazarene" from the "tribe of David," which Sanon interprets to mean that Jesus subjected himself to the cultic rites of his people. He expressed solidarity with his people and finally descended to the dead, which means that he was with his family and maintained his affiliation to them.[9] But which references does the New Testament provide for Jesus as a master of initiation?

(a) The life, death, and resurrection of Jesus as the way of initiation. Sanon sees in the meaning of the Greek word *teleiosis*, "fulfillment," a key allusion to initiation in the context of the New Testament. He takes the word to refer to a path of religious development.[10] From this perspective, passages like Hebrews 2:10 and Hebrews 1:1-3 indicate a progressive dynamic. For Sanon, the theology of the letter to the Hebrews comes to serve as the most important evidence for his initiation Christology. He points especially to Hebrews 10:14—"For by one sacrifice he has made perfect forever those who are being made holy" (NIV). Furthermore, in Hebrews 12:2 Jesus is called

---

[6]Ibid., 47. Emphasis removed.

[7]In the case of the Bobo tribe, the connection becomes clear on a linguistic level: "Do-non = the son of Do, i.e. the mask;—Do-bere = the luo, the secret language;—Do-da = the hidden secret of the do, i.e. the mystery." Ibid., 48.

[8]Ibid., 88.

[9]Ibid., 87-88. Note that he did, however, descend to all (!) the dead, not only to those belonging to his people. This shows the universality of his scope.

[10]In terms of the religious-historical background, Sanon points to the mystery religions.

the "author and perfecter of faith." Sanon takes this to mean that Jesus Christ is "the great master of initiation of our faith." It is crucial for him that "no one can be a master of initiation without having first been initiated himself, inasmuch as initiation comprises knowledge gained by experience of that which needs to be done."[11] It follows that since Jesus had been initiated, he could become a master of initiation. Besides, Jesus being first an initiate and then a master of initiation shows the significance of the correlation that knowledge is made possible *by experience*.

Consequently, Sanon now proceeds to trace salvation history in Jesus Christ, reading it as a story of initiation in order to arrive at an understanding of Jesus Christ as the true and only master of initiation from the perspective of Easter. The life of Jesus serves essentially to warrant his claim; his resurrection serves authoritatively to confirm his claim by putting it into effect. Sanon adds the following observations: Jesus lived among brothers, which Sanon takes as a community of initiates. The presentation of Jesus in the temple (newborn children were shown to the priests) demonstrates that he lived in accordance with the given traditions. Over and above those, Jesus voluntarily subjected himself to many trials and learned obedience through suffering (Heb 5:8), ultimately by facing the greatest trial of all, death on the cross. In so doing, Jesus mastered the subject content and the tests set for all initiates, namely to display patience and to pass trials.

Now the difference between Jesus and normal people becomes significant. First, Jesus is the son of God; he not only suffered trials, but he *actively* chose them. Besides, second, he is the older brother (which generally plays an important role in African tribal traditions) and, what is more, he is also the first brother of the human beings; he is the brother who passes through the trials as the first and authoritative one, as the first initiate. The community that forms around him (the disciples) for its part continues down the path of initiation. Hebrews and Philippians are to be interpreted within the context of initiation, especially in terms of what their statements on the death and resurrection of Jesus Christ: through the death and resurrection a new role is assigned to death, one that it did not play before, namely that death now allows the dying to enter the freedom of a superior life, of the resurrection life.

---

[11]Sanon, *Das Evangelium Verwurzeln*, 108.

The initiation that comes from Jesus thus leads through death (on the cross) and through the resurrection to life (eternal life). In this way, the character of Jesus' life comes into effect. Sanon then proceeds to interpret the life of Jesus from the perspective of initiation. We may briefly outline his interpretation as follows: It is said that Jesus was in the temple—presumably, according to Sanon, together with boys of his own age. This means, first, that he sequestered himself from women, as is the case in the initiation rites of tribal religions also, where the boys remain in their age group in an initiation camp outside town for between two months and three years. Second, this means that Jesus is joined by a community of fellow initiates. Third, this means that Jesus, like all initiates, listens to what the old and the wise have to say. In other words, Jesus begins by listening and learning. The wise are extremely astonished at his understanding. But the reason why Jesus understands so well is that he comes from the Father (from God). The messianic secret is constituted by Jesus' submitting to the pedagogy of the phases of initiation. According to Sanon, the miracles of Jesus are signs and symbols, of which Jesus makes use. In so doing, Jesus avails himself of initiation rhythms, thus for instance in Luke 13:32-33. At issue here already is the Easter rhythm.[12] Finally, Jesus goes to Jerusalem, i.e., to the place of initiation. Jesus comes from the tribe of the prophets. The Passover and the cross mean that the initiation is concerned with both the beginning of a path and the completion of a path. Sanon summarizes,

> Does Jesus serve as our master of initation? Yes! And how consummately so! Jesus is our master of initiation because he showed us the highest values in the form of symbols, the way experienced masters of initiation do. These values are: The love of God and the neighbor, adoration and intercession, mercy and forgiveness, childlike obedience, devoting one's life to serving others even to the point of suffering and death, and the spirit of service and sharing. He makes these absolute life values understandable for us by using familiar symbols: By means of the tree of the cross, the water of baptism, the bread and the communal family meal, the wine, the washing of the feet, the night (of prayer on the mountain or in the desert), life and death.

---

[12]Ibid., 115-17.

The consequence for Christians is that they cannot walk the path of initiation alone but only in community with others.[13]

(b) Is there a wider use for such a theological concept? Some might question whether this concept represents anything more than an intellectual giving of account. That this is not so is shown by the fact that the concept itself calls for liturgical implementation. The Christian church can only be considered as an initiation community to the extent that it adequately gives expression to the stages of initiation in its liturgical life. It is especially in the domain of the Roman Catholic Church that many points of contact may be found in this regard. This becomes clear when one remembers that this church recognizes a total of seven sacraments, namely baptism, confirmation, marriage, holy orders, confession, the Eucharist, and extreme unction. From the perspective of a theology of initiation, it is especially baptism, confirmation, marriage, and extreme unction that suggest themselves as rites of passage (or *rites de passage*, as van Gennep calls them). Holy orders may be understood along the lines of an initiation helper (as long as the role of the master of initiation is reserved for Christ), whereas confession and the Eucharist would need to be localized elsewhere.

So we need to ask, first, whether and in what form such approaches are to be implemented liturgically. In the case of the Roman Catholic Church, this would need to be discussed within the church and decided by the magisterium. Thus in Zaire a new missal has already been introduced. Yet, second, to what extent the liturgy is able adequately to reflect the cultural character of each individual people without losing sight of the universal and transcultural quality of the worship service is a separate issue. After all, the Roman Catholic Church is a *global player*, a world church that has taken great strides in the areas of universalization and standardization in the last 250 years.

THE CHURCH AS A FACILITATOR OF INCULTURATION?

When we ask the reciprocal question as to the correlation between gospel and culture, we find that Sanon allocates a special role to the church, that of a protagonist in the process of inculturation.

---

[13]Ibid., 118-19. For his comments on the cross and resurrection of Jesus Christ, see 120ff. He uses the image of the grain of wheat.

When it comes to cultural traditions, the church has a revelatory function—not only in its capacity as an evaluating body, but by allowing these traditions to say what they do and why they do it that way. Once these traditions come to a knowledge of themselves, they are enabled to open up to a new dimension. In the new light of that which outlives them, they take responsibility for themselves and reconsider what they are in view of what they are to become. To re-evaluate traditional initiation—does that not mean to provide it with a favorable opportunity, with the kairos to re-evaluate itself, not within the framework of a particularistic and ethnic horizon, but rather on the basis of the human and divine calling of the people who came out of the womb of this tradition?[14]

It is remarkable that in this view, the church is seen as the agent of inculturation. The church is able to provide a kairos, to lead, to decide, to guide. Traditional initiation thus takes on the role of "serving" baptismal faith. Traditional culture sees itself in a new light—made possible by the church—and takes hold of itself in the kairos provided by the church! Perhaps one may say that instead of pulling the strings, the church guides traditional culture in this way. While traditional culture now is under administration, it still reserves a certain amount of autonomy and continues to exercise its own creative drive to a certain extent. It provides the cult of baptism with its cultural points of contact. Seen in this light, evangelization comprises both dialogue and confrontation. At any rate, it is through the church that culture "comes to a knowledge of itself," since this is not about the intrinsic importance of, say, initiation rites, but rather about their significance within the horizon of understanding of the church's doctrine.

---

[14]Ibid., 100-101.

12

Jesus Christ and an African Women's Theology

When it comes to the issue of the inculturation of the gospel in Africa, several areas of tension may be discerned. First, there is the tension between the alien Christianity of the mission churches in Africa, whose theology and forms of expression are not truly African, and the issue of African traditions. Second, there is the intra-African tension between the drive to maintain the older tribal traditions and the need to face the challenges of societal change, which make many traditions seem old-fashioned or obsolete, if they have not already died out. Third, from the perspective of women, there is a tension in African theologies between positive elements of tradition and those that sanction the oppression of women in the opinion of African women theologians.[1] These include patriarchal institutions as well as cultural traditions in three areas, namely (1) the traditions of Western mission churches, (2) the traditions of African traditional tribal cultures, and (3) the biblical traditions of the books of the Bible and especially of the New Testament, which were authored by men.

THE ROLE OF WOMEN IN AFRICAN TRIBAL CULTURES
The aim of African women theologians as a group—notwithstanding all the individual differences—is to lift the liberating aspects of the praxis of Jesus Christ out of the New Testament, to exegete them in the context of everyday reality of life in Africa, and critically to apply them. To begin with, this means that they acknowledge the positive aspects of African tribal cultures

---

[1]For an overview of African women's theologies, see Doris Strahm, *Vom Rand in die Mitte: Christologie aus der Sicht von Frauen in Asien, Afrika und Lateinamerika*, 2nd ed. (Lucerne, Switzerland: Edition Exodus, 1997), 158-59.

while criticizing them at the same time. A few examples will serve to illustrate this approach. Most African traditions share an emphasis on the correlation between the individual and community. While African women theologians see this emphasis as positive, they insist that it may not be used to justify the continuation of those traditions that are used to cast aspersions on the dignity of women or oppress them. As a result, male inculturation theologians might promote certain African traditions in an effort to counteract foreign influences, while female African theologians might criticize those same traditions as patriarchal. One example might be women being barred from ecclesiastical offices or positions of leadership in African churches on the basis of African traditions.

The same is true for the image of women—African traditions generally hold women in high regard in their function of giving life. However, in so doing the image of women is restricted to their function as mothers and wives. This finds expression especially in oral traditions such as legends, stories, proverbs, and titles. For African women theologians, the liberation of women is not just a matter of criticizing certain societal forms of unequal treatment; rather, above and beyond that it is a matter of fundamentally criticizing and transforming the image of women in and of itself. The reason for this is that the traditions have a lasting effect on the perceptions and attitudes of both men and women, such as when obedience, submission, and service are simply demanded of women.[2]

In addition, restricting women to their biological function of motherhood also corresponds to the *devaluation of women who do not conform to this image*. This applies especially to women who are not married and thus defy the conventions of society, divorced women, and women who have children out of wedlock. Even more blatant, moreover, is holding women in contempt who have not yet had children or who cannot do so.[3] These women are denied status and dignity in society.

Criticism is also voiced over ritual actions to which women are subjected in the process of becoming mothers, if and to the extent that these rituals contribute not to the empowerment of the women but to their humiliation and subjugation under pejorative traditions. Instead, the aim is to *create a*

---

[2]Ibid., 162-63.
[3]Ibid., 178ff.

new view of the female body and of female sexuality. For instance, in certain traditional religions, women's blood is seen to have an ambivalent status. The Akan tribe in Ghana, say, considers the menstrual blood of women to be dangerous. It is said to cause impotence among men and to render religious rituals ineffective. On the whole, ritual impurity is surrounded by many religious taboos, and women are often excluded from the religious cult for long periods of time. Even in matrilineal societies women are barred from serving in leadership positions.[4]

THE LIFEWORLDS OF AFRICAN WOMEN AND THEOLOGY

Many African women theologians are convinced that the only legitimate way to pursue theology is to do so from within the lifeworlds in which people in general and women in particular exist, in which they live and must survive. To pursue theology therefore means to consider not only one's own biography from a theological perspective but also the life contexts of African women in general. Methodist Mercy Amba Oduyoye[5] hails from Ghana. She studied in Cambridge (England) and Accra (Ghana) and then worked for a time for the WCC in Geneva. She also taught at the University of Ibadan (Nigeria), at the University of Birmingham (England), and at the Harvard Divinity School in Cambridge (Massachusetts). One would be justified in describing her as the most well-known African woman theologian of our time.[6]

For Oduyoye, theology has to be relevant, which it only is when it proceeds from the understanding of people in their everyday life and its cultural and religious traditions as well as its social and economic contexts.

---

[4]Ibid., 206-7.

[5]Mercy Amba Oduyoye, *Hearing and Knowing: Theological Reflections on Christianity in Africa* (Maryknoll, NY: Orbis Books, 1986). See also Mercy Amba Oduyoye, "Naming the Women: The Words of the Akan and the Words of the Bible," *Bulletin of African Theology* 3 (1981): 81-97; Oduyoye, "Churchwomen and the Church's Mission," in John S. Pobee and Bärbel von Wartenberg-Potter, eds., *New Eyes for Reading: Biblical and Theological Reflections by Women from the Third World* (Geneva: WCC, 1986), 68-80; Elizabeth Amoah and Mercy Amba Oduyoye, "The Christ for African Women," in Virginia Fabella and Mercy Amba Oduyoye, eds., *With Passion and Compassion: Third World Women Doing Theology* (Maryknoll, NY: Orbis Books, 1988), 35-46; Mercy Amba Oduyoye, "A Critique of Mbiti's View of Love and Marriage in Africa," in Jacob Obafemi Kehinde Olupona and Sulayman S. Nyang, eds., *Religious Plurality in Africa: Essays in Honour of John S. Mbiti* (Berlin: Mouton de Gruyter, 1993), 341-65; and Mercy Amba Oduyoye, "Christianity and African Culture," *International Review of Mission* 84 (1995): 77-89.

[6]Strahm, *Vom Rand in die Mitte*, 199-226.

Her own mother came from the Asante tribe, which belongs to the Ghanaian ethnic group of the Akan, a matriarchal people. Oduyoye brings out how her grandmother and her mother played a formative role for her faith life. At the same time, she also factors in the general experiences of African women, with the result that her theology owes itself to a least three dimensions, namely (1) the biographical dimension, (2) the actual cultural dimension of her surroundings, and (3) the dimension of the living conditions of African women, which—in spite of the many differences—are similar across many African countries. Theology develops out of these contexts and leads back to these contexts. As a result, Oduyoye is sensitized to elements that would contribute to or seek the oppression of women, be it in biblical traditions, in Western traditions, or in African traditions. One example of a biblical tradition that has been misused to justify the oppression of women is the interpretation that the woman is the origin and embodiment of sin (Gen 3). A corresponding example of a Western tradition is the practice of name giving, a European custom introduced by the colonial powers by which a woman would receive the name of her father as her own second name. African tribal traditions along these lines are constituted by, for example, certain taboos and purity codes and also by certain other rituals.

Jesus Christ as the Companion of Women: Merci Amba Oduyoye

For Oduyoye, the fullness of womanhood was revealed in Jesus Christ in the sense that he performed "mothering" roles, by which she means the caring, nurturing, and, in this sense, "motherly" actions of Jesus. However—and this is a particular concern of Oduyoye's—this applies not only to women but also to men. Thus for her, mothering is a life orientation that pertains to both sexes. The question of why Jesus as a historic figure was a man may be answered as follows: it enabled him very specifically to challenge the prevalent androcentric cultural patterns of his day and to demonstrate a holistic way of life. Doris Strahm notes that for Oduyoye,

> the significance of Jesus' historical existence as a man was not an essential, but rather a functional one, because it was precisely in his capacity as a man that he was able to proclaim that faithfulness to God is more important than

faithfulness to one's family, clan, or people, that serving is better than ruling, and that love (and not control) promotes the well-being of a community.[7]

One might therefore abstractly speak of the subversive power of the man Jesus in the face of an androcentric society, religion, and culture. As Oduyoye puts it,

> Jesus of Nazareth . . . has become for us the . . . true "Child of Women"—"Child of Women" truly because in Christ, the fullness of all that we know of perfect womanhood is revealed. He is the caring, compassionate nurturer of all. Jesus nurtures not just by parables, but by miracles of feeding. With his own hands he cooked that others might eat; he was known in the breaking of the bread. Jesus is Christ—truly woman (human) yet truly divine, for only God is the truly Compassionate One.[8]

For Oduyoye, Jesus Christ is above all the servant, the good shepherd. He is the one who embodies wholeness of body and soul, wholeness of both men and women, and he does so in that he helps people emerge from their social isolation and from the isolation in which they exist due to cultural and religious commandments. In his relationship to women, Jesus lives a new reality, and in so doing he makes it possible to live a new culture between men and women. As Oduyoye says, "we are baptized into Christ as persons, irrespective of our social status, so that just as the humanity of the male is taken into Christ so is the humanity of the female. There is no sexual distinction in the Trinity, but qualities labeled feminine and masculine are all manifested in Christ Jesus who is the image par excellence of God."[9]

In this way the idea of mothering is applied to both women and men; this is inclusive feminism. But this also means that the idea of woman is no longer fused exclusively to her biological role or to her function as birthgiver and mother. Oduyoye therefore sharply distinguishes between *motherhood* and *mothering*. For her, mothering is more of a lifestyle, one that is expressed by cultivating relationships and acting within a relationship paradigm. It is about the fullness of human existence that every human being should be able to experience individually. In consequence, Oduyoye believes, it is necessary to develop a *new understanding of marriage*, one that goes

---

[7]Ibid., 222.
[8]Amoah and Oduyoye, "Christ for African Women," 43-44.
[9]Oduyoye, *Hearing and Knowing*, 137.

beyond focusing only on reproduction. She also criticizes that particular ancestor concept, or more specifically that concept of immortality, that is contingent on the birth of descendants—the idea found in many ethnic groups that the ancestors return in the form of their descendants.

The Trinity as the perfect community. Oduyoye sees the divine harmony between the three persons of God as the original image of a successful community.

> The Christian proclamation that God is not a nomad but rather a center of relations in which Father, Son, and Holy Spirit act and interact without subsuming or subordinating any of the Persons and yet act as One toward the world—may provide us with a model of the integrity of persons within community and their interrelatedness. . . . The doctrine of the Trinity may yield models for building the human community—not on a hierarchy of beings but on the diversity of gifts that operate in an integrative manner.[10]

Here Oduyoye picks up on an aspect of the discussion taking place within the World Council of Churches. It is one that played a role in the talks held between the Protestant churches and the Orthodox churches: the *filioque* issue, i.e., the question whether the Holy Spirit is "breathed forth" by both the Father and the Son (as the Western tradition holds) or whether the Spirit is breathed forth only by the Father (as the Eastern tradition holds). It was German systematician Jürgen Moltmann, among others, who submitted a proposal to harmonize the two standpoints.[11] At any rate, what struck a chord was the idea that the intradivine Trinity could serve as an archetype and as a role model of a human community constructed on the basis of equality and reciprocity. Oduyoye picks up on this idea from the perspective of an African feminist theology.

Feminist Theology Between Locality and Globality

Mercy Amba Oduyoye's work clearly shows that the issue of an equitable position for women in African societies serves as the main criterion of her theological thought. The overarching feminist perspective challenges not

---

[10]Ibid., 136-37.

[11]See Jürgen Moltmann, "Is the Filioque Addition to the Nicene Creed Necessary or Superfluous?," in *The Spirit of Life: A Universal Affirmation*, trans. Margaret Kohl (Minneapolis: Fortress, 1992), 306-9.

only the traditions of the mission churches, i.e., Western traditions in Africa, but also the conventional understanding of biblical texts. Conversely, its criticism is also aimed at the traditions of the African tribal cultures, most other aspects of which are valued highly. Thus what is at issue here is no longer simply the demand for an *authentic Africanness* as a presupposition for those who would be African Christians or represent African churches. Rather, she critically examines such simplistic approaches to ascertain whether they continue to promote a patriarchal understanding of the relationship between men and women, be it implicitly or explicitly. It is openly conceded that older African traditions tended quite clearly to devalue or even oppress women. This is no longer about authenticity as such but rather about a clear and deliberate selection of those religiocultural elements that from the perspective of the women in question might help women to achieve equality of status and respect for their dignity.

These approaches are quite clearly liberation theological in nature. Not in the sense of sociopolitical struggles for power and influence on the level of goods of production, capital, income, or economic codetermination, but rather in the sense of religiocultural traditions that put women at a particular disadvantage within their immediate surroundings. This is about all the consequences to which these disadvantages lead in the legal, cultic, social, and thus also psychological and economic spheres. While these religiocultural patterns differ tremendously from one ethnic group to another and from one place to another, their effects truly are comparable in terms of the discrimination and/or oppression of women. Thus it would be legitimate to describe the gender issues occupying center stage here as a *crosscultural context*, yet also as one that can only be processed within the *patterns* of each specific *local culture*. This could be achieved by abolishing older inheritance procedures, naming customs, and ritual taboos; by identifying older proverbial wisdom sayings as misogynistic and replacing them with alternative proverbs; or by implementing new rituals in place of the older ones that discriminate against women. One area in which this conscious selection of traditional elements takes place is in the ancestor issue. Whereas a great many male theologians subscribe to an ancestor Christology, almost no African women theologians do so. This might have to do with the fact that in many ethnic groups, only men were permitted to wear the ancestor masks. This continues to be the case in most ethnic groups that continue to follow the custom today. Whenever men invoke the spirits of the ancestors through the masks and ask for ethical guidance, the simple fact that it is men wearing the masks (and not women) continues to promote a patriarchal attitude in and of itself.[12] To conclude, while we recognize that there is a need to relate the Christian faith to African traditions, we must admit that attempts to do so tend to meet with varying success.

---

[12]Strahm, *Vom Rand in die Mitte*, 264-65.

13

The Contextual Theologies of African Evangelical Theologians

In what follows, we will need to analyze how concepts like "context" or "hermeneutics" are understood in evangelical theology; how the relationships between contexts, interpreters, and the Bible are viewed; and which role is allocated to the individual determinants in the process of contextualization. The list of well-known theologians who either served in leadership positions in evangelical organizations or were closely affiliated to them includes Nigerians Byang H. Kato (1936–1975)[1] and Tokunboh Adeyemo (1944–2010),[2] Kenyan Anglican David Mukuba Gitari (1937-2013),[3] Ghanaian Kwame Bediako (1945–2008),[4] and Tite

---

[1] Byang H. Kato, *Theological Pitfalls in Africa* (Kisumu, Kenya: Evangel Publishing House, 1975); Kato, *Biblical Christianity in Africa: A Collection of Papers and Addresses* (Achimota, Ghana: Africa Christian Press, 1985); David J. Hesselgrave and Edward Rommen, "Contemporary Understandings of and Approaches to Contextualization: Africa: John S. Mbiti and Byang H. Kato," in David J. Hesselgrave and Edward Rommen, *Contextualization: Meanings, Methods, and Models* (Leicester, UK: Apollos, 1989), 96-112. For more on Byang's person and work, see Keith Ferdinando, "Byang Kato: 1936 to 1975; Evangelical Churches of West Africa; Nigeria," in *Dictionary of African Christian Biography*, Center for Global Christianity and Mission at Boston University School of Theology, www.dacb.org/stories/nigeria/kato_legacy.html (accessed April 16, 2015).

[2] For more on his person and work, see "Tokunboh Adeyemo: 1944 to 2010; Evangelical; Nigeria," in *Dictionary of African Christian Biography*, www.dacb.org/stories/nigeria/adeyemo_tokunboh2.html (accessed April 16, 2015).

[3] For more on his person and work, see Alfred S. Keyas, "Gitari, Mukuba David: b. 1937; Anglican Church; Kenya," in *Dictionary of African Christian Biography*, www.dacb.org/stories/kenya/gitari_david.html (accessed April 16, 2015).

[4] Kwame Bediako, "Biblical Christologies in the Context of African Traditional Religions," in Vinay Samuel and Chris Sugden, eds., *Sharing Jesus in the Two-Thirds World: Evangelical Christologies from the Contexts of Poverty, Powerlessness, and Religious Pluralism* (Grand Rapids: Eerdmans, 1984), 81-122; and Bediako, *Jesus in African Culture: A Ghanaian Perspective* (Accra, Ghana: Asempa Publishers, 1990).

Tiénou (b. 1949),[5] who is originally from Burkina Faso and to whom we now turn our attention.

CONTEXTUAL EVANGELICAL "PRESCRIPTION THEOLOGY": TITE TIÉNOU

Although Tite Tiénou was born in Mali (in 1949), he spent a number of years living in Burkina Faso, where he later founded a Bible school. He received his doctorate in 1984 from Fuller Theological Seminary in Pasadena (California), having written his dissertation on the methodology of African Christian theologies. He was a member of the Theological Commission of the World Evangelical Fellowship for many years and taught at various institutions of theological education in the United States.[6] In terms of his theological approach, Tiénou wants to avoid what he calls a "mnemic hermeneutics," a hermeneutics of remembrance that only adopts those aspects of the Bible that fit into one's own theological preconceptions. He believes that in this approach, the religiocultural context dominates the text of the Bible, leading to a selective reading that results in turn in the loss of the critical impulse of the biblical message. For Tiénou, the *Sitz im Leben* of a theology is of utmost significance. On the one hand, he criticizes the theology pursued at the university level because in his view it is far removed from congregational praxis and also elitist, since it does not consider the context of poverty, suffering, and injustice to any real extent. On the other hand, he recognizes the widespread presence of a "popular theology" in the churches and congregations that is expressed in music, the sermons of the evangelists, and the ideas of congregation members but that is not biblically based. He sees this as a theological state of emergency because—to paraphrase—the biblical message is often in danger of being absorbed into a milieu of syncretism. Tiénou proposes to do theology in a "third way"; he believes that the true *Sitz im Leben* of theology is and must be the *local*

---

[5]Tite Tiénou, "The Theological Task of the Church in Africa: Where Are We Now and Where Should We Be Going?," *East Africa Journal of Evangelical Theology* 6, no. 1 (1987): 3-11; Tiénou, ed., *The Theological Task of the Church in Africa*, 2nd ed. (Achimota, Ghana: Africa Christian Press, 1990); Tiénou, "Indigenous African Christian Theologies: The Uphill Road," *International Bulletin of Missionary Research* 14, no. 2 (1990): 73-77.

[6]Byang Kato took an approach that was similar in style to that of Tiénou but stricter. He played an important role in the church politics of the evangelical movement in Africa from the end of the 1960s to the beginning of the 1970s but unfortunately died young.

congregation. A contextual theology can only come into being in the congregation and *out of the congregation.*

THE CONGREGATION AS *SITZ IM LEBEN*

For Tiénou, this demand is based on the Bible's own process of origination, for the Bible constitutes in the first instance not a book but the Word. Notwithstanding its unity, the biblical message is conveyed in diverse narrative forms such as poetry, preaching, or admonition. The reason for this, Tiénou believes, is that the needs of the hearers are also diverse. The biblical message came into being in the personal interaction between God, people, and their life contexts; that is to say, the web of relationships making up the congregation is the true *Sitz im Leben* of the Bible's message. Tiénou therefore considers it important to relate the local congregation, its religiocultural context, and the Bible to one another and to do so in such a way that the transforming power of the biblical message may come into its own. The author recommends a number of steps to achieve this.

Theologians make it possible for theology to benefit the local congregation. Therefore their first step must be to *analyze the individual circumstances of a particular congregation,* i.e., to consider its relationship to its religiocultural and social milieu. As a second step, they need to utilize the *biblical message to address both needs and aberrations.* Thus a three-part relationship structure emerges between the congregation, its contexts, and the Bible. The theologian serves as a fourth element, as an intermediary. Tiénou calls his approach *prescriptive theology,* i.e., prescription theology, because he sees the theologian acting like a physician treating a case of anamnesis. The theologian plays the role of the physician; he examines the situation of the congregation, which for its part plays the role of the patient. In the process, questions and problems are discovered, which correspond— in the metaphorical sense—to the illness that needs to be cured. The theologian then tries to identify suitable answers in the biblical message. The Bible thus plays the role of the medicine that is to be administered. Just as in the case of the physician's therapy, this is a matter of life and death.

Tiénou explains what he means by using the example of Bobo Christians in the area of Upper Volta. These Christians continue to revere the god Do, since they see him as a mediating god. Tiénou argues that an appropriate diagnosis will show that while there are indeed functional similarities between the god Do and Jesus Christ, the mediator of salvation, it is also imperative to recognize several key differences. Ultimately, the theologian must use the biblical message to point out both the inconsistencies of the Do religion and that Christ's mediation is superior to that of the god Do: Christ is the only and the universal mediator of salvation who benefits not just individual tribes but *all* people and who can thus help the Bobo Christians overcome the limitations of tribal thinking. The congregation's medicine then consists in abolishing older elements of the Do religion such as the veneration of ancestors.

THE HERMENEUTICAL IMPLICATIONS OF TIÉNOU'S APPROACH: SOME QUERIES

In general, evangelical theologians take pains to ensure that the authority of the Bible serves as the yardstick for their theological thought. They assert not only the inerrancy but also the infallibility of the Bible. However, as the examples of both Byang Kato and Tite Tiénou (to a lesser extent) show, in reality this approach does not address the issue of a biblical hermeneutics. If evangelical theology would incorporate some insights from the oft-maligned academic theology of the universities, it might regain some much-needed flexibility.

It is impossible to avoid contextual preconceptions: Although Kato and Tiénou recommend *obedience to the Bible*, that does not mean that the exegesis of the biblical text and the selection of relevant passages have been satisfactorily addressed—not by a long shot. In other words, their recommendation serves little purpose, since many ethical behaviors, sociocultural patterns, or political convictions can be justified on the basis of a variety of biblical contexts. What does it actually mean to be "more obedient" or "more Christlike"?[7] Tiénou assumes that when a message is sent, there is a *sender* who sends the message, a *receiver* or *receivers* who receive it, a message *content*, and a *context* in which the communication takes place. Using examples from the New Testament, he points out that people appropriated the gospel within the setting of Hellenistic congregations. For him, it is their

---

[7]Detlef Kapteina, *Afrikanische Evangelikale Theologie*, 2nd ed. (Nuremberg, Germany: VTR, 2001), 209.

day-to-day reality that constitutes the *Sitz im Leben*. He concludes that the same must be true today, that the Bible is understood in the context of congregations. At the same time, Tiénou allocates a leading role to the theologians in this regard.

Tiénou argues that there are two theologies today. One is the superficial and in part heretical popular theology of the congregations. The other alternative is what he calls "university theology," one that exists in a vacuum. Tiénou now proposes to remedy the dichotomy by asserting a third possibility: a congregation theology that is obedient to the Bible and that aspires to be Christlike. Such a theology trusts that the Bible can inform the context and be critical of it. Now, any rational observer would agree to this proposal; however, when it comes to putting it into practice, we need to ask: What will prevent the biblical texts from being used arbitrarily? After all, this is very likely when the exegete selects biblical passages directly, quasi while being personally affected by her circumstances, and when she interprets them for the benefit of others who are also being affected.

Kato, for instance, criticizes historical-critical approaches and contextual approaches (whatever those might be) for being anthropocentric, experience oriented, and relativistic. Instead, he claims, Scripture is to be the only source of theology. Kato insists on both the inerrancy and infallibility of Scripture.[8] However, in his essay "The Christian Leader and His Family," he calls for monogamy on the basis of Genesis 2, 18 and 24, and he argues that according to the Bible, only adults may marry (as opposed to the marriage of children) and that parents do not have the right to arrange the marriages of their children (as opposed to the majority of families who conduct marriage negotiations). For the most part, he believes, women should remain at home and be there for their children; while it is possible for them to work outside the home, it is dangerous for women to be too independent financially. Women should submit to their husbands, while both marriage partners should respect each other.

However, Kato's attempt to skip over his own context fails. People from a variety of different cultures might well ask whether the biblical message does in fact provide such clear direction on the issue of marriage or whether Kato

---

[8]Ibid., 68.

as a theologian has not perhaps read his own unacknowledged preconceptions into the text. Even though evangelical theologians claim that the knowledge of the truth must be given by the Holy Spirit, they have to consider whether the Holy Spirit might not also work through the means of historical recontextualization. After all, what is the goal of any historical exegesis of the biblical texts but to determine their original meaning on the basis of the contexts in which they came into being? However, since these contexts may be very different from those of today, recontextualization always implies a certain degree of alienation for the readers of today. The meaning that a text may have for a present-day reader is flanked by the meaning that the text presumably had for the original readers (on the basis of historical reasoning). As we realize this, we become conscious of the perspectivity and contextuality of all knowledge—things we generally take for granted.

THREE POSSIBLE POINTS OF CRITICISM FROM A HERMENEUTICAL PERSPECTIVE

From a hermeneutical perspective, we must answer by asking Kato and Tiénou some critical questions. These have to do with, first, the meaning of African cultural patterns; second, gender issues; and third, the understanding of Scripture itself.

(1) In terms of African moral values, or in terms of what various authors mean when they talk about them, the question arises as to whether too great an individualism in matters of marriage might not result in negative social consequences. Bénézet Bujo, for instance, argues along these lines when he states that from an African perspective, the applicable freedom rights documented in the 1948 UN Human Rights Charter need to be criticized. Following Bujo's lead, we could see Kato as an African who reiterates Western cultural patterns, as an African convert who considers himself to be more of an advocate of Western mission Christianity than an African Christian. In this sense Kato prefers to identify himself by his affinity to the global evangelical discourse rather than to the specific cultural patterns of his home culture. Granted, this is a legitimate preference. Yet his claim that this view is the *only biblical one* does not hold water, especially since he would have to admit that Old Testament authorities such as Abraham, David, or Solomon had no problem with taking more than one wife and that Jesus did

not say anything on whether individuals are free to decide who to marry or not, etc. In short, even Kato's and Tiénou's assertions are predicated on the context in which they are made and are thus relative.

(2) Kato's view of gender issues is just as relative. From the perspective of an African women's theology, Kato's attitude appears coterminous with that of Protestant conservatism. In contrast, feminist exegesis alerts us to the fact that the New Testament provides a great deal of evidence that women played a much more significant role in the early phase of Christianity as leaders, missionaries, and preachers than the male-dominated history of tradition is willing to admit.

(3) Further proof of the relativity of evangelical approaches is provided by their emphasis on the inerrancy or infallibility of the Bible itself. This emphasis is a thoroughly modern phenomenon. It is no accident that both the Roman Catholic dogmatization of papal infallibility and the Protestant accentuation of the infallibility of the Bible came about toward the end of the nineteenth century. Both may be understood as reactions to higher criticism, which questioned the credibility of biblical accounts and ecclesiastical traditions. Fundamentalist Christians responded by attempting to demonstrate the infallibility of the Bible to the same extent that it seemed possible to prove the laws of physics. In consequence, a scientific epistemology was applied to the Bible, with the result that the way people interacted with the Bible changed. The recontextualization of biblical texts was interpreted as a threat, since the asserted historical relativity of biblical statements seemed to undermine their authority. Thus when ethical doctrines that had hitherto been taken as divine revelation now seemed to be predicated on their historical context, or when it became legitimate to view elements of theological doctrines as having been adopted from the setting of other religions, then what could still truly count as divine revelation?

What we criticize about evangelical approaches is not that they consider certain ethical maxims and theological doctrines to be biblically mandated. Every form of exegesis needs to do so. Rather, what we criticize is the notion that one's own exegesis is the only legitimate one and that all others are illegitimate. This approach is problematic because there is no scholarly justification for it. On the contrary, we may well ask: Does appreciating the contextuality *necessarily* undermine the authority of biblical statements? It is very possible that reconsidering the efficacy of the Holy Spirit might provide a solution for the quandary.

Scriptural hermeneutics and the work of the Holy Spirit: Tiénou's approach creates the impression that the work of the Holy Spirit consists only in enabling the exegete to find the "pertinent" biblical texts for any given issue and then to understand their meaning correctly. Consequently, he disregards the contextuality of the Bible. Its contextuality simply features as a background, which the exegete may blend in or out at will. At the same time, the context of the congregation's own lifeworld is not really factored into the process of understanding either, since Tiénou's model accords no theological dignity to the congregation's cultural paradigms, social structures, and religious elements. It is as if the congregation exists in a neutral vacuum, as if God works in any given situation only through the Bible. In contrast, theologians like Bujo, Mbiti, Oduyoye, and others wonder whether it is not possible to explain *why* certain biblical texts suggest themselves or attract attention, i.e., why the exegete selects certain passages from among the wealth of biblical narratives, by analyzing one's perspective against the backdrop of a particular situation and context. Particular contexts raise particular questions, and particular experiences within those contexts either consciously or unconsciously determine the exegete's interests as he looks for answers in his reading.

In concrete terms, by his experiences with initiation Bishop Sanon is inspired to interpret Christ's title as the "perfecter of faith" in a new way. He comes to see Jesus Christ as the master of initiation precisely in and because of his history (life, work, cross, and resurrection). Bujo's ancestor experiences suggest to him that Jesus may be understood as the proto-ancestor, viz. also throughout his history. I believe therefore that critics would not be justified in faulting these approaches as insufficiently christocentric unless they were to define the term *christocentric* on the basis of a particular theology of the cross, like that of the Baptists. This perspective suggests the need to consider whether the Holy Spirit might not also be at work in societal processes, within cultural paradigms, yes, even within elements of other religions, continually finding new ways (which are contextual and thus relevant) to help people to understand and articulate the gospel of Jesus Christ. We will need to revisit this topic in greater depth at a later point.

14
∙∙

African Theologians and
the Reality of the Congregation

The approaches discussed in the previous section consisted of theological proposals formulated in essays and books. Yet how much influence do such proposals have on the congregation level? Could it be that academic African theology represents the actual reality of the congregations and churches in various places only to a very limited extent? Could it be that these titles for Christ that seem so appropriate, such as "ancestor" or "healer," are actually unsuitable and that entirely different aspects play a much bigger role in reality? Could it be that it is impossible to cover the topic of inculturation "all at once"—that each aspect and each level of inculturation needs to be addressed separately instead? We will address these questions in the following section, joining Wilhelm Richebächer in identifying metaphors for Christ actually used in various Lutheran congregations in Tanzania today.

NAMES FOR CHRIST IN BUHAYA, ANYILAMBA, IRAQW, AND MAASAI CONGREGATIONS

The Lutheran church in modern-day Tanzania is constituted of regional synods, each of which is predominantly characterized by the traditions of a particular ethnic group. Richebächer, for instance, studies Lutheran congregations among the Buhaya, Anyilamba, Iraqw, and Maasai peoples. According to the conceptions of African theologians like Mbiti, Pobee, Bujo, Sanon, or Nyamiti, one might expect to find the issue of an ancestor Christology to play a significant, if not seminal, role among all of these ethnic groups. Is this the case? Which designations for Christ are predominantly used in the congregations, and why?

Wilhelm Richebächer states that "King" (*Mukama*) or "Lord" is the title most commonly used for Christ among the Buhaya people. The frame of reference for this metaphor for Christ is the social system that existed among the Buhaya people from the seventeenth century onward: a type of "feudal system of administration" that encompassed "an elaborate system of royal power administered by a hierarchy of governors extending from the palace down to the village level." Richebächer concludes that it is inaccurate to speak of "chieftaincies" here; rather, this is indeed a matter of "kingship" within a society clearly structured according to social classes. The semantic content of the title *Mukama* (King) was transferred to Christ; this included such aspects as designating Jesus as "Lord over all goods and over the life and death of his subjects," the belief that he was drenched with blood at his coronation (which symbolized that the blood of his people, i.e., their fate, lay in the hand of the king), or that the king reunited the clans. Thus Christ comes to be seen as the Lord over life and death who shed his blood on the cross and wants to extend his protection over all people. Meanwhile, the image of the king breaks down at the point that Christ does not rule from a seated position and is feared by the people; rather, he is the king who is close at hand, the one who *goes after* people, who anyone (even the women, the sick, etc.) may approach.

Another name that occurs frequently is "healer," whereas the shepherd image occurs less frequently. Lutheran theologians favor the designation "blood brother," since blood brotherhood corresponds to an ecumenical perspective, i.e., one that goes beyond the clan to whom one is related. Even so, this designation does not occur very often either. In addition, Lutheran Buhaya Christians struggle to describe Christ as an ancestor, since this would mean that his significance is limited to their own tribe and since it would degrade him to the level of the angels and spirits.[1]

In the case of the Ilyamba tribe, Christ is often designated as "Lord" (*Shekulu*), which denotes a person of superior status. This designation is

---

[1]Wilhelm Richebächer, *Religionswechsel und Christologie: Christliche Theologie in Ostafrika vor dem Hintergrund religiöser Syntheseprozesse* (Neuendettelsau, Germany: Erlanger Verlag für Mission und Ökumene, 2003), 307-9. In the following section I will summarize some of the findings from Richebächer's excellent study.

used within the clan. Richebächer states that "the maternal and paternal grandfathers as well as the maternal uncle or 'Mnalume' were addressed as 'Lord,' whereas this honorific was not used for any other elder."[2] This means Ilyamba people readily address Christ as both Lord and *maternal uncle*. According to the view of many Ilyamba Christians, designating Christ as an ancestor would mean associating him with the realm of the spirits of the dead and not with the new life, for which reason most Ilyamba Christians refuse to designate him as such. The title of the maternal uncle signifies a relationship of deep trust, since the maternal uncle plays a significant role in the acephalous (i.e., decentralized) and matriarchal culture of the Ilyamba. Another title used for Christ is that of the "Rainmaker Priest." "What the maternal uncle does on the clan level, the rainmaker priest does on the level of society as a whole: He intercedes with the supernatural powers and with God. His task is to bestow blessings on a supra-clan level for the benefit of many, which also suggests analogies between his office and the work of Christ."[3] Until as late as the colonial period, the office of the rainmaker priest was an apolitical one and not comparable to that of a chieftain. But for clans who lived in arid areas, it was a vital one, for the people living on sandy soil depended on regular rain. In addition, other titles such as "Savior," "Healer," and "Son of God" are commonly used. The latter title in particular, Son of God, lent itself to use among the Ilyamba, for they saw themselves as "children of the sun," i.e., of God.[4]

For Lutheran Iraqw Christians, an ancestor Christology is irrelevant for the very reason that—contrary to Bantu societies—the ancestors are of hardly any significance for this ethnic group. Since this people group also has no centralized cults, very few names used for Christ are common to all the tribes. The expression *Aako* designates Christ as the eldest of the family and as a healer-diagnostician. Another healer title that is used is *qwaslermo*, which connotes charismatic leader figures. But to use this title for Christ means to place him in a category of his own as the "true" healer, as opposed to the many profit-seeking traditional healers, and as the healer

---

[2]Ibid., 317.
[3]Ibid., 319.
[4]Ibid., 321.

par excellence who provides not only physical healing but also holistic healing from sin, evil powers, and death.

Since the Maasai are pastoralists, one might assume that "the Good Shepherd" might be a title commonly used for Christ. However, the life-world of the Maasai militates against overly superficial comparisons. For the Maasai, shepherding is an everyday occupation usually carried out by children.[5] So this title is actually unsuitable, because it is impossible to associate any special dignity or authority with it. In contrast, the title "Herald of the Age Groups" seemed much more appropriate to the Maasai, since the Maasai people are classified according to age categories. Thus the Herald of the Age Groups is one who represents exemplary behavior; he acts for the benefit of the entire society. He fights for a just order.

> In this regard, the significance of Christ as a teacher (Matthew 5–7) and as an intercessor or mediator between God and all people (1 John 2) dovetails in an ideal way with the strong desire of the Maasai to maintain the discipline of the age groups, to which they are committed. More than anything else, this means that by way of analogy, [Jesus is identified with] the most permanent authority and identification figure with the greatest effect in the life of a Maasai, and in such a way as to extend his significance way beyond the kraal boundary.[6]

There is another Maasai title that portrays the role of Jesus Christ in a particularly apposite manner. Richebächer explains,

> It is the honorific "Olkikau," the "Firstborn Heir of the Father" in the family tradition. This heir does not just receive all of the possessions of the father and the responsibility and duty to care for the entire kraal when his father dies. No, he also serves as the father's direct representative to his descendants. This is already true even before the father dies and only more so afterwards. It is believed that the father himself is present in the son. That means that he must necessarily fulfil the testamentary will of the father; indeed, he personifies this will. It goes without saying that he faithfully carries out everything which the father commanded. Yet above and beyond that and in the spirit of his father, he is free to change whatever he likes—or not. His decisions determine the

---

[5]For more on various aspects of inculturation among the Maasai, see Moritz Fischer, *Maasai gestalten Christsein: Die integrative Kraft traditionaler Religion unter dem Einfluss des Evangeliums* (Erlangen, Germany: Erlanger Verlag für Mission und Ökumene, 2001).

[6]Richebächer, *Religionswechsel*, 333.

fate of the entire community. It is expected of him to bring peace and unity, and to ensure a viable future for all.[7]

We might easily add other metaphors and motifs to this name for Christ.

METAPHORS FOR CHRIST, TITLES OF CHRIST, AND SOCIAL STRUCTURES

The comparison clearly demonstrates that the metaphors for Christ reflect the social structures of each individual ethnic group, as it were. While the Bahaya, who had been ruled centralistically, prefer to designate Jesus as the "King," this is not an option for the Anyilamba because of their decentralized organization. This matriarchal ethnic group conceives of Jesus as a matriarchal uncle, who is responsible for interceding on behalf of the family, and as a rainmaker priest, whose duty it is to advocate for the fertility of the land and for the survival of the clan. Thus the titles used for Christ evidently convey the specific experiences of these people groups, even though in each case the traditional use of the names allows for an ambivalent interpretation: the distant king who one should dread or the lying and self-serving rainmaker priest. However, as a countermeasure the stories and teachings of the New Testament are used to redefine these titles; in the process, they are *disambiguated* and, in a sense, transcended.

According to what was said above, the relevance of the metaphors for Christ is constituted within the medium of certain sociocultural patterns, on the one hand, and in the medium of the witness of the New Testament, on the other. We need not pursue the complexities of this process at this point. Yet it is important to recognize that, quite obviously, simply "translating" the designations for Christ is not enough and that the process of appropriation clearly takes place on the basis of the self-evidence of ethnic-cultural lifeworlds.

Do "African Christologies" exhibit any supracultural patterns? Despite the cultural diversity in Africa, it is nevertheless possible to distinguish some supracultural characteristics of African contextual theologies. We will

---

[7]Ibid., 335. "But this person could also be an adopted person from among the children's generation. In order to forestall an adoptionist interpretation, one should append the designation 'Oinoti' to the word 'Olkikau' (which would then mean the 'authentic son of the same substance as the father')" (336).

content ourselves with furnishing a (by no means exhaustive) list of four such characteristics, at any rate.[8] First, Christian contextual theologies in Africa see the God mediated by the Christ event as an *imminent God* and no longer as a distant one, which had been the case in many tribal religious contexts. Secondly, the *new Christian identity is seen as an identity with supracultural validity*. The salvation event recorded in the New Testament pertains to all people without distinction, with the result that in the religious domain, cultural boundaries have become meaningless. Third, the *metaphor for God is disambiguated, together with all the elements of traditional tribal cultures* to which it refers. In concrete terms, this means that whether Jesus Christ is viewed as (proto-)ancestor, healer, eldest family member, maternal uncle, chieftain, king, master of initiation, or rainmaker priest, each of these analogies is disambiguated. All that is adopted from the motif of the powerful, distant, and possibly also cruel king is the image of a good king who is close at hand; all that is adopted from the image of the healer who is able to use his powers for both good and evil is the image of the unambiguously good healer; and all that is adopted from the image of the rainmaker priest who can bestow blessings but also act in his own interests is the image of the good and unselfish priest. Fourth, *the message of the death and resurrection of Jesus Christ introduces a new horizon of meaning to the concept of life after death*. What ultimately matters from this point on is no longer life in the here and now, nor blood ties. Rather, life comes to be understood in a much larger framework extending beyond the creaturely life, one that includes all people one way or another.

These characteristics all derive from the basic narrative of the books of the New Testament. Despite all the differences in the detail, none of the twenty-seven books of the New Testament bears witness to anything other than the soteriological centrality of the events surrounding Jesus of Nazareth as the Christ, the Son of God, the Lord (*kyrios* in Greek), or whatever other title is used. Furthermore, all of these writings bear witness to the supracultural purport of this event, namely that the proximity of God may be experienced through Jesus Christ, and also to the connection between cross, resurrection, and a future with God.

---

[8]Ibid., 277.

CHALLENGES POSED BY CULTURAL CHANGE

One of the difficulties posed by the prospect of inculturation consists in the circumstance that every culture is subdivided into various generations, each of which have their own attitude toward life and their own collective experiences, which they gathered over time (such as political events like war or natural catastrophes like drought). Each age group (cohort) is characterized by certain interests. Since cultures are subject to constant change, the generations occasionally experience conflict with one another, such as when the older generation is intent on maintaining certain cultural customs that the younger generation sees as already obsolete. The issue of cultural change is thus always associated with issues of interests and power structures; one example of this is the question as to who claims to have the authority to define the identity of a certain culture. Culture is subject to a constant process of rigidification since it tends to be expressed in certain behavioral patterns, convictions, values, and cultural artifacts that each generation must appropriate for itself over the course of time. If this does not happen, vibrant cultural traditions are reduced to merely peripheral folklore.

Social structures in urban and rural areas: Also of importance for the issue of inculturation is the locality. While the simple social structures typically found in rural areas make it easy to conserve uniform cultural patterns, the plurality of urban contexts makes this far more difficult. Global trends toward urbanization also make themselves felt in Africa. It is only a matter of decades until half of the world's population will live in cities of more than one million people. This implies that there is a need to acknowledge multiculturalism as a new context.

INTERNATIONALIZATION AND MODERN LIFE

The internationalization of modern life that is facilitated by the global flow of information via television and the Internet poses yet another challenge. For example, anyone wanting access to the mass of data available online must be proficient in either English, French, Spanish, or Arabic. It has long been observed that the process of internationalization may elicit quite ambivalent responses. The term *glocalization* (Roland Robertson) was created to signify that globalization, with its trend toward uniformity, also elicits a simultaneous backlash of people emphasizing the uniqueness of their own cultural character and campaigning for its conservation by means of strategic delimitation, educational efforts, etc. In short, increasing globalization also elicits counterreactions of increasing localization.[9]

All three aspects, namely the negotiation of identity between the generations, the cultural differences between urban and rural areas, and the phenomenon of internationalization raise the question of what defines truly "African" Christian theology and praxis.

---

[9]It must be clarified that these localizations do not constitute a return to the "pure" traditions of yesteryear; rather, they reformulate certain aspects of the tradition within the framework of an ongoing globalization. Roland Robertson, "Glocalization: Time-Space and Homogeneity-Heterogeneity," in Mike Featherstone, Scott Lash and Roland Robertson, eds., *Global Modernities* (London: SAGE, 1995), 25-44.

15

On the Contextuality of Contextual Theologies

An Interim Appraisal

The question of the contextuality of contextual theologies is the question of the discourse-theoretical locus. The simplistic assumption that a contextual theology comes into being as a result of the *interaction* between the biblical text and the cultural context proves to be inadequate. To be sure, this interaction does play a role, since people appropriate the biblical message through the medium of very specific cultural patterns and preconceptions. But what is very important above and beyond that interaction is *who* formulates such a theology and from *what position*.

Stabilization: Jesus Christ as Proto-Ancestor and Master of Initiation

For instance, in the case of Bujo and Sanon, we are dealing essentially with *men* formulating a theology of inculturation; to be precise, they are priests within the Roman Catholic Church, which indicates that they hold an elevated status within the hierarchy. In this capacity, then, they are writing in view of a church that features a large membership in a particular area. *Since they hold this discourse position, they are concerned with stabilizing the social order*. Initially, this order manifests itself in a kind of *church culture* that finds expression in the liturgical-ritual life of the congregations. This church culture may serve as a stabilizing force within the society as a whole. At the same time, the concern with stabilization awakens an interest in an interregional theology, i.e., one that formulates this social order for larger subareas of what is in other respects one single church body. Here the operative understanding of culture is essentially a functional one: a culture is a structure shaped by human beings that serves to stabilize and promote a life of communal togetherness. The African heritage is considered to be acceptable to the extent that it corresponds to this orientation. As a result, dissociation takes place on two levels. On the one hand, the church dissociates itself from the alienation caused by the imposition of Western cultural forms, an aspect commonly criticized in the praxis of the mission churches, and on the other hand, it dissociates itself from (or rather limits) what it considers too rapid a cultural change.

In the case of Roman Catholic theologians with a high level of education, the theological interpretation of culture and cultural elements is derived from the Thomistic theology taught at most Roman Catholic institutions of education, which developed out of the work of Thomas Aquinas. One of the tenets of this theology is *gratia non tollit, sed perficit naturam*—grace does not destroy nature but perfects it. Culture may thus be acknowledged as a part of human nature. The Christian gospel becomes comprehensible in the medium of a culture even though it also invalidates certain elements that cannot be reconciled with the message of the New Testament. According to Bujo, the church enables culture to understand itself better. In this case, the church and the contextual theologians serve as the main actors in the inculturation event, and the inculturation itself is expressed in liturgical forms (i.e., in ritual events), art, architecture, customs, and also in new theological paradigms.

Dynamization: How African Women Theologians Portray Jesus Christ

African women theologians who pointedly represent an African women's theology occupy a very different discourse-theoretical locus. As women and as women theologians, they usually do not occupy any ecclesiastical leadership positions—in the Roman Catholic Church they do not do so at all, and in many Protestant churches they do so only to a very limited extent. The locus of their theological articulation is one of theological institutions of education or state universities. The intended audience consists for the most part of women both within and outside the women's own ecclesiastical traditions. In contrast to the approaches discussed above, the proponents of these kinds of contextual theologies are not concerned so much with stabilizing as they are with *dynamizing the social order*. They are not concerned with church culture as such; rather, theirs is a wider perspective that focuses on the *critical power of the gospel to affect a societal culture*, i.e., on changing the way men and women relate to each other in society. Christian churches enter the picture as possible loci for exemplary behavior in the area of gender equality, thus in a secondary sense as places where the intended contextualization will occur. Here too the proponents are interested in an interregional theology.

The operative understanding of culture in these approaches may be described as an *axiological understanding of culture*. This is about the quest for a true culture, for a liberating and thus value-oriented culture, a culture that both enables and gives expression to an authentic life together between men and women. In so doing, cultural elements are assessed transculturally according to the standard of whether they are conducive to the equal treatment and status of women and men or not. The criticism that is implicit here is directed toward both the biblical writings and their exegetical traditions, thus to both African traditions and Western traditions of the past and present.

The process of theologically interpreting cultures and cultural paradigms is not carried out according to any set pattern; rather, it comprises an unsystematic approach, a search for liberating elements of culture, a theological heuristic. The point of reference is constituted by the subversive power ascribed to the model of Jesus Christ, who is seen as the archetype of mothering, of a nurturing approach, for both men and women. In this sense, contextual theology does not take the form of a fully formulated system of theological doctrine of Christ within the medium of African cultural patterns; rather, it takes the form of a "negative Christology" that criticizes paternalistic paradigms and attempts in order to put a stop to them using a divine imprimatur. Cultural paradigms may be appropriated eclectically as long as they correspond to an axiological understanding of culture that espouses an appropriate gender culture. It might be better to describe this approach as one of "contextualizing theologies." It may be communicated in various forms such as song lyrics, proverbial folk sayings, and Bible studies or in the form of new labels for and a heightened awareness of those areas where paternalistic interpretive paradigms are still evident. Thus these contextual theologies initially manifest themselves in decentralized forms of action. The actors are women in the lifeworlds of women. At the same time, these women theologians constitute an elite serving and intending to serve as catalysts for new processes.

LOCAL ELITES AND GLOBAL DISCOURSES

The concepts we considered above claim to identify and represent those aspects that are intrinsic to an uniquely African theology. This is both legitimate and necessary. Nevertheless, the question must be asked: Who is speaking here, and, more importantly, on whose behalf? In most cases, African theologians belong to the educated elite of the respective churches of a particular country. They pursue theology using a medium commonly used in the academic domain worldwide and particularly in Europe and North America: theological treatises in the form of articles and books. Furthermore, they write as intellectuals, i.e., as people whose education has enabled them to analyze complex theological, ethnological, sociological constructs and constructively to arrange them into a coherent and systematic framework. They belong to an elite group of intellectual pioneers who serve their Christian countrymen by submitting proposals to their individual churches in the hope of a favorable response. The medium of their theology, the locus of their theology, their positions in society and in the church—all of these things set them apart and enable them to serve as actors in the area which we are addressing here.

These theologians are writing for an audience within their own milieu (church, society, culture, nation, and continent), but in doing so they simultaneously also take a stance in the global Christian discourse. Thus on an international level this concerns the interpretation and in a certain sense also the prerogative of interpretation of Christian traditions (the Bible, confessional and denominational traditions, etc.), which means that these theologians are contending and competing for prominence, influence, and the recognition of certain interpretations. Articles and books serve as the means to attract attention in the global discourse in general and specifically on the level of academia and church leadership or on the level of the overarching associations or organizations, as the case may be. Despite the contextuality of the approach—one could also speak in more concrete terms about the locality of the approach—the pursuit of theology at this level implies that it is necessary to declare the universal validity of the proposed approach, since the aim is to postulate that it is generally relevant, i.e., for other contexts as well. In other words, the locus in the global discourse forces the proponents of these kinds of contextual theologies to argue that their findings are universally relevant. The discourse locality introduces into these kinds of contextual theologies a tension between contextuality and universality, between locality and globality.

But that is not all. It is necessary to consider not only the significance of the discourse locality but also the significance of the confessional or denominational character of a contextual theology. A great deal depends on whether the theologians who propose a certain contextual approach belong to the Roman Catholic, Baptist, Presbyterian, Reformed, or Lutheran tradition. In spite of the great amount of diversity that occurs even within these traditions, and in spite of the variety of ethnic, cultural, sociocultural, or other characteristics, certain basic patterns keep on resurfacing, even if it is in the area of significant technicalities. An example of this is the theological significance of ecclesiology, which plays a very different and far greater role for Roman Catholic theologians than it generally does for Protestant theologians. To be sure, such patterns are always eclipsed, displaced, intensified, or weakened by other factors to a greater or lesser extent. However, the fact remains that confessional and denominational characteristics continue to be of considerable significance.

One might ask, for example, whether Charles Nyamiti's attempt to develop a comprehensive, quasi pan-African African theology is based on the Roman Catholic ecclesiology, a church body that aims (either consciously or unconsciously) at formulating a universal theology precisely because it sees itself as the universal church. Another example is constituted by the restraint demonstrated by Baptist and Reformed churches and congregations worldwide when it comes to ritual practices (in this case too the exceptions prove the rule). At any rate, these factors continue to be of significance for an intercultural hermeneutics of Christian forms of life. What is just as significant is the circumstance that in many churches and congregations theology is "implemented" and "put into effect" very differently, i.e., not according to some kind of plan but rather by "establishing itself," as it

were, not as a result of conscious effort but rather of unconscious adoption—
not in theory but in practice. Peter Sandner describes this phenomenon
very well:

> In the Western tradition, concise formulations, uncompromising delimita-
> tions, and binding doctrinal statements are important. . . . What we must
> learn from African Christians is that confession is not primarily a matter of
> documentation, but of consummation; not a weapon, but a hymn of praise
> for what Christ is doing; not a splendid achievement of the intellect, but the
> renewal of human life and thought; not the privilege of a few theological
> specialists, but the mandate of the entire congregation over against the world.[1]

Conclusion

According to what was said above, contextual theologies are contingent, first,
on the interaction of the biblical message and a given context with its various
dimensions. Second, contextual theologies are contingent on the discourse
locality of those who formulate them. If the persons in question belong to
an elite, then it needs to be ascertained whether this elite forms part of the
ecclesiastical-religious hierarchy or whether it plays the role of a critical
minority that lacks its own power base. Third, we need to pay attention to
the discourse locality at the intersection of the local audience and the global
discourse. Fourth, we must point out that the confessional character of
churches and congregations—inasmuch as they consider themselves to
belong to a certain confession or denomination—can play an important role.
The contextuality of contextual theologies thus proves to be a far more
complex and multifaceted issue than it initially seems to be.

---

[1]Peter Sandner, quoted in Wilhelm Richebächer, *Religionswechsel und Christologie: Christliche Theologie in Ostafrika vor dem Hintergrund religiöser Syntheseprozesse* (Neuendettelsau, Germany:
Erlanger Verlag für Mission und Ökumene, 2003), 302.

PART IV

· ·

Christian Missions and Foreign Cultures

Historical Perspectives

In this part we will consider the significance of theological constructs for the processes of intercultural encounters and exchanges. It will be shown that political, geographic, social, and other contexts have indubitably and substantially influenced these processes.[1] It will also be demonstrated that the actual progressions of intercultural interactions were characterized by many coincidences and, in the case of purposeful actions, also by unforeseeable factors. However, it is possible to discern certain interpretive models shaped by certain theologies and worldviews, by which that which is perceived to be culturally foreign and alien is interpreted. These interpretive models were common to many people

---

[1]For instance, in terms of whether these contexts were shaped to any great extent by the military and political dominance of a particular cultural configuration, such as by various forms of colonial constellations.

over long periods of time and thus had a significant impact. Spatial limitations permit only a brief survey of these models. Yet we hasten to add that these models probably did not occur in their "pure form" very often; it was far more common for them to occur in combinations and with a degree of overlap. We must also emphasize that these models should not be seen in terms of a chronological succession but rather as occurring simultaneously and in some cases even up to the present day. Nevertheless, these models of theological interpretation are clearly discernible. They are of considerable significance in terms of how people engage in and experience intercultural interaction, since people's motives and actions are determined not just by contexts and utilitarian considerations (as *rational choice* theories suggest) but also and to a significant degree by the interpretive models contingent on one's worldview, which often distinctly contradict considerations of "what is useful" and "what works."

We will use examples of intercultural interactions from the past five centuries to illustrate each model. We will begin by studying (1) variations of the *replacement model* with reference to what was later called "Latin America," followed by (2) the *indifference model* as illustrated by the first major Protestant mission (the mission of the Herrnhut Brethren), which would dominate the mission scene of European Protestant churches for about two hundred years. Next, we will consider (3) the *ennoblement model*, which became more and more significant especially from the second half of the nineteenth century onward, though its counterpart was constituted (4) by a number of variations of an *indigenization model*. Over against all of these models, in which an established church body served as the main protagonist, we will finally present (5) a viable alternative: the *appropriation model*. This applies when religious leaders adopt aspects of Christianity outside established Christian structures (churches, congregations) after receiving them through transcendental experiences (dreams, visions, etc.). These are then implemented in ritual ways that are new from a religious-historical viewpoint and that result in the formation of either independent Christian religious configurations or independent religious configurations that do not consider themselves to be Christian despite having adopted a number of Christian elements.[2]

---

[2]Spatial limitations prevent us from studying such movements. In the case of Africa, one might cite hero worship cults; for Latin America, one might point to cults such as Candomblé or Umbanda; for Oceania, one could consider the Cargo cults, etc.

The Replacement Model and Covert Resistance in the New World

MISSIONS IN THE NEW WORLD

Historian Horst Gründer has pointed out that the Spanish never stationed a colonial military of their own in South America and also that the administration did not extend beyond the core regions.[1] Most of these core regions were located in coastal areas, while colonial forces occasionally ranged over but did not occupy the interior, especially the jungle and mountain regions. This meant that the weak forces were unable to achieve comprehensive rule over the entire territory. The pope issued a legal mandate to the Spanish kings in the form of the so-called *universal patronage*, which enabled them more or less to rule the church in the New World autonomously. The Spanish kingdoms in turn commissioned certain Christian orders to

---

[1]Horst Gründer, "Conquista und Mission," in *Christliche Heilsbotschaft und weltliche Macht: Studien zum Verhältnis von Mission und Kolonialismus; gesammelte Aufsätze* (Münster: LIT Verlag, 2004), 23-46; for a general overview of the subject, see also Giancarlo Collet, "'Wir aber schätzen das Leben und die Seele eines Indianers höher ein als alles Gold und Silber': Kontext, Ziele und Methoden der Mission," in Michael Sievernich et al., eds., *Conquista und Evangelisation* (Mainz, Germany: Matthias-Grünewald-Verlag, 1992), 223-41. See also Arnulf Camps, OFM, "Begegnung mit indianischen Religionen: Wahrnehmung und Beurteilung in der Kolonialzeit," in Sievernich, *Conquista und Evangelisation*, 348-72; Mario Cayota, "Die franziskanischen Missionen: Prophetische Alternative oder kolonialistische Kollaboration?," in Sievernich, *Conquista und Evangelisation*, 373-412; Richard Konetzke, "Die Bedeutung der Sprachenfrage in der spanischen Kolonisation Amerikas," *Jahrbuch für Geschichte von Staat, Wirtschaft und Gesellschaft Lateinamerikas* 1 (1964): 72-116; Konetzke, *Süd- und Mittelamerika*, vol. 1 (Frankfurt: Fischer, 1988); Bartomeu Melià, "Und die Utopie fand ihren Ort . . . Die jesuitischen Guaraní–Reduktionen von Paraguay," in Sievernich, *Conquista und Evangelisation*, 413-29; F. Amado Aymoré and Michael Müller, "Die Globalisierung des Christentums durch die Überseemission der Jesuiten: Das Beispiel zentraleuropäischer Missionare in Südamerika im 17. / 18. Jahrhundert," in Artur Bogner, Bernd Holtwick, and Hartmann Tyrell, eds., *Weltmission und religiöse Organisationen* (Würzburg, Germany: Ergon Verlag, 2004), 137-61.

convert the Indians to the faith—and in so doing to pacify them and gradually to incorporate them under Spanish rule. Only a few select orders were permitted to engage in these missionary endeavors, namely the mendicant Franciscan and Dominican monks as well as the Augustinian and Jesuit orders. Certain territories were allocated to each in which they had to work. Somewhat later, a number of women's orders such as the Clarissines also became involved.[2] The so-called Council of the Indies in Spain oversaw the licensure of every missionary from these orders since it controlled all traffic between Spain and South America.

When the Spanish crown commissioned the monastic orders, it did so in the attempt to harness the Christianization of the Indian population and its simultaneous pacification for the purpose of establishing a homogenous Christian-Hispanic population structure. Thus what played an important role, besides the motivations of faith, was the overt power-political calculus as well as the economic interests.[3] This missionary initiative spanned approximately three hundred years. After the landing of the Europeans in the Americas in 1492, from 1493 to 1800 a total of about fifteen thousand members of these orders left Europe for the New World as missionaries, with the "New World" being the area that would later become known as Latin America.[4] How did these missionaries proceed? Here it must be recognized that there was a whole range of different missionary methods that varied from one territory and order to the next. Nevertheless, there was a certain basic model that was used in many different places, and we will now endeavor to provide a broad outline of it.

The tabula rasa method. We may designate this missionary method as the *replacement model* or as the *tabula rasa method.* The intention was to "wipe the slate clean" (the Latin *tabula rasa* = a "blank slate"), which means that the old religion was to be replaced abruptly and immediately with the new faith and the new religion. The fundamental justification for this approach was taken by way of analogy from the exodus of the people of Israel and its occupation of the land of Canaan. Passages like Deuteronomy 7:5 were pressed into service as proof texts, where the divine command states: "This is what

---

[2]Camps, "Begegnung," 366.
[3]Gründer, "Conquista und Mission," 23-46, and especially 33.
[4]Ibid., 33.

you are to do to them: Break down their altars, smash their sacred stones, cut down their Asherah poles and burn their idols in the fire" (NIV).[5]

Two theological leitmotifs are of importance in this regard. First, the Indian religions were seen by many missionaries *as animalistic, as idol worship, and as the work of the devil,* while Indian culture was seen as uncivilized, unjust, inane, shameless, etc.[6] Second, the Christian Spaniards viewed their own arrival as an *event of divine providence.* They believed themselves to have been commissioned by God to propagate the true faith in these new lands.

Let us now consider the question of how the foreign religions were interpreted. Two patterns emerge. For Dominican Bartolomé de Las Casas, the idolatry[7] of the Indians was not demonic as much as it was *a natural phenomenon.* He argued that this was a case of spiritual confusion that had come about because of the construction of the tower of Babel, i.e., because of the confusion of language. He believed that the confusion redirected the natural human desire to worship the *one* God into the practice of worshiping many gods and that the devil now took advantage of this natural human inclination to deceive people. Thus it was essentially still a matter of worshiping God, only in a misguided manner. Jesuit missionary José de Acosta saw things rather differently. For him, idolatry was not a natural phenomenon, but rather *a demonic one.* Instead of tracing its origins back to the tower of Babel, he saw it as the work of the devil himself.[8] Whereas both men agreed that the foreign religion needed to stop, they clearly differed in terms of the theological interpretation of the Indian religions, which would result in turn in some significant political consequences, as will be shown below.

---

[5]See also Ex 34:13; Deut 12:1; et al. See Mariano Delgado, "Inkulturation oder Transkulturation? Der missionstheologische Charakter der Evangelisierung der altamerikanischen Kulturen am Beispiel der Übertragung des abendländisch geprägten trinitarischen Gottesbegriffs," *Neue Zeitschrift für Missionswissenschaft* 48 (1992): 172.

[6]Gründer, "Conquista und Mission," 31-32, 34-35.

[7]"Especially during the first two centuries of the church's presence in America, idolatry or idol worship were all-inclusive terms." Non-Christian religions were viewed as the work of the devil. Camps, "Begegnung," 354.

[8]Ibid., 353. De Acosta went on to distinguish between several different types of idolatry, which he ranked from bad to worse. Thus the "worship of heavenly bodies and the elements" was valued somewhat higher, while the "deification of the dead" represented a second category, and the third category consisted of the "veneration of clean or unclean animals," as Camps summarizes.

In practical terms, this *mission method* took the form of the destruction
of Indian temples and idols, especially in the period between the arrival of
the Spaniards and the year 1560, i.e., in the time when the actual conquest
(the destruction of the Mayan, Aztec, Toltec, and other empires) was accomplished. In 1531, for instance, Franciscan padre and bishop Zumárraga
(1476–1548) boasted that five hundred temples and twenty-six thousand
cultic images had been destroyed at his command. While Zumárraga
claimed on the one hand that "we however rate the life and soul of an Indian
as more valuable than all the gold and silver," thus distancing himself from
the greed for gold of the military conquistadors, on the other hand he also
described the Franciscan missionaries as *conquistadores espirituales,* i.e., as
spiritual conquerors.[9] Yet the monks kept the *places* of worship, instructing
the Indians to build churches or chapels on the sites of the former temples,
using the rubble as building material. Naturally, these church buildings were
constructed in the Iberian-European style of the Spanish Christians. In this
way they came to stand on the former places of pagan worship.

This approach served a double purpose: For one thing, people's long-
standing habits of coming to a certain holy place to pray were not disturbed.
This ensured continuity in terms of the locality of worship. In view of the gods,
however, the complete destruction of the old temples showed the Indians
quite plainly that their former gods were now completely powerless. In contrast, the God of the Christians—symbolized by the form of the newly constructed church and the implementation of the new cult—was presented as
strong and victorious. This God had to be stronger, the reasoning went, because he had achieved a lasting victory. Furthermore, the combination of
the takeover of the locality, the construction of the church, and the cult
made it impossible for local Indians to fall back into their old religion.[10]

---

[9]Collet, "Wir aber schätzen," 231.

[10]Gründer, "Conquista und Mission," 35. Meanwhile, not only idols and temples were destroyed but
also the holy writings of the Indians, wherever they were found. For instance, in 1562, the entire
body of literature of the Mexican Yucatán peninsula, the thousand wise books of the Mayans, was
burned. These actions were called *autodafé,* which meant the burning of heretics and books. Franciscan monk Diego de Landa became the first bishop in this area. He wrote the following concerning these book burnings: "We found among them (the Mayans) a great number of books filled with
this script, and because they contained nothing that was not tainted by superstition and the deceptions of the devil, we burned them all, which the Indios lamented and bemoaned" (as cited in
Gründer, "Conquista und Mission," 35). These burnings were carried out particularly because the
books in question were the *liturgical books* of the Mayans and Aztecs. Camps, "Begegnung," 359.

The children of priest and warrior families of, say, the Aztec people were placed in Christian boarding schools and raised by the padres. Structurally speaking, in many respects the institutional methods of the boarding schools resembled the traditional educational methods that had been formerly used for these special children in Aztec society. In later years, these same grown-up young Christian Aztecs were the ones who helped propagate the work of the padres.[11] Thus here education was used to facilitate the adoption of cultural and religious content on the part of young indigenous people.

The basic mission model. What did this prevailing *mission model* involve, leaving aside the fact that it was found in many different shapes and forms? *The view of the other*: In this model, the foreign religion is viewed as the deception of the devil, as an ungodly power to which one should not expose oneself and from which nothing is to be learned; rather, from the missionaries' perspective, it should be destroyed for the sake of God's honor and for the salvation of humankind. At the same time, it was held that certain cultural goods like *language* and *certain customs* could be adopted, and indeed they were. That being said, there was little agreement and certainly no uniform praxis between and within the various orders in this regard. *The view of the self*: The foreign religion was to be replaced by the true religion, which in this case undoubtedly meant the Christian religion as represented by the Catholic faith. At the same time, in this instance Catholicism's cultural character, i.e., its particular manifestation as *Spanish Catholicism in the context of the European civilization* was not taken into consideration; it was simply taken for granted. For the Spaniards, it went without saying that this form was "the" true religion per se.

Mission as replacement. In this sense, mission can only be understood as a radical break with the old religion: the old must be replaced by the new because light has nothing in common with darkness, because God has nothing in common with the devil and his accomplices, and because the true faith has nothing to do with the reprehensible paganism. Besides the break, however, one may also discern a certain amount of continuity: the localities of the old faith are kept, for it is here that the power of the true God becomes

---

[11]Gründer, "Conquista und Mission," 34.

manifest; these localities are some of the places where the enduring demonstration of the truth of the Christian faith and the superiority of the culture to which the Christian faith gives rise are most visible. *Mission as expansion*: Here mission means the *expansion of the sphere of Christianity into what had been non-Christian territory up to that point*; it means the incorporation of that territory into the *corpus Christianum*. It is still the concept of the one (Catholic) Christianity under the one shepherd (the pope) in the one church, whose outward form should remain the same in all places; for this reason, the churches in the New World were to have the same Ibero-Catholic character as those in Spain (or Portugal) itself.[12]

Justification for mission. The justification for this kind of mission is based on the idea of *divine providence*: the claim that God elected the Spanish/Portuguese to promulgate the Christian faith—and that means the Catholic Christian church—in this land. It is not only the discovery of these lands that is interpreted in this manner but also their victorious conquest and annexation. The success of these endeavors also appears to reflect God's will. *Mission and upbringing*: It follows from the premises that were articulated above that the Indians must first be brought up to become good Christians. This happens by means of catechesis, prayer, training; it happens by the Indians working and adopting a Christian ethos—after all, from the perspective of the padres, the Indians had no track record or credentials with which they could corroborate a work ethic of their own. Thus the missionaries see themselves as the ones who impart, who teach, who train. The way most of the padres saw it, this is a one-way process: the missionaries bring the true religion, and the indigenous people must let them bring it and accept it. Whether this reflects the actual state of affairs will need to be discussed at a later point.

Various Attempts at Implementation: Some Examples

In what follows, we will describe some examples of how these principles were implemented. Again, we need to clarify that the various *orders* were responsible for the actual mission work, but that the nature and method of the work differed considerably from one to the other, while various regional

---

[12]See Camps, "Begegnung," 350.

differences are also apparent within the same order. Due to our spatial limitations, we can provide only a basic overview of the methods and models.[13] Let us begin by examining the model of the attempt to decree a type of lay mission—the *encomienda system*. The encomienda system was originally an attempt to Christianize the indigenous people by forcibly allocating groups of them to individual Spanish colonists. Hence the name *encomienda*, which is derived from the Latin *commendare*, meaning to "commend" or "entrust." Queen Isabella of Castile and León introduced this system in a decree she issued for the New World in 1503. Thus Indians were forcibly allocated to Spaniards; yet at the same time, Isabella did not want the Indians to be seen as slaves but rather as free persons who were to be treated well and paid for their services.[14] More details followed in the "Laws of Burgos"—for instance, the Spanish masters were to construct churches in their territories, and teach the Indians the *Pater Noster* (Our Father)—in Latin, of course—as well as the *credo* (creed of faith) and the *Salve Regina*. The masters were to pray with the Indians when the day's work was done, and, once they had fifty Indians or more in their service, they were to ensure that the children were to receive religious instruction and be taught to read and write. The masters were also instructed to pay the salaries of the priests and for the upkeep of the churches in their territory.

In other words, the idea made provision for both economic profitability and the attempt to use the Spanish colonists as lay missionaries, as it were. For the most part, the theory did not translate well into practice. The colonists resisted the imposition in many ways because prayer times would have meant a reduction of working hours, because the education of the Indian youth (reading and writing) would have endangered their own position of superiority, and because the presence of priests and missionaries in their own estates would probably have led to some unwelcome observations of the way the colonists treated the Indians. As a result, the encomienda system factually developed into an institution that resembled slavery rather closely,

---

[13]Camps is correct when he states that "thus the cultural and religious methods of the Spaniards were complex. The utopia of universal Christianity, together with the connection between Spanish humanism, the renewal of the church, and the continuation of the idea of the crusades fundamentally influenced the conquest (*conquista*) of the American lands and islands." Ibid., 352.

[14]Klaus Koschorke et al., eds., *Außereuropäische Christentumsgeschichte: Asien, Afrika, Lateinamerika 1450–1990* (Neukirchen-Vluyn, Germany: Neukirchener Verlag, 2004), 221.

including the exploitation and cruel abuse of the Indians. Despite royal attempts to mandate reforms in form of the "New Laws" (1542), the situation did not change to any great extent. In 1720, the encomienda system was abolished completely. This model was quite naturally based on the premise that the Indian culture was to be replaced by a Spanish-Christian religion and culture. No attempts were made to adapt these concepts to local contexts, with the result that the Indians were taught to pray in Latin.

Christian villages. Various orders, especially the Franciscans[15] and Dominicans at first, tried to gather baptized Indians in many different places into separate Christian villages, which were usually located in the vicinity of outposts of the cloisters. The Franciscans initially imagined that Indians and Spaniards would be able to live in such villages together and have the same rights. However, this visionary concept was soon replaced by a more pragmatic approach. It turned out that the Indian Christians needed to be protected from the influences of the Spanish colonists.[16] The decision was then made and carried out to relocate such Christian villages away from Spanish colonial territories. But a relocation of this nature can also have been motivated theologically, which in this context sheds some new light on the basic model of the tabula rasa method. According to an idea common to many orders at this time, it was held that one could reestablish the *original* Christianity in the New World—a pure Christianity, not one that had been corrupted by various influences. Against the background of this idea, Mario Cayota points out, "When the members of the orders viewed the Indians as blank slates (*tabula rasa*), then they did so not because they wanted to impose the European lifestyle on them, but because they wanted to use them to forge a 'different humanity,' a truly Christian humanity, one in line with the model of the ancient church."[17]

To paraphrase, it was held, at least in theory, that the Indians had praiseworthy aptitudes and a commendable lifestyle (as far as peaceableness,

[15]Cayota, "Die franziskanischen Missionen," 385.
[16]For more on the "utopian" visions of the Franciscans, which were inspired by the humanism of Erasmus of Rotterdam and the influence of a certain Thomas Morus, see Cayota, "Die franziskanischen Missionen," 390. Cayota writes about the Franciscan padre Jerónimo de Mendieta, concluding, "Mendieta and many other Franciscans idealized the Indian to such a degree that some authors identified this idealization as the root of the myth of the 'noble savage,' an idea later expanded upon by Jean Jacques Rousseau and the Enlightenment" (ibid., 390).
[17]Ibid., 388.

contentedness, etc., were concerned). Despite the perception that the religion of the Indians should be abolished, it was believed that a new Christianity could develop, building on the positive attributes of the Indians, one that would not take on the forms of Spanish-European Christianity. *Thus in this instance mission was seen not in terms of the expansion of an already existing formation with a uniform religion and culture but rather as the creation of an independent form of Christian community.*[18] *It was hoped that Christianity could experience a new beginning here, based on the unspoiled aptitudes of the natural human being.*

Elite mission: the educational mission of the Jesuits. While the Franciscans and Dominicans were active especially among ordinary people—we may recall the ideals of preaching and poverty held by these orders—in contrast, the Jesuit order frequently focused on educating the elite segments of the various people groups. At various places, the sons of Indian chiefs and of the Indian upper classes in general received instruction in Jesuit centers of education. One of the aims behind this was that many Indians would follow the lead of their chiefs and rulers once these had been converted and baptized. Meanwhile, this method was only one among many implemented by the Jesuits in their missionary endeavors. The approach of the Jesuits differed markedly from one continent, area, and local context to another. As far as South America is concerned, it is especially the mission reductions model that deserves attention.

The system of reductions. The Indian Reductions of the Jesuit order were in a certain sense protectorates established for indigenous people far away from the zones of Spanish settlement.[19] The term was derived from the Spanish word *reducir*, meaning "to bring together," and it refers to the settling of formerly seminomadic Indians in one place. In the heyday of the Jesuit missions, there were approximately thirty such settlements in existence, with about 170,000 Indians of the Guaraní tribe living in them. They

---

[18]The extent to which this was practically feasible would have to be ascertained on a case-by-case basis.

[19]The following discussion is based primarily on the following works: Horst Gründer, "Der 'Jesuitenstaat' in Paraguay: 'Kirchlicher Kolonialismus' oder 'Entwicklungshilfe' unter kolonialem Vorzeichen?," in *Christliche Heilsbotschaft und weltliche Macht* (Münster: LIT Verlag, 2004), 47-70; and Bartomeu Melià, "Und die Utopie fand ihren Ort . . . Die jesuitischen Guaraní-Reduktionen von Paraguay," in Sievernich, *Conquista und Evangelisation*, 413-29.

were located in remote places in the jungle or in mountainous regions in what are today Paraguay, Uruguay, and Argentina. There were also settlements located in the lowland areas of Bolivia and Peru, so that the total number of Indians living in such settlements in 1767 came to around two hundred thousand. Similar projects had been attempted earlier already,[20] particularly by the Franciscans, but also by other orders. However, the Jesuits, who arrived in the New World somewhat later, implemented this model to the most significant extent.

Administratively, these areas, which were located in, say, the jungle, were allocated to the Jesuits by the respective governor. He would assign sites to them while retaining administrative control of the area. He stipulated the tributes to be paid, retained jurisdictional authority, and scheduled visitations every so often. What was unique to the reductions was that no Spaniards lived within the territory in question—not even administrative officials. On the contrary, the *Spanish were prohibited even from entering* the reductions. These were run and administered by the Jesuit padres alone. Furthermore, in these areas the *encomienda system was abrogated*—that is to say, the Indians resided in the reductions *voluntarily*. There were usually two Jesuit padres assigned to each reduction, one of whom acted as the leader and occupied the rank of a royal official (including the salary). Within the reduction, he served as the final court of appeal. The padres ran the reductions by means of their personal authority and example. No revolts are known to have taken place in the reductions, which indicates that the Indians placed great trust in the padres.[21]

The reductions were constituted in such a way that a piece of land was set aside as communal property[22] and was worked by all, with the result that the basic foodstuffs for the Indians as well as export products were harvested from it. In this way, provisions could be secured for communal institutions, the church, and the care of widows, orphans, and others. In addition, each family had its own piece of land as well as a house, household goods, and some livestock, which enabled the family to be self-sufficient. Furthermore,

---

[20]One example is the Dominican mission among the warlike Indians of the Guatemalan highlands, whom Las Casas served as bishop for a time. Gründer, "Der 'Jesuitenstaat,'" 51.
[21]Ibid., 55.
[22]Called the *tupambae* = "God's business." Ibid., 56.

the formerly seminomadic and now settled Indians were free to hunt, fish, etc., which corresponded well with their former way of life. Popular export products were livestock surplus from the reduction's animal husbandry efforts, leaves from the *Yerba* trees (used for making *mate* tea), and other commodities like tobacco, wood, sugar, or furs.[23] The padres built schools, hospitals, and craftsmanship training centers, in which they instructed the Indians in woodwork, carpentry, the production of musical instruments, woodturning, weaving, dyeing, spinning, and many other trades besides. They also devised a system of writing for the *Guaraní* language and designated it the *official language.*

The rhythm of daily life was determined by regular work and religious life. Even though the Jesuits adopted many elements of Guaraní culture (such as the language, customs, artwork, symbols, and behavioral norms), when one compares their new way of life to the old, one must conclude that the life of the Indians had been rearranged substantially. Horst Gründer provides the following summary:

> These former hunters and gatherers had become settled fieldworkers and craftsmen. Their daily routine was laid out in detail and determined by others. The village association of the reduction now came to represent the new social unit, in which Christian-European norms and values for the most part regulated life together. The missionaries demonstrated little tolerance when it came to many of the so-called heathen customs and traditions. A new system of ethics, a new division of time, a new legal system, and the imparting of education, which they had not known before—these things redefined the Indians' rhythm of life. It seems this was the price they had to pay for their survival.[24]

It is legitimate to understand this mission model as the attempt of the Jesuit missionaries both to protect the Indians living in the reductions from enslavement and oppression by the Spanish settlers and to enable them by means of education and training to meet these challenges. But historically, the appraisal of this model has varied from the positive verdict that this was a triumph of the cause of Christian and humane anthropology to the negative verdict that the Indians had been placed under the yoke of a paternalistic

---

[23]Ibid., 57-58.
[24]Ibid., 61.

system, i.e., one determined by the Jesuits. Yet it is important that any criticism rendered take into consideration what was actually possible given the circumstances at the time.[25] Gründer believes that the enduring legacy of the Jesuits and of their reductions was that in this manner they successfully protected the Indians from exploitation and destruction.

THEOLOGICAL RATIONALES FOR INTERNATIONAL HUMAN RIGHTS ISSUES

Let us return once more to the issue of the reasons for the entitlement by which the Spanish justified their conquests, most of which they carried out in a very brutal manner. Here we may observe a range of legal opinions—the outlook of some is rather moderate, others are pacifistic, others again generally sanction just wars. At issue here is the concept of the human being in general and the distinctions that are applied. Let us consider as the first of these three streams the arguments of the moderate, late scholastic School of Salamanca. It was made up of theologians and scholars of law belonging to the Dominican order who developed international law concepts. The most renowned among them was Francisco de Vitoria (1492–1546). They taught, first, that there were indeed rightful rulers among the pagans, for natural law had been instituted by God the Creator, which included the stipulation that a rule of law should exist; for this reason, even among pagans the rule of law should be considered to be a work of God, irrespective of other aspects. It followed, second, that the plenipotentiary powers of the pope did not permit him summarily to allocate the sovereign rights over hitherto unknown foreign peoples and areas to the Spanish kings or the Portuguese king, who then simply and "rightfully" took possession of them, i.e., conquered them. Third, this stream of thought did not consider the unbelief or the heathenism of the non-Christian peoples to constitute sufficient reason in and of itself for waging a "just war" (*bellum iustum*) against them. After all, it was believed, faith is subject to the "law of freedom," and besides, God will render his verdict over belief and unbelief in the hereafter. Indeed, the

---

[25]Ibid., 48-49. "The reductions differed from the colonial state church system in that they were not integrated into the system of colonial exploitation by the expropriation of land, forced labor on the part of the Indians ('encomienda'), nor the payment of tributes ('tithes')" (ibid., 64). Any surpluses were reinvested for the benefit of the Indians, and there was no forced labor.

dissenting view at the time was that the unbelief of the Indians was cause for a just war in and of itself and that the pope could simply allocate the title deeds of the land in question to whomever he chose. We will return to this point at a later time.

Meanwhile, we need to acknowledge that even the proponents of this moderate stream of thought like Francisco de Vitoria allowed for certain exceptions, for example in a treatise formulated in 1539, which historian Horst Gründer summarizes as follows. Waging a just war against the Indians was warranted if the Indians "refused to reply to natural communication and to permit the exchange of goods, or rejected mission efforts, if the caciques forced the Indians to return to idolatry, if the caciques thwarted the desire of the Indians to be ruled by the Spanish, or if any party called on the Spanish to intervene in an interethnic war."[26] This makes it very simple to declare war, for "legitimate" reasons could easily be produced or manufactured. It meant that in order to prevent war, the Indians had no choice but to permit missionary proclamation and trade, and if they failed to do so, their territory could legitimately be conquered.

Radical criticism of colonial Spain: Bartolomé de Las Casas. Meanwhile, members of religious orders such as Dominican friar Antonio de Montesino (1480–1540) and Bartolomé de Las Casas (1484–1566), the bishop of Chiapas (Mexico), raised their voices to castigate the criminal excesses of the Spanish conquerors and colonists fiercely, to call for an end to the enslavement of the Indians, and to decry every form of violence and war as being profoundly unchristian.[27] Prior to them, from as early as the year 1500 onward, members of the Franciscan order had also repeatedly protested against the cruelty of the conquistadors.[28] This stream of thought, represented especially by the tireless efforts of Las Casas, moved the Spanish kings to promulgate the so-called new laws in 1542, which were formulated to improve the lot of the Indians. However, due to lobbying efforts by Spanish settlers in the New World, important statutory regulations were rescinded as early as 1545. De Montesino and Las Casas viewed the Indians in a much more positive light than did many Spanish colonists and indeed many other

---

[26]Ibid., 41.
[27]A number of these voices were silenced in turn by means of violence and murder.
[28]Cayota, "Die franziskanischen Missionen," 373.

members of religious orders, even if they—like all others—did not doubt
that the Indians should accept the Spanish-European form of civilization.
We can affirm that the slavery of Indians declined after 1542, whereas the
importing of African slaves continued, and nothing changed as far as their
fate was concerned for quite some time.[29]

Proponents of a just war: Juan Ginés de Sepúlveda. We come now to the
third stream of thought. Legal scholars such as the influential court chaplain
of Emperor Charles V, Juan Ginés de Sepúlveda (1489–1573), proceeded on
the assumption that the Spanish crown was duty bound to establish and
govern a global empire and that the church should be understood as the
church militant (*ecclesia militans*). They believed that mission is only possible once foreign nations have been subjected. These proponents referred
to Aristotle to argue that some people are slaves "by nature," citing the
apostle Paul and the Scholastic Thomas Aquinas as additional authorities.[30]
They denied the humanity of the Indians because of their idolatry, on the
one hand, and because of their crudeness,[31] on the other; Indians were
placed on the same level as wild animals.[32] It was claimed that they had no
culture and were unable to make proper use of their freedom. It was necessary therefore to proceed by subjugating them totally in order then to
propagate the faith among them. Spanish chronicler Gonzalo Fernández de
Oviedo reflected the sentiments of many Spaniards during the early time of
conquest when he said, "The powder used against the heathen (is) as incense
to our Lord."[33]

When Pope Paul III stated in the bull *Sublimis Deus* (1537) that "1. All
peoples of the world are by nature true human beings; 2. as such they enjoy
their freedom and their property, and they may not lawfully be robbed of it
and enslaved; 3. all are to be invited to join the Christian faith by means of

---

[29]See also Horst Gründer, "'Bin ich nicht ein Mensch und ein Bruder?'—Vom Sklavenhandel der
Christen zur christlichen Antisklavereibewegung," in *Christliche Heilsbotschaft*, 175-88. From the
sixteenth to the end of the nineteenth centuries, about ten million blacks were transported from
Africa to the New World as slaves; approximately the same number did not survive the voyage.
These slaves were seen as "chattel" (moveable property) until as late as the nineteenth century.
[30]Gründer, "Der 'Jesuitenstaat,'" 40-42.
[31]That is to say because of their nakedness, their customs, their eating habits, and not least because
of their sins, as demonstrated by the human sacrifices and instances of cannibalism (which are
indeed known to have taken place).
[32]Ibid., 41-42.
[33]As cited in Collet, "Wir aber schätzen," 228.

proclamation and good behavior," Charles V prohibited the promulgation of this bull in the colonial territories, and copies of it were destroyed. Even if the slavery of Indians was abolished after 1542, the importation of black slaves from Africa continued for centuries. This practice only came to an end in South America toward the end of the nineteenth century.

CONQUEST AND COVERT RESISTANCE: A SECOND GLANCE

In some areas, the Christianization of the population proceeded very rapidly. For instance, in 1524 Franciscan friars arrived in Mexico, and vast numbers of them continued working after the Aztecs had been defeated by the conquistadors. After approximately seventy-five years of catechesis, the land had been completely Christianized, at least outwardly. At second glance, however, many things appear to be very different. Mission studies scholar Arnulf Camps points out that some of the Franciscan missionaries realized over time that while the Indian population and the people of mixed descent in, say, Mexico participated in the life of the church outwardly, the question remained as to the extent to which the people had truly internalized the Christian faith. Diego Durán, OP (1537–1588), born and bred in Mexico, was one who addressed this question, demanding that it was necessary to understand the old religion better in order completely to destroy it.[34] Thus in this context the desire to understand is fused with the desire to complete the mission and to establish a "pure" Christianity. It is in this regard that Durán writes that it is necessary to understand the language of the people. He goes on to say,

> It is unfortunate that so many books [of the indigenous religion] were burned [by the conquistadors] during the first five years of evangelization, because it has made evangelization very difficult. The Indians venerate their idols in our presence, yet we do not realize what they are doing and what they are expressing in their dances [such as during public festivals], in the marketplaces, in the public baths, in their singing, and during their meals and banquets.[35]

Diego Durán vacillated. On the one hand, he wanted to prevent hybridization between the religions, yet on the other hand, he wondered whether

---

[34]See Tzvetan Todorov, *Die Eroberung Amerikas: Das Problem des Anderen* (Frankfurt: Suhrkamp, 1985); for more on Durán, see ibid., 240-59.
[35]Camps, "Begegnung," 361.

similarities between the ancient Aztec religion and Christianity might not have come about because a Christian preacher such as the apostle Thomas had been active in this region in former times. Were certain symbols, doctrines, and rights of the old Aztec religion not perhaps vestiges of the work of a Christian apostle in days of yore, whose work had passed out of memory entirely?[36] At any rate, many Franciscan friars felt certain that Indian Christians held dual affiliation and lived somewhere in between the old religion and the new.

Let us move on to a second missionary who was active as an ethnographer. Bernardino de Sahagún was born in 1499 in Spain, came to Mexico in 1529, and lived there until his death in 1590. He was a Franciscan friar and was appointed professor of Latin at the Franciscan college in Tlatelolco in 1536, where he instructed young men from the upper class of the Aztec society.[37] He taught the young people Latin, and in return he simultaneously learned from them Nahuatl, the language of the Aztecs. In terms of the study of languages, one would be justified in describing this as a reciprocal learning process. Later, Sahagún composed his main work over a course of about forty years. He wrote it in Nahuatl and entitled it the *General History of the Things of New Spain*.[38] This work encompasses twelve volumes, but was only—and tellingly!—published in the nineteenth century. Here the Aztecs themselves have a chance to speak. The work contains descriptions of the Aztec faith that Sahagún received from informants. The whole work is about the history and customs of the Aztecs. Sahagún was also able to incorporate Aztec manuscripts into it, which had been composed in Aztec pictographic script and which had been preserved from the destructive efforts of the Spanish. Thus Sahagún functioned as an ethnographer, and it is thanks to men like him and Durán that the language, the script, and much of the history, religion, and culture of the Aztecs were conserved for the collective history of humanity. Meanwhile, Sahagún was naturally also interested in

---

[36]Durán said, "Either people in this land knew of our sanctified faith—as I have said already—or the devil, our accursed foe, compelled them to mimic the Catholic ceremonies of the Christian faith for his service and cult, in order to serve and worship him in this way." As cited in Todorov, *Die Eroberung*, 249.

[37]Camps, "Begegnung," 362.

[38]For an English translation, see *General History of the Things of New Spain: Florentine Codex*, trans. Arthur J. O. Anderson and Charles E. Dibble, 12 vols. in 13 books (Salt Lake City: University of Utah Press, 1950–1982).

abolishing idolatry; however, this did not have a negative effect on his portrayal of the Aztec materials, since Sahagún distinguished categorically and consistently between the Nahuatl accounts and his own commentary. After its completion, the work was translated into Spanish. The text was also illustrated by Aztecs.[39]

Sahagún realized that in many instances, hybridization occurred between Christian and Aztec symbols, festivals, songs, doctrines, rituals, and places. He was critical when he noticed that the veneration of the Dear Lady of Guadalupe, the Mother of God (i.e., Mary), was coterminous for the indigenous people with the veneration of the Aztec goddess (earth mother) Tonántzin.[40] Sahagún undoubtedly desired a new form of Christianity for Mexico—a Mexican Christianity, not a Spanish Christianity. However, at this time there were no progressive interpretive models in place that could speak to the issue of the mutual influencing of cultures and religions. In practice, many Indians were practicing a folk religion, and those in charge allowed this to happen even when they suspected that Indian deities continued to be worshiped in the guise of Christian rites.

Around the year 1585, things changed in Mexico. The Franciscan friars began to be replaced more and more by secular priests. The privileges that the members of religious orders had enjoyed up until that point (such as being permitted to lead congregations themselves) were withdrawn. The profound understanding that the Franciscan friars had had of the Aztec religion was lost for the most part, since the secular priests, most of whom came from Europe, were seldom interested in these things. Arnulf Camps sums it up in this way: "It may be asserted that thanks to the mendicant orders, the Indians both became Christians and continued to be Indians up to the present day."[41] It came to be seen as inevitable that various interpretations and practices

---

[39]Camps, "Begegnung," 363-64. Besides, Sahagún did not consider the Mexicans but rather Satan himself to be responsible for the negative aspects of their culture and religion. Cayota points out ("Die franziskanischen Missionen," 383) that the Franciscans learned the indigenous languages for the additional reason that they wanted to identify with the suffering of the indigenous peoples.

[40]Richard Nebel, *Altmexikanische Religion und christliche Heilsbotschaft: Mexiko zwischen Quetzalcóatl und Christus* (Immensee, Switzerland: Neue Zeitschrift für Missionswissenschaft, 1983), 243. The name *Tonántzin* means "our little mother"—local people preferred to use diminutives in addressing the gods.

[41]Camps, "Begegnung," 365.

would exist alongside one another. Today, we would maintain that in the end, the Indians themselves (in this case) were and are the main actors, who develop(ed) their own ways of living and practicing the Christian faith.

Indigenous artists as interfaith mediators. During the first years of the mission in Mexico, hundreds of thousands of Indians accepted Christianity and were baptized. But what did this mean? Since there were very few members of the religious orders present, it could not fail that in most cases, the practice of the new religion was little more than an outward participation in ritual actions (worship services, celebrations of saints' days, etc.). Of course, many of the young Indian Christians received more in-depth instruction in the Christian faith. The Franciscan friars recruited artists from the ranks of the newly converted in Mexico, such as sculptors, and instructed them to fashion sacred objects, many of which have survived. From old baptismal fonts, for example, one may deduce how the first Indian Christians associated the symbolism of the old religion with that of the new. In the Franciscan monastery in Zinacantepex in Mexico, for instance, there is a baptismal font featuring a strange kind of symbolism, namely a "helical line with four or five water droplets inside it" coming out of a flower-like structure.[42] The symbol in question is that of the Aztec rain god Tláloc; it is a symbol of the old religion used to decorate that Christian cultic object that represents the transition from the old to the new, namely baptism. An inscription states that a Franciscan friar commissioned the baptismal font in 1581; thus one may infer that the friar must have accepted the depictions even though he must have known their significance for the Aztecs.

Catholic mission studies scholar Richard Nebel summarizes the significance of this as follows:

> The god Tláloc played an important role in the life of the indigenous people. It was he who provided fertility at seedtime with his life-giving water and who made the maize flourish. It depended upon him whether people had enough to eat or whether they had to suffer hunger. The idea of water as a blessing-bestowing element was deeply rooted in the mentality of the population. The missionaries could therefore easily tie into the old religion, emphasize the significance of water for human life in general, and go into detail regarding

---

[42]Nebel, *Altmexikanische Religion*, 143-45 (quotation drawn from 144).

the meaning and function of water during the Christian rite of baptism: Water purifies and revives. Without water, there would be no life in nature. But it can also be deep and dangerous. To be submerged in it means death; to be saved from it means new life. Thus being baptized with water represents the death of the old man and his resurrection to new life as he is united with Christ and incorporated into his church. Four circular reliefs around the baptismal font depict themes from Christian doctrine [in addition to animal and plant ornamentation, which also possibly depicts Aztec symbolism]: The annunciation of Mary, the flight into Egypt, the baptism of Jesus, and the overthrow of Satan, who lies defeated at the feet of the archangel Michael. The interpretation of these depictions with reference to Christian baptism is easily recognized and understood. The purpose was to strengthen the conviction of the indigenous people that with the advent of Christ, the true Son of God, the power of the old gods and demons was broken forever.[43]

The old is replaced by the new—yet the new is (also) interpreted by the old. The examples show that despite the obvious power imbalance (in this case, for example, the military power of the Spanish immigrant culture over against the Indian cultures), the web of intercultural relationships shows *no trace of unilinear developments*. Granted, as far as culture and religion were concerned, it may be seen how temples and idols were destroyed and replaced by Christian churches and symbols. *The (converted) indigenous people, however, associated many Catholic saints with the former gods, and in this way they were able to continue venerating the older gods in the form of religiocultural hybridization. In this way, the two traditions of origin (Roman Catholicism of a Spanish-European character and Indian religions respectively) were amalgamated to form something new,* namely a "Christian–ancient Mexican" religious mix.[44] Accordingly, the relationship between the European-Christian missionaries and the indigenous population cannot be defined as an association between subjects and objects since the indigenous people continued to be the protagonists in the way they appropriated the new symbols, interpreted, and reinterpreted them, and in the way they followed the ritual practices either in public or in private. The process of relational interaction was thus a very complex one.

---

[43]Ibid., 144-45.
[44]Ibid., 330.

From a theological-normative view, we must address the question: When considering this process, when is it appropriate to speak of a successful "indigenization" of the gospel into a certain culture (i.e., Mexican Christianity), and when should one describe it as an "amalgamation of religions" (i.e., syncretism)? Which aspects of the Christian message are indispensable? Who determines these aspects? Who interprets the symbols, practices, liturgies, rites, doctrines, and ethical values? In closing, we might append a very popular example—it concerns the madonna figure of the Dear Lady of Guadalupe. Let us consider the legend and the symbolism.[45] Virgil Elizondo supplies the following summary of the legend:

> When Juan Diego, an Indian from the ordinary people who had converted to Christianity, left his abode in the part of town close to Tepeyac, he heard the sound of some wondrous *music*. When he tried to find the source of the music, a woman appeared to him and spoke to him in Nahuatl, the language of the conquered. She told him to go to the palace of the archbishop of Mexico and to give him the message that the Virgin Mary, "the Mother of the true God, the Author of Life," desired that a temple be built in this place, so that "I may show and grant to all residents of this land all of my love, my compassion, my help, and my protection, . . . and alleviate all their privation, pain, and suffering." After two unsuccessful attempts to persuade the bishop of the authenticity of the woman, the Virgin performed a miracle. She told Juan Diego to pick *roses* in a place where usually only desert plants grew. She wrapped the roses in Juan Diego's coat and sent them with him to the archbishop as the sign for which he had asked. When Diego unfolded his coat in the prisons of the Archbishop, the roses fell to the ground, and the image of the Virgin appeared on his coat.[46]

This led to the construction of the chapel. A place of pilgrimage had come into being, or rather had been reestablished. In 1709, a basilica was constructed here at the site; today, it is perhaps one of the most important pilgrimage sites in Central America.

---

[45]Virgil Elizondo, "Unsere Liebe Frau von Guadalupe als Kultursymbol: Die Macht der Machtlosen," *Concilium* 13 (1977): 73-78; Enrique Dussel, "Christliche Kunst des Unterdrückten in Lateinamerika: Eine Hypothese zur Kennzeichnung einer Ästhetik der Befreiung," *Concilium* 16 (1980): 106-13, in this regard especially 108-10.

[46]Elizondo, "Unsere Liebe Frau von Guadalupe," 74-75.

How is the story of its origin to be interpreted? What happened here? Who were the role players here? How did native heritage and foreign beliefs, foreign heritage and native beliefs combine to produce something new? Let us begin with the two human protagonists, Indian Christian Juan Diego Cuauhtlatoatzin (1474–1548) and the bishop. Ten years after the conquest of the territory, an ordinary Indian came to the bishop in the name of the Virgin Mary, who had allegedly spoken with him in Nahuatl, his own language, demanding the construction of a chapel on the very hill on which previously a sacrificial temple to the Aztec goddess Tonántzin (now destroyed) had stood. *The archbishop is encountering his own heritage (the Virgin Mary) in a foreign form (the Nahuatl language) from the mouth of a foreigner.* He cannot believe that an ordinary Indian should convey such a message to him, the powerful bishop. He mistrusts Juan Diego. By the same token, let us now consider the Indian Christian, Juan Diego, a poor, simple, uneducated man who had converted to Christianity maybe ten years before—perhaps as little as two or three years before (this detail is not known). He is, according to the legendary account, the one in whom the encounter between the old Aztec religion and a new Christian religion is taking place; at the victory of the Spanish (1521) he was already an old man of perhaps fifty or sixty years of age.

It is to him that Mary appears. In the person of Mary, the novel subject matter that had been foreign to him until very recently now appears in the guise of the old and familiar, but—and this is significant—in a way that betrays reciprocal interaction. The first familiar element is the *music* that attracts his attention. In the Aztec religion, music was a means of divine communication. Additional familiar elements presented themselves to him in the visual aspect of the apparition (fig. 4), such as the clothing, for in the Aztec religion, the matte red of the dress represented the color of sacrificial blood and of the life-giving god Huitzilopochtli. The coat features a blue-green color, which is the color in which the gods were usually depicted in the Aztec religion. She wears a black sash around the body, which signifies that she is pregnant. Another familiar element is Nahuatl, his native language, in which the apparition addresses him. A further familiar element is the place at which she prompts him to have the bishop build her a chapel, namely the hill Tepeyac, where the sanctuary of the earth and mother goddess Tonántzin had stood. From an Indian perspective, the personage in question might well have been the goddess Tonántzin herself.

However, other aspects seem to rule out this possibility. The apparition introduces itself as "the Mother of the true God" and instructs him to go to

Figure 4. Virgin of Guadalupe

the archbishop and have him build a Christian church. After the bishop refuses repeatedly to do so, the floral miracle and the wondrous image on the coat of Juan Diego effect the turnaround. The image depicted Mary according to the description provided above. Flowers are Aztec signs for the presence of the divine, but the figure is standing in front of rays of light emanating from the sun, the symbol of the Aztec sun god, whom she obscures, and she stands on a crescent moon, the symbol of the Aztec moon god, on whom she stands victoriously. This is a superlative comparison: there is more here than in the old religion. Also, she wears no mask—contrary to the Aztec gods—and her face shows compassion, which unequivocally symbolizes that she is loving and benign. According to her own words, in the new location she will "be there" for all residents—this constitutes a new beginning. The stars on her cloak signify the same thing; while they were seen as a bad omen in the time before the arrival of the Spaniards, they now signify something new.

To sum up, the example shows how an encounter between two religious configurations "happens." It happens in the person of Indian Christian Juan Diego; it happens with reference to an apparition, in which in this case the Virgin Mary herself comes to play the role of a protagonist. It results in a folk-religious practice expressed in symbols and actions that are very open to interpretation. This means that the apparition and the madonna image may be interpreted on the basis of both the Christian-European set of cultures and the Indian-Aztec set of cultures and system of symbols. The two symbolisms overlap each other, leading to delimitations and adjustments in the process. In each case, the interpretation depends on the perspective of the interpreter. It is probable that some people venerated the Aztec goddess Tonántzin in the person of the Dear Lady of Guadalupe, others venerated Mary the Mother of God in an Indian guise, others venerated both Tonántzin and Mary, while yet others again considered this polarity no longer to represent either one. All manner of hybrid forms are conceivable. Thus the question remains unresolved: Is this a matter of syncretism (and thus illegitimate from the perspective of Christian theology) or a matter of successful inculturation, i.e., of the indigenization of the gospel in the form of the Indian culture? We will need to revisit this question at a later stage.

17

The Indifference Model

The Example of the Herrnhuter Mission

The Herrnhut Congregation of the Brethren may serve as an example of a theology and method of mission in which the relationship between gospel and culture is hardly mentioned at all.[1] Count Nicolaus von Zinzendorf, born in 1700, was a member of the European high nobility. From 1721, he lived on his estate of Berthelsdorf in Upper Lusatia. Having grown up in a pietistic home, he first came into contact with Danish Halle missionaries during his childhood and school days via mission journals and later encountered several of these missionaries in person. After an expatriate congregation made up of Moravian religious refugees had gathered in 1727 on the territory that he ruled in Herrnhut, it was constituted that same year as a congregation of Brethren. Zinzendorf became its spiritual leader.[2] In 1732, only five years later, this revivalist congregation sent its first two missionaries to the island of St. Thomas in the West Indies. Hundreds more male and female missionaries would follow in the next decades. By 1760, the year Zinzendorf died, around 230 persons had been sent out; by the end of the

---

[1]See Hartmut Beck, *Brüder in vielen Völkern: 250 Jahre Mission der Brüdergemeine* (Erlangen, Germany: Verlag der Ev.-Luth. Mission, 1981); Peter Zimmerling, "Zinzendorf und die Brüdermission," in *Pioniere der Mission im älteren Pietismus* (Giessen, Germany: Brunnen Verlag, 1985), 30-45; Carola Wessel, "'Es ist also des Heilands sein Predigtstuhl so weit und groß als die ganze Welt': Zinzendorfs Überlegungen zur Mission," in Martin Brecht and Paul Puecker, eds., *Neue Aspekte der Zinzendorf-Forschung* (Göttingen: Vandenhoeck & Ruprecht, 2006), 163-73. For source texts, see Werner Raupp, ed., *Mission in Quellentexten* (Erlangen, Germany: Verlag der Ev.-Luth. Mission, 1990), 164-72, especially 166-67 and 170-71.
[2]Zimmerling, "Zinzendorf und die Brüdermission," 31.

century, the number had grown even more.[3] In 1900, 431 missionaries (both men and women, most of them laypeople) were serving worldwide.[4]

ZINZENDORF'S THEOLOGY OF MISSION

Count Zinzendorf's understanding of mission would become foundational for the mission of the Herrnhut Moravian church, since the latter was profoundly shaped by the former. Zinzendorf saw Jesus Christ as the protomissionary, whose goal was to use his life of poverty and his redeeming work of the cross to lead people to God. The Holy Spirit, who as the Spirit of Christ corresponds to the Christ event, continues this work. Zinzendorf viewed the mission of Christians as an imitation of this mission of Christ. Christ continues to serve as the prototype. This has some far-reaching consequences in terms of carrying out the mission: according to the count's views, Christian missionaries are to imitate the itinerant life of Christ, beginning with his exile to Egypt as a kind of *pilgrimage* that is not primarily oriented toward making oneself at home in any one place. Accordingly, mission is no meticulously planned undertaking; rather, according to Zinzendorf's view, mission corresponds to the model of Jesus by following the improvisation method. Any restless wanderer has constantly to improvise. And this is the reason why the count did not provide the missionaries with comprehensive instructions before their departure. The Moravian mission was therefore characterized during the first decades by a kind of restlessness. However, this restlessness was clearly intentional.[5]

Also characteristic for Zinzendorf was his stated intention not to convert masses of people but only *individual souls*. This was predicated on his ecclesiology. He saw the *invisible church* as existing within institutionalized and thus visible churches, some composed of more and others of fewer people. The goal of the mission is therefore not to prop-

---

[3]Peter Zimmerling, *Nikolaus Ludwig Graf von Zinzendorf und die Herrnhuter Brüdergemeine* (Holzgerlingen, Germany: Hänssler, 1999), 122.

[4]Wolfgang Gabbert, "Phasen und Grundprobleme protestantischer Mission im kolonialen Afrika—Die Brüdergemeine bei den Nyakyusa in Tansania," in Artur Bogner, Bernd Holtwick and Hartmann Tyrell, eds., *Weltmission und religiöse Organisation* (Würzburg, Germany: Ergon Verlag, 2004), 517-40, especially 519. In the nineteenth century, missions were founded in "Eastern South Africa (1828), British Guyana (1835), Nicaragua (1849), West Himalaya (1856), Alaska (1885), California (1890), Northern Queensland, Nyassa (1891), and Unyamwezi (1898)" (ibid.).

[5]Zimmerling, "Zinzendorf und die Brüdermission," 37-38.

agate any particular confessional church or to reestablish one in a new place, but rather to gather small groups of sincere Christians. The idea is to found an *ecclesiola in ecclesia*, a community of real believers within the larger institutionalized church. This puts paid to the objective of achieving as many conversions as possible. Zinzendorf was not interested in reaching the masses. It is for this reason that as far as the method of proclamation was concerned, the count preferred one-on-one conversations over public sermons. He saw churches and Christian groups as nothing more than preliminary phenomena. According to the so-called doctrine of tropes, Zinzendorf believed that various congregations and churches are nothing more than manifestations (in Greek, *tropoi*) that are endowed with various gifts. Thus they should be free to accept each other. In this regard, the strong *ecumenical dimension* of Zinzendorf's thought becomes apparent.

THE MISSION METHOD OF THE MORAVIANS

Zinzendorf's thoughts on mission were strongly characterized by the awareness that he had only a *limited role* to play in God's comprehensive plan of salvation. In this regard he referred to the model of Jesus Christ, who personally converted not masses of people but only a handful of disciples (both male and female) and other people, who became his hearers and companions of their own volition. Accordingly, the missionaries of the Moravian Brethren sought to lead only a "selection of firstfruits" to Christ, and they saw this "gift of firstfruits" in turn as a type of preparatory work for the actual mission work of Christ, which he himself would bring about in the future. Another aspect of the imitation of Christ (*imitatio Christi*) was *serving in lowliness* and caring for the poor, just as Christ had devoted himself to caring for the poor and despised. It was no accident that the first mission initiative was directed at black slaves on the West Indies island of St. Thomas.[6]

---

[6]For more on the initial phase of this work, see Beck, *Brüder in vielen Völkern*, 41-60. Even though the Herrnhut missionaries became slaveholders themselves by purchasing and running a plantation (49), this may be attributed for the most part to the inescapable political circumstances prevailing at the time. Slaves both here and elsewhere certainly understood that these missionaries treated them very differently. This explains both the many slaves who requested baptism and the mistrust and rejection shown toward the missionaries on the part of white slave owners. At

The *imitatio Christi* is the attempt to orient every action toward Christ. This ideological approach was intensified by Zinzendorf's willingness to have Christ take individual decisions (such as assigning an area of service to missionaries or selecting marital partners for them) in person. Zinzendorf also favored the unusual (and scriptural!) procedure of *casting the lot*—after all, the disciples of Jesus Christ determined the replacement for Judas by casting the lot (namely Matthias, Acts 1:26). For example, the selection of the specific location to which missionaries would be sent took place by writing the names of various possibilities on slips of paper and drawing one of them at random. It was believed that this drawing of lots would reveal the will of Christ. This procedure was also used for other purposes, such as determining whether to proceed with a new mission initiative or not, allocating marital partners, filling certain offices, and the like. All of this demonstrates that for Zinzendorf, aligning himself with the model of Christ and according to the message of the cross meant that he refused to see mission as the expansion of the Christian area of influence and that he decried the political, economic, or educative consequences in which this thinking resulted.[7]

Zinzendorf saw the mission message as something that people were free to accept—or not. It was for this reason that he refused to organize the mission as an authority structure in its own right; instead, the congregation functioned as the sponsor of mission, the missionaries were laypeople, and mission was conducted in areas in which it was incumbent on the missionaries to participate in the colonial apparatus of power as little as possible.[8] Thus the agents of the Herrnhut mission were primarily lay missionaries, farmers, and craftsmen who earned their own living. For the most part, small trading companies, craft industries, or plantations were founded to this effect. Missionary couples or missionary families lived on the mission

---

any rate, a balanced historical judgment will need to take into account the limited amount of feasible changes at the time as determined by the framework of the historic situation and the position of the actors within the societal hierarchy.

[7]Zimmerling, "Zinzendorf und die Brüdermission," 34.

[8]For instance, in the case of the mission to Suriname/Berbice, which commenced in 1735, the missionaries came to this Dutch colony as settlers. For this reason, their passage was paid by the Dutch trading company. In other territories, the Herrnhut missionaries earned their keep by means of various trades (such as blacksmithing) and livestock farming (such as in Jamaica) or by processing sugar (St. Thomas), to cite just a few examples. See Beck, *Brüder in vielen Völkern*, 72-89, especially 73-74.

stations—another special feature of the Herrnhuters—in *communal* house-holds. As it was, marriage was seen along the lines of Zinzendorf's own example as "marriage in battle for Christ," i.e., oriented primarily toward benefiting the mission of Christ.[9]

There were a number of reasons why the relationship between gospel and culture was not addressed as such. First, the efforts in question were not intended to be permanent. Second, the purpose was to win individual souls for Christ, not to Christianize entire people groups and cultures. There was no question of employing long-term strategies or conducting ethnographic studies of people groups with the purpose of expressing the gospel in their particular cultural patterns. True, Count von Zinzendorf did impress on his missionaries that they were "not to measure everything according to Herrnhut standards" overseas, i.e., not to evaluate everything according to their own ideals. Nevertheless, the missionaries seldom adopted the cultural forms of expression of the indigenous people they served. Instead, they maintained the European treasury of songs that they brought with them, the familiar construction form of the church in Herrnhut,[10] and other such aspects. The operative principle was not to do away with an existing religion and culture and to replace them with one's own, but rather the under-estimation of the culture factor for mission, that is to say the indifference toward this issue.

For instance, in the case of the work among the Arawak Indian tribe in Berbice, the educated theologian Theophil Schumann did succeed in learning their language and in developing a writing system for it, even going so far as to write a grammar and a dictionary for the language. At the same time, the Indians were subdivided according to the Herrnhut model into so-called clusters (literally *Banden*, groups meant to facilitate pastoral care), a liturgical foot-washing ceremony was instituted, the cemetery was named "Hutberg" just like the one in Herrnhut, a visit was paid to the cemetery every Easter Sunday just as it was done in Herrnhut, Herrnhut hymns were sung in German and in Arawak, the unmarried Indian brothers lived in a

---

[9]Zimmerling, "Zinzendorf und die Brüdermission," 41.

[10]For more on the symbolism of the Herrnhut church in Herrenhaag, see Peter Zimmerling, "Die Architektur der Brüdergemeinde als sichtbarer Ausdruck der Theologie Zinzendorfs," in *Nikolaus Ludwig Graf von Zinzendorf*, 57-67, particularly 61-63.

"brother-house" (*Brüderhaus*), etc. It seems as if many aspects of the European practice of the Herrnhuters were replicated.[11]

Yet to respond to this finding by claiming that the missionaries should have adapted more to the culture of their hearers would do decidedly little justice to the complexity of the situation. One needs to bear in mind that the Herrnhut missionaries frequently had to endure a difficult life and to make many sacrifices. Unfamiliar living conditions, harsh climates, illnesses, hostilities on the part of white settlers or colonial authorities, setbacks in their work—all of these were the order of the day. Many missionaries died soon after arrival. For instance, of the twenty-nine missionaries sent to St. Thomas, within a few years twenty-one had died. Elsewhere too the mortality rate was high.[12] *In view of these circumstances, it is understandable when people cling to familiar ways of life and devotional practices as an anchor, as a way of affirming their identity, and as an expression of a sense of community. These people served in and belonged to a mission movement that was active in different places all around the globe; they remained united with each other not only through reading reports of mission from around the world but also through prayer and intercession, and they viewed the devotional practice that they kept the same wherever they went as helping them to remain part of a greater—transcontinental—whole.*

ASPECTS OF A THEOLOGY OF RELIGION

The aspect of mission as an individual, often spontaneous occasion—limited in every instance to the event in question—is also significant for that which one may label as Zinzendorf's theology of religion. This becomes evident from the following short section from a speech Zinzendorf held in Zeist in the Netherlands in 1746:

> What should people think about our "heathen work"? I do see our work in those lands where—as no sane person would dispute—the common people truly believe in false gods as "heathen work." . . . We act like courtiers when they approach the rooms of a great lord and *do not dare to knock; they only scratch [at the door]*, so that those who are close to the door can pay attention

---

[11]See Beck, *Brüder in vielen Völkern*, 79-80.

[12]For instance, a total of 157 missionaries came to Suriname between 1735 and 1800, and seventy-one of them died there. See Beck, *Brüder in vielen Völkern*, 89.

and open it if they wish, but if they do not wish, they can ignore it and pay no attention: We do not knock, we only tap when *get the impression that the Holy Spirit has souls in attendance* who are silently listening. For our commission does not state *that we should convert nations, lands, and islands, no, our instructions say nothing about that;* rather, just as we *ourselves are an eklogé [selection],* so we too may only hope for an aparché *[gift of firstfruits] from among the heathen here and there,* and particularly from among the unspoiled heathen who have had as little contact with the so-called "Christindians" [*Christianer*] as possible, and of whom by grace we have seen more than one with our own eyes.[13]

The first thing that is striking is *what he says about the Holy Spirit.* While he uses the term *false gods,* he does see indigenous people as human beings, in some of whom the Holy Spirit is already at work. Thus the work of the Spirit is neither comprehensively affirmed nor denied; rather, the work of the Spirit is seen as an individual process, differing from one person to another, subject to the leadership of Christ and obedient to his counsel. Second, it may be observed that Zinzendorf compares the *proclamation event* to tapping lightly at the door of another person's heart. In this figure of speech, which is taken from the world of a nobleman's home, the hearers are seen as free people who can choose to listen to the tapping or not. It is their decision whether they choose to answer the tapping. Third, in the proclamation event, the person tapping is taking special care that the hearer—we may paraphrase—does not lose face. Zinzendorf asserts that the hearers are able to "ignore" the tapping and "pay no attention" to it. These basic premises from Zinzendorf's theology of religion have far-reaching consequences, for the act of mission is seen to be subject to certain restrictions from the outset; Zinzendorf sees it as the conversion of the individual.

Christian mission does not aim at the conversion of people groups but of individuals who are to be gathered in congregations of the revived. The intention was thus not the expansion of the Christian world or the church; it was to win individual souls wherever they may live. In consequence, remote territories were often selected in which few "nominal Christians" lived, whose bad example was seen as an obstacle to mission[14] (geographical delimitation).

---

[13]Quoted in Raupp, *Mission in Quellentexten,* 170. The italicized text has been edited.
[14]Gabbert, "Phasen," 522.

The mission follows in the Spirit's footsteps: According to Zinzendorf, the missionary does not bring light into the darkness of heathenism; rather, he pays attention to the preparative and in this sense preceding action of the Holy Spirit, who alone can open people's hearts for the gospel. Thus great value is placed on listening (pneumatological delimitation). *Some, not all—there is no quantitative goal*: The goal of mission is not to gain as many as possible, i.e., a quantitative mission success; rather, due to the eschatological hour, the goal is only to seek a selection of people, a group of firstfruits. The selection of firstfruits is seen in connection with a divine plan. However, Christ himself will bring about the great harvest (quantitative delimitation). *No expansion of church or culture*: When gaining individual souls, the intention is not to expand an ecclesiastical organization or a Christian-European culture. Zinzendorf impresses on the missionaries that they are not to measure everything according to "Herrnhut standards." Wherever possible, the idea is not simply to reproduce the European forms of Christianity (cultural delimitation). *No systematic approach*: Zinzendorf did not systematize his thoughts on mission, since his theology is essentially a conversational theology, one that entrusts itself to the work of the Spirit. As was shown, the Herrnhut mission initiatives also featured no detailed systematization; for instance, mission goals were selected by lot, i.e., by the process of casting lots, in which God was leading and revealing his will, as the Herrnhuters believed (structural delimitation).

Zinzendorf's thoughts on mission were endorsed by his successor, August G. Spangenberg (1704–1792), but also slowly and gently developed to include the establishment of Christian communities in which the congregations became virtually indistinguishable from the civil community. This was a tribute to the actual developments on the ground, in which masses of people flocked to the gospel, to the extent that it would have been impossible for the Herrnhut missionaries to care for every individual person. Meanwhile, it took until 1899 for the Herrnhuters to take the step of recognizing the Christianization of people groups as a legitimate mission method in addition to that of the conversion of individuals, which had been propagated since the 1870s by German mission studies scholar Gustav Warneck and by Lutheran mission director Karl Graul (1814–1864).[15]

---

[15]Johannes Christiaan Hoekendijk, *Kirche und Volk in der deutschen Missionswissenschaft* (Munich: Chr. Kaiser Verlag, 1965), 54.

FURTHER DEVELOPMENTS AND THE RELATIONSHIP BETWEEN
GOSPEL AND CULTURE(S)

The Herrnhut Congregation of the Brethren engaged in a number of mission initiatives in rapid succession, first in the West Indies island of St. Thomas, then in Greenland; little congregations formed in both places. The Herrnhuters worked in Suriname as settler missionaries. A kind of "people's church" finally came into being, just as it did among the Nyakyusa in what is today Tanzania.[16] Here and elsewhere the missionaries of the Moravian Brethren worked toward entrusting the responsibilities of proclamation and leadership to indigenous Christians as soon as possible; both for this reason and because the mission sought to discern the guidance of Jesus Christ in the most immediate manner (such as by casting lots), the Herrnhuters did not retain control of the mission for long but allowed it to develop its own dynamic instead. Such developments sometimes took on unintended forms, which even contradicted the original views of the Herrnhuters at times. *For instance, mission initiatives generally commenced with the intention of converting individuals. When the converted indigenous people began to serve as preachers, however, they were sometimes able to win over whole tribal groups to the Christian faith. This happened, for example, in the unity provinces of Tanzania,[17] where whole family and clan confederations came to faith. When this happened, it did so against the convictions of the Herrnhuters, who doubted the inner conviction of such converts and the genuineness of such mass conversions to Christianity; at the same time, they had little choice but to go along with them. In this way, the mission theory was frequently outstripped and rendered obsolete by the mission praxis, i.e., by the actual course of events.*

Among the Nyakyusa, the Herrnhuters had originally established mission villages at some distance from local population centers. These villages consisted of buildings for the missionaries and for Africans, a church, a school, stables for livestock, buildings for agricultural use, and some artisanal enterprises. Very few Africans were converted in the first few years; for the

---

[16]Beck, *Brüder in vielen Völkern*, 206-27, especially 225-26. See also Gabbert, "Phasen," 517-40.

[17]The mission work of the Herrnhuters in this area commenced in 1891, approximately at the same time as that of other German mission societies (such as the Bethel Mission Society, the Berlin Mission Society, and others); Beck, *Brüder in vielen Völkern*, 364-409, and especially 367. For more on indigenous preachers, see especially 370ff.

most part, the Africans living in the villages were mostly day laborers, orphans, and refugees. Most of the first converts were disowned and evicted
by their families, with the result that the mission villages came to serve as
replacement families for them in the full sense of the term. Since the Herrnhuters had to earn their own living, the flow of goods became a significant
economic factor for the transport operations of local chieftains, to the extent
that a number of them gave up the slave trade to cater to the transport of
goods for the mission stations.[18] The system of segregated mission villages
was abandoned after 1905, when satellite stations were established for evangelization tours in order to compete with Catholic mission initiatives and
more and more indigenous helpers needed to be equipped and engaged for
this task.[19] As early as 1914, there were as many as two hundred indigenous
elders, deacons, and evangelists, as compared to fourteen European missionaries. Whereas there had been only fifty-six satellite stations in 1910, by
1928 these had increased to 181. The Christianization of the people took on
such a strong internal dynamic that the few European missionaries were
hardly able to keep up with the administration. The issue of education took
on increasing importance; in this region, just as in many others, the missionaries ran the only schools.

A comparison of Zinzendorf's theology of mission and of religion and of
the practice of the Herrnhut Moravians with that of the replacement model
in Latin America shows that in both cases the respective theology of mission
had implications for how people interpreted theologically the concept of
foreignness, and it also predicated a certain theology of encounter. Zinzendorf's theology of imitating Christ also determined the way in which the
Herrnhuters encountered people from other nations, cultures, and religions.
Whenever the Christian missionaries engaged in such encounters, they were
instructed to do so circumspectly, cautiously, and gently. Even when they
considered the foreign religion to be an expression of human sin or demonic
deception, they were nevertheless instructed carefully to examine whether
the working of the Holy Spirit might not also be in evidence among the

---

[18]Gabbert, "Phasen," 524-28. On the stations and surrounding pastures and farmlands that the
chieftains had allocated to the missionaries, the latter assumed the leading role both legally and
politically.

[19]Ibid., 531.

foreigners. *The model of individual conversion remained in force for the Herrnhut missions from 1732 until around 1900; the missions were tightly and centrally managed by the general synod as the highest executive board of the Moravian church.*[20] *Their indifference toward the issue of culture is clearly seen from the establishment of remote mission stations and villages, a method that only fell into disuse when it was replaced by the internal dynamic of mass conversions within the context of tribal cultures.*[21]

---

[20]Ibid., 520.

[21]Naturally one needs to bear in mind that when it came to the practical implementation, the model was seldom realized in a pure and unadulterated form and that the efforts of putting it into practice were limited by a great many specific conditions that ultimately contributed to its abandonment. Nevertheless, in many cases such basic mission theological ideas as that described above were very effective over long periods of time.

18
....

The Ennoblement Model

The mission model of the Moravians of Herrnhut remained definitive in the area of Protestant missions until as late as the first half of the nineteenth century. In essence, the overriding goal of mission was the conversion of individuals. Whereas the Herrnhut mission was probably the most significant European mission in the eighteenth century, a whole wave of new mission societies were founded at the turn of the century that initially oriented themselves toward the Herrnhut model and aimed at the conversion of individuals. During the course of the nineteenth century, however, the theological justification for the conversion of entire people groups (ethnic groups) became an increasingly important issue. These approaches will be discussed under the "indigenization model" in the next section. For now, we will focus on the relationship between gospel and culture(s) as it was defined and seen toward the end of the nineteenth century; at issue here is the so-called cultural mission approach, which will be discussed here under the rubric of the ennoblement model.[1] The proponents of this model trenchantly argued that mission and the cultural ennoblement of the recipient culture should go hand in hand. Yet the basic principle found support in a broad stream of consciousness throughout the entire century; this was a secular sense of mission often titled "the white man's burden," which held that the European (and North American) civilization had been tasked with

[1]See Ferdinand Hahn, "Das theologische Programm von Ernst Buss," in Ferdinand Hahn, August Bänziger and Winfried Glüer, eds., *Spuren . . . Festschrift zum hundertjährigen Bestehen der Ostasien-Mission* (Stuttgart, Germany: Evangelisches Missionswerk in Südwestdeutschland, 1984), 10-18; Wolfgang Eger, "Zur Geschichte der Ostasien-Mission," in Hahn, Bänziger and Glüer, *Spuren*, 56-61; Wilhelm Brachmann, "Die Ostasien-Mission in Vergangenheit und Gegenwart," *Zeitschrift für Missions- und Religionswissenschaft* 46 (1931): 238-53; Johannes Witte, "Was veranlasst die Ostasien-Mission zur Bitte um Aufnahme in den Deutsch-Evangelischen Missionsbund?," *Zeitschrift für Missions- und Religionswissenschaft* 46 (1931): 225-38.

elevating other cultures to the niveau of its own state of development.[2] Yet we must also clarify that this was no uniform phenomenon. Besides, it is not legitimate to make sweeping statements and to tar both Christian mission-aries and the model of civilizing mission in the colonial context with the same brush. After all, there were an exceedingly great number of different streams, and many of them took an expressly anticolonial approach. These eschewed entirely the infrastructure (schools, farms, artisanal enterprises, printing presses, etc.) that would have tied them to the context of colonial administration. The most prominent example of this is constituted by the *faith missions*, which were modeled on Hudson Taylor's (1832–1905) China Inland Mission.[3] In addition, as the example of the language issue in the work of the North German Mission Society demonstrates, there was a wide range of ideas about what "ennoblement" or "elevating the recipient culture" was supposed to mean exactly.[4] After these preliminary remarks, we now turn to an example of a cultural mission in the narrow sense of the word.

MODELS OF CULTURAL MISSION

Whereas the Herrnhuters aimed to convert individual people while de-voting little attention or theological consideration to their cultural identity, for the approaches we discuss in this section, the issue of culture occupies the center of attention. The aim was nothing less than to *Christianize all of humanity*. The Christianization of entire people groups was seen merely as a stage along the path of a more comprehensive development of humanity as a whole. One significant advocate of this line of thought was Swiss pastor Ernst Buss (1843–1928). He published his basic ideas on the theology of mission in a book in 1876.[5] Having been influenced by the religious his-torian Max Müller (1823–1900), Buss tried to see mission objectively in a manner that was free of the bias of confessionalism or of particular camps

---

[2]See Boris Barth and Jürgen Osterhammel, eds., *Zivilisierungsmissionen: Imperiale Weltverbesser-ung seit dem 18 Jahrhundert* (Konstanz, Germany: UBK Verlagsgesellschaft, 2005).
[3]See Andrew Porter, "Christentum, Kontext und Ideologie: Die Uneindeutigkeit der 'Zivilisier-ungsmission' im Großbritannien des 19. Jahrhunderts," in Barth and Osterhammel, *Zivilisier-ungsmissionen*, 125-47.
[4]See chapter eight, under the heading, "Ethnic Identity as a Construct and Language Issue: The Example of the Ewe."
[5]Ernst Buss, *Christliche Mission, ihre principielle Berechtigung und practische Durchführung* (Leiden: E. J. Brill, 1876).

within the churches. He understand mission as an exchange between
Christianity and the elements of truth found in non-Christian religions.
According to his opinion, studies in comparative religions and liberal theology were to play an important role in the education of missionaries, in
order to enable them to engage in a scientific exchange with non-Christian
religions. Buss was president of the General Evangelical Protestant Mission
Association (*Allgemeiner Evangelisch-Protestantischer Missionsverein*) from
1884 to 1892. This association began work in Japan and China in 1929 and
later changed its name to the German East Asia Mission Society (*Deutsche
Ost-Asien-Mission*).

Buss believed that it was necessary to educate humanity in a systematic
and pedagogical manner in order for it to become Christian.[6] In so doing,
he was less concerned about conversion and more about education, i.e., with
elevating the niveau of the recipient culture, since, as he put it, "Christianization and Civilization must necessarily go hand in hand the world over."[7]
In this sense, mission aims at having a civilizing effect on the masses, which
is why the phrase "Christianization of the peoples" was used. The term
people is not used to denote a cultural unit such as a (small) ethnic group
(for instance, a tribal confederation in Africa); rather, *people* is used in the
general sense to mean *the mass of people who need to be civilized* in order to
mirror the Christian-European culture. Mission theologian Johannes Hoekendijk critically notes, "The secularized corpus Christianum that spread out
across the world in the form of Western culture did not encounter people
groups, much less heathen; instead, it encountered only populaces civilized
to a greater or lesser extent—not the goyim, but rather the barbaric pagani.
Sermons meant education. The school took priority over the church."[8]

Let us recap: The concern of the replacement model was to do away with
the religion of the recipient population and to replace it with Christianity
(in European form), with the non-Christian religions and their followers

---

[6]Horst Rzepkowski, *Lexikon der Mission* (Graz, Austria: Verlag Styria, 1992), s.v. "Buss, Ernst."
The East Asia Mission Society later became a member of the Evangelical Mission Association in
Southwestern Germany (EMS). Buss founded the journal *Zeitschrift für Missionskunde und Religionswissenschaft*, which was issued from 1886 to 1940 and was then amalgamated with the
journal *Evangelische Missionszeitschrift*.
[7]For more on Buss, see Johannes Christiaan Hoekendijk, *Kirche und Volk in der deutschen Missionswissenschaft* (Munich: Chr. Kaiser Verlag, 1965), 83-87; quotation drawn from 84.
[8]Ibid., 85.

being painted with a broad brush as "heathen." In contrast, in the indifference model the concern was to recognize the recipients of mission as individuals, as persons in whom the Spirit of God was believed to have been at work already, leading them to Christ. Here non-Christians were seen as members of foreign people groups, as individuals. However, in the cultural mission model as defined by Buss, the recipients of mission are seen as a mass of people civilized to a greater or lesser extent, who are to be advanced slowly by means of education until they reach the niveau of the Christian-European culture. In a programmatic article published in the newly founded journal *Zeitschrift für Missionskunde und Religionswissenschaft*, Buss stated,

> In consequence, helping the nations progress from their state of retarded religious development, pouring new, healthy blood into their sick heart, aiming at achieving the inner regeneration of their quintessence, in this way guiding them on the path toward a superior ethos and culture, rousing the individuals from their religious and moral misery and directing them toward true life from God and in God—all of this contributes toward improving their happiness (in the best sense of the word) and helping them advance. . . . All of this is based on the presupposition that Christianity does not only constitute a higher stage of the religious development of humanity and the other religions, but that it is *the* truth. Even if it does not do justice to its nature as the absolute religion as far as its ecclesiastical manifestation is concerned, it still is the absolute religion in principle; it is the fulfilment and completion of all religious desire and hope of the human heart.[9]

Arguably the most prominent theologian of the so-called cultural Protestantism was Ernst Troeltsch. He also viewed mission as education and the exchange of religious ideas. He believed that mission was not to be pursued as a general task but with greater nuances of *relational* differentiation and due regard to the cultural level of the recipients. For the *lower levels of civilization*, education and instruction were to take priority, so that these cultures would become able to understand and accept Christianity in the first place. In contrast, for the *higher levels of civilization* the approach of exchanging religious ideas was to be used instead of the mission approach. Even Europeans could learn something every once in a while from the great

---

[9]Ernst Buss, *Zeitschrift für Missionskunde und Religionswissenschaft* 1 (1886): 2. See also Hahn, "Das theologische Programm von Ernst Buss."

cultures of, say, China and Japan. Even so, he believed that it is still necessary to disseminate the collective ideas of Western Christianity, since these are superior in all main points. As a third alternative, according to Troeltsch, the mission approach is to be used for *middle levels of civilization*, i.e., for cultures that are neither tribal cultures nor "high cultures."

Troeltsch thus—like Buss—saw humanity as constantly progressing along the scale of cultural and religious advancement, the peak of which is constituted by Protestant Christianity. Therefore, this is the culture that is most likely to prevail in the end. Conversely, Christianity can only be disseminated through the medium of this culture. Troeltsch was convinced that the Christian faith can only be disseminated through the medium of Christianized culture and that, conversely, the recipients can only receive the blessings of cultural progress once they have also accepted its religious basis. The reason for this, Troeltsch believed, is the fact that world domination through science and technology is only possible because Protestants are beholden neither to a religious hierarchy of priests nor to a religious law. *Priests are an obstacle to free thought; immutable religious laws inhibit societal development;* and *the belief that the world is animated* (e.g., that trees have spirits dwelling within them and therefore one may not fell trees, etc.) makes scientific research impossible. All of this is ruled out in Protestantism because, *first*, believing Christians are only answerable to God and to their consciences, which makes priestly hierarchies and religious laws dispensable; and *second*, faith sees the world as God's creation, which rules out a belief in the animation of plants, animals, and objects. Troeltsch's view serves as a classic example of the mission model of trying to civilize people by way of Christianization.

AN ATTEMPT AT IMPLEMENTING THE MODEL: THE EAST ASIA MISSION

The General Evangelical Protestant Mission Association was founded in 1884.[10] Wolfgang Eger persuasively proposes the following periodization of the association's focus of activity:

> During the first phase of mission work between 1884 and 1900, the focus was on literary, spiritual, and educational work, and on establishing contacts with the

---

[10]It was renamed as the East Asia Mission Society in 1929.

country's intelligentsia. . . . During the second phase of work between around 1900 and 1930, the focus shifted to practical and social work. Kindergartens were opened and mercy work was begun in hospitals and nursing homes. During the third phase, which is still ongoing, the focus has shifted yet again; emphasis is placed on the individual, on strengthening the congregations, and on finding ways to maintain people's Christian identity, with the difference that this takes place in cooperation with the churches in Japan and Korea, who have now assumed control of and responsibility for the mission society themselves.[11]

The 1876 book by Ernst Buss is imbued with the spirit of the nineteenth century. Instead of the expansion of confessional Christianity, Buss, who endorsed the tenets of academic theology, called for the distilling of a pure "Christendom of Christ" and for its transmission on a supraconfessional level. After all, he reasoned, the goal was "to facilitate the progressive development of the world, so that it can become the kingdom of God by way of Christianity."[12] The way to achieve this was by focusing on *large* nations with an advanced culture and within them on the well-educated section of the population. While acknowledging the positive aspects of these cultures, Buss believed that the long-term goal should be to lead the nations to Christianity by means of education and intense efforts. In consequence, Buss demanded that missionaries should study at universities in order to receive a thorough academic education.

THE CHRISTIAN GOSPEL AND THE PROGRESSIVE DEVELOPMENT OF CULTURES

The following characteristics apply to the operative use of the term *culture* in this model: (1) It is used in a broad, sweeping sense to refer to large cultural groups in the inclusive sense (for instance, when speaking of "ancient cultures"), meaning such cultures as the Japanese or Chinese. Today, people would probably prefer the term civilization. (2) In addition, the term *culture* is used in an "elitist" sense, since it is used to denote especially those cultures that may be described as particularly developed from a contemporaneous European perspective. Cultures were generally seen considered "developed" if they had developed *a system of writing* and, whenever possible, had also

---

[11]Eger, "Zur Geschichte," 59-60.
[12]Buss, *Christliche Mission*.

produced scientists and philosophers of their own. (3) Furthermore, the term *culture* is used in an *optimistic sense*, since the assumption is that cultures are located somewhere on a scale of progressive development. Cultures are considered to be capable of development, albeit only to the extent that they are able to adapt to the European-Christian culture. (4) The term *culture* is thus defined in a certain sense as "universal," since it is believed that advanced cultures can be integrated with each other. (5) In essence, *culture* is seen as an abstract term, since both Buss and Troeltsch emphasize certain spiritual principles that allegedly operate in cultures regardless of the actual material form taken by the cultures at the time. For example, Chinese academics would be allowed to continue to address and act according to Chinese custom as long as they developed these spiritual principles of independent thought, individual responsibility, worldview, etc.

From the perspective of the theology of religion, it is important that in this model, foreign cultures and religions are no longer interpreted demonologically, as had been the case in the replacement model, but rather through the lens of ethics and civilization. Accordingly, the ethics produced by cultures and religions serves as the yardstick to determine their acceptability, at least inasmuch as it accords with the ethical maxims prevalent in Christian Europe. Thus the true yardstick is the virtuousness of a particular culture, i.e., the extent of its philosophical development, its scientific development, its artistic development, etc. *In so doing, both the term* culture *and the term* religion *are used in a strongly normative sense.* Thus on the basis of the elitist sense in which the term *culture* is used, a distinction is being made between the recipients of mission according to their respective level of education.

In 1931, Witte critically appraised the first forty-five years of the work of the East Asia Mission Society. From his appraisal it emerges that Witte was no longer able to agree with Ernst Buss's optimistic view of history and culture. Although Witte offers many criticisms of Buss's book,[13] it is clear

---

[13]Witte criticized Buss's method as follows: "Buss' dream of Christianity influencing foreign religions to the point that they begin to take on the form of Christianity was indeed realized in Eastern Asia, especially by the Anglo-Saxon mission societies, and particularly in Japan. Yet this process did not make things easier for the missionaries, as Buss had hoped, but rather more difficult. These religions used the means of Christianity to reinvigorate themselves, and now put up even more resistance to Christianity than they did before." Witte, "Was veranlasst die Ostasien-Mission," 230.

that a number of characteristics of the East Asia Mission Society were retained. These allow us to continue to define the model as an ennoblement
model. Witte writes,

> We value true, noble culture very highly, and we do want to renew and in-
> tensify it through the Spirit of Christ, but we also recognize the limitations of
> all culture and the restrictions on its development. Wanting the world pro-
> gressively to develop into the kingdom of God is a pipe dream; ever since the
> rise of secularism in the West and in the East, it has become clear that this is
> an impossible task and a contradiction in terms.[14]

While Witte acknowledges the individual value of different cultures, he believes that Buss overemphasized the significance of having the mission efforts progress from the upper to the lower strata of society.[15] At the same
time, the East Asia Mission Society continued to focus on the "ancient cultures of Asia." Its aim continued to be to "influence the national spirit of
those peoples by engaging in strong lecturing and instruction efforts among
the public at large."[16] Also, the target group continued to be the "educated
classes," and for this reason the mission society continued to send only "academically educated" missionaries.[17]

THE GOSPEL AS A CULTURE-SHAPING FORCE: HOW OTHER
CULTURES ARE PERCEIVED

In contrast to the replacement model, in the ennoblement model there is
in essence a high regard for aspects of other cultures; the latter model does
not endorse the former's categorical rejection of especially religious traditions. All cultures are believed to be capable of development. On the other
hand—in contrast to the indifference model—these cultures and religions

---

[14]Ibid., 232.

[15]"Our mission society will continue to devote itself to its special task of exercising a Christian
influence on the national spirit, and to direct its efforts at the educated, but today its emphasis
is on helping people attain complete salvation through repentance. While Buss did have this in
mind, he did so to a far lesser extent." Ibid., 231.

[16]However, according to Witte, promoting literature and schools did not suffice (any longer) to
"exert a Christian influence on the national spirit"; rather, he believed it was necessary to present
living examples to the people—of Christian families, for example (keyword: the image of women
in Asian cultures)—and for this reason the East Asian Mission Society began to have a preference for founding congregations. Ibid., 230-31. In so doing, the views and methods of this
mission society began to resemble those of others more and more.

[17]Ibid., 233.

are acknowledged as significant for the reason that religion is seen as something mediated by culture, as an inseparable aspect of a greater holistic religious-cultural construct. Furthermore, the ennoblement model is fundamentally distinct from the other two in the sense that it is a dynamic model in which all cultures and religions are believed to be moving along a global process of upward development. Thus from the perspective of intercultural theology, we might well ask: Of all the models we have considered thus far, is the ennoblement model not the one that views other, foreign cultures and religions in the most positive light? Could it not perhaps even serve as a model of an intercultural hermeneutics for us today?

It is at this point that we can no longer overlook its limitations. For instance, in this model, other cultures and religions are not valued *in and of themselves*; rather, they are viewed unilaterally according to the standard of European moral concepts and evaluated accordingly. It is the European perspective that allocates to each culture and religion its position on the global scale of human development. Instead of judging religions as either "true" or "false," this model categorizes them as either "more" or "less" true. Despite the partial appreciation for the cultures and religions in question, the premise continues to be that they need to move past their respective status quo, that they are in need of continued ennoblement until they reach the degree of truth, morality, and scientific knowledge that is considered to comprise the highest stage of development—as defined and embodied by Protestant Christianity. It seems doubtful whether this view allows for a truly mutual intercultural process of learning. Besides, the operative understanding of culture is a holistic one that does little justice either to the tensions and fragmentation within cultures or to the overlaps, hybridizations, and mutual influences between cultural formations.

In addition, we must also face up to the basic question: Is it not legitimate or even inevitable that in the process of intercultural and interreligious exchange, each party *necessarily* assumes—and may well assume—that its own position is the ultimately correct one? To put it plainly, is it not either naive or dishonest to claim that one can evaluate all the different options without prejudice? Is it possible for people engaging in intercultural encounters to "factor out" their own presuppositions entirely? Would this even be desirable? Or should the aim not rather be to *become* as *conscious* of one's own presuppositions as possible in order to "factor them in" whenever possible? We will revisit these questions at a later point. Let us now consider the fourth model: the indigenization model.

19

The Indigenization Model

The Example of Bruno Gutmann

Let us begin by providing a brief explanation of the concept: The word *indigenization* is derived from the Latin word *gens*, which may be translated as a "tribe" or "people." Indigenization refers to the gospel becoming indigenous to an ethnic group[1]—or, to use modern terminology, to a small-scale society, to a tribal confederation, to people related by a common progenitor (a group of some hundreds of thousands of people at the most), but not to a national entity. This model was favored by missionaries who were committed to the ideal of Christianizing whole nations and establishing national churches. Among the most prominent (and successful) German representatives of this group are Lutheran missionaries Christian Keysser (1877–1961) in Papua New Guinea and Bruno Gutmann (1876–1966) in Tanzania. In what follows, we will focus on Bruno Gutmann as a case study.[2] Gutmann was born in 1876 in Dresden and worked as a missionary of the Leipzig Mission Society from 1902 to 1938 among the Chagga people in the Kilimanjaro area of what is today Tanzania.[3] As he did so, Gutmann began by studying not only the language but also the culture and morals of the Chagga people. He created a substantial body of literature in which he

---

[1]Borrowing from the concept of the incarnation of the eternal *Logos* in the person of Jesus of Nazareth, the operative concept here is one of relating the gospel to a tribal culture.

[2]See Klaus Fiedler, *Christentum und afrikanische Kultur: Konservative deutsche Missionare in Tanzania, 1900 bis 1940* (Gütersloh, Germany: Gütersloher Verlagshaus, 1983); Christoph Bochinger, *Ganzheit und Gemeinschaft: Zum Verhältnis von theologischer und anthropologischer Fragestellung im Werk Bruno Gutmanns* (Frankfurt: P. Lang, 1987), 17ff. See also Johannes Christiaan Hoekendijk, *Kirche und Volk in der deutschen Missionswissenschaft* (Munich: Chr. Kaiser Verlag, 1965), 139-65.

[3]He had to return to Germany from 1920 to 1925.

dedicated himself to describing and interpreting this tribal African tradition and religion. How did Bruno Gutmann view the Chagga tribal culture? We find an initial indication of Gutmann's appraisal of tribal cultural traditions in his critical remarks on what was described as "European civilization" at the time.

CIVILIZATION VERSUS PRIMORDIAL TIES

Gutmann's critical view of civilization becomes understandable when viewed against the backdrop of his biography. Gutmann grew up in a rural family severely affected by the economic depression of the late 1870s, as demonstrated by the bankruptcy of the little family business in 1879.[4] The only way for family members to survive was by rendering mutual assistance to each other. This was a formative experience for the young Gutmann. During this time, industrialization and urbanization led to the establishment of poorhouses in many cities. The masses of people who crowded together in these poorhouses lacked both proper medicinal care and access to education in schools. Gutmann later explained that this came about because of the difference between urban and rural areas, a figure of thought fairly common at the time:

> When the urbanized man—which includes everybody in Germany no longer belonging to the rural classes—thinks of friendship, he thinks of elective community, of a brotherhood among people who are foreigners to each other, one which comes about on the basis of some or other mutual appreciation and which may be dissolved again at will. In the urbanized world, which proudly calls itself "civilization"—an unnatural phenomenon—each individual has been worn by constant friction into a rock-hard piece of grit. He prides himself on grinding against some blue fellow grit the one day and some red the next, yet remaining yellow himself no matter what! We see him glittering in the water, being swirled along by the flow; yet the grumbling and rumbling of the cogs and gears, which propel the water and rush him and all the other pieces of grit along relentlessly, he calls progress, development.[5]

---

[4]Fiedler, *Christentum und afrikanische Kultur*, 38.
[5]Bruno Gutmann, *Freies Menschentum aus ewigen Bindungen* (Kassel, Germany: Bärenreiter Verlag, 1928), 12. See also Gutmann, "Urtümliche Bindungen und Sünde," *Neue Evangelische Missionszeitschrift* (1934): 20-31.

Gutmann here describes the individualization of human beings that accompanies urbanization as "unnatural," as a social consequence of that societal change that in Gutmann's view does not deserve to be called "civilization," "progress," or "development." Family ties and neighborly ties characterized by commitment and responsibility are replaced by "elective communities" that may be formed to one's own taste but also dissolved again very quickly. Gutmann contrasts this with rural society, which is—to put it abstractly—a social configuration delimited by area and thus clear and defined.

According to Gutmann, the freedom of a human being only begins to take shape within the security and nurture of personal ties, which he also called "organic ties," i.e., committed relationships within the association of relatives and neighbors. Gutmann believed such ties to be fundamental for the Christian proclamation as well, since God elected to provide an answer to the fate of humanity within the medium of these ties:

> [God] founded the eternal kingdom of divine filiation and located it within the network of these organic ties. As a man, he entered his kingdom by this portal. He decreed that his kingdom should be proclaimed as the kingdom of the Father and of the Son. And he also instructed this same only-begotten Son of his to engage in battle here on earth in order to maintain the order of God. Yet this means also that he fought for our ongoing commitment toward those who are tied and related to us—a commitment which surpasses all artificial relationships.[6]

Thus the gospel of Jesus Christ relates to these "organic ties," which Gutmann also calls "primordial ties" elsewhere. In contrast to the program of cultural Protestantism, according to which the Christian faith is to be disseminated together with the European culture and civilization (note the singular!) that it produced and formed, Gutmann believed that the influence of Europe on other countries, on other people groups, and their cultures was corrosive and thus destructive. Gutmann criticized the civilizations and Christianity of Europe; there, he said, "people live out an individualized form of Christianity, and Christian congregations are culture clubs and nothing more. To live the European life means to care for nobody but

---

[6]Gutmann, *Freies Menschentum*, 7-8.

yourself."[7] As Gutmann saw it, whenever this mindset was exported any-where else, it meant that people groups that had hitherto been healthy would now be harmed in that the organic ties would be destroyed and replaced by individualistic self-interest. *Thus for Gutmann, the yardstick for "civilization" was not technological development, rational thought, and the ethos of self-determination, but rather the preservation of a community that is and con-tinues to be characterized by stable and responsible relationships.* For instance, before the Europeans arrived, the Chagga had complex social networks. This may be seen in the cooperative organization of the irrigation systems, which featured miles and miles of canals that conducted water to banana planta-tions and fields. But it also manifested itself in institutions such as the con-joining of two individuals in "shield fellowships," as was practiced among tribal warriors, peer groups, and neighborhood groups. As a missionary, Gutmann witnessed how in the wake of colonization, the intrusion of Eu-ropean influences in eastern Africa led to the gradual destruction or dis-solution of these structures.

With his criticism of civilization, Gutmann was a child of his time. He was influenced among others by the theories of famous German philosopher and "social psychologist" (*Völkerpsychologe*) Wilhelm Wundt (1832–1920) and by the sociological studies of Ferdinand Tönnies (1855–1936), who pro-posed the distinction between *community* (*Gemeinschaft*) as an organic as-sociation of human beings and *society* (*Gesellschaft*) as an artificial com-munitizing construct.[8] Similarly, Gutmann differentiated between an organism (having organic ties) and an organization (a construct of artifi-cially created associations).[9] This appeal placed Gutmann and many other missionaries of his time squarely in the tradition of Romanticism, whose most famous intellectual representatives include Englishman Edmund Burke (1729–1797) and German Johann Gottfried Herder (1744–1803). Ro-manticism, which may be dated to the time period between 1790 and 1825, took a critical view of rationalist thought. It emphasized emotion as opposed to rationality, metaphysics as opposed to faith in science, and the value of

---

[7]Ibid., 56.
[8]In Gutmann's often not very consistent terminology, this distinction corresponds with the differ-ence between "organic ties" and "elective community."
[9]See Fiedler, *Christentum und afrikanische Kultur*, 37.

societal traditions as opposed to what it considered excessive belief in progress. After this movement gradually receded (by the end of the 1840s at the latest), a revival of romantic ideas took place in the form of the so-called neo-Romanticism at the end of the nineteenth century (after 1880).[10] However, the ideas of Romanticism continued to have an effect in various circles throughout the entire century, as may be seen for instance in the German use of the term *Volk* ("people" or "nation").

In German Romanticism, *people* was a key term. Whereas the term had hitherto been used in the sense of the "common people," i.e., as referring to the uneducated lower classes, Romanticism redefined the term. It was precisely among the common people (in the countryside), the hypothesis went, that the cultural traditions of the people have been preserved in an unadulterated form. It is no coincidence that at this time people like the Brothers Grimm began to collect German folk traditions, stories, myths, songs, and the like. Oral traditions, i.e., the stories, myths, songs, etc., that had only been preserved by oral communities but not written down before, were now accorded a high value. A striking contrast to the courtly and elitist culture of the eighteenth century with its etiquette, French as lingua franca of the refined society, and the emphasis on the fine arts! It was Johann Gottfried Herder who defined Romanticism's use of the term *people*. Herder saw every people as a delimitable entity, as an organism with its own individual characteristics such as its own language, a national character, and its own stories, songs, proverbs, or cultural institutions. Both linguistics and ethnology would later develop on the basis of Romanticism.[11]

The neo-Romantic movement, which began in the years following 1880, may be understood as a reaction to the increasing industrialization taking place at the end of the nineteenth century. Industrialization, technologization, urbanization, and rapidly increasing social change perceptibly altered

---

[10]F. Lampart, *Religion in Geschichte und Gegenwart*, 4th ed., s.v. "Romantik. I. Als Epochenbegriff."

[11]It already became clear during the late Romantic period that the term *people* is vulnerable to ideological exploitation, particularly after philosopher Johann Gottlieb Fichte (1762–1814) added a political dynamic to the term by declaring the German people to be an "ancient people" (*Urvolk*) and thereby giving expression to the idea of German superiority (in the context of the fight against Napoleon). After the Romantic era ended, the years after 1880 ushered in a neo-Romantic phase. At this time, the term *people* was redefined on the basis of the idea of race. Thus the individual character of a people was no longer seen as defined merely by culture and language but also biologically by the race of its members.

living conditions. In Germany, the so-called village church movement (*Dorf-kirchenbewegung*) sought to counteract this development. Here the preservation of rural customs and the emphasis on family ties and neighborly ties came to be associated with Christian ideas, since family and nationhood came to be seen as divine ordinances. At this time, contrasting pairs of binary opposites, such as "urban versus rural," "fleeting versus abiding," "artificial versus simple," became pervasive. Gutmann himself belonged to the village church movement. The youth movement (*Jugendbewegung*) was characterized by similar ideals. Calling for a life in harmony with and in nature, it attempted to live according to the ideals of purity and truth by promoting the celebration of folk music and particular festivals.

Adopting Tribal Cultural Traditions into the Framework of Creation Theology

What theological reasoning did Gutmann provide for his view of peoples and cultures? Gutmann's premise was that God had established the primordial ties in his order of creation. In other words, these ties constitute anthropological constants that may assume different cultural forms from one people to another while still comprising the basis for the "body politic" of each people or nation. To be created in the image of God (Gen 1:26-27) means to live in mutual responsibility within a system of primordial ties. Thus, for Gutmann, these ties predate the fall into sin (Gen 3) and are not compromised by it.[12] While they may be weakened or perverted, Jesus Christ as the Son of the Father not only restores them but also elevates, strengthens, and in so doing fulfils them. *Jesus Christ himself is the prototype of communality.* In terms of local tribal traditions, this means that Christ does not dissolve the ties already present within people groups, which occur in unique cultural and religious forms, such as those of the Chagga; instead, they are preserved and elevated to become an "eternal childship." They are appropriated and simultaneously transcended. *As a result, Gutmann believed that an integral part of mission work was to use, shape, and cultivate these ties; for him, missionaries needed to understand the type of communality of a people before they could relate the Christian faith to it.*

---

[12]Gutmann, "Urtümliche Bindungen und Sünde," 20-31.

As far as intercultural hermeneutics is concerned, the first implication of this is that the tribal traditions of various peoples are not measured by the default yardstick of European civilization and thereby dismissed as substandard. Rather, these tribal traditions are essentially considered to be superior to the alleged European civilization, since and to the extent that responsible communality structures have been preserved within them. In other words, the yardstick is not a particular cultural configuration (such as European civilization or European Christianity) but rather a transcultural social structure. The benchmark to gauge whether a culture conforms to or is proper to human nature is defined with reference to the framework of creation theology. This framework, it is claimed, establishes the basis for all human communities. The entire body politic of a people must be "internally" structured on this basis. Here Gutmann differentiated between civilization as the "world of auxiliary aids" (meaning science, technology, and modern administrative structures) and civilization as a corrosive factor, as exemplified by European civilization. Gutmann's critical verdict stated, "Civilized man is an entirely new type. He has lost his creaturely structure and lives disjointed from his own people."[13]

Gutmann viewed African peoples as having remained fundamentally more in line with God's order of creation and believed that this is what gives them their particular value. The cultural and religious elements of the tribal configurations thus come to comprise an indispensable medium by which the kingdom of God is established among human beings. To this end, the gospel appropriates these elements and raises them to a high level. *Only those customs that directly conflict with the gospel are to be abolished. Among these, Gutmann counts such practices as sacrificing to the dead, polygamy, and sorcery.* He sees many others (such as the chiefdom, drinking beer, circumcision, or paying bride prices) as *adiaphora*, i.e., as things neither commanded nor forbidden in Scripture, which one is free to keep or not.[14]

Gutmann thus rejected every type of mission work aiming at the conversion of individuals, for this would mean separating converts from their relational and social ties. This approach would be inappropriate, according to Gutmann. *Even if mission succeeds only in converting individuals at first,*

---

[13]Gutmann, *Freies Menschentum*, 27.
[14]Fiedler, *Christentum und afrikanische Kultur*, 29, 36.

from the start its aim must be to become a Volksmission, *a people's mission; that is to say, the aim must be to convert an entire ethnic communal association, since it is only in this way that the relationship structures remain intact and may be purified and reordered by the Christian gospel.* Mission must take the form of *Christianizing an entire people* (*Volkschristianisierung*), not so as to bring about an inauthentic Christianization but an authentic one, i.e., one that connects with the individual endowments of a people. The aim should not be merely to Christianize the people's morals in an outward fashion; rather, a distinctive Christianity is to come into being on the basis of the primordial ties present among the people. *In this way, the work of the missionaries reveals once more what is distinctive to the particular tribal culture in question; after all, the primordial ties are inherent within it on the basis of the order of creation.* The aim thus continues to be the Christianization of the people as a whole.

According to Gutmann, civilization leads to individualization, and individualization in turn leads to the disintegration of the community. Gutmann observed how this took place in eastern Africa, where the colonial influence became stronger and stronger during the first decade of the twentieth century. The law code introduced by the colonial powers recognized only the responsibility of the individual, not the significance of the group, i.e., of the clan, any longer. This was the first aspect. Second, he observed that the value of the individual was determined by his or her performance; that is to say, the individual was being economized. This in turn led to the economization of the ties within the group. Every individual is considered to be replaceable, which means that instead of being segmented and structured, the community becomes a crowd of (otherwise replaceable) individual monads.[15] All that ultimately matters is money. The thought progression thus goes as follows: civilization creates individuals who are considered to be autarchic beings, who are organized economically, and who form a society, which is viewed as a crowd of monads.

By comparison, tribal societies are very different, as demonstrated by the example of the Chagga. According to Gutmann, Chagga society was organized into three systems of ties, namely ties of *relationship* (the clan), spatial

---

[15]The term *crowd* as it is used here would need to be analyzed in greater detail. For instance, the 1895 book *Psychology of Crowds* by Frenchman Gustave Le Bon was very influential in this regard.

ties of the *neighborhood*, and finally chronological ties of *age groups*. In Christianizing a people, Gutmann's concern was to integrate the various entities or institutions of the people, i.e., the communal bonding structures, into the body of Christ. Gutmann attempted to identify Christian equivalents to them in order to replicate the networks of ties among the people (family, neighborhood, age groups) using such Christian terms as, first, *childship*, second, the *kingdom of God*, and, third, the *neighbor*. Concerning the first of these, when Jesus says, "Truly I tell you, unless you change and become like little children, you will never enter the kingdom of heaven" (Mt 18:3 NIV), Gutmann interprets this to mean that human beings experience their humanity by being entirely dependent on other human beings and living in relatedness to one another. Concerning the second, the kingdom of God also manifests itself in these ties. As Gutmann said, "the kingdom of God exists in the form of the primary construct of divine indwelling in the world of human beings— the primordial ties—and also in the form of the supreme construct of divine revelation—the Son of God."[16] Concerning the third, the neighbor, the kingdom of God exists both within us and between us. According to Gutmann, the primordial ties are *the* points of contact of the gospel. In terms of the doctrine of the church, Gutmann's structural analogy between structures among the people and structures in the church should not come as a surprise after what was said before. To apply this christologically, for Gutmann both reconciliation and the work of the Spirit do not lead to the creation of a new basis; rather, they deepen and ennoble and purify the primordial ties. The following illustration of circumcision will serve to clarify this principle.

Gutmann himself saw the circumcision of both girls and boys as an *adiaphoron*, as something neither commanded nor forbidden in Scripture. However, a number of the African leaders in his congregations—elders and teachers—viewed circumcision as unscriptural and rejected it as a backward practice. When Gutmann had to leave Tanzania from 1920 to 1925 because of a stipulation to this effect in the Treaty of Versailles, the African leaders decided to prohibit circumcision. They attempted to put the prohibition into effect in 1923.[17] This may be seen as *an inner-African struggle between the*

---

[16]As cited in Hoekendijk, *Kirche und Volk*, 157.

[17]In this issue, I side with Fiedler, *Christentum und afrikanische Kultur*, 76ff. Those who decided to circumcise their children regardless were not excommunicated as such but rather "thrust aside."

progressive teachers, who were the de facto leaders of the congregations, and the conservatives within the congregations, represented by the majority of the elders. The latter were, however, unable to prevail against the former, since these had the advantage of having been educated in the schools (keyword: mission schools).

After Gutmann's return in 1925, a confrontation took place between the separately convening white missionaries—led by Gutmann—and the African elders and teachers. Gutmann was of the opinion that the practice of circumcision should continue, that it had nothing to do with the gospel, that it did not warrant church discipline, and that if it were abandoned, it would lead to further decay of the communal structures. In the compromise that was reached, circumcision was neither prohibited nor permitted, but it was stipulated that the congregations would strive to do away with this custom.[18] Afterward, children continued to be circumcised. However, since the practice was left up to the family, the communal character of this ceremony ceased to apply.[19] This example shows that Gutmann's understanding of the original traditions of the people collided with the attempts of African leaders to dispense with older traditions. Thus in this instance, Gutmann's thought model had a conservative effect, and as a result, he acted so as to restrict even *such changes* within the African tribal traditions of the Chagga that were *considered desirable* (by some people).

In an attempt to pick up on tribal cultural traditions, Gutmann tried to adopt certain elements of the initiation rites and to integrate them into confirmation classes and the confirmation ceremony. In the traditional rituals, two boys at a time were made to lie on the ground following the circumcision procedure. A circle was drawn around them to signify that they had been symbolically assigned to each other. The association between the two was a lifelong relationship of mutual aid. While Gutmann did not adopt circumcision, he did adopt the practice of assigning two people to each other—constituting the so-called shield fellowships. Many people welcomed

The names of the families were read out in the Sunday announcements (78). Whereas the white missionaries of the Presbyterian Church of Scotland Mission became involved in the controversy surrounding the circumcision of girls among the Kikuyu between 1925 and 1930 (the missionaries rejected the practice), the missionaries in the Kilimanjaro area remained neutral.

[18]Fiedler, *Christentum und afrikanische Kultur*, 79.

[19]Ibid., 82. In the 1970s, the circumcision of girls became less and less common.

the move. Two hours of confirmation classes were held each week; in addition, the two-person shield fellowships met for an hour on Saturdays to help other people in the congregation. At first, the shield fellowships consisted of only two people, but then Gutmann also formed four-person and six-person shield fellowships for reasons of practicality. Now, in the tribal religions, solidarity was limited to the defined relationship of the shield fellowship. In contrast, Gutmann tried to have his people foster solidarity toward everybody (the "neighbor" in the Christian sense), in accordance with the gospel. However, for a long time the majority of the congregation members refused to help those to whom they *had not been assigned*. In this case, the missionary worked tenaciously—in accordance with his understanding of the gospel as a transcultural value—to wear down the resistance of the African Christians.[20] By this time, age classes and shield fellowships had already ceased to be part of the societal reality of the Chagga people as a whole (although the older congregation members had still been initiated this way in their youth). Gutmann, however, in a certain sense reintroduced them in the Christian congregations (which still constituted a minority), although he did not form large age classes but only small shield fellowships (he was clearly being selective).[21] The reason for the acceptance of this structure by the Chagga Christians was the societal function that this newly minted "tradition" served in its capacity as a combination of African and European elements (confirmation classes).

In neighboring Mamba, missionary Georg Fritze took a different approach from that of Gutmann. Fritze wanted to reinstitute the initiation of entire age classes. The second-to-last traditional initiation camp took place in 1913, lasting two months, followed by the last one of its kind, a two-week camp that took place in 1914. In this way, the traditional practice came to an end. No further initiations of this nature took place in Mamba from 1915 onward. In 1930—fifteen years later—Fritze attempted to reinstitute the practice in a Christian garb. Missionaries, elders, and congregation members backed him in his attempt. To this end, Fritze began his confirmation classes by having his forty-one male confirmation students aged between fourteen and twenty meet for fourteen days at a group retreat held in a camp outside

---

[20]Later, Gutmann applied the shield fellowship concept also to schools.
[21]Fiedler, *Christentum und afrikanische Kultur*, 84-85.

the village. Thereafter, they met first for one day and night each week, then
every two weeks, and finally for a second two-week retreat, followed by
confirmation. In so doing, Fritze picked up on a number of elements from
the tribal cultural traditions. Klaus Fiedler summarizes this as follows:

> After a festive worship service, the boys formed a procession and entered the
> camp. They approached the camp on a path bordered by draecene palms. At
> the entrance, they had to pass through a six-and-a-half-foot-deep hole filled
> with water, and then jump over a fire to get into camp. The boys had dug the
> hole the previous day, and when the boys asked Fritze why they were digging
> the hole, he answered that they would bury an elephant there the next day.
> Yakobo Lyimba [a teacher] received them in the camp, saying, "Welcome to
> the house of the age classes. You left your childhood behind you in this water.
> Here you will learn to live as a Christian and a warrior. Be brave, be manly,
> and be strong." Then Fritze held an impressive speech in which he explained
> what it all meant. The water was supposed to remind the boys of their bap-
> tisms; it signified that they would now enter a new phase of the spiritual life.
> They were to leave everything that was sinful or of no use (the old elephant)
> behind them or burn it in the fire, and in so doing prepare themselves for a
> new life. Life in camp was strictly regulated. Physical work, exercise, and
> confirmation classes were the order of the day. The evenings were reserved
> for *mapfundo*, instruction, which was provided the same way it had been in
> the traditional initiation camps.[22]

Quite obviously, Fritze was combining European elements like night
vigils (boy scouts), trumpet signals, and exercising with tribal cultural elements such as the initiation camp outside the village, the "liminal" status of
the initiates (Victor Turner)—a kind of in-between phase between childhood
and adulthood—the symbolism of dying to the community (passing through
the water), reintegration in the form of a type of rebirth (the confirmation
worship service), and many others. These examples reflect the dynamic between the white missionaries, the indigenous Christians, and the leaders
among the latter. Many attempts by conservative missionaries to retain or
even revive the older traditions of the tribal cultures were met with resistance on the part of the African Christians. This happened, for instance,
when Fritze attempted to cut the boys' hair before they entered the initiation

---

[22]Ibid., 86. Italics indicate edited passages.

camp. It is likely that the African Christians felt that such practices were too close to the religious traditions they had left behind them when they converted to the Christian faith. This is understandable on a psychological level, since the new identity was still somewhat fragile and needed to be protected. Meanwhile, Fritze's experiment was terminated after a little less than ten years, following the fourth cohort. Ostensibly, the elders opposed Fritze's practice of allowing uncircumcised boys to participate in the camp; however, one might also induce that the elders and teachers were feeling threatened because the loyalty of the age classes to Fritze was weakening their power and fortifying his own.[23]

Overall, we may state that the issue of preserving traditional structures and of the necessity of social change affected both the African Christians and the white missionaries. Simplistic explanations are unhelpful here—the Africans certainly did not view social and cultural change as a threat only; rather, depending on the individual social positions, some at least also saw such change as an opportunity. The missionaries certainly did not intend summarily to abolish African culture; rather, they were the ones trying to preserve or even revive certain cultural traditions. In the case study provided above, the process of interaction was a very complicated one, and simply labeling the participants as active or passive does not do justice to the complexity of the situation.

Do Religions and Cultures Die Out? A Provisional Appraisal

Under Zinzendorf, mission was conducted in the *horizon of eschatology*, i.e., in view of the circumstance that the kingdom of God could come at any time, with the result that the aim of the mission was to gather firstfruits in a somewhat improvised manner. In contrast, Gutmann located and established mission in a *protological* context—that is to say, not from the perspective of the end of all things (eschaton), but conversely from the perspective of the order of creation as represented by primordial ties. Whereas for Zinzendorf and for the proponents of cultural Protestantism, the issue of *tribal cultures* was of no significance theologically, Gutmann considered

---

[23]Ibid., 88. The elders also complained that structuring the classes in this way was encouraging the boys to become arrogant.

tribal cultures to be the fundamental point of contact for the gospel.[24] Whereas Zinzendorf saw the *church* as essentially consisting of the sum of individual converts, in the model of cultural Protestantism the church is more of an institution of education, while for Gutmann church develops out of a body politic. The church and the body politic should become one and the same thing, with the newness of the kingdom of God consisting of the transformation of existing ties into a service of love to the neighbor— whoever that may be. Whereas it is legitimate to speak in Zinzendorf's case of individualism in terms of converting individuals, in Gutmann's case one may speak of individualism in terms of Christianizing a people.[25]

Let us recap. Whereas the ennoblement model is oriented toward an *evolutionary model of human civilization*, Gutmann's indigenization model, being oriented toward primordial ties, is diametrically opposed to the former and aims at the *restoration of divine orders of creation*. Both models operate with an abstract understanding of culture, with the former being predicated on *certain spiritual values* (individuality, freedom, independent thought) and the latter on *certain structures* (family ties and neighborly ties, responsibility, the preservation of tradition). The consequence is that the ennoblement model aims at the development of a certain cultural formation, namely that of modern European civilization, while Gutmann's indigenization model aims at preserving the *plurality of cultural individualities* and at anchoring the Christian values in indigenous Christianities within the medium of this plurality. The ennoblement model aims to use education as a means, operating with an *elitist view of culture*, whereas Gutmann's model is oriented toward *ethnic givens* and sees their value in the extent that people act in responsibility toward the community.

Even though Gutmann's concern was to preserve the individuality of indigenous cultures, there is something about his model that smacks of paternalism, since it is the missionary coming from the outside who tries to influence the cultural processes etically—*even against the will of the indigenous*

---

[24]Whereas Zinzendorf was thinking in terms of eschatology, cultural Protestantism took an evolutionary position, while Gutmann's indigenization approach was a protological one.

[25]The concept of a "people" takes on considerable significance here in the sense that the church comes into being not only by the preaching of the gospel and the celebration of the sacraments any longer, but now also by the harnessing of the primordial ties already present among the respective people—i.e., within the "body politic" of the people—and by their infusion with the Spirit.

people. Consider, for example, the role of women among the Chagga: Gutmann complained that during his absence, the Chagga voted to permit women to hold leadership roles even in the church. He claimed that this was contrary both to the culture of the Chagga and to female nature.[26]

This example clearly demonstrates the problem of Gutmann's "people" concept: (1) According to this model, it is imperative to protect and preserve the cultures of tribes and people groups. While this might sound pretty good initially, the question remains: Does this model do justice to the fact that cultures are constantly changing? (2) Does the way women are viewed not show that Gutmann denied the validity of certain innovations because he insisted on using older cultural patterns as his yardstick? *Does the postulate of a national spirit, a national body politic, various national agencies, and the like not entail the image of a timeless cultural entity?* And does this definition not establish the basis for distinguishing between healthy and sick cultures, between national cultures that are "natural" and those that are "unnatural"? And what does this mean for those individuals who refuse to submit to the cultural patterns, values, and conceptions of the majority? What does it mean for marginalized groups, minorities, young people, the oppressed, and, last but not least, for women? Is it not legitimate to conclude that this *understanding of people groups and cultures is highly vulnerable to ideological exploitation?* (3) Gutmann distinguished between unstructured companionableness, which he rejected, and the community of a people group, which he considered imperative. Freedom is constituted in configuring primordial ties so as to conform to the gospel, not in dissolving them. But what does this mean for the relationship between the individual and the community? Is it not so that the community then becomes absolute, to the point that the individual is ultimately unable to defend against it? (4) In addition, the hypothesis about the nature of the culture of a people begs the question: What exactly does the identity of a

---

[26]Gutmann stated that even in the case of Lutheran congregations, "leaders were selected by way of the organization and not by way of tapping into organic feeder groups. In every single scenario, this would mean laying the ax to the root of true Africanness and surrendering the soul of Africa to the civilization template. Limiting the influence of women to their own sex would mean inhibiting the flow of forces in the circulatory system of the body politic; conversely, directly involving women in the outward control of the affairs of a collective would mean dishonoring their own nature. Women rule indirectly." Gutmann, *Freies Menschentum*, 32.

culture consist in, and who gets to define and decide it? Who is entitled to the prerogative to analyze cultures, people groups, or communities?[27] Is it the educated and the powerful? If so, what interests do they have? Could it not also be the weak? Is it possible and permissible for the majority to assume this function? Or can that only be the case for an elite group among the indigenous people? Who defines what comprises identity, for whose benefit, and with which power-political calculations?

---

[27]With regard to the German mission movement of the nineteenth and early twentieth centuries, historian Thorsten Altena notes, "It is remarkable that the frequent use of the term 'culture' . . . is offset by the fact that nobody ever bothered to define it." Thorsten Altena, *"Ein Häuflein Christen mitten in der Heidenwelt des dunklen Erdteils": Zum Selbst- und Fremdverständnis protestantischer Missionare im kolonialen Afrika 1884–1918* (Münster: Waxmann, 2003), 99.

20

The Appropriation Model

The Example of "Intuitive" Inculturations

Many of the examples we have considered thus far show reflexive processes taking place. The missionaries served as the observers; they were the ones who saw cultural and religious parallels and differences, evaluated other religions as heathen or demonic, or tried to replace them. Others paid less attention to these religions and cultures, focusing on individual conversions instead, which they saw as a matter of the heart. Other missionaries regarded certain cultures and religions as underdeveloped, as occupying a low position on the scale of the development of humanity, and as being in need of ennoblement, which was to be effected by mission, education, and civilization in general. Others again believed that a primordial God-given ordering is present in tribal cultures, one that needs to be preserved and filled with Christian content. Now, in each of these cases, the leading role (or at least the more comprehensive role) was played by the missionaries; the understanding of the "older" Christians was seen as the yardstick that established what it meant to be a true believer, a true church, or a true Christian, not the understanding of the recent converts.[1] Meanwhile, during the last few decades, missionary

---

[1] The protagonists in each case are (believed to be) either the missionaries themselves—which is tantamount to self-deception, as we have seen—or both missionaries and indigenous people interacting with each other to determine power balances, competency, and social position. The missionaries contribute the new message and also such things as new technology, money, education, and international connections; the indigenous people in turn contribute local knowledge, knowledge of indigenous languages, cultural and religious customs, authority in social configurations of tribes and clans, the trust of regional leaders, etc. When seen against the background of the complexity of these relationships, various interpretive models of such processes of inculturation are of very little value. This was the case, for instance, when one assumes the primacy of the biblical message, or conversely of the religiocultural context, or of a combination between

agencies have increasingly espoused a different model, one that reverses this relationship: it is not the missionaries who are acting as such; instead, the recipient cultures are seen as the actors, as actors who actively appropriate the gospel for themselves.[2] When compared to the term *assimilation*, the term *appropriation* has the advantage that it does not *stipulate the manner* in which the process of appropriation takes place. In contrast, the term *assimilation* would imply an approximation, i.e., A becoming similar to B. This of course begs the question: What is B? To whom or what should A become similar? After all, the similarity could only be "measured" by using either a relatively stable cultural formation or a defined form of Christianity as the yardstick.[3]

As far as the broader subject matter is concerned, it is crucial to note that the setting of inculturation processes is very diverse. One must begin by differentiating between those inculturation processes that take place within the context of existing churches and those that do not. Existing churches project their particular unique characteristics into the process, such as in the case of the Roman Catholic Church, which hardly compromises when it comes to its hierarchy (the priestly office, celibacy, ordination) or its ordinance (order of the mass), although it has begun to adopt cultural elements in the form of certain rites ever since the late 1960s.[4] For Orthodox churches, the

---

the two. This model and others like it are unhelpful, since they do not address the real problem: the operative understanding of culture.

[2] Birgit Meyer uses the term *appropriation*. She is correct in her criticism that terms like *acculturation, cultural contact,* or *syncretism* continue to reflect the conception of cultures as relatively homogenous units. Birgit Meyer, "Beyond Syncretism: Translation and Diabolization in the Appropriation of Protestantism in Africa," in Charles Stewart and Rosalind Shaw, eds., *Syncretism/Anti-Syncretism: The Politics of Religious Synthesis* (London: Routledge, 1994), 45-68, quotation drawn from 45-46.

[3] Thus the term *assimilation* presupposes an understanding of cultures as relatively homogenous entities. However, if one defines cultures as open configurations in a constant state of flux, then the issue of *assimilation* becomes redundant.

[4] In the case of the Roman Catholic Church, it would be legitimate to state that ever since the papacy of John Paul II, the liturgical and canonical forms of expression deriving from the European history of tradition are being increasingly seen as an own "culture" and are being mandated also for other continents and contexts. This tendency continued unabated during the papacy of Benedict XVI. See Stefan Silber, "Inkulturation und Befreiung in der Politik des Vatikan," in "Die Befreiung der Kulturen: Der Beitrag Juan Luis Segundos zur Theologie der inkulturierten Evangelisierung" (PhD diss., University of Würzburg, 2001), 152-75, especially 161-62, where Silber refers to the 1994 publication of the Sacred Congregation for Divine Worship, "The Roman Liturgy and Inculturation," which only provides limited latitude for cultural adaptation.

form of the liturgy is essentially nonnegotiable, whereas for Protestant churches, the respective cultural, confessional, and denominational background needs to be taken into account. All of this leaves little "wiggle room" for inculturation.

A Theoretical Model: Leonardo Boff

In the face of such limitations, theologians like Leonardo Boff have pointed out that the missionaries are not the ones who adapt the message of the gospel to a certain context, nor is it the church or some particular form of Christian religiocultural configuration; *on the contrary, the indigenous, non-Christian cultures appropriate the gospel for themselves.* In so doing, Boff rejects the tendency to view foreign cultures as passive, malleable masses but sees them as the real actors in the inculturation process instead: cultural formations appropriate elements of the biblical message (or of the Christian praxis which they observe in others) in their own unique way, and in so doing they also appropriate—in the best case—the gospel. According to Leonardo Boff, the *cultures* are the ones who "assimilate" the gospel.[5] Thus on the one hand, by making such programmatic statements as "the Gospel does not identify itself *with* the cultures, but rather *in* the cultures," Boff deemphasizes the subjectivity of the gospel.[6] On the other hand, he clearly emphasizes the active role of the culture in the process of inculturation, stating,

> That is to say: The permanent and foundational datum is culture. Culture has always been shaped by revelation, the Gospel, and God. As soon as the societal bearers of a culture bring it into contact with the positivity of faith and the Gospel . . . , it appropriates [faith] and expresses it, using the range of codices to which it has access.[7]

As a result, a dialectic process takes place, which one might describe as a "double osmosis," in which the culture changes due to the contact with the gospel and in which the gospel enters into a relationship with the basic

---

[5]Leonardo Boff, *Gott kommt früher als der Missionar: Neuevangelisierung für eine Kultur des Lebens und der Freiheit*, trans. Horst Goldstein (Düsseldorf, Germany: Patmos Verlag, 1991), 52.
[6]Ibid.
[7]Ibid., 57.

patterns of the culture.[8] In other words, a number of subjects relate to one another in the process of inculturation: on an anthropological level, it is humans with their cultural conditionality and limitations; on a theological level, it is the gospel and the cultures, both of which are seen as God's doing. The intent behind this approach is to maintain the equality of all cultures before the gospel. Latin American liberation theologian Paulo Suess (b. 1938) therefore states that the "Gospel is equidistant from all cultures."[9] The strength of this model of thought undoubtedly consists in the inability to distinguish between the sender, the message, and the recipients in the process of inculturation, which one generally does when one sees inculturation as the transfer of a fixed message from one context into another. *However, the real problem of this approach is that it is difficult to imagine how "the gospel" is to be described apart from a specific cultural instantiation. How is it possible to conceive of the gospel as a direct object when one conceives of it in a "pure form," as it were?*[10] How would such a "pure," i.e., transcultural, gospel be defined? And, above all, who would define it? This dilemma becomes evident when one attempts conversely to determine what comprises the essence of such a gospel. We will return to this question at a later stage.

The example of Isaiah Shembe, which we shall presently discuss, will show that such appropriation processes, which Boff considers from a theoretical aspect, in practice most often take place intuitively. When this

---

[8] It is evident that Boff's thinking is based on the Thomistic model, which states, *gratia non tollit, sed perficit naturam*—grace does not destroy nature but perfects it. Accordingly, Boff sees human cultures as a work of God in the sense of a *praeparatio evangelica*.

[9] Stefan Silber, "Typologie der Inkulturationsbegriffe: Vier Aporien; Eine Streitschrift für einen neuen Begriff in einer notwendigen Debatte," *Jahrbuch für Kontextuelle Theologien 97* (1997): 124. For more on Suess's theology of inculturation, see Markus Büker, *Befreiende Inkulturation—Paradigma christlicher Praxis: Die Konzeptionen von Paulo Suess und Diego Irarrázaval im Kontext indigener Aufbrüche in Lateinamerika* (Freiburg, Switzerland: Universitätsverlag, 1999).

[10] To be sure, Juan Carlos Scannone, speaking of "faith" instead of the "gospel," says the following: "Between . . . two inculturated views of faith, e.g. between the European and the Latin American views of faith, faith itself constitutes in a sense the primary and normative 'magnetic field' which transcends both cultures and both inculturated theologies to the extent that faith 'incarnates' itself in both. In this way, faith can promote, direct, standardize, and evaluate from within the exchange of knowledge between the old and the newly formulated inculturated theology." Juan Carlos Scannone, *Weisheit und Befreiung* (Düsseldorf, Germany: Patmos, 1992), 75. Meanwhile, this theory does not solve the problem of who gets to define what "faith" and "praxis" are.

happens, inculturation is not the result of contemplation but rather something that takes place in the life of a human being who "finds herself" located between various religiocultural configurations. Often (from an analytical perspective) unanticipated reciprocal interaction takes place between the religiocultural configurations. When it takes place in the lives of religious people, such interaction finds expression in the form of their *dreams and visions. From their own perspective, something is happening to these people (caused by spirits, ancestors, gods, God, apparitions, or whatever the label may be), which prompts them to act in certain ways (e.g., to perform rituals, utter revelations, find a ritual place, understand the causes of an illness, design role and objects).* Such persons and events in particular often have such an intense effect on their surroundings that they result in the founding of religious movements that can gain several million followers within the space of a few decades. This is evident in the case of a number of AICs.

INTUITIVE INCULTURATION: THE EXAMPLE OF THE SHEMBE CHURCH (NBC)

When I label inculturation as an "intuitive" event, I use the term *intuitive* to speak of religious leaders who implement ritual innovations, justifying the implementation on the basis of special encounters with transcendent powers (to use as generalized a term as possible)[11]—usually in the form of dreams or visions. This then leads to the formation or formulation of religious traditions (the founding of communities with a particular set of rituals, stories told about the prophet, etc.) that are passed down among their followers. We will now proceed to illustrate this using the example of the Nazareth Baptist Church (NBC), founded by the prophet Isaiah Shembe (1867–1935) in southern Africa. Thousands of similar examples may be found in sub-Saharan Africa. Many of these prophetic movements lead to the founding of distinct religious configurations, while many others result in the formation

---

[11]Naturally, from the perspective of religious studies or mission studies, this term could also be criticized as being too "Eurocentric," too "Christian," or what have you. I would certainly agree with such criticism in the sense of a hermeneutic reserve, although I do believe that the term is eminently suitable for our topic of discussion, even if—and I will gladly repeat this commonplace to be on the safe side—the understanding of "transcendence" varies widely from one culture or religious configuration to another.

of African Independent Churches[12] or African Instituted Churches.[13] The
Nazareth Baptist Church, often referred to as the Shembe Church, is one of
the larger AICs and has a following of approximately four million people in
South Africa today.[14] The church is, however, currently divided into four
factions. We are unable to elaborate on this development at this point. Instead, we will concentrate on the founding of this church and on the significance of its founder. Researchers interpret Isaiah Shembe's legacy very differently. For instance, Gerhardus C. Oosthuizen describes it as "nativism,"[15]
while Hans-Jürgen Becken[16] sees the Shembe church as a thoroughly
Christian phenomenon.[17]

---

[12]We need to distinguish the AICs from the so-called Ethiopian movement, which began when
groups of blacks broke away from mission churches in Africa (such as the Lutheran Bapedi
Church, which split off from the Berlin Mission in 1889, or the Africa Church, which split off
from the Anglican Church in 1889). The name of the movement is derived from the Ethiopian
Church, which split off from the Wesleyan Church in 1892. These churches have for the most
part preserved the European profile of the praxis of faith. This is clearly a different phenomenon
from the churches founded in the course of the Zionist movement, which were founded by indigenous prophet figures and have a much stronger "African" character. This movement takes
its name in turn from the Afro-American Christian Catholic Apostolic Church in Zion, United
States, which maintained contact to such churches at the beginning of the twentieth century.

[13]Other variants of these names are African Initiated Churches or African Indigenous Churches.

[14]Another large AIC is headquartered in the Limpopo province of South Africa: the Zion Christian Church, founded by Engenas Lekganyane.

[15]Gerhardus C. Oosthuizen, "Isaiah Shembe and the Zulu World View," *History of Religion* 8
(1968): 1-30; Oosthuizen, "Diviner-Prophet Parallels in the African Independent and Traditional Churches and Traditional Religion," in Gerhardus C. Oosthuizen and Irving Hexam, eds.,
Empirical Studies of African Independent/Indigenous Churches (Lewiston, ME: E. Mellen, 1992),
163-94; Gerhardus C. Oosthuizen et al., eds., *Afro-Christian Religion and Healing in Southern
Africa* (Lewiston, ME: E. Mellen, 1989); Gerhardus C. Oosthuizen and Irving Hexam, eds., *Afro-
Christian Religion at the Grassroots in Southern Africa* (Lewiston, ME: E. Mellen, 1991). After
surveying forty-two followers of the Shembe Church, Oosthuizen summarizes, "The messianism
of the Bible is centered around Jesus Christ; the messianism of the Nazarites is centered around
the Shembes. Jesus Christ is not proclaimed there. Rather, he serves as an example of the meaning of salvation for Shembe. If this movement is to count as Christian—those surveyed denied
this—then the person of Jesus Christ and his work should take center stage. But this is a post-
Christian movement. One should not refer to it as Christian." Gerhardus C. Oosthuizen, "Wie
christlich ist die Kirche Shembes?," *Evangelische Missionszeitschrift* 31 (1974): 140-41. For more
on religious symbolism among the Zulu, see especially Axel-Ivar Berglund, *Zulu Thought Patterns and Symbolism* (London: C. Hurst, 1976).

[16]Hans-Jürgen Becken, *Wo der Glaube noch jung ist: Afrikanische Unabhängige Kirchen im Südlichen
Afrika* (Erlangen, Germany: Verlag der Mission Erlangen, 1985); Becken, "Die Entstehung einer
prophetischen Großkirche in Südafrika," *Zeitschrift für Missionswissenschaft* 18 (1992): 99-108;
Becken, "Isaiah Shembe und der Heilige Geist," *Zeitschrift für Missionswissenschaft* 20 (1994):
145-52; and Becken, "Christliche Kirchen und Bewegungen im neuen Südafrika," *Zeitschrift für
Missionswissenschaft* 20 (1994): 19-26.

[17]See also B. E. Ngobese, "The Concept of the Trinity Among the AmaNazaretha," in Oosthuizen

This debate will need to be ongoing. At any rate, playing a very significant role for the life and expansion of this church are the topic of healing, the work of the Holy Spirit, its ritual manifestations, and its communal character throughout.[18] Western theologians will tend to view the praxis and doctrine of this church critically and question its orthodoxy, especially when Shembe people say things like, "Shembe is the Holy Spirit!" or when they refuse to use the title "Son of God" for Jesus Christ. Yet whether this truly comprises heterodox teaching will only gradually "become clear" once the critics begin to take the religiocultural characteristics of this church seriously, without prematurely passing judgment on it.[19] We will proceed by first sketching out some of the characteristics of this church and then using these to aid us as we reflect on issues regarding intuitive inculturation.

Isaiah Shembe: The "Umbrella Thorn Tree from Zululand"

The followers of Isaiah Shembe use many honorary titles for him, such as the (shade-giving) "umbrella thorn tree from Zululand," the "horned viper of grace," the "Lord of Ekuphakameni," or the "liberator of the cripple and the oppressed."[20] Who was this man who would become the founder of what is today one of the largest independent churches in southern Africa? Isaiah Mdliwamafa Shembe was born around the year 1867 in the vicinity of Giant's Castle in the Natal Colony in southern Africa. As a child, he lived with his family in an area farmed by whites. He is reported to have had dreams and visions and also the gift of healing from an early age. The young Shembe was initially associated with a Wesleyan church but left when conflict broke out after he demanded that people should take off their shoes when they entered the church, celebrate Holy Communion at night, conduct

---

et al., *Empirical Studies*, 91-109; and Reiner Mahlke, "Nazareth Baptist Church (Shembe Church)," in *Prophezeiung und Heilung: Das Konzept des Heiligen Geistes in Afrikanischen Unabhängigen Kirchen (AIC) in Südafrika* (Berlin: D. Reimer, 1997), 194-215.

[18]Hans-Jürgen Becken, *Theologie der Heilung: Das Heilen in den Afrikanischen Unabhängigen Kirchen in Südafrika* (Hermannsburg, Germany: Missionshandlung, 1972).

[19]In this respect, the empathetic exegesis of Hans-Jürgen Becken is a good example for how such doctrines, which seem rather heterodox from a European perspective, may be deciphered by means of an applied intercultural hermeneutics. For more on the subject, see Edley J. Moodley, *Shembe, Ancestors, and Christ: A Christological Inquiry with Missiological Implications* (Eugene, OR: Pickwick, 2008).

[20]Becken, "Die Entstehung," 100. Ekuphakameni is a place in the vicinity of Durban where the headquarters of the Shembe Church is located.

baptisms in the river, and not use the churches for concerts. He joined a Baptist church for a while, where he served as a preacher. Allegedly, he was struck by lightning during a storm, during which time he received a word from God that he was being sent to the land of the East. It is said that he later received the following message:

> I am sending you to my suffering people, who have naked hips, to free them from their slavery. Tell them that they are to serve me, the God of their ancestors, and to keep the vows of the Nazarites: They are not to drink beer or wine, they are not to cut their hair or their beard, or use medicine, and they are to keep the Sabbath day holy; on this day they shall do no work and light no fire in their houses.[21]

Shembe responded by leaving his wives and going about as a missionary, healing the sick, and driving out demons. When people converted to the Christian faith, he referred them to the local congregations of various denominations.

On July 22, 1906, Shembe was baptized in a river by the Baptist pastor W. M. Lushisha and received the name Isaiah. He was ordained shortly afterward. From 1908 onward, Shembe was active in the area of Durban. Here a church settlement was constructed, called Ekuphakameni, in the vicinity of Durban. Another important site for this church is the mountain Nhlangakazi, located a little less than twenty miles from the church center. Here Shembe is believed to have received his calling, which the church tradition tells as follows:

> When Shembe was in the area of Maphumulo to conduct marriage negotiations for Jan Dambuza's son, the Word of God came to him at night: "I am sending you to the mountain Nhlangakazi; there you must pray, and I will meet you." The next morning, when he asked the people about this mountain, they showed him a high table mountain and said: "There are dangerous wild animals up there; one should not go there." So Shembe decided in his heart to go to his homeland instead, for the Drakensberg Mountains are even higher, but not as dangerous. So he got on the train. But the locomotive came to a stop at Botha's Hill, and it only started moving again once he had disembarked. As soon as he reached the top of Nhlangankazi, he experienced visions. A lion promised him power, spirits promised him wealth; but he turned

---

[21]Quoted in ibid., 103.

them all down. After twelve days of fasting and prayer, God came to Shembe and made a covenant with him; he fed him with Holy Communion, anointed him with oil, instructed him to build an ark of the covenant, and sent him to gather his church on earth.[22]

What we are told is that during the night, Shembe is directed to go to a certain place, but he only finds it by "coincidence" (the train comes to a stop), which is interpreted as a sign of divine guidance. The vision that is told sounds like an African adaptation of elements of the story of the temptation of Jesus, with a strikingly parallel narrative structure—first the temptation, then the sending. The call to construct an ark of the covenant clearly illustrates that this is a case of justifying ritual innovations on the basis of divine revelations in dreams and visions; in this sense, they are "intuitive" and not "reflexive" (as was the case in the models we have described thus far). In terms of church ritual, two festive seasons take on special significance. One of these takes place in July every year: an approximately three-week-long meeting takes place on the mountain Nhlangakazi—a kind of pilgrimage, actually, with many ritual actions, including *dances*.[23] Shembe performed

---

[22]Quoted in ibid., 106.

[23]Shembe introduced dancing into the ritual life of this church. The mission churches frowned on dancing and prohibited it. However, this is not to say that the church members imitated traditional Zulu dances; rather, this was an innovation in that, unlike the Zulu, the Shembe dancers *closed ranks and danced only two steps* forward and then back again. Also, he introduced *new clothing*—a white shirt (Zulu tradition) and a kilt, a knee-length skirt corresponding to the parade uniforms of Scottish Highland regiments. These regiments had been stationed in South Africa as the spearhead of British colonial power for around one hundred years and were famous and feared for their fighting abilities. Shembe had presumably seen such troops and their dances in his youth and then later adapted them. The *colors of the Scottish kilts*, white, red, and black, corresponded to *the basic colors* most commonly used in African traditions as well. Yet Shembe adapted the colors, clothing, and dances in his own unique way, which *assuredly also constitute an* (either conscious or unconscious) *attempted ritual appropriation of power* by taking on the articles of clothing and colors of the powerful and dreaded opponents. For more on this point, see the analyses in Andreas Heuser, "Die sakralisierte (Kon-)Version eines Kriegstanzes," in *Shembe, Gandhi und die Soldaten Gottes: Wurzeln der Gewaltfreiheit in Südafrika* (Münster: Waxmann, 2003), 224-37. *To sum up, ritual processes of appropriation are often motivated by the desire to appropriate the power of those whose culture and religion are foreign.* This must be emphasized over against a culturalistic, apolitical reading of religiocultural symbolisms.

At the same time, Shembe subjected this dancing tradition to an inversion, such that the dance is no longer warrior-like but rather oriented toward prayer, encouragement, and peaceable actions. Heuser provides an apposite summary: "By their Scottish and Zulu dress, the *Nazarites* reveal themselves to outsiders as a community that resists every kind of resignation and apathy. The dance-like movements reassign symbols of war and destruction in a collective demonstration of religio-ecclesiastical determination, *for Shembe preserved the dance, a characteristically expressive form of the African understanding of life, for use in the Christian worship service.* The

the first of these pilgrimages in 1916. During this time, people live in huts made of leaves and in tents.[24] Today, several hundred thousand people participate every year; it is one of the most substantial pilgrimages in South Africa today.[25] The other festive season takes place in January every year, mainly in the church settlement of Ekuphakameni itself. We will turn our attention to the symbolism of these festive seasons at a later point. At this point we will consider Shembe's healing ministry.

Current reports about Shembe's healing ministry might cause disconcertment among Western observers. For instance, consider the following example, drawn from a tract written in Zulu by an author closely associated with the milieu of the Nazareth Baptist Church, as translated in the research of Hans-Jürgen Becken:

> As Shembe was traveling, a man came to him and told him that his wife was childless. He explained: "Every time she is pregnant, she dreams of a big bird with an enormous beak, and then she suffers a miscarriage." The prophet entered with him into the house in which the woman was sleeping, and he commanded that the inside of the hut be plastered with fresh cow dung. This happened at the time during which the bird usually came. After Shembe had prayed, he spent the night in the hut; and when the bird came during the night, Shembe captured and killed it. The woman recovered and gave birth to children.[26]

Overall, one would be justified in saying that the church founded by Shembe incorporates many elements of the traditional Zulu religion. In Shembe's view, in this manner the God of the Bible, who is also the god of the Zulu, comes to the Zulu himself. Shembe died in 1935. His son Johannes Galilee Shembe (1904–1976) was the first to take over the leadership of the

---

energetic repurposing of military traditions took place not in the form of a principally intellectual mindset, but rather as a 'prayer to God' expressed through dance, one that reinforces itself in the corporeal experience of the individual. It is precisely by means of the internalization that the liturgical dances signify an ethical reorientation" (ibid., 235, italicized passages edited).

[24]See the description in Becken, *Wo der Glaube noch jung ist*, 98-120.

[25]The homepage of the church allows for a first impression of providing pictures and explanations: Nazareth Baptist Church, "Friday, May 15, 2009: Nhlangakazi," http://nazarethbaptistchurch. blogspot.com/2009/05/nhlangakazi.html (accessed May 14, 2015). It is estimated on one of the pages that the annual number of pilgrim attendees is around one million people, although it is likely that this is a slight exaggeration. Elsewhere, a number of around three hundred thousand people is given. Sbonelo McDee, "Shembe pilgrimage, www.youtube.com/watch?v=ep6LfqRXFn8 (accessed May 14, 2015).

[26]Quoted in Becken, "Die Entstehung," 104.

church, followed by other male family members. In order to understand the examples provided above, we would first need to familiarize ourselves with both the basic principles of black African anthropology[27] and the symbolic world of the Zulu traditions.[28] However, it is impossible to do justice to this desideratum within our framework. Instead, we will focus only on the parallels between the Zulu traditions and the traditions of the Shembe Church.[29]

At Shembe's calling (which is retold in many versions today), lightning plays an important role, which is also true for the Zulu tradition. In the Zulu traditions, the shape and color of "sacred" clothing is revealed in dreams, just as it was in Shembe's case. In the Zulu tradition, the color white is the color of the clothing of diviners, in whose dreams the goddess of fertility, known as Nomkhubulwana, appears, dressed in white, while white also plays a role in the dreams of Christian prophets and in Shembe's own dreams—in such dreams, it is particularly angels and Christ who appear dressed in white.[30] In the Zulu traditions, sticks are also revealed in dreams, with specifications as to their length, form, and color, which is also true for Shembe, in whose church a stick (i.e., a staff) is revealed in a specific form for each new convert. The stick is then fashioned accordingly sometime after the convert's baptism, with the purpose of serving as his "weapon."[31] In the Zulu traditions, people sense the working of the ancestral spirits between their shoulder blades; in the Shembe Church, believers sense the working of the Holy Spirit between their shoulder blades.[32]

Oosthuizen also points out the similarity between the diviners (traditional healers) of the Zulu traditions (Zulu *isangoma*) and the prophets of the AICs (Oosthuizen does not speak of "churches" but rather of "movements"), who also essentially function as healers.[33] Both believe that they receive calls through dreams and visions given to them by the ancestors or,

---

[27]Theo Sundermeier, *Nur gemeinsam können wir leben: Das Menschenbild schwarzafrikanischer Religionen*, 2nd ed. (Gütersloh: Gerd Mohn, 1990); and John Mbiti, *African Religions & Philosophy* (New York: Praeger, 1969).

[28]Bengt G. M. Sundkler, *Bantupropheten in Südafrika* (Stuttgart, Germany: Evangelisches Verlagswerk, 1964).

[29]See Sundkler, "Heidnischer Wahrsager und christlicher Prophet," in *Bantupropheten*, 384-88; and Oosthuizen, "Diviner-Prophet Parallels," 163-94, and especially 169ff.

[30]Sundkler, *Bantupropheten*, 235.

[31]Ibid., 236.

[32]Sundkler, "Heidnischer Wahrsager," 385.

[33]Oosthuizen, "Diviner-Prophet Parallels," 169ff.

in the case of the prophets, by the ancestors and the Holy Spirit; both then experience a phase of illness; both are trained by older diviners (in the case of the former) or prophets (in the case of the latter), first, to experience dreams and visions, which then allow them, second, to diagnose a patient's illness and its causes, and enable them, third, to identify suitable methods of treatment (medicine, pastoral care, surgical procedures). Both consider fasting to be an important part of their preparation to experience dreams and visions. In the process, the ancestors/the Holy Spirit serve as intermediaries. Vomiting plays a fundamental role for both as a purification ritual; both use water, ash, or a mixture of the two for their healing practices; for both, the custom of dancing, clapping, singing, circling around the patient, burning incense (in the case of the diviners, who do so in order to summon the ancestors by means of the scent), or lighting candles (in the case of the prophets) plays a role. Both use a stick/staff in their service.

Critics argue about whether Jesus Christ is the focal point in the praxis of this church or whether he is being eclipsed by the mediator figure of Isaiah Shembe. Of course it is very difficult to answer this question, since even different research (including surveys) yields very different results.[34] From a Western perspective, it seems quite offensive when Nazarites say that "Shembe is the Holy Spirit." However, in an empathetic research paper, Hans-Jürgen Becken points out that the followers do not distinguish between the Holy Spirit as the third person of the Trinity, on the one hand, and the way God operates using "a holy spirit" as a messenger, on the other. Becken believes that it is imperative not to engage in one-sided criticism from a Western perspective; rather, one should seek to understand what is truly at issue here.[35] According to Ngobese, in terms of the designation "Son of God," the Zulu traditions distinguish between aspects of ancestry, on the one hand (vertical line), and extension (horizontal line), on the other. Mahlke summarizes Ngobese's argument as follows:

---

[34]While Oosthuizen states that for those surveyed, Jesus Christ hardly features, Ngobese finds that 90 percent of those he surveyed see Jesus Christ as the second person of the Trinity, while 98 percent see him as mediator of salvation. Ngobese, "Concept of the Trinity," 100. The blatant difference between the two may be explained either by means of the (possibly leading?) manner in which each survey was carried out or, alternatively, by the fact that over the course of decades certain things have been clarified among the followers of the church.

[35]Becken, "Isaiah Shembe und der Heilige Geist," 152.

Jesus is seen as God only in his role as Savior; this role places him on the same level as God, namely on the "horizontal level." As an "extension of God," this role makes sense to the Zulus of the Shembe Church; it underscores the perfect deity of Jesus Christ, to which all believers are required to subscribe. In contrast, as a figure in human history, Jesus Christ is seen as a Jew who came to the whites to preach salvation to them. Buddha and Mohammed assumed this same function for other people groups; in the case of the Zulu people, it is Shembe who did so. In terms of this function, which may be located below *uMvelingqangi* [a designation for God in Zulu] on the vertical line, Jesus Christ stands on the same level as Shembe; however, this is not the case in terms of his function as "Jesus Christ as Savior—extension of God," which is seen as a universal function, one that is superior to that of Shembe.[36]

This brief overview will need to suffice for the present. Let us draw some conclusions: *First,* the Nazareth Baptist Church serves as an example of a church that came into being entirely without the influence of people associated with mission churches (even though it must be admitted that there were some Christian influences on the young Shembe).[37] *Second,* in essence, the religious customs (such as rituals, clothing, places, healing ministry) were revealed in the dreams and visions of the founder, Isaiah Shembe; that is to say that, according to the understanding of the church, they did not come about as a result of human decisions but rather as a result of divine actions. *Third,* it is evident that many of the elements and conceptions of the Zulu traditions were integrated into the outward form of the church and its practices, but that these were reinterpreted and rearranged. *Fourth,* it is very significant that in terms of the way the members of this church see themselves, a clear line of demarcation is drawn between the older Zulu traditions and their own church traditions. *Fifth,* this line of demarcation is based and justified precisely on their derivation from Shembe's dreams and visions. Thus, as the members see it, the authority of these Christian reconfigurations consist in the particular circumstance that they were not "brought about" by human beings.

In this sense, then, the Shembe Church serves as an example of intuitive inculturation, one that is separate from any form of influence on the part of

---

[36]Mahlke, "Nazareth Baptist Church," 201.

[37]Of course Isaiah Shembe received impulses from the churches to which he belonged; however, as far as the form of the rituals of his church is concerned, it is his dreams and visions that are of fundamental importance.

colonial authorities or mission churches *in terms of the morphogenesis* of the church's rituals and customs. We have already considered an example of intuitive inculturation in a colonial context, namely that of Juan Diego and his experience with the apparition of the Dear Lady of Guadalupe.[38] Here too a vision plays a particularly important role. At the same time, it must be recognized that while the Roman Catholic Church displayed a significant amount of tolerance for centuries when it came to matters of popular devotion, i.e., to Marian piety, the veneration of saints, or pilgrimages, it did not do so when it came to Sunday Mass.[39] Not so for the Shembe Church, the entire organization of which was shaped by Shembe's unbounded actions, being "guided" only by dreams and visions. So in this instance there is no trace of normative influences from the outside. The biblical writings serve as the only norm, although the more this church matures, the more time will tell which role the oral traditions about Isaiah Shembe play for the church. His son began the process of ensuring that many of the traditions were recorded.[40] It remains to be seen what the balance between the biblical writings and the Shembe traditions will be.

From a cultural perspective, whereas the Shembe Church constitutes a *regionally* oriented church body (even though it naturally also maintains a website these days), in what follows we will turn our attention to examples of intuitive inculturation in which the area of influence extends into the international domain due to the regional cultural "impregnation."

INTUITIVE INCULTURATION: THE EXAMPLE OF THE RCCG IN NIGERIA

Let us consider another example, one that at first glance appears to be the polar opposite of the previous one. Since the 1990s, a "Pentecostal explosion" has been taking place in Nigeria in terms of both an undreamed-of growth of Pentecostal churches and a "charismatization" of the mainline churches.[41]

---

[38]See chapter nineteen under the heading "Civilization Versus Primordial Ties."

[39]If it did, then only to a very limited extent.

[40]Joel Cabrita, "Texts, Authority, and Community in the South African 'Ibandla lamaNazaretha' (Church of the Nazaretha), 1910–1976," *Journal of Religion in Africa* 40 (2010): 60-95, especially 69ff. and 73ff.

[41]For a selection of literature on the subject, see the following: Ayuk Ausaji Ayuk, "The Pentecostal Transformation of Nigerian Church Life," *Asian Journal of Pentecostal Studies* 5, no. 2 (2002): 189-204; André Corten and Ruth Marshall-Fratani, eds., *Between Babel and Pentecost:*

The list of the largest Pentecostal churches includes the Redeemed Christian Church of God,[42] with about two million followers at present,[43] and the Deeper Life Bible Church of Nigeria[44] and the Church of God Missions,[45] having approximately one million followers each. These churches are different from the older Aladura churches in a number of ways. First, these churches managed to reach new people groups and enlist their support for the churches—especially people from university circles and from urban areas. Second, the power of prayer receives significant attention in these churches. Yet this is associated with the expectation that God has promised to grant people not only eternal salvation but also earthly riches. The term used for this was *prosperity gospel*.[46] This orientation led—third—to a *new lifestyle*, i.e., to changes in the worship services, such as a new worship style with electronic music (bands) and a lively and spontaneous progression

---

Transnational Pentecostalism in Africa and Latin America (Bloomington: Indiana University Press, 2001). The Pentecostal approach is even being followed in Islamic circles: "For instance, the Nasir Llahr Fathi (NASFAT), a Muslim group with nationwide branches now organizes night vigils, prayer camps, fasts, and prescribes rituals similar to those of Pentecostals." Olufunke Adeboye, "'Arrowhead' of Nigerian Pentecostalism: The Redeemed Christian Church of God, 1952–2005," *Pneuma* 29 (2007): 30.

[42] Adeboye, "'Arrowhead,'" 24-58.

[43] Afeosemime Adogame, "HIV/AIDS Support and African Pentecostalism: The Case of the Redeemed Christian Church of God (RCCG)," *Journal of Health Psychology* 12 (2007): 477.

[44] Matthews A. Ojo, "Deeper Life Bible Church of Nigeria," in Paul Gifford, ed., *New Dimensions in African Christianity* (Ibadan, Nigeria: Sefer, 1993), 161-81. See also Matthews A. Ojo, "Deeper Life Christian Ministry: A Case Study of the Charismatic Movements in Western Nigeria," *Journal of Religion in Africa* 18 (1988): 141-62; and Afeosemime U. Adogame, *The New International Dictionary*, s.v. "Deeper Christian Life Mission (International)."

[45] Founded in the 1970s by Benson Idahosa.

[46] Researchers debate the extent to which this emphasis was adopted from the US-American Pentecostal scene. Adeboye submits that it did so to a great extent, stating that the "faith gospel," which is characterized by emphases on prosperity, on the one hand, and healing, on the other, was introduced by US-American preachers: "The 'faith gospel' has been traced to American preachers such as Kenneth Hagin, Kenneth Copeland, Oral Roberts, E. W. Kenyon, A. A. Allen and John Avanzini. It came to Africa through the literature of Kenneth Hagin, T. L. Osborn, Oral Roberts, and through the evangelistic crusades of preachers like R. Bonnke. Its first principal exponent in Nigeria was Benson Idahosa whose ministry has a close relationship with Oral Roberts." Adeboye, "'Arrowhead,'" 30. In so doing, the author picks up on the hypotheses of James Gifford. See for instance Paul Gifford, "Ghana's Charismatic Churches," *Journal for Religion in Africa* 24 (1994): 241-65. Other research criticizes this view as a sweeping simplification and as a perpetuation of the mission historiography of the nineteenth and early twentieth centuries, as a one-sided perspective that sees the initiative coming only from Western mission societies and those whom they influenced. Opposing views to that of Gifford may be found in, say, Ogbu Kalu, *African Pentecostalism: An Introduction* (Oxford: Oxford University Press, 2008); and in Allan Anderson, "The Newer Pentecostal and Charismatic Churches: The Shape of Future Christianity in Africa?," *Pneuma* 24 (2002): 167-84, especially 181-82.

including well-known phenomena like speaking in tongues, prophecies, healing ministry, and exorcisms. All of this took place in modern settings, such as large and stylishly decorated church buildings, shopping centers, large conference centers located in hotels, cinemas, and the like. In addition—fourth—one may observe a trend toward *internationalization*, as may be seen especially in the selection of English as the language of worship; in the names given to many churches, which often feature words like *international* or *global*; and also in the sense of a transnational expansion of missionary work.[47] Currently, the RCCG has daughter congregations in more than 30 African countries and in more than 50 countries worldwide, including 183 daughter congregations in the United States, 127 in Great Britain, 33 in South Africa, and 25 in Kenya.[48] The mission statement of the church, which is available online, leaves no doubt that this internationalization is intended and will continue to be pursued:

> It is our goal to make it to heaven. It is our goal to take as many people as possible with us. In order to accomplish our goals, holiness will be our life-style. In order to take as many people with us as possible, we will plant churches within five minutes walking distance in every city and town of developing countries; and within five minutes driving distance in every city and town of developed countries. We will pursue these objectives until every nation in the world is reached for Jesus Christ our Lord.[49]

This very clear intention forms part of the reorientation that the RCCG experienced when the mantle of leadership passed after the death of founder Josiah Olufemi Akindayomi (1909–1980)[50] to Dr. Enoch Adejare Adeboye (b. 1942) in the 1980s. Adeboye introduced the abovementioned new forms of worship services as well as other elements when he founded the so-called model parishes.[51] Tension arose between the congregations that emulated

---

[47]Olufunke Adeboye, "Transnational Pentecostalism in Africa: The Redeemed Christian Church of God, Nigeria," in Laurent Fourchard, André Mary and René Otayek, eds., *Entreprises reli-gieuses transnationales en Afrique de l'ouest* (Paris: IFRA-Ibadan, 2005), 439-65.

[48]Adeboye, "'Arrowhead,'" 46.

[49]The Redeemed Christian Church of God, "Mission and Vision," www.rccg.org (accessed November 12, 2011).

[50]For more on his person, see Adeboye, "'Arrowhead,'" 31-37. Akindayomi received the name "Akindolie" at birth but adopted the name "Akindayomi" in 1951 (ibid., 34; see the same page for the meaning of the names).

[51]Ibid., 37-38. For more on the worship style that had been rather more "traditional" up until

the concept of the model parishes and those that preferred traditional worship; as a result, there were efforts in the mid-1990s to unite both streams in so-called unity parishes.[52] But the model parishes represented that part of the church with the greatest growth. The years from 1990 to 2010 marked a time of especially significant growth. During the same period, new initiatives were carried out, such as the Redemption Camp, a church camp where around five hundred thousand people gather for certain occasions every year.[53] The church is also active in schools and in the medical sector. It currently maintains more than forty-four primary and secondary schools, its own university (the Redeemer's University, established in 2005), more than fifty centers for "primary health care," two hospitals, and an orphanage.[54] The church also runs programs aimed at fighting HIV/AIDS and drug abuse, to name just two examples. The church is also active in the area of the media and in the banking sector. Adeboye provides a good impression of the economic power and media presence of the church:

> The RCCG operates four banks, one of which is called Haggai Community Bank, the strongest community bank in Nigeria. Its Jubilee Investment Corporation has gradually metamorphosed into a mortgage bank. The church also operates a travel agency and controls over 60 per cent of the importation of blank audio-visual tapes and CD's in Nigeria with which it produces and markets the sermons of E. A. Adeboye. In addition, the RCCG owns a satellite television (the Dove Media Group) with headquarters in Texas, USA, with Dove Vision as its major subsidiary. Its Nigerian arm is represented by the Trumpet Internet Television (TITV) which offers a banquet of television channels and high speed (satellite download) internet services.[55]

In terms of the HIV/AIDS pandemic, two aspects of the church's work need to be mentioned.[56] On the one hand, the church believes the illnesses

---

that point in time, see Asonzeh F.-K. Ukah, "Mobilities, Migration and Multiplication: The Expansion of the Religious Field of the Redeemed Christian Church of God (RCCG), Nigeria," in Afeosemime Adogame and Cordula Weissköppel, eds., *Religion in the Context of African Migration* (Bayreuth, Germany: Eckhard Breitinger, 2005), 317-41, specifically 320.

[52]Adeboye, "'Arrowhead,'" 39.

[53]Ibid., 41.

[54]Ibid., 43-44.

[55]Ibid., 44-45 (quotes drawn from 45). For more on Dove Media Vision, see Olufunke Adeboye, "Running the Prophecy: The Redeemed Christian Church of God in North America; 1992–2005," *Missionalia* 36 (2008): 259-79, on 271-73.

[56]On what follows, see especially Adogame, "HIV/AIDS Support," 477ff.

and other impairments of human life to be caused by demons. From the church's perspective, it is taking part in a cosmic battle between the forces of God and the forces of the devil and his demons. This is known as "spiritual warfare." The gods, spirits, rituals, and doctrines of the traditional religions are unequivocally seen as the work of the devil, while the followers of the church see themselves as being on God's side, strengthened and fortified by the power of the name of Jesus Christ and by the power of the Holy Spirit. Their aim is to do battle against Satan and his demons by means of prayer, fasting, confession of sins, and absolution, exorcisms, and healing ministry. On the other hand, and at the same time, the church also makes efforts to combat illness, HIV/AIDS, poverty, alcoholism, promiscuity, lies, and other phenomena detrimental to human life, since these are believed to be caused by evil spirits.[57] *The bottom line in this context is the church's commonly held perception that every human being may fall victim to demons.* As a result, people with HIV/AIDS are *not* stigmatized (as opposed to many other churches) but receive comprehensive and holistic assistance instead. This assistance, which is rendered by such organizations of the church as RAPAC, is considered to be an integral aspect of the mission of this church. This is a very significant phenomenon as far as the theology of mission is concerned.[58]

VISIONS, DREAMS, MISSION, AND MANAGEMENT

In the Redeemed Christian Church of God, too, many forms and practices of church life may be traced back to dreams, visions, and prophecies given to the founders. This is true for the naming of the church, issues relating to the healing ministry, exorcisms, worship style, and the church's orientation toward mission. At the same time, a wide variety of the church's activities

---

[57]Adogame's portrayal of the topic of spiritual warfare closely follows US-American examples. One wonders whether there might not be other factors playing a role in the context of the Yoruba culture. If this is not the case, then the practice of spiritual warfare may serve as a good example of the globalization of exorcistic practices. Ibid., 478-79.

[58]The Africa Missions Committee of the church describes its task as follows: "Recruiting brethren that can reach out to missions in various ways; to identify the needs of the missions and prioritise them, thereby making these missions self-supporting; to train pastors and missionaries to satisfy the large manpower need in Africa; to assist with the establishment of more mission schools and bible colleges throughout Africa; to eradicate poverty by providing self-enrichment courses and community development programmes; to educate on and reduce the spread of the AIDS epidemic in many African countries." See www.africanmissions.org/aboutus.htm (accessed January 12, 2011).

are packaged in a highly professional manner, creating a picture of a modern, forward-looking, and committed church that is socially relevant. In urban areas in particular, this picture has to do with a global lifestyle: both the members and the leading figures of the church are fashionably dressed; many drive expensive cars (Mercedes, BMW, etc.); in order to appeal to high society, presentations are made in the most exclusive hotels; cruise trips and such are organized; and the church has a strong presence on the Internet, television, and the media. This lifestyle has a missionary quality in and of itself, since it embodies the dream of upward mobility for many people, using real people as models. At the same time, this whole setting is embedded in a dualistic worldview, according to which the forces of God are locked in battle with the forces of Satan and his demons.

In this way, what the church offers on a spiritual level serves as a direct means to share in the hope and the vision of life in abundance (according to Jn 10:10). It is for this reason that many of these churches bear the name "Full Gospel Church." According to this outlook, *spiritual warfare* and the modern lifestyle are inextricably linked, since the former is the prerequisite for the latter. The emphasis on believing in the spirits and in spiritual warfare should, however, not be put off as something unique to Africa or as something borrowed from the Yoruba traditions (even though these may have a particular meaning), for this would mean disregarding the global discourse on the subject of spiritual warfare, which is of considerable significance for certain practices, such as that of exorcism.[59] A widespread debate on this topic rages in places like the United States, with a multimillion-dollar book industry catering to the subject; conferences are held with people attending from far and wide, there are educational institutions in Africa, Asia, and Latin America that are networked to each other, and there are networks of people worldwide exerting an influence on each other. *Thus the question as to which elements of spiritual practice in our case study may be traced back to local traditions of origin and which came about as a result of the global*

---

[59]It is frequently brought home to me in conversations with both Pentecostals and pastors of various "traditional" churches (Lutheran, Presbyterian, Roman Catholic, Orthodox) in countries such as Indonesia, India, Egypt, or Tanzania how important international connections in this area are for people actively involved in spiritual warfare or healing ministries—regardless of the ongoing significant cultural differences, needless to say. This too is an instance of "glocalization" (R. Robertson).

discourse is everything but settled. In addition, we can and should ask which elements of African or Asian origin (to the extent that they are identifiable) have an effect on, say, countries in the northern hemisphere like the United States in turn.

These observations demonstrate that hermeneutical paradigms commonly used in the inculturation debate, such as "text and context" or the priority of the context as opposed to the priority of the biblical text, should be considered insufficiently complex, if not naive. Here the most diverse factors interact and mesh together, of which we will only name a few (in no particular order and without being exhaustive): biblical texts that serve as references, dreams and visions, the demands of and laws germane to the media, global lifestyle fashions, the internal dynamics of business and trade, mechanisms of institutionalization (such as the trend in academia to garner as much prestige as possible by means of advanced degrees), and many others. For this reason, in what follows we will need to focus our attention on the terminology from the fields of cultural studies and religious studies that is used in the research field of the discipline of intercultural theology/ mission studies.

PART V

. . . .

Theology and Interculturality

Systematic Perspectives

Even though intensive theological debates about the topic of inculturation (and similar terms) are a comparatively recent phenomenon, the issue that they address is as old as Christianity itself and may naturally also be found in other religious configurations. In what follows, we will focus our attention on some of the terms used in debates in mission studies during the last few decades and critically appraise and contextualize them. We will then endeavor to show that the use of terminology is extremely contingent on the context, so much so that there is a need for a discourse about the discourse. The question then becomes, Who uses which term to signify what on the basis of which contextual parameters and challenges?

21

....

Inculturation

During the last few years, the term *inculturation* played an important role for the discipline of mission studies.[1] The term is intended to circumscribe in a new way that phenomenon for which the entire history of Christianity offers a plethora of examples, such as the specific ways in which Christian churches were founded and configured in Egypt or Ethiopia.[2] As far as the history of Western Christianity is concerned, one might mention by way of example the significance of Pope Gregory I (590–605), whose instructions for dealing with heathen Germanic traditions defined mission practice for centuries.[3] One could also draw attention to such examples as the Nestorian mission to China, which led to the formation of some unique cultural patterns, or to the so-called rites controversy, which proved to be so very significant for the Roman Catholic Church. The rites controversy was a dispute over whether and how missionaries should adapt European forms of Christianity so as to conform to cultural customs in China. Prominent missionaries like Matteo Ricci (1552–1610) or Roberto de Nobili (1577–1656) were in favor of adapting Christianity to local customs such as the veneration of

---

[1]For a selection of literature on this topic, see the following: Robert Schreiter, *Constructing Local Theologies* (Maryknoll, NY: Orbis Books, 1985); Theo Sundermeier, "Inkulturation und Synkretismus: Probleme einer Verhältnisbestimmung," *Evangelische Theologie* 52 (1992): 192-209; Fritz Frei, ed., *Inkulturation zwischen Tradition und Modernität: Kontexte—Begriffe—Modelle* (Freiburg, Switzerland: Universitätsverlag, 2000).

[2]An interesting overview is provided in the following history of (mostly Western) Christianity: Karl-Heinz Ohlig, *Fundamentalchristologie: Im Spannungsfeld von Christentum und Kultur* (Munich: Kösel, 1986).

[3]Pope Gregory I sent a letter containing instructions for mission to Augustine of Canterbury in 601, recommending that the outward forms of pre-Christian religions (such as sacred sites) be retained and given a new Christian interpretation. See Horst Rzepkowski, "Das Papsttum als eine Modell frühchristlicher Anpassung," in Theo Sundermeier, ed., *Die Begegnung mit dem Anderen: Plädoyers für eine interkulturelle Hermeneutik* (Gütersloh: Gütersloher Verlagshaus, 1991), 88ff.

Confucius and of the ancestors in China. While the *propaganda fidei* (the papal institution responsible for the propagation of the faith) initially welcomed this approach, it eventually came to favor a different approach after a lengthy dispute took place between the proponents of various positions. The result was that Benedict XIV finally issued the bull *Omnium sollicitudinem* in 1744, mandating a restrictive approach.[4]

In consequence, for about two hundred years Roman Catholic missionaries had no choice but to use Latin as the language of worship and to implement church customs in European form. And for the most part, their practice was not to translate the Bible into local languages either. In contrast, nineteenth-century Protestant mission societies prioritized translation work and schooling efforts.[5] On the Protestant side, it was particularly Briton Henry Venn (1796–1873)[6] and American Rufus Anderson (1796–1880)[7] who pushed for the rapid creation of indigenous (say, African, or Asian) churches. Both men were proponents of what would come to be known as the "three-self formula," which stated that indigenous churches should become *self-governing, self-supporting,* and *self-extending.*

In many cases, however, such demands remained little more than theory, since the white missionaries found it rather difficult to cede the leadership

---

[4]Rivalries between different orders played a significant role in the rites controversy. For example, the Dominicans and Jesuits took very different approaches. The Dominicans focused on ordinary people and saw their ancestor veneration as a form of worship and thus as idolatry. In contrast, the Jesuits elected to focus on the educated segment, and they had no problem with the ancestor veneration practiced by these people.

[5]See chapter eight under the heading, "Colonial Indirect Rule and Ethnic Identity: The Example of the Fulani."

[6]Venn served as the director of the Church Missionary Society (CMS) from 1841 until his death. He created a step-by-step plan to facilitate what he called "indigenization," according to which the mission would be "euthanized"—that is to say, the white missionaries would voluntarily surrender their leadership and bow out over time. Venn's plan played a significant role in the development of the church in West Africa, which was a significant field of activity for the CMS. This work led to the implementation of strategic innovations in the mission field, such as the dissolution of the society's central mission stations and the creation of village congregations, the practice of ordaining indigenous pastors as soon as possible (which continued to be an area of conflict within the CMS), and the involvement of mothers in primary school education (reasoning that mothers play a pivotal role in Christian education and thus in the education of indigenous leaders).

[7]Anderson began serving as assistant and secretary of the American Board of Commissioners for Foreign Missions in India in 1826; from 1832 to 1866 he served as its foreign secretary. In his most important work, *The Theory of Missions to the Heathen* (1869), Anderson called for, among other things, the implementation of the three-self formula.

of their own mission initiatives (i.e., congregations and churches) to indigenous people. This often led to considerable frustration among indigenous leaders, since they were denied ordination and thus full leadership rights. As a result of these tensions, from the last third of the nineteenth century onward a number of schisms took place (leading in Africa to what became known as the so-called Ethiopian movement). Whereas many mission churches continued to be very European in character until as late as the 1960s, this changed more and more when independence was granted to the former colonial territories (from around 1945 to 1969). The churches that had originally been founded by the mission societies now became independent, which led in turn to increasing efforts to merge the practice of the Christian faith with cultural traditions.

SOME REMARKS ON THE TERMINOLOGY

When we consider the terminology commonly used in the debates, we find that the term *accommodation* came to signify a primarily outward adaptation of Christian traditions to a given culture.[8] This refers to the alteration and adaptation of the method (or *modus* in Latin) that is used. The term *accommodation* was used especially by Catholic mission studies scholar Joseph Schmidlin (1876–1944) and his student Johannes Thauren (1892–1954). Most Protestants preferred to use the older term *indigenization*, which refers to the gospel becoming indigenous to an ethnic group, since the Latin word *gens* means "a tribe" or "a people." In contrast, many Roman Catholics preferred to use the term *inculturation*, a neologism that became popular in the 1960s as a result of the work of Pierre Charles (1883–1954) and Joseph Masson. This term suggests a combination of the term *incarnation* (i.e., the divine Word—in Greek, *logos*—becoming flesh in Jesus of Nazareth) and the subject of culture.[9] It is believed that just as the divine Word became incarnate, the gospel now also needs to take shape in various

---

[8]By rights, I should direct the reader to Richard Niebuhr's classic: Richard Niebuhr, *Christ and Culture* (New York: Harper, 1951). However, even if Niebuhr's typology is helpful for an initial orientation, I will devote no further attention to the rubrications that he proposes, such as Christ above culture or Christ against culture, since Niebuhr's operative understanding of culture seems to me to be superficial and overly homogenous.

[9]Michael Sievernich, "Von der Akkomodation zur Inkulturation. Missionarische Leitideen der Gesellschaft Jesu," *Missionskunde und Religionswissenschaft* 86 (2002): 260-76.

cultures. This term began to be used officially in 1974 in official statements released by the Asian Bishops' Conference of the Roman Catholic Church at its meeting in Taipei.

Here—just as in Africa, Latin America, and other parts of the world—the conference picked up on the important and far-reaching reform impulses of the Second Vatican Council (1962–1965). The emphasis now shifted from European expressions of catholicity to regional and local forms of expression. In the 1980s and 1990s, however, the Vatican attempted to scale back this development to some extent.

The founding of the Ecumenical Association of Third World Theologians (EATWOT) in 1976 was of particular importance as far as the global ecumenical movement was concerned. For the first time, an international platform had been created that could lend a voice to theological efforts aimed at contextualizing the Christian message. During the initial phase especially, a significant influence by Latin American liberation theologians made itself felt in this regard.[10] The term *contextualization* that now came into vogue emerged from the work of the Theological Education Fund in the 1970s. It emphasizes context in the broader sense, as opposed to the emphasis on culture favored by the term *inculturation*. *Contextualization* is derived from the Latin word *textus*, meaning "texture" or "woven fabric." The operative assumption here is that a theology that aims to be both indigenous and relevant needs to consider the setting in which Christians live, i.e., their lifeworld. At issue are the con-texts, i.e., various aspects inherent to the surrounding lifeworld. The term *contextualization* alerts us to the fact that this lifeworld includes not only cultural aspects but also social and political ones, contexts such as poverty, a lack of health care, illiteracy, political oppression, chauvinisms of various kinds, violence, war, ecological conditions, or pandemics such as those later caused by HIV/AIDS, to name just a few. Such contexts are of considerable importance and worthy of theological attention in their own right, since their significance surpasses the interests of particular cultures or nations and is sometimes even global in scope.

---

[10]For more on inculturation from a liberation theology perspective, see Juan Carlos Scannone, "Volksreligion, Volksweisheit und inkulturierte Theologie," in *Weisheit und Befreiung* (Düsseldorf, Germany: Patmos, 1992), 66-88. For an overview of the debate see Paulo Suess, "Inkulturation," in Ignacio Ellacuría and Jon Sobrino, eds., *Mysterium Liberationis: Grundbegriffe der Theologie der Befreiung*, 2 vols. (Lucerne, Switzerland: Exodus, 1995–1996), 1011-59.

INCULTURATION IN THE MATRIX OF SEVERAL DETERMINING FACTORS

Our deliberations thus far have shown that it would be far too simplistic to describe the event of the indigenization of the gospel against the backdrop of only one particular context. As important as the cultural, lifeworldly, political, or other parameters may be, these are not the only definitive factors; another factor that is of paramount importance is the theological presuppositions by which various participants orient themselves, the way they define inculturation, culture, justice, community, or whatever else is always predicated on their own cultural background. This means that it does not suffice simply to be aware of various theological rationales and definitions of culture on an intellectual level, as was often suggested in the past; rather, it is also necessary to take into consideration the operative definitions of inculturation that vary from one context to another. This will be clarified in the following units. For now, we need to point out once again that the following discussion can only proceed by way of example and with the aim of cultivating both a greater hermeneutical sensitivity for issues of intercultural theology and a more nuanced appreciation of the problem at hand.

After these preliminary remarks, let us now return to the concept of inculturation, which will occupy our attention in what follows. We have already pointed out that many treatises on the topic of inculturation proceed on the basis of rather superficial argumentation, since *they often fail to consider the cultural and contextual contingency of inculturation models.* A (by no means exhaustive) list might include the way confessional or denominational (say, Roman Catholic, Lutheran, Presbyterian, Baptist, Pentecostal, or Episcopal) groups are typically perceived, the way national entities are typically defined (in various places like Germany, South Africa, Brazil, or North America), typical macrocultural perceptual patterns (such as how "Indian" or "African" cultures are collectively perceived), and microcultural perceptual patterns (such as how Indonesian Batak people groups are typically perceived). Let us begin with typical ways in which nations are perceived: Volker Sellin[11] proposes the distinction between a "political-subjective" and

---

[11]Volker Sellin, "Nationalbewusstsein und Partikularismus in Deutschland im 19. Jahrhundert," in Jan Assmann and Tonio Hölscher, eds., *Kultur und Gedächtnis* (Frankfurt: Suhrkamp, 1988), 241-64.

a "cultural-objective" concept of "nation." The concept of nation used in the United States, for instance, was formulated in a context in which the citizens to which it pertained were affiliated with one another not by a common progenitor, language, history, or geographical area but rather by the *collective will* to found a nation on the basis of a certain constitution. In contrast, the cultural-objective concept of nation used in central Europe saw a nation as constituted by a common history and language; here, the political and cultural status quo, namely a plurality of dominions each featuring various local traditions, was contraposed to the image of a shared, collective national history.[12] The nation was thought of as a present reality; even if people had forgotten it, they just needed to be reminded of it again.

When seen as a frame of reference for theological inculturation theories, one may surmise that the privileged status many US-American theologians accord to the "translation model" is at least partly contingent on the narrative of American society. It is the congregation and not the culture that generally constitutes the reference framework of the gospel, because for the longest time there simply was nothing even remotely resembling a homogenous cultural configuration. In contrast, in the nineteenth-century European context, the issue of cultural identity was of supreme importance. This was demonstrated earlier by reference to the German concept of culture and the significance of the "mother tongue" for the mission praxis of German mission societies. We may recall that Napoleon's intervention led to the formation of new dominions in the domain of the German territories; after the end of the Napoleonic wars, these dominions now went about constructing their own "national" identities. In the process, various actors (the ruling dynasties, representatives of the educated middle class, as well as a variety of historical societies, societies for the preservation of folklore elements like songs and stories, etc.) came to endorse different identity constructs. Some invoked the unity of the pan-German nation, believed to have existed until as late as the Middle Ages; others invoked the national identity of territorial states. In short, anyone giving thought to the subject of inculturation must take into account these diverse perceptual patterns. And it logically follows that various conceptions of inculturation are contingent on

---

[12]Ibid., 257.

the cultural, national, confessional, and general contexts of the subject in question, which must also be taken into account. In what follows, we will consider two examples in this regard.

INCULTURATED UNDERSTANDINGS OF INCULTURATION? SEARCHING FOR TRACES

In his semiotic theory of culture, Clifford Geertz has shown that it is culture that defines what people see or do not see as self-evident or, as Geertz puts it, "common sense."[13] Müller-Funk states,

> Culture establishes what is unconscious, self-evident, or . . . what each person perceives as specifically real. One of the principal mechanisms of culture is to make itself disappear, especially that element which Musil designates the "sense of the possible" [*Möglichkeitssinn*]. It could also be different. One of the functions of ethnology is critically to scrutinize such self-congratulatory certainties which are reflected not least in a pronounced ethnocentrism.[14]

The concern of African women's theology is to unmask these cultural "self-evidencies" and to call them into question. Culture needs a certain level of coherency to function, but at the same time, this coherency is often somewhat ambiguous. For this reason, the task of the observer is not as simple as identifying a code and then decrypting it, since every code can be used in various ways.

This is the paradox of inculturation: On the one hand, inculturation must necessarily establish a sense of what is self-evident, but in the process the awareness of being inculturated is gradually lost. At the same time, inculturation implies maintaining a critical distance when considering the biblical metanarrative. This corresponds to Aleida Assmann's distinction between lifeworld and monument: inculturation leads to the construction of a self-evident lifeworld, and at the same time it lends expression to a monument, namely the biblical texts. The biblical texts shape the cultural memory, and in so doing they establish a fixed distance to the immediacy of the lifeworld. There are, therefore—to agree with New Testament scholar Gerd Theissen—sound

---

[13]Clifford Geertz, "Common Sense as a Cultural System," in *Local Knowledge* (New York: Basic Books, 1983), 73-93.

[14]Wolfgang Müller-Funk, *Kulturtheorie: Einführung in Schlüsseltexte der Kulturwissenschaften* (Tübingen: Francke, 2006), 251.

reasons for keeping the concept of religion distinct from that of culture. One of these is that followers of religions like Judaism, Christianity, and Islam each have a distinct and particular sense of affiliation.[15] Another is that this distinction consists in more or less consciously transmitting religious traditions containing an implicit claim to validity and, in the case of the Jewish and Christian traditions, also a claim to obedience. This means that both intercultural and interreligious encounters never consist simply of commingling traditions or each participant adding certain elements. Instead, the process is an active adoption or rejection of elements from the other tradition, i.e., it implies that each participant consciously preserves or alters her own tradition. The modus of such adoption or rejection is essentially determined by what the traditions themselves demand. It is therefore the biblical texts themselves that elicit a certain form of transmission. Gerd Theissen demonstrates this as he discusses how Judaism and Christianity approach tradition.[16] Understanding the present situation from the perspective of the story of the Bible enables the observer to maintain a certain distance to it, and this distance allows the necessary room to maneuver and to act. Thus the goal of inculturation may never be total "indigenization," since the message itself subverts such attempts and since the power of the message is contingent on maintaining the distance. The Christian metanarrative is always a counternarrative at the same time. It transcends every given situation.

After these deliberations, it will not come as a surprise that members of different cultures view the issue of the inculturation of the gospel very differently. In what follows, we will illustrate this using two models. Although the respective proponents of these models belong to one and the same church (the Roman Catholic Church), one approaches the subject matter from within the Indian context and the other from within the African one. It will be shown that what each respective culture takes for granted is of

---

[15]This is not true for all religious configurations; one might question whether it applies, for instance, to certain Japanese Shinto cults found before the mid-nineteenth century. See Shingo Shimada and Jürgen Straub, "Relationale Hermeneutik im Kontext interkulturellen Verstehens: Probleme universalistischer Begriffsbildung in den Sozial- und Kulturwissenschaften—erörtert am Beispiel 'Religion,'" *Deutsche Zeitschrift für Philosophie* 47, no. 3 (1999): 449-77.
[16]Gerd Theissen, "Tradition und Entscheidung: Der Beitrag des biblischen Glaubens zum kulturellen Gedächtnis," in Assmann and Hölscher, *Kultur und Gedächtnis*, 170-96.

paramount importance, with the result that very different conceptions of inculturation arise.

INTERCULTURALITY AS A TRANSRELIGIOUS EVENT: FRANCIS D'SA (INDIA)

Indian Jesuit Francis X. D'Sa (b. 1936) distinguishes between *in*culturation on an ontological level and *in*culturation as an action, which he designates *inter*culturation. Ontologically, *in*culturation signifies overcoming an initial alienation; its focus is on life as a whole. Thus he sees *in*culturation as both a paracultural and a parareligious event.[17] The aim is to bridge the "gap between knowing and being known," to deconstruct the ontological biases, psychological biases, and the biases that determine the way one acts, and in the process to restore the human being—no matter to which religion she might belong—to wholeness. In this way, D'Sa postulates a parareligious onto-theology as the basis for an interreligious *inter*culturation, which he goes on to explain in greater detail.[18]

According to D'Sa, as an *action* the term *inter*culturation means, first and fundamentally, to *recognize the validity* of other cultures with which Christians come into contact. Second, it means being cognizant of the fact that different cultures *"touch" and "influence" each other*. Third, it refers to the *reciprocity* of the event; fourth and finally, to the fact that this event concerns not only the area of religion but *also other areas* such as economy, culture, and politics, since the aim is to achieve wholeness. The author attempts to demonstrate these points using the example of encounters between the Christian religion and Hindu religions. He distinguishes between an anthropocentric and a cosmocentric worldview[19] and recommends that the anthropocentric worldview pay more attention to the significance of the

---

[17]See Francis X. D'Sa, "Inkulturation oder Interkulturation? Versuch einer Begriffsklärung," in Michael Heberling, ed., *Inkulturation als Herausforderung und Chance* (Aachen, Germany: Riese Springer, 2001), 21-54, especially 33-36. For the many uses of the term *interculturation*, see Younhee Kim, "Interkulturation: Der immerwährende Missionsauftrag der Kirche," in Richard Brosse et al., eds., *Für ein Leben in Fülle. Visionen einer missionarischen Kirche* (Freiburg im Breisgau, Germany: Herder, 2008) 223-32; Wolfgang Pauly, "Mission—Inkulturation—Reziproke Interkulturation: Aspekte zur Begegnung zwischen Christentum und anderen Kulturen," *Orientierung* 73, no. 11 (2009): 123-25.

[18]D'Sa makes use of Heidegger's philosophical terminology.

[19]D'Sa, "Inkulturation oder Interkulturation?," 44ff.

cosmos, while conversely the cosmocentric worldview should pay more attention to the significance of history. He demands that both sides relinquish their respective claims to absolute truth.[20] In this way—i.e., by participating in *inter*culturation, by mutually recognizing and learning from each other—both parties may experience more and more *in*culturation (on an "ontological level," to use Christian terminology). "For the search for inculturation is essentially the search for wholeness." For this reason it is not limited to the area of religion but also concerns the areas of politics, culture, and economy, since these too relate to love and justice, i.e., to wholeness.[21]

D'Sa's approach intends to undermine the claim that any one culture is superior to another. Everything that happens, happens by the process of *inter*culturation; when that process succeeds, then it is for the better. Yet the author also allows for the possibility that *inter*culturation can lead to a negative outcome.[22] This clearly shows that the term of *inter*culturation is defined as an action and thus comes without theological baggage. *Successful interculturation enables greater inculturation in the sense of a transreligious wholeness experience.* What emerges is a very dynamic image of the processes of cultural encounters and interaction.

On closer inspection, however, it is evident that D'Sa continues to operate with a holistic concept of culture. This becomes evident, for instance, in his choice of illustrations. The author compares cultures with the colors of the rainbow: "The colors touch and determine each other; at the edges they blend with one another, such that it is impossible to ascertain where one color begins and the other ends. The reciprocal contact determines the identity of each color." The author goes on to postulate that it is important to determine the "points of contact," i.e., where people come into contact, where they meet each other, and what such encounters set in motion. Yet this image presupposes homogenous cultural units, for although it is legitimate to see the areas of transition as a blending of the primary colors, *this does not warrant any intracultural heterogeneity.* One also senses a holistic

---

[20]Ibid., 51.

[21]Ibid., 52. The author seems to sense that his suggestions are profoundly theoretical in nature. He states, "The task of inculturation cannot be completed on the drawing board; just as little can it be begun without the drawing board of hermeneutics" (52). Among other things, this hermeneutics demands that one see the other person the way one would like to be seen by him (44).

[22]Ibid., 43.

understanding of culture underlying such statements as the following: "A culture (or a system) which does not know of any encounters with other cultures also cannot know its own deficiencies."[23] *Such a statement presupposes that cultures are homogenous entities.* D'Sa goes on to say: "Had the Hindu traditions never come into contact with other cultures, they would never have realized the inhumane consequences to which the caste system gives rise. Likewise, if the Christian traditions had never encountered other traditions, they would never have realized the extent to which they have instrumentalized the cosmos."[24]

Even if one were to admit that a culture's self-perception is enhanced when it sees the image of itself that the other culture reflects back, D'Sa's statements are nevertheless overblown, for they simply skip over the intracultural disunity, opposition, struggles and negotiation processes. Granted, D'Sa attempts to subvert claims of cultural superiority and to clarify that the process of Christian proclamation is only one part of a transreligious inculturation event. However, his holistic and homogenous concept of culture does not allow for the complexity of the negotiation processes, and so he ends up presenting very theoretical characterizations of two religiocultural entities.

INCULTURATION AND TRIBAL CULTURES: TERESA OKURE (NIGERIA)

Teresa Okure understands inculturation as an open process. This sets her model apart from others, such as the translation models.[25] For her, inculturation must be based on the concept of the incarnation of the divine Word in Jesus of Nazareth. As she sees it, two distinct realities, the divine reality and the human reality, become united in the person of Jesus.[26] In the process, the divine nature enriches the human. This raises the question whether the human nature conversely also enriches the divine one. From a human perspective, Okure answers in the affirmative under two aspects.

---

[23]Ibid., 42.

[24]Ibid., 43.

[25]"Genuine inculturation should be based upon the mystery of the Incarnation, seen not only as a mystery and as an event in the person of Jesus of Nazareth, but as a process to be carried on in history till the end of time." Teresa Okure, "Inculturation: Biblical/Theological Bases," in Teresa Okure et al., *32 Articles Evaluating Inculturation of Christianity in Africa,* Spearhead 112-114 (Eldoret, Kenya: AMECEA Gaba Publications, 1990), 55-86. Thus for Okure, the understanding of inculturation must be based on the understanding of incarnation (57).

[26]Ibid. (reference drawn from 57 in particular).

First, it is impossible for human beings to conceive of God apart from his union with the human reality. Second, without Jesus of Nazareth, the fullness of humanity would never have been achieved. These aspects still need to be explored. *In contrast to the incarnation, however, the Christian message did not come to the Africans directly, but rather in the form of Christianity as characterized by European culture.* For Okure, inculturation in Africa does not mean finding suitable cultural patterns to express the Christian faith; on the contrary, the very existence of such expressions is the fruit of inculturation.[27] Okure joins Pope John Paul II in speaking of cultures as fertile soil in which the good news is planted, with the result that mutual enrichment occurs. Allow me to make a critical observation at this point already: the image that Okure uses is not very helpful because it ascribes a largely passive role to culture, in that the plant already encapsulates its "agenda" within itself (in the form of the genetic code). Even though elements of the soil enter into the plant, they have no effect on its form.

At any rate, Okure herself assumes not only that a particular culture tends toward Christ but that Christ also tends toward a particular culture. This is about change, which Okure sees as given in the incarnation as the prototype of inculturation: regarding the association of the divine and the human reality, she writes that "in this union, neither reality is destroyed, down-graded or absorbed. Yet each is enriched and mysteriously transformed by the other."[28] It is not only the reality of human beings that is accepted, transformed, and saved in Jesus Christ, but also the reality of nature. Jesus Christ lived entirely as a Jew, as a Galilean, and as a Nazarene, and by living this cultural existence, he expressed the transforming will of God in *a countercultural lifestyle.*[29]

> Indeed, the personal life-style of Jesus Christ was largely counter-cultural, with respect to his attitude towards riches, wealth and greatness; towards women, the poor and sinners . . . ; towards the Sabbath, that very revered of Jewish religious institutions. . . . In all this, and similar instances Jesus Christ concretely and effectively challenged his Jewish culture, in order to purify and transform it.[30]

---

[27] "The finding of suitable cultural expressions is only the fruit of inculturation." Ibid., 59.
[28] Ibid., 57-58.
[29] Ibid., 62ff.
[30] Ibid., 63.

As Okure sees it, this countercultural mission resulted in opposition to Jesus and finally in his crucifixion. Thus the mission of Jesus Christ was to live a life of self-emptying. *This self-emptying allowed room for the true humanity that Christ lived out in community with others, criticizing outward ritualism, false distinctions between pure and impure, and other religiocultural forms that exclude people or discriminate against them.*[31] Christ's steadfastness, selflessness, and courage, based on his divine existence, made it possible for his incarnation to function as inculturation. Okure summarizes,

> In the last analysis, the personal and cultural transformation of humanity, the birth of the new creation, happened first and foremost in Jesus' own person, in his own life, passion, death and resurrection (Col 1:15-20). In the past we may not have regarded Jesus Christ's entire life on earth as one sustained act of inculturation, but that is what it was.[32]

In his capacity as the "constitutive model" of inculturation, Jesus Christ demonstrates the following aspects: (1) Inculturation is a matter of cultural transformation. (2) This transformation can only take place from within a culture, i.e., from within a relationship of immediate cultural proximity. (3) This means that inculturation has both cultural and countercultural aspects. (4) Inculturation is characterized by self-emptying. (5) The event of inculturation is also characterized by conflict. This calls for trust in God, courage, selflessness, and sometimes also for preparedness to suffer. The early church continued to exhibit these characteristics, as Okure demonstrates by pointing to the example of the Jewish Christians.[33] Ultimately, this served to emphasize the theological recognition that in Jesus Christ all people become a "new creation" (2 Cor 5:17).[34] For the Roman Catholic woman theologian Okure, it goes without saying

---

[31]"Christ emptied himself, not of his nature as God, but of the divine mode of operating. He did this in order to create space in himself substantially, for the humanity, which he was to assume, own and live as a full human being. This is a mystery, which we accept in faith, but it constitutes an integral part, a necessary aspect of inculturation." Ibid., 62. See also 63ff.

[32]Ibid., 64.

[33]"Thus, self-emptying for the Jewish Christians entailed rejecting most of their inherited prejudices and sacrosanct Torah-based narrow 'theology' and religious practices, changing their elitist self-image and derogatory or separatist attitude towards gentiles." Ibid., 65.

[34]Ibid., 68.

that the mission of Jesus Christ continues in the mission of the church.[35] Thus Okure understands the mission of the church as the continuation of the mission of Christ, which has significant consequences for the understanding of inculturation: (1) Inculturation is an integral part of the mission of the (Roman Catholic) church. (2) Through Jesus Christ, cultures are to be restored in the church. (3) This presupposes that inculturation is seen not as endangering the universality of the church but as realizing it.[36] (4) Since the various cultures come together within the church, the transculturality of the Christian message finds its expression in the transculturality of the church itself. *Thus Okure understands inculturation as ecclesiogenous transculturality.* (5) Conversely, the church is only able to live in this form when the members of the church allow enough room for cultural plurality. But the church is only able to tolerate this plurality when it continues to orient itself by the mission of Christ and to submit to the process of self-emptying.[37] *Thus for its part, ecclesiogenous transculturality is only possible in the form of kenotic ecclesiogenesis.*

According to Okure, inculturation is to be carried out in the form of a dialogue between experts and the people at the grassroots level.[38] *That being said, African experts who have received their education in the West and have subsequently returned to Africa must first undergo an intercultural reorientation of their own before they are able to render truly effective help in Africa.*[39] The gospel of Jesus Christ is to serve as the yardstick in this dialogue. As an essential expression of the mission of the church, inculturation implies not only criticizing those cultural elements that contradict the gospel but also

---

[35]"Jesus Christ entrusted to the Church the task of making subjectively present for every people and culture, what he had accomplished objectively once and for all, in their regard. Thus, the subjective restoration of all cultures to Christ (and culture defines the collective self and identity of a people), institutes as much an integral part of the mission of the Church as does the subjective redemption of every human being." Ibid., 60.

[36]Ibid., 60: "Such an understanding of inculturation rests finally upon the mystery of the Church itself. Theologically, the Church is believed to be universal, because it embraces people from every tribe, tongue, nation, and hence from every culture (Rev 5:9). But, this theological universality becomes a physical reality only when the Church is seen to embrace all cultures in their concrete manifestations, instead of adopting one culture as the norm to which all other members from other cultures have to conform."

[37]"The Church today will also need to undergo the process of self-emptying, and of selective assumption for transformation." Ibid., 70.

[38]Ibid., 77.

[39]Ibid., 79.

that the church draws its strength from this process. After all, the church itself should be understood as a dynamic process.[40]

In Okure's model, inculturation comes across as something achievable, as something that takes place in the church, and as something that contributes to the enrichment and nourishment of the church. Critical elements exert an influence on society itself, such as the criticism of tribalism, witchcraft, the oppression of women, and the cultural systems that sanction the oppression of women.[41] It is in the church, however, that inculturation takes on form, and also, say, in the hierarchy of the magisterium, which Okure— from her African (or rather Roman Catholic?) perspective—portrays as a very positive institution for Nigeria.[42] The difference between Okure's estimation in this regard and that of other African women theologians indicates her discourse location: Okure writes as a nun.

INCULTURATION: A MULTIDIMENSIONAL PHENOMENON

These deliberations may have shown that it is hardly possible to "nail down" the definition of phenomena related to inculturation. It would be far more helpful to highlight the various dimensions of the inculturation process instead. One needs to take into consideration first the *particular circumstances* of the culture(s) in question and what is taken for granted there. Second, one must pay attention to the *discourse locations* of those advocating particular forms of inculturation—whether they are men or women, whether they belong to hierarchies or authorities (i.e., whether they are leading figures in the church or teachers at institutions of education), or whether they represent subordinate groups or movements. Third, it is important to take into

---

[40]"It would enable us to see God constantly at work in the Church through successive ages, and to see the Church itself as an ever-growing, developing and changing body, led by God's Spirit who delights in making 'all things new' (Rev. 21:5). . . . Such a sense of mission has been given further impetus in the repeated appeals of Pope Paul VI and Pope John Paul II: that we nourish and enrich the universal church through effective inculturation, and that this inculturation be 'an impulse arising from the heart of Africa itself.'" Ibid., 78.

[41]"The current socio-political and economic climate in Nigeria, as elsewhere in Africa, serves as another great resource for fostering inculturation. The call for self-acceptance, self-reliance and self-development, is being made on all fronts: politically, economically and culturally. . . . One may, therefore, see this as the favourable time, when God has brought about for us the conditions and dispositions favourable to successful take off and implementation of inculturation in our African countries. God forbid, that we should miss this unique opportunity, and so fail Christ and his Church." Ibid., 79.

[42]Ibid., 78-79.

consideration the way in which an instance of inculturation takes place (i.e.,
what form inculturation is meant to take in a particular setting). It is just as
important, as the examples of D'Sa and Okure and also the example of the
US-American concept of culture have shown, to remember that the basic
model of what inculturation is, or may be, is itself culturally contingent.
Fourth, the nature of the phenomenon is determined by whether the process
is a *reflexive* one (as is the development of rituals among the Gbaya people,
which we will discuss below in chapter twenty-two) or an *intuitive* one (as
was seen in the examples of the Shembe church and other AICs in chapter
twenty). Fifth, a great deal depends on *which particular church body* is involved since, as we have seen in the Roman Catholic Church, for instance,
certain liturgical forms are subject to greater control than, say, expressions
of popular piety; in contrast, for other churches it is the individual congregation that serves as the frame of reference (to mention just a few of the
examples we have discussed).

We might enumerate other dimensions as well, but since this would
exceed the limited scope of a textbook, we are unable to do so here. Yet the
few dimensions we have mentioned suffice to indicate the complexity of the
phenomena at issue here. Simple models of text and context are both too
static and too naive even to come close to doing justice to the phenomena
we are discussing. After all, cultures are dynamic formations in which many
factors play a role—economic factors, issues of power and influence, the
prerogative of interpretation, identity, issues of affiliation and exclusion or
of recognition and denigration. From this perspective, the so-called translation models, for instance, which assume that inculturation consists of the
cultural application of a universal gospel, are in fact characteristic of a discourse of power. The reason is that their proponents claim for themselves
the exclusive right to decide on the interpretation (the monopoly of interpretation) or at the very least the prerogative in doing so.[43] Proponents of
this model claim that it is especially "biblical," which is yet one more way of
bolstering their claim to the right of interpretation. It is only possible

---

[43]The topic of translation models will not be pursued any further in this book. These kinds of
models are especially popular in the United States. One of the most prominent representatives
in this regard was American linguist Eugene Nida (1914–2011). Other proponents of translation
models include Paul G. Hiebert, Charles H. Kraft, David J. Hesselgrave, Edward Rommen, and
Lamin Sanneh.

successfully to recognize such paradigms for what they are once the multi-dimensionality we described above is recognized and also acknowledged to a certain extent. To be sure, many role players reject this viewpoint most vehemently. However, the reason for this is located in the manner in which they *experience* phenomena of inculturation (which they themselves frequently tend not to designate as such). That being said, in my opinion, taking this seriously would again allow us to take a step forward on the unsteady ground of intercultural understanding.

22

Syncretism

What Is That?

Much has been written on the topic of syncretism in the last few decades. This wealth of literature necessitates a selection and limitation on our part. Besides some very helpful anthologies,[1] there are some monographs that stand out because of the systematic nature of their contents. We will discuss the approaches presented in them in what follows. For the sake of clarity, we will again proceed by presenting an example in each case, which will provide the basis for the following brief sections of theoretical analysis.[2] I have purposely selected examples that are truly relevant for the everyday life of people in congregations and churches first in the United States, and then, following the trajectory, also in churches in African and Asian countries, and finally in the Lutheran church of the Central African Republic. This approach must be emphasized because it stands out from those treatments

---

[1]Wolfgang Greive and Raul Niemann, eds., *Neu glauben? Religionsvielfalt und neue religiöse Strö-mungen als Herausforderung an das Christentum* (Gütersloh, Germany: Gütersloher Verlagshaus Mohn, 1990); Hermann Pius Siller, ed., *Suchbewegungen: Synkretismus—kulturelle Identität und kirchliches Bekenntnis* (Darmstadt, Germany: Wissenschaftliche Buchgesellschaft, 1991).

[2]Theo Sundermeier, *Religion—Was ist das? Religionswissenschaft im theologischen Kontext*, 2nd ed. (Frankfurt: Lembeck, 2007), 187-206. Sundermeier distinguishes between *vertical syncretism*, which is the blending of secondary religions with paradigms from primary religions, which he refers to as *symbiotic syncretism*; and *horizontal syncretism*, which is an exchange on the level of primary religions among themselves, or on the level of secondary religions among themselves, which he designates as *synthetic syncretism*.

For some examples from the global discussion of the issue (which has become almost impossible to overlook) drawn from, say, a liberation-theological perspective, see Leonardo Boff, *Kirche: Charisma und Macht* (Düsseldorf, Germany: Patmos Verlag, 1985), 164-94. Boff's suggested typology of addition, accommodation, mixture, agreement, translation, and adaptation comes across as associative and hardly persuasive on a systematic level. For the intra-Christian discussion in India, see Francis X. D'Sa, SJ, "Der 'Synkretismus' von Raimundo Panikkar," in Siller, *Suchbewegungen*, 117-29.

of the topic that refer only to the now-famous presentation by South Korean woman theologian Hyun Kyung Chung (b. 1955) held at the plenary assembly of the WCC in Canberra in 1991. The reason is that the *performance* she gave was not a true reflection of the actual state of affairs, at least not in the sense of the actual reality of Christians belonging to the various denominations; rather, it was an ad hoc convention event. While this event evoked a lively discussion, the discussion remained a very abstract one because it did not refer to specific material.[3]

In my opinion, one of the important tasks of intercultural theology is to reflect on the true state of affairs, on what is done in practice, rather than to join the ranks of those who give the impression that intercultural theology's only purpose is to discuss books written by theologians from the so-called Third World. Many of those who claim to pursue intercultural theology actually lack the necessary background to do so and end up constructing a stylized image, a distortion of it. This becomes clear by the fact that they frequently ignore subjects like prayers of healing, exorcisms, and ritual actions carried out on the grassroots level; that they overlook such extremely influential institutions of education as Fuller Theological Seminary, the graduates of which exercise considerable influence in many institutions of theological education worldwide; and that they completely fail to address the praxis of local Christians, local congregations, and their local fields of action. The image they construct instead only depicts a very limited selection of the theologically acceptable positions of the theological elite; it is an image that has very little in common with the reality on the ground in the countries, congregations, churches, and movements at issue. Again, intercultural theology should be based on an intercultural hermeneutics that caters for theological and practical divergences and aberrations, for deviations and abnormalities, for that which is odd and comes across as offensive, perhaps, and allows room for it in the bigger picture of Christianity as a pluriform global religious configuration. This is about nothing less than grasping what intercultural theology truly is about.

---

[3]Hyun Kyung Chung, "Come Holy Spirit, Renew the Whole Creation," in Michael Kinnamon, ed., *Signs of the Spirit: Official Report, Seventh Assembly, Canberra, Australia, 7-20 February 1991* (Geneva: WCC Publications, 1991), 37-47.

DRIVING OUT DEMONS: EXORCISMS AS "SPIRITUAL WARFARE" IN THE UNITED STATES

Let us begin with an example from the Pentecostal movement and from those parts of the evangelical movement that dedicate a great deal of attention to the topic of *spiritual warfare*. Other parts of the evangelical movement, while conceding the existence of demons as attested by the New Testament, see this topic as only marginally important. From a central European perspective, the entire subject matter may seem somewhat outlandish, but it is precisely such "outlandishness" that constitutes the object of analysis of the subject of intercultural theology/mission studies. To accuse the other side of obscurantism is simply a way to avoid engaging the intellectual debate.[4] This is not productive, however. Let us therefore proceed with a brief overview. We find that in North America, the praxis and theory of spiritual warfare are contested even within the movement itself.[5] US-American mission studies scholar Scott Moreau presents a typology in which he distinguishes between "traditionalists," with a strong bias against spiritual warfare,[6] and "experience-based warriors," who formulate doctrinal positions predominantly on the basis of exorcistic experiences. Examples of the latter include the internationally renowned John Wimber (1934–1997), Charles Kraft (b. 1932), and Claus Peter Wagner (b. 1930). The other types Moreau proposes are "evangelical confronters," who prefer a

---

[4]We have to question how "ecumenically" or "interculturally" minded those people are who choose simply to ignore phenomena pertaining to world Christianity, phenomena that play a significant role for hundreds of millions of others. Naturally, this does not mean that everybody has to adopt the demonological paradigm, but it does mean that everybody should take it seriously as a legitimate object of study. It is an entirely different question how to deal with it in practical terms in everyday life. Meanwhile, as far as practical issues go, a more profound understanding of the phenomena is not only helpful but also fundamentally important. For some excellent academic analyses in addition to those already mentioned by Birgit Meyer, see also the publications by Andreas Heuser in the area of mission studies and cultural studies. Examples include Andreas Heuser, "'Put on God's Armour Now!'—The Embattled Body in African Pentecostal-Type Christianity," in Sebastian Jobs and Gesa Mackenthun, eds., *Embodiments of Cultural Encounters* (Münster: Waxmann, 2011), 115-40.

[5]For an introduction to the US-American discussion and scene, see the remarkably self-critical deliberations of A. Scott Moreau in his "A Survey of North American Spiritual Warfare Thinking," in A. Scott Moreau et al., eds., *Deliver Us from Evil: An Uneasy Frontier in Christian Mission* (Monrovia, CA: World Vision International, 2002), 117-27. See also the following overview: Charles H. Kraft, "Contemporary Trends in the Treatment of Spiritual Conflict," in Moreau et al., *Deliver Us*, 177-202.

[6]Especially Thomas Ice, Dan Korem, John MacArthur, and others.

direct confrontational approach;[7] "spiritual healers," who emphasize a close connection between spiritual warfare and pastoral care;[8] biblical scholars, who engage the subject of spiritual warfare from an exegetical perspective (such as Walter Wink, Clinton Arnold); "truth encounter advocates," who focus on the doctrine of truth rather than on exorcisms as such (like Neil Anderson, Jimmy Logan, Timothy Warner, and others); and finally "cross-cultural spiritual conflict analysts," who try to understand spiritual warfare in light of an intercultural comparison (such as Scott Moreau, Gailyn Van Rheenen, and others).[9]

Scott Moreau himself teaches courses on the subject of spiritual warfare at Wheaton College, an institution of theological education. That being said, Moreau takes a decidedly self-critical position as far as the intention of some authors is concerned when he points out, "As surprising as this sounds, the feeling I sometimes have in reading the literature is that for some authors it is easier (and more fun) to expel a demon than to walk through realities of broken, shattered lives built on foundations of relational disfunctionality." In terms of the *vocabulary* that is used, Moreau believes that some terms like "binding Satan/the demons" are in danger of becoming fetishized; in terms of the *praxis* he points out that the danger of ritualism exists when authors describe exorcistic techniques as almost mechanical procedures that must be followed with painful precision. Moreau sees this as a symptom of the desire to find quick answers to serious problems or of the desire to be seen as a hero by resorting to violence in the name of good in order to combat violence committed in the name of evil—just as in the Rambo movies—but completely ignoring the topic of forgiveness. In such a case, exorcists assume the role of superheroes.[10] Furthermore, in terms of the afflicted, the belief in demons encourages patients to externalize conflicts, which prevents them from taking responsibility for their own contribution to the problems. Moreau cautions that too little thought is given to the possibility that exorcists could also abuse their power (and that in some cases, the possibility is intentionally ignored altogether). This could lead to a kind of spiritual rape

---

[7]Especially Mark Bubeck, Thomas White, and Fred Dickson.
[8]Paula Sandford, Leanne Payne, and David A. Seamands.
[9]Moreau, "A Survey," 117-19.
[10]Ibid., 121-22.

(such as when indiscreet questions are asked that serve to gratify the exorcist rather than the afflicted person or that pander to his desire for power). From a methodical perspective, a theologically questionable disambiguation is brought to bear. To paraphrase Moreau, the allegedly unambiguous distinction between good here and evil there prohibits the pastoral caregiver from developing a sensibility for the potential sinfulness of every human action, including exorcistic endeavors. In short, there is an internal debate within the movement that we do well to consider.

But let us now proceed to the issue of syncretism. Ever since the 1980s especially, an intense debate has raged in the United States concerning how to deal with demons.[11] While some believe that demons should be *silenced* with words of power since they can only spread lies anyway, others believe that it is necessary to make use of the services of the demons as quasi-*informants*. They believe that *spiritual warfare* is only truly successful when the secrets, plans, strategy, and means of the demons become known. Exorcists need to ensure that the demons tell the truth by *forcing them to do so* by means of invoking the Holy Spirit or the name of Christ. If this has been done, it is believed that the information will be trustworthy. Most noteworthy among those who believe that the information given by demons can and should be trusted when they have been forced by the Holy Spirit to tell the truth is Charles Kraft, a former missionary to Africa who is well known in these circles and who later served as a professor at Fuller Theological Seminary in Pasadena, California. Other authors, however, saw and continue to see this very notion as evidence of "missiological syncretism."[12] How so?

Robert Priest and others point out that any information gained from conversations with the possessed reintroduces into Christianity the concepts and practices of traditional religions, concepts and practices that the

---

[11]*Global discourses* on the subject of demonology have been taking place for a long time. For more on the influence of the US-American persons and their publications in Ghana, as well as on the new forms of *deliverance* occurring there as people adopt elements from the global discourse against the background of local religious traditions, see Opoku Onyinah, "Deliverance as a Way of Confronting Witchcraft in Modern Africa: Ghana as a Case History," *Asian Journal for Pentecostal Studies* 5, no. 1 (2002): 107-34, esp. 114ff. This source also elaborates on the research debate.

[12]Robert J. Priest, Thomas Campbell, and Bradford A. Mullen, "Missiological Syncretism: The New Animistic Paradigm," in Edward Rommen, ed., *Spiritual Power and Missions* (Pasadena, CA: W. Carey Library, 1995), 9-87.

Christian faith is in fact supposed to overcome. These include the notion that objects can be infused (or infested) with good or evil powers and used accordingly, either for protection or to cast malicious curses (fetishes). They also include the notion that even Christians may be possessed by evil spirits or that curses can remain effective over many generations. Charles Kraft, for instance, believes that evil power may emanate from Buddha statues that people bring along as souvenirs. He also assumes that Christians may readily become possessed by evil spirits and accepts the existence of generational curses. Critics of these beliefs—which, as we have said, are held also by many other authors—point out that the New Testament does not recount such details, that the writings of the New Testament are conspicuously reserved on this issue, and that those who subscribe to such beliefs essentially deny or at least call into question the assurance of faith that they are protected in Jesus Christ against all the powers of evil.

The debate shows that the various actors are very much agreed on their struggle against that which they consider to be demonic powers, but that they differ considerably as to which line of attack to take. This tension is also evident in other contexts, for instance when it comes to the use of cultural and religious symbols, the use of ritual elements, of linguistic expressions, and the like.

THEOLOGICAL CONCEPTS OF SYNCRETISM

These examples help us to articulate an essentially theological and thus normative concept of syncretism. Thus some theologians see syncretism as something fundamentally negative, as something endangering the Christian identity. German proponents of this negative use of the term include Peter Beyerhaus (b. 1929)[13] and others. Proponents of this view see an "illegitimate commingling of religions" taking place in various contexts, whereby the operative interpretation of religion and religions plays a seminal role. Beyerhaus, for instance, proceeds on the basis of a *tripolar* understanding of religion, according to which religion is something God intended but which has become corrupted by both *human sin* and the *work of Satan and*

---

[13]Peter Beyerhaus and Lutz von Padberg, eds., *Eine Welt—Eine Religion? Die synkretistische Bedrohung unseres Glaubens im Zeichen von New Age*, 2nd ed. (Asslar, Germany: Schulte & Gerth, 1989).

the demons. Other religions are thus under general suspicion of being demonic deceptions even when they lead to initially positive social effects.
After all, it is argued, they might immunize people against recognizing
Christ as their only Lord and Savior. Good deeds and the institutions of
other religions are therefore potentially expressive of a kind of immuni-
zation strategy conceived by evil powers.

Other authors see what they call "syncretism" as something very positive.
Thus Indian theologian M. M. Thomas believes himself at liberty to call for
a "Christocentric syncretism."[14] According to this view, if the Christian faith
does not relate to the elements and forms of other cultures and religions, it
will remain irrelevant for people. For this reason, it is vital bravely to step
out in faith and to adopt and adapt such elements and forms. Systematician
Wolfhart Pannenberg (1928-2014) is also among those who hold a progressive, positive view of the term *syncretism.*[15] He argues that it was especially due to the *adaptability of the Christian faith* that Christianity was able
to express itself in ever new ways in a plurality of religiocultural forms, i.e.,
that it was able to express itself in ways relevant to the everyday life of people.
Its missionary strength is located above all—to paraphrase Pannenberg—in
the Christian faith's "ability to syncretize."[16]

Meanwhile, we must qualify these assertions and caution that both M. M.
Thomas and Wolfhart Pannenberg use the term *syncretism* in a way that
does not conform to its original meaning. After all, naturally both of them
admit that it is possible for the Christian identity to be endangered in theology and praxis, that it is even possible for the Christian identity to be lost,
which would correspond to genuine syncretism. It would appear, however,
that the normative-theological approaches briefly presented here are not
able to differentiate well enough in their perception of the actual nature of
the processes of exchange at issue here. A group of scholars in the field of
religious studies resorted to a systems theory approach in order to shed light

---

[14]Madathilparampil Mammen Thomas, "The Absoluteness of Jesus Christ and Christ-Centred
Syncretism," *The Ecumenical Review* 37 (1985): 387-97. By contrast, H. K. Chung, who we mentioned earlier, opted for a *life-centered syncretism.*

[15]Wolfhart Pannenberg, "Erwägungen zu einer Theologie der Religionsgeschichte," in *Grundfragen systematischer Theologie: Gesammelte Aufsätze*, 2nd ed. (Göttingen: Vandenhoeck & Ruprecht, 1971), 252-95.

[16]For more on Pannenberg, see Hennning Wrogemann, *Mission und Religion in der Systematischen
Theologie der Gegenwart* (Göttingen: Vandenhoeck & Ruprecht), 147-73.

on this issue. Let us turn then to a second example and inquire after an illustrative, purely descriptive way of defining syncretism.

WARDING OFF DANGER: CHRISTIAN PURIFICATION RITES IN CENTRAL AFRICA

In the Central African Republic (*Republic Centrafricaine*, RCA) too, people's fear of evil spirits, the ancestors, and evil powers plays an important role. Here, however, ritual actions take on a greater significance than they do in the United States and other countries. Among the Gbaya people, for instance, who lived in a tribal-religious context up until the beginning of the twentieth century, many traditional rites, or at least elements of such rites, continue to be well known. Since many people here believe that it is possible to be bewitched, the Lutheran church, which was founded in the 1960s among the Gbaya people, began in the 1990s to develop a variety of liturgical-ritual forms in order to respond to fears often prevalent in the congregations. What distinguished these Christian liturgical rites was that the sequence, i.e., the flow of the liturgy, was modeled after the sequence and flow of the traditional rites and that they also feature the repeated use of elements drawn from the traditional rites (such as pieces of wood, water, smoke from a fire, a forked branch, pieces of coal, etc.). This raises the question: Does the adoption and adaptation of ritual forms from the older, i.e., traditional, religion of the Gbaya people equate to "syncretism"?

Before we turn to a ritual of washing, on the basis of which we will consider this question in greater detail, allow me to tell a short story in order to demonstrate the relevance of the rite. The story is set in a little village located in the northwest corner of the Central African Republic. The local police have arrested Antoine and thrown him into prison, highhandedly accusing him of having committed a certain crime.[17] Everyone in the village knows that the government has not paid the salaries of the police for two years. Everyone survives by resorting to a subsistence economy. The police frequently carry out actions like this in order to extort money from the general population. Prisons did not exist in central Africa until they were introduced

---

[17]I base the following discussion on the excellent study of Markus Roser, *Hexerei und Lebensriten: Zur Inkulturation des christlichen Glaubens unter den Gbaya der Zentralafrikanischen Republik* (Erlangen, Germany: Erlanger Verlag für Mission und Ökumene, 2000).

by the colonial powers as recently as the nineteenth century. After some time, it turns out that the accusation against Antoine was spurious. He is released, but he is now no longer able to return to his village. Why? Because people believe that while in prison, Antoine contracted *simbo*. In the language of the Gbaya people to which he belongs, this means an evil curse, if you will, that people conceive of as something like a substance clinging to Antoine and to everybody coming out of prison, innocent or not. It is feared that in every case, *simbo* will cause misfortune for somebody in the village. It will lead to illness or perhaps to murder, infertility, miscarriage, or whatever the case may be. In the eyes of the residents, the danger is very real.

Now, the majority of the village population consists of Christians— Baptists, some Catholics, Brethren, a significant number of Lutherans, also a Muslim and a Baha'i here and there. Antoine is a Lutheran Christian. Now, what would happen if something like this were to happen to, say, a Baptist? Well, the Baptist Christians would not take him back into the village, but on Sunday they would confess that believing in *simbo*, in witches, sorcerers, evil powers, and the like is superstitious, and that Christ the Lord is stronger than all these things. So Antoine would secretly go to a medicine man or a diviner, perhaps on Monday, subject himself to a rite featuring elements of the tribal religion, and then, when the news of this had spread, he would be able to return to his village. The rite would have purified him; the danger would have been averted—Jesus or no Jesus. This rite would include circling around a termite hill three times, taking a ritual bath in a dammed-up stream with leaves of the Soré tree floating in the water, jumping over a fire, tossing pieces of coal in a westerly direction, and, naturally, chanting incantations.

There is a widespread fear of evil and of witchcraft in the Central African Republic. In the past, during times of great poverty, corruption, and HIV/ AIDS, often accusations of witchcraft were leveled, resulting in mob justice even before it came to a hearing. The Evangelical Lutheran Church in the RCA responded in the 1990s by drafting a liturgy that catered for a case like Antoine's. The liturgical rite that it offered contains prayers and Scripture readings that interpret what happened. The central aspect of the rite is a baptismal reminder, during which water is sprinkled on the shoulder (not on the head!) of the person released from prison. At the end, the person who has been released shakes hands with a representative of the home village. A sign of friendship?

By no means. This represents the visual confirmation of an invisible transformation, one that is seen as very real: in the name of Jesus Christ, the village dissociates Antoine from any possible *simbo* infection. At the same time, the adoption and adaptation of a water rite both establish and invalidate continuity with the tribal religious rite, for the rite serves as a reminder of baptism, which guarantees that nothing can separate us Christians from God. This guarantee finds expression in the freedom to reestablish *physical contact* with the person released from prison, as signified and sealed by the shaking of hands.

Thus the purpose of the ritual is to make faith visible, to show that faith is applicable to the causalities arising from a worldview associated with tribal religious thinking and to show that it helps overcome them. The aim is *to liberate people from the fear of (evil) powers in the name of an even stronger power, and the ritual serves as a reminder of the presence of this power. The aim is to achieve certainty of faith by means of a visible, public, tangible ritual that makes a new social reality possible. Thus this rite serves as a medium of cultural liberation.* We will now study in detail the textual form of this rite (the spoken parts) and the instructions it contains for liturgical actions (what is to be carried out). Since it helps us see some important correlations, we will need to consider a somewhat lengthy excerpt. The instructions enclosed in square brackets refer to the sections describing physical actions in the liturgy. I have italicized certain words to make it easier to recognize the structure.

> 1. Introduction. Officiant: We are gathered here because Christ has called us out of slavery to freedom, in order that we may always live in freedom. Formerly, we lived as prisoners in this world. But now we are heirs of God, who is rich, and we address Him as: "Abba," which means "Father." Therefore we too are no longer slaves, but rather children and heirs.
>
> [I. Proclamation]
>
> 2. Invocation. Officiant: In the Name of the Father and of the Son and of the Holy Spirit. [Here the sign of the cross is made.] All: Amen.
>
> 3. Prolog. Officiant: Jesus said to them: "I have told you these things, so that in me you may have peace. In this world you will be afraid.[18] But take heart! I have overcome the world." (John 16:33)

---

[18]Translator's note: Scripture passages cited in this ritual are taken from the NIV. In this instance, the translation deviates from the NIV in order to correspond more closely to the German text. The NIV original reads, "In this world you will have trouble."

4. Brief Prayer. Officiant: Almighty God, we come to you as people oppressed by the slavery of fear: The fear of the *simbo* curse. Help us that we may remain in Your love and that evil may have no power over us. Send us Your Holy Spirit, so that His light may scatter the darkness. In the Name of Jesus Christ, our Lord. Amen.

5. Scripture Reading. "Formerly, when you did not know God, you were slaves to those who by nature are not gods. But now that you know God—or rather are known by God—how is it that you are turning back to those weak and miserable forces? Do you wish to be enslaved by them all over again?" (Galatians 4:8-9)

6. Address/Admonition. Officiant: *Formerly*, when someone discovered a corpse, when people died in a traffic accident, if some other disaster occurred, if someone was released from prison, or if someone had killed another person, then he was washed clean of the *simbo* curse. But *now* the people know God. He is the God of Life. He cares for the people. He protects us the Father, the Son, and the Holy Spirit. Just as you know Him, He also knows you. He calls to you: "Don't be afraid; just believe." (Mark 5:36; Luke 8:50) For by your faith He will overcome your fear.

Formerly, the ancestors were washed clean of the *simbo* curse in the river valley, circling around the trees.

But *now* the cross of Christ is the new Tree of Life for the people. This new tree gives peace to the people. That is why we can say: *Christ is our* Soré-*tree-peace!* For the cross was raised up among the people as a sign of new life in Christ through his death and his resurrection from the dead.

Formerly, our ancestors were washed clean of the *simbo* curse in deep water, into which they had cast the bark of the trees they had circled around. But *now* Jesus Christ has purified us by the water of Baptism and has established a covenant of blood with us. Because we have already been purified by the water of Baptism, we no longer need to act as our ancestors did.

Formerly, after they had been washed, they jumped over the fire. But *now* the fire of the Holy Spirit shows us that God has already made us new people.

Formerly, our ancestors cast a piece of coal at a bird so that it would bear away the curse that oppressed them. But *now* Jesus Christ is the Lamb of God that takes away all the evil that oppresses us. He restores our relationship with God.

The God of Life desires that we become free of every curse. We no longer need to walk in the way of the ancestors; rather, we turn to the Living God. He calls to us: "Don't be afraid; just believe." (Mark 5:36; Luke 8:50)

II. Reconciliation

7. *Renunciation of Evil.* Officiant: When we purify ourselves of evil, *it means that our life is changed.* Therefore each person will respond to the purification of evil by *shaking hands.* Let the person who desires to be purified of evil now answer my question: Officiant: Are you resolved to renounce the works of the evil one and to renounce his guile? All: Yes, we are resolved! Officiant: Are you resolved to renounce the evil that rules the darkness, and to follow Christ, walking and abiding in the light, in life, and in love? All: Yes, we are resolved! Officiant: Do you know that when people are purified from evil, new faith awakens within them? That Jesus Christ is risen from the dead, that he lives, and is seated here among us? All: Yes, we know this!

8. *Liberation from evil.* Officiant: Human beings know evil and their own desires, but now they experience the mercy of God. As our Lord Jesus Christ commanded, I say to you: He has already banished all the evil that weighs you down; in the Name of the Father and of the Son and of the Holy Spirit. (+) All: Amen.

9. Proclamation of Grace. Officiant: Everything that separated us from God and from our brothers and sisters has been cleansed. Let us rejoice in this truth of His.

10. Greeting of peace. Officiant: The peace of the Lord be with you! All: And also with you!

III. Symbolic Actions

11. Provision of the symbols: A cross made from a *Soré* tree; water; and a candle. When the *objects* are in place, the officiant says the following: [The officiant takes the cross, lifts it up, and says:] Officiant: *Let us look to the cross of Christ!* Formerly, our ancestors circled around trees. But now we do so no longer. We look to the cross of Christ. For Christ gives us life by His death and His resurrection from the dead. He has taken away our fear of death. In Him we already have peace. [The officiant takes the bowl of water, lifts it up, and says:] *Let us turn our eyes to this water!* Formerly, our ancestors purified themselves of the *simbo* curse in the water, using bark from various kinds of trees. But now we do so no longer. This water is no new Baptism; it is meant to remind us of our Baptism. In Baptism, we have already died and been saved through the death of Jesus Christ. For in our Baptism, God has established a covenant of blood with us. He saved us in our Baptism. We are clean, like newborns. The old evil can harm us no longer. For we know that by His death on the cross, our Lord Jesus Christ won for us life itself. Through the Holy

Spirit, He remains among us. [The officiant takes the candle, lifts it up, and says:] *Let us turn our eyes to the candle.* Formerly, our ancestors jumped over the fire. But now we do so no longer. The candle's fire symbolizes the Holy Spirit. It illumines the darkness by giving of itself, consuming itself. In the same way, Christ gave Himself up to death, and died. He truly died and won for us true life. The candle's fire is similar to the Holy Spirit, the Spirit of Power, the Spirit of Faith, and the Spirit who delivers people from their fear.

[The officiant takes the bowl of water, dips his fingers into the water, makes the sign of the cross, and says:] I mark you with the sign of the cross on the forehead and on the heart as a sign of the Holy Spirit and to remind you that God has already purified you. God loves you! Put your trust in Him! "Don't be afraid; just believe." (Mark 5:36; Luke 8:50) In the Name of the Father and of the Son and of the Holy Spirit. Amen! (+)

IV. Conclusion

12. Prayers of Intercession. . . .

13. Blessing. . . .

14. At this point, the person is permitted to wash as normal.[19]

Let us proceed by summarizing the distinctive aspects of the rite: The first part contains an interpretation of the situation of fear and insecurity (introduction) and a characterization of the Christian image of God (proclamation). After praying, the cause of the fear is stated, following which the older tribal-religious rites are contrasted repeatedly with the Christian alternatives: Formerly, people circled around trees, washed themselves in water that had been dammed up and infused with medicines, jumped over a fire, and cast a piece of coal at a bird in a westerly direction. But now the following symbols replace these ritual elements: the cross (a tree as a cross), baptism (water, washing), and fire (the Holy Spirit). Instead of casting a piece of coal at a bird, people are directed to the Lamb of God. As the service proceeds, the reconciliation part calls the participants to renounce evil, and it provides for physical contact in the form of a handshake. Then in the symbolic actions a Christian rite of washing is followed, in which the sequence of the symbolism of the tribal-religious rite is duplicated, yet at the same time a liturgical text is interpolated throughout. The ritual action now consists of the presentation of the physical symbols of the cross, the bowl of

---

[19]Liturgy translated from the German in Roser, *Hexerei und Lebensriten*, 320-30. Emphasis added.

water, and the candle ("Let us look . . ."), at which point the contrast between "formerly" and "now" is repeated again. Finally, as a symbolic action and also as a reminder of baptism, the officiant dips his fingers into the bowl of water and marks the person accused of being afflicted by the *simbo* curse with the sign of the cross on the forehead and on the heart. After the ritual is over, an opportunity is provided for the washing of the whole body.

This raises the question of whether this liturgical rite equates to a kind of syncretism, since it not only mentions the older rite but also follows the sequence of the older rite. Furthermore, does this not serve to perpetuate the older tradition in a certain sense? Is it not also possible that this will lead to the perpetuation of people's fears? We conclude that it remains to be seen what the long-term effects of the practice of the rite will be. Let us note: here a church is attempting to provide a ritual answer to a specific problem. The form demonstrates a very elaborate theological framework, as the selection of biblical texts clearly shows. At the same time, the focus of the rite is a holistic one that devotes attention to the whole person, together with all of her existential concerns. From the 1990s until the present, this rite has proven to be most helpful for the Gbaya people.

SYNCRETISM FROM THE DESCRIPTIVE PERSPECTIVE OF RELIGIOUS STUDIES

Ulrich Berner and other researchers have suggested distinguishing between syncretism on the level of religious elements and syncretism on the level of religious systems.[20] According to this distinction, if we approached our example from the world of the Gbaya people descriptively from the perspective of religious studies, we might speak of syncretism on the level of religious elements. In contrast, it is far more difficult to identify examples of syncretism on the level of systems. It is perhaps legitimate to speak of such religious configurations as the Afro-Brazilian Umbanda and Candomblé cults (to name just two) as dual religious systems, as Robert Schreiter has suggested.[21] We are not at liberty to pursue such issues here.

---

[20]Ulrich Berner, *Untersuchungen zur Verwendung des Synkretismus-Begriffes* (Wiesbaden, Germany: Harrassowitz, 1982).

[21]Robert J. Schreiter, "Synkretismus und duale Religionsysteme," in *Abschied vom Gott der Europäer* (Salzburg, Austria: Atnon Pustet, 1992), 220-40. Schreiter allows for four different types of syncretism. The first is the integration of elements of other religious traditions into the

However, from the descriptive perspective of religious studies, it is to be expected that there will be a considerable need for clarification as far as intra-Christian processes of interaction and communication are concerned. This becomes evident from the significant contribution to the discussion by Andreas Feldtkeller.[22]

Feldtkeller begins by conceptualizing the term *syncretism* from the perspective of those who use it. After all, processes of exchange between religious configurations are not "syncretistic" as such; rather, corresponding phenomena are designated as syncretistic *from the specific perspective* of various role players. This usually happens for a very specific reason that arises from their specific positioning vis-à-vis the phenomena in question. In order to gain a better understanding of these positionings, Feldtkeller goes on to distinguish whether the role players are *individuals* or *groups*. An additional dynamic is whether such a phenomenon takes place within the *immediate presence* of the role player(s) or only *after some time has passed*. These four categories yield a grid, which is constituted as follows:

When an individual considers whether his own exercise of religion is syncretistic or not, then his *perspective* is that of his own *religious biography*. The individual is considering his exercise of religion and his faith, asking where there is *continuity* and where there is *discontinuity*. To illustrate this using an example: Even though converts (i.e., people who have switched one religion for another) tend to view their earlier exercise of religion as false or deficient, after some time many of them claim that there were powers at work

---

framework of Christianity. The second is the integration of Christian elements into the framework of another religious configuration. The third is the amalgamation of two traditions into an entirely new framework. In contrast, dual systems occur when people belong to two different religious configurations concurrently and allow these, as far as they themselves are concerned, to exist alongside each other. Meanwhile, a critical observation reveals that Schreiter's operative definition of what constitutes a "religion" is somewhat deficient; essentially, he has in mind religions like Christianity, Judaism, and Islam, with their fixed canons of sacred writings, fundamental doctrinal systems, certain similar rituals (for the most part, anyway), religious specialists, etc. In contrast, S. Shimada is correct when he points out that the term *syncretism* is not applicable to certain other religious configurations at all, since they lack fixed forms—and since such fixed forms are needed in order to define syncretism in the first place as an aberration from the norm in general. Shingo Shimada and Jürgen Straub, "Relationale Hermeneutik im Kontext interkulturellen Verstehens: Probleme universalistischer Begriffsbildung in den Sozial- und Kulturwissenschaften—erörtert am Beispiel 'Religion,'" *Deutsche Zeitschrift für Philosophie* 47, no. 3 (1999): 449-77.

[22]Andreas Feldtkeller, "Der Synkretismusbegriff im Rahmen einer Theorie von Verhältnisbestimmungen zwischen Religionen," *Evangelische Theologie* 52 (1993): 224-45.

in it that guided them toward their new religious identity. However, when an individual considers his current religious practice, then this analysis of his religion is oriented toward its *similarity* and *contradistinction* to others.

Meanwhile, whether the party carrying out the analysis is an individual or a group makes a significant difference, since the cohesion of a group demands a minimum of coherency, whereas that same coherency may be called into question by the verdict of syncretism. If the analysis is a diachronic one, then the perspective of religiocultural exchange (selection) predominates. The example of the Gbaya liturgy clearly shows how both *adoption* and *rejection* are interpreted theologically, justified, and then staged liturgically. From a synchronic perspective, the parallel exercise of religion results either in *reaching an understanding* or in *conflict*. It then comes either to the toleration of certain religio-ritual innovations or to conflicts within the group concerning the appropriate religious praxis. An example of this, as we have seen, is that of the Aladura churches among the Yoruba people that separated from the mission churches over issues regarding the prayer for healing (one example is the split between the church of the Church Missionary Society and the newly constituted Cherubim and Seraphim). In summary, we may conclude that the term *syncretism* is quite obviously self-referential, which means that it says less about the phenomenon as such and more about the position of the particular individual or group using the term.

BEYOND SYNCRETISM, OR WHAT ACTUALLY DEFINES IDENTITY?

After what has been said thus far, we would be justified in asking whether it is actually legitimate to continue using the term *syncretism*. However, this question will remain an academic one for as long as other persons and groups within world Christianity continue to use the term. As long as this continues to be the case, it is helpful to clarify the various uses of the term for ourselves. One important aspect that we have covered consisted of identifying the self-referential character of the term. Beyond that, however, we must answer a more elementary question: If this is about determining Christian identity, or more precisely about determining which form of Christian doctrine and practice may still be considered either authentically Christian or legitimately Christian, then we must ask: What actually defines identity? In other words, the term *syncretism* refers back to the term *identity*. Allow me to conclude with a few brief remarks.

During the past few decades, the term *identity* has truly come into vogue.[23] The difficulty with the identity debate already begins with the term *identity*. From a philosophical perspective, identity may initially be understood as *identity with itself*. Something is identical with itself. Strictly speaking, this understanding raises the question: What does such self-identity consist in? Thus philosopher Ludwig Wittgenstein was correct in his assertion: "To say of *two* things that they are identical is nonsense, and to say of *one* thing that it is identical with itself is to say nothing."[24] We can only speak metaphorically about identity, since for logical reasons there can be no such thing as pure identity. Thus because identity always consists of "*something being identical with something else*," it presupposes the existence of something with different gradations or aspects of incrementation that is identical with something else. That is not to say that these are two entirely different things.[25] Rather, the question is, In what sense are these two things one and the same?

We can simplify the issue by distinguishing between two areas in which this question is debated on an academic level: In the field of *cultural studies*, it is the issue of how a member of a society is "identical" with this culture of hers and with its symbol system, i.e., the shared symbols, patterns of observation, life orientations, values, etc., common to all members of the society. Thus the focus is on the *spatial dimension*, which connotes the shared space of a culture or a society as its identity. This culture (and religion) is reflected by its individual members. In contrast, in the field of *ego psychology*, it is the issue of a person's identity, which should be observable as remaining "identical" with itself over a long period of time. The issue of the continuity of the subject with itself thus presupposes the *temporal dimension* of the perdurability of an identity and is centered on the degree to which the subject may

---

[23]In the humanities, the word first came to be used during the 1940s, namely in Erik Erikson's ego psychology. Once introduced, other academic disciplines soon adopted the term. In the process, the term was broadened and then integrated into very different theoretical concepts. For more on this issue, see Aleida Assmann and Heidrun Friese, eds., *Identitäten*, vol. 3 of *Erinnerung, Geschichte, Identität*, 2nd ed. (Frankfurt: Suhrkamp, 1999); Aleida Assmann and Heidrun Friese, "Einleitung," in Assmann et al., *Identitäten*, 11; Wilhelm Schmidt, *Philosophie der Lebenskunst* (Frankfurt: Suhrkamp, 1998); Jürgen Straub, "Personale und kollektive Identität: Zur Analyse eines theoretischen Begriffs," in Assmann et al., *Identitäten*, 73-104.

[24]Ludwig Wittgenstein, *Tractatus Logico-Philosophicus*, ed. David Pears and Brian McGuinness (London: Routledge, 2001), 5:5303.

[25]See Peter Wagner, "Fest-Stellungen: Beobachtungen zur sozialwissenschaftlichen Diskussion über Identität," in Assmann et al., *Identitäten*, 44-72.

be said to have remained identical with itself despite or precisely because of the way it changed over the course of time.

From a cultural-semiotic perspective, an intercultural hermeneutics will need to consider which similarities various actors "discover." Put differently, it will need to examine which things suggest themselves to the actors as signs in order to serve as the medium of that which they see as being incrementally identical with themselves or with their group. To come at the issue with a broader scope, an intercultural hermeneutics will need to study what the actors see as compatible or tolerable, either consciously or unconsciously. From a discourse-theoretical perspective, a crosscheck will need to be performed: Namely, which actors see which phenomena as constituting a successful present-day praxis, and which discourse position do they occupy? Here we may recall the example of Bruno Gutmann following his return from Germany to Tanzania: in his absence, the indigenous African leaders had for the most part abolished the circumcision of both boys and girls and had come to understand this abolition as an appropriate form of Christian-African praxis. In contrast, as a result of his desire to conserve and safeguard Chagga culture, Gutmann declared the circumcision issue to be of secondary importance theologically and opted to reintroduce circumcision again. Again, which actors act in which historic constellations, in which religio-politico-cultural contexts, coming from which social positions (because the issue of power and of the prerogative of interpretation always plays a role as well)? How are majority and minority constituted, and how do they relate to one another? We might recall the example of Christian minorities in India and the efforts by activists there against the backdrop of a Hindu majority, activists intent on putting a stop to any and all attempts to adopt the religious symbolism of the Hindu traditions.

23

The "Postcolonial Turn"— and Then What?

On the Newer Terminology

The term *postcolonial* initially came to be used as an historic term designating the time after the colonial era, but its definition was then broadened to refer to the continuation of colonial dependencies ("neocolonial") in the economic and cultural spheres following the independence of former colonial territories. In this sense, *postcolonial* was used as a systematic term designating a discourse formation. Let us begin by discussing *postcolonial* as an historic term: In connection with the independence movements, we may list such authors as Léopold Sédar Senghor or Frantz Fanon (with his famous book, *The Wretched of the Earth*, 1961), who resisted the colonial system in their capacity as intellectuals. They developed terms like *négritude* to call attention not only to the economic and political factors of independence but also to the cultural self-consciousness of African actors. Using the motto "black is beautiful," they protected integral aspects of their own identity from the way others were characterizing them in the colonial discourse. They rejected the way others characterized blacks as belonging to a lower cultural level. Such characterizations were used to justify the right and duty of the colonial powers to annex foreign territories and to civilize their populations, i.e., to grant them a share in the "blessings" of Western civilization. This still constituted a political discourse, one in which people were responding to essentialist characterizations by others (blacks are backward) with similarly essentialist self-characterizations ("black is beautiful," "African values," etc.).

THE DEVELOPMENT OF POSTCOLONIAL THEORY

Yet from the 1980s onward, the debate began to change. *Postcolonial* came to be understood more and more as a term designating a discourse formation. This happened especially in the so-called field of postcolonial studies. Here "hegemonic power structures" were analyzed that were observed to operate across national boundaries, analyzed especially with a view to how people were characterized by others or how they characterized themselves. The term *othering* was coined to describe how people classify the world according to a binary code, i.e., when people consciously or unconsciously dissociate themselves from others by simultaneously stylizing both themselves and others.[1] The hypothesis stated that colonial power is maintained not only by means of economic dependencies but also and especially by means of patterns of cultural interpretation, which the Western academic tradition presents as self-evident and then propagates institutionally.

The wide appeal of postcolonial studies led to the postulation of a *postcolonial turn*. This term is generally used to designate the turn toward a more general postcolonial criticism. The object of study is now no longer the manner in which a certain colonial power operated within a certain territory, but rather in a more general way how the Self and the Other were represented in the colonial discourse. This perspective was demonstrated in an exemplary manner by Edward Said (1935–2003) in his 1978 book *Orientalism*.[2] Said was a native of Palestine who then resettled in the United States and taught comparative literature studies at Columbia University in New York. In his work he criticized, first, that the Western academic tradition was characterized by a binary classification between the Self and the Other, between insiders and outsiders. He believed, second, that this led the observer to project his own preconceptions onto the Other, which in turn served to justify the colonial appropriation of other countries on an intellectual level. In Said's opinion, this program continued to be in effect long after the actual colonial era, which came to an end in the 1960s. His basic hypothesis states that the Western academic tradition defines its own identity by dissociating itself from the Other and by interpreting both cultural "entities"

---

[1]For more on the discussion, see Doris Bachmann-Medick, "Postcolonial Turn," in *Cultural Turns: Neuorientierungen in den Kulturwissenschaften*, 3rd ed. (Hamburg: Rowohlt, 2009), 184-207.
[2]Edward Said, *Orientalism* (New York: Pantheon Books, 1978).

as homogenous units. In contrast, authors of the postcolonial turn point out that these contradistinctions (such as Europe being active, Asia being passive; Europe academic, Asia mythical) need to be broken up to allow interstices to develop. Overall, Said demanded that what is incomplete, contradictory, and fragmentary also needs to be taken into account.[3] At issue for him was the deconstruction of the image of homogenous cultures. One of the pioneers of deconstructionism was French philosopher Jacques Derrida (1930–2004), who used deconstruction to help liberate people from the way their cultures were characterized by outsiders.[4]

Multiculturality or Interculturality?

The development of postcolonial theory focused, on the one hand, on the discourses of alterity observed to be taking place between the cultures and continents, while the other area of intense focus was the makeup of culturally plural societies. In the process, significant attention was initially devoted to the concept of "multiculturality."[5] The prevalence of significant migratory streams then led researchers to question just what makes for cohesion in culturally plural societies. This led to the development of very divergent models. The model of the *melting pot*, for instance, proceeded on the assumption that every immigrant society will continue to be subdivided into cultural subgroups, but that as assimilation takes place over time these groups tend to conform to one another and to amalgamate into a new shared culture more and more. Critics rejected this as hegemonic. The *salad bowl* model was then developed to allow for ongoing plurality and in so doing to take into consideration the continued existence of culturally independent groups. Yet some criticized that this model downplayed the togetherness of a society. Others again censured the idea of the continued parallel existence of relatively autonomous and "pure" cultures as illusionary; they claimed that to have cultural groups existing parallel to one

---

[3] Among the significant theoreticians in this regard, we may list especially Homi Bhabha (b. 1949) and Gayatri Chakravorty Spivak (b. 1942).
[4] Jacques Derrida, *Grammatologie* (Frankfurt: Suhrkamp, 1974); for more on the discussion of postmodernism, see Jürgen Habermas, *Der philosophische Diskurs der Moderne* (Frankfurt: Suhrkamp, 1985).
[5] See Andreas Reckwitz, "Multikulturalismustheorien und der Kulturbegriff: Vom Homogenitäts-modell zum Modell kultureller Interferenzen," *Berliner Journal für Soziologie* 11 (2001): 179ff.

another was not worth striving for and that describing the shared existence of such groups as a mere coexistence did not do justice to the existing relationship patterns. In response, a number of theoreticians began to prefer the term *interculturality*.

With respect to the term *interculturality*, Jürgen Gebhardt is correct when he points out that the term *culture* derives from the domain of the German academic tradition. He shows that around 1900, the term *culture* (*Kultur*) came into widespread use with a political connotation in Germany. Here, *Kultur* was generally paired with its counterpart, *Zivilisation* (whatever that was supposed to mean), i.e., the two were used in combination as a binary pair.[6] In contrast, in the Anglophone (and Francophone) world the term *civilization* was the preferred one up until the 1940s. This only changed under the influence of the work of US-American anthropologist Edward B. Tylor, with the result that *cultures* were now spoken of in the plural. The scope of the term was broadened to include political and economic aspects, and it became widespread in this sense through the work of Alfred L. Kroeber and Clyde Kluckhohn.[7] Talcott Parsons then took the term (which originally came from the field of anthropology) and redefined it as a sociological term: *cultural system*.

It is especially in the area of the applied sciences that there is a tremendous interest in this kind of functional use of the concept of culture, since it is here that intercultural communication is understood as the communication between two cultural sense systems that may be optimized by following certain rules. Gebhardt criticizes this approach because one important area of application for a theory of this nature is the advising of government and business delegations, as frequently happened in the United States from the 1950s onward.[8] It is imperative that the interests driving the demand for such approaches also be taken into account. The difficulty of these kinds of theories, like those of intercultural psychology, for instance, consists in the

---

[6]Jürgen Gebhardt, "Interkulturelle Kommunikation: Vom praktischen Nutzen und theoretischen Nachteil angewandter Sozialwissenschaft," in Lars Allolio-Näcke, Britta Kalscheuer and Arne Manzeschke, eds., *Differenzen anders denken* (Frankfurt: Campus, 2005), 275-86, especially 277-78.

[7]Alfred L. Kroeber and Clyde Kluckhohn, *Culture: A Critical Review of Concepts and Definitions*, Papers of the Peabody Museum of American Archaeology and Ethnology 47 (Cambridge, MA: The Museum, 1952).

[8]Gebhardt, "Interkulturelle Kommunikation," 280.

fact that the theoreticians in question continue to presuppose the existence of cultural units (i.e., of entities)—a view that does not do justice to the complexity of mutually interacting cultural configurations. It may be assumed that there is a tendency in this regard to generalize any (alleged) cultural patterns with the intent of delivering the most practicable instructions possible. Thus the motivation behind the theorization implies a willingness to "reify" cultural patterns.

As far as *intercultural theology* is concerned, this immediately raises the question: What is the motivation behind this discipline? Is the aim here also to optimize intercultural activities on the basis of a certain means-end rationality? To what end should intercultural theology actually be pursued? Which interests are driving the research? We also need to ask whether the terms *multi*cultural and *inter*cultural do not presuppose overly homogenous conceptions of culture. Is it actually possible to distinguish cultures from one another to the necessary extent when people constantly move and function within culturally plural contexts? Would that not call for the development of new concepts? In fact, such attempts have been carried out for some time with the aim to analyze culturally plural contexts, using such terms as *hybridity, mélange,* or *creolization.* We will now turn our attention to these concepts.

HYBRIDITY, MÉLANGE, OR CREOLIZATION?

In the last few years, the concept of "hybridity" has grown in popularity.[9] *Hybridity* is a term used to designate the increasing blurring of cultural boundary lines in the wake of globalization. Hybridity thus basically means an "amalgamation" of a sort, a process that may highlight the increasing complexity and efficiency of the product or, alternately, the resulting contamination and the lowering of standards, depending on how such processes are interpreted. Meanwhile, it is difficult to nail down a definition for

---

[9]See Jan Nederveen Pieterse, "Hybrid Modernities: Mélange Modernities in Asia," *Sociological Analysis* 1, no. 3 (1998): 75-86; Nederveen Pieterse, "Globale/lokale Melange: Globalisierung und Kultur; Drei Paradigmen," in Brigitte Kossek, ed., *Gegen-Rassismen: Konstruktionen—Interaktionen—Interventionen* (Hamburg: Argument, 1999), 167-85; Nederveen Pieterse, "Hybridität, na und?," in Allolio-Näcke, Kalscheuer and Manzeschke, *Differenzen anders denken*, 396-430; Nora Räthzel, "Hybridität ist die Antwort, aber was noch mal die Frage?," in Kossek, *Gegen-Rassismen*, 204-19.

hybridity, since every metaphor used to explain it generates a momentum of its own. For instance, some texts use the example of hybrid engines in order to illustrate the concept of hybridity as one of "amalgamation." I find such illustrations less than helpful, because hybrid engines are not about amalgamation as much as they are about com-bi-nation, i.e., about the con-joining of two distinct entities (an electric motor and a combustion engine).[10] Now, for other phenomena of hybridity, the metaphor of "mixing" may be more appropriate, although one would have to ask whether this should be seen as taking place in a vacuum (i.e., two things that mix the way colored liquids do) or whether ascriptions of status and power might not also play a role. After all, this would imply that hybridity should be located from the outset within societal negotiation processes between various actors. These few remarks will suffice to indicate the many challenges surrounding the definition of the term hybridity. We might go so far as to join Jonathan Friedman, to whom we will turn our attention shortly, in asking whether there is any point to this concept at all.

At any rate, the artificial "theoretical" language used by a number of pro-ponents of this concept produces little more than wordplay. This becomes evident already by the haphazard use of contradictory metaphors: it makes a significant difference which metaphors are used to explain the concept of hybridity. If people mean by it the overlapping of various cultural patterns, then the implication of this choice of image is that the respective patterns continue to exist and to influence each other; the image of "overlapping" suggests the existence of a hidden sublayer covered by another layer that is "visible" because it lies on top. Both are present, but one of them has a greater effect, even though the other also has effects of its own. In contrast, the term mixture allows for a range of possibilities, such as that distinct elements are brought together and combined in a certain sense, the way distinctly dif-ferent vegetable pieces (lettuce, peppers, onions) are combined in a bowl to make a salad. The elements are—and continue to be—different. The point of the salad bowl image would be that the elements initially remain distinct and then combine to give rise to a new taste sensation only when they are

---

[10]Arne Manzeschke, "Introduction," in Allolio-Näcke, Kalscheuer and Manzeschke, Differenzen anders denken, 355-60, especially 355. In general, the wording used in this anthology comes across as either hypertrophic or arbitrary.

consumed. It is difficult to imagine how this image is supposed to apply to cultural constellations. It is, however, also possible to conceive of a mixture as a fusion of different liquids, say, of colors that are mixed to produce a new shade of color. But this image too is difficult to apply, because it for its part suggests both the uniformity of the base colors and the uniformity of the resulting color. If, however, we were to turn to the image of water and oil, which repel each other but emulsify when agitated, only to separate again, then we would be allowing for the fragility of cultural configurations while also continuing to presuppose the uniformity of cultural configurations. Let us therefore go one step further. Some prefer to speak about hybridity using the term *multiple affiliation*. This refers to individuals (and groups) located in an environment featuring a range of social configurations; or, rather, it refers to a certain interaction of the individual or group defined by these social configurations and their demands and values. For instance, a young man belonging to the second generation of Indian immigrants in London might identify and position himself as Asian over against English society, as Hindu over against Muslims of Indian descent, and as a British intellectual and cosmopolitan over against his rural relatives. The multiple affiliations in his case would have come about as a result of the expectations of various social configurations, on the one hand, and his own interests, on the other. The result is a complex process in which certain ascriptions of affiliation are activated only when they are of interest for the individual or the group.[11]

Jonathan Friedman's astute analysis refers to this regard. He subjects the concept of hybridization to radical criticism, hypothesizing that it constitutes an ideological discourse.[12] Friedman begins by pointing out *that an objectively hybrid culture represents a contradiction in terms, since it would*

---

[11]Famous US-American golfer Tiger Woods is said to identify himself as "Cablinasian" at times, truncating his multiple origins ("Ca" for Caucasian, "bl" for black, "in" for Indian [as in Native American], and "Asian"). Nederveen Pieterse, "Hybridität, na und?," 407. It would have to be examined whether the purpose of such self-positioning would be to establish ties with the assignment options to which it refers or to subvert such assignment options. Other metaphors are those of "intersections" and "interconnections." Kum-Kum Bhavnani, "Rassismen entgegnen: Querverbindungen und Hybridität," in Kossek, *Gegen-Rassismen*, 186-201, specifically 187. Here Bhavnani also attempts to persuade her readers—unsuccessfully, in my opinion—to distinguish between "situative" and "organic" hybridity.

[12]Jonathan Friedman, "The Hybridization of Roots and the Abhorrence of the Bush," in Mike Featherstone and Scott Lash, eds., *Spaces of Culture: City-Nation-World* (London: SAGE, 1999), 230-55.

be impossible to determine hybridity under these conditions. In other words, the language of hybridity always presupposes the ongoing existence of distinguishable cultural configurations that serve as the criteria as to whether a phenomenon of "hybridization" has taken place, and if so, in what way. As it is, Friedman asserts, all cultures are mixed to a certain extent. Even though this is a trite observation, as far as the term *hybridity* is concerned, it means that something can only "be" hybrid when someone *observes* a certain phenomenon to be hybrid (i.e., mixed). *Accordingly, hybridity only becomes an issue once certain persons or groups draw attention to the mixing of cultures.* Thus one might well ask: In whose interest is it when certain phenomena are identified as "hybridizations" that would otherwise have gone unnoticed? Assuming that such hybridizations are not understood as cultural decay, i.e., as impurity, but rather as cultural gain, then of course those actors who represent such a hybrid culture would stand to benefit. This brings Friedman to another important point: "The rise of a discourse of hybridity, creolization, etc. is a social phenomenon and not the reflection of a neutral fact that has finally been discovered. The discourse appears to be located among certain groups, usually cultural elites and harbors hegemonic pretensions, as suggested above."[13] Thus for Friedman, the concept of hybridity does not result in knowledge gain but rather serves to express a hegemonic mindset, since it seeks—in contrast to his own criticism of such approaches—to explain plurality using *a single* pattern.[14]

Let us proceed by focusing our attention on a single aspect: the topic of hybridity is all about the question of status. Wherever a certain societal status exists, it is also protected by boundary lines.[15] Now, because status is not an issue on the level of popular culture, it means that the mixing of cultural elements is also generally unproblematic at this level. The same is not true, however, when it comes to "higher" levels of culture.[16] This state of affairs makes it clear that while processes of hybridization take place on many levels, these often go unnoticed, as attested for instance by the "nacho

---

[13]Ibid., 249.
[14]Ibid., 237.
[15]We may recall those forms of sport that earlier served as indicators of a high social status (such as tennis or golf) but have become more and more popular today. In the process, earlier conventions such as clothing lose their distinctiveness and become more and more arbitrary.
[16]Nederveen Pieterse, "Hybridität, na und?," 419.

pizza," a modern dish that combines elements of the "Mexican" nachos and the "Italian" pizza—but does not offend anybody.

This shows that some hybridizations go unnoticed, while others are seen as foundational by some and dangerous by others, as the case may be. It follows, therefore, that the boundary lines are what draws attention to hybridity. For this reason we must agree with Nederveen Pieterse when he asks the critical question: "If hybridity is real, yet boundaries stand out, how can hybridity be a way of self-identification: In a world of boundaries, what opportunity and what justification are there for boundary-crossing identities, be they political or cultural?"[17] Furthermore, Nederveen Pieterse believes it is important to realize that very different forms of hybridity exist. The phenomenon is certainly not new.[18] Mixed relationships are ubiquitous. *Thus if the term hybridity is to make sense, it must be analyzed together with factors such as power, status, and equal rights.* In this regard we soon come across striking differences. In the Caribbean, for instance, the term *creolization* was commonly used. Here the term meant the mixing of people of different backgrounds and with it various shades of brown skin color—but this did not generally translate into the establishment of a hierarchical system or pecking order. The same does not hold true for the term *mestizaje* in Latin America; due to the long colonial history, the term continues to be associated with a very explicit hierarchical classification ranging from white through dark to black. This corresponds to the social structure, with its upper class of whites of European descent, a middle class of people of mixed race, and a lower class of blacks, the descendants of Africans who had been brought into the area as slaves.[19]

We may affirm the following: (1) Hybridity has become an *everyday experience*, with different societies interpreting various aspects of mixed relationships quite differently. (2) Thus the *interpretation* of different patterns of hybridity *varies widely depending on the context*. At issue, therefore, is not only the fact *that* mixing takes place but rather also *how* various actors interpret it. (3) At the same time, this interpretation means that boundaries are drawn. How the boundaries are drawn depends on the actors drawing

---

[17]Ibid., 411.
[18]One term used for it in older approaches was *bricolage*, for instance.
[19]Nederveen Pieterse, "Hybridität, na und?," 422.

them, defining them, postulating them, or trying to perpetuate them. *Thus the boundaries are not fixed; rather, they are the product of processes of negotiation.* (4) For this reason, boundaries cannot simply be eliminated, for boundaries are part of life and a necessary prerequisite for being able to orient oneself. The problem that arises in a mobile global society driven and expressed by the multimedia is evident: overall, if boundaries are becoming more porous because TV, the Internet, and telecommunication are causing spatial boundaries and social barriers to fall, if national boundaries are becoming less and less important, and if a global hyperculture is leading to the diminishing relevance of mores, aesthetic norms, and taste, how then is it still possible to orient oneself when existing boundaries are becoming ever more blurred, on the one hand, and new lines of demarcation are being drawn, on the other? At any rate, the term *hybridity* draws attention to the fact that, contrary to "fabricated" or merely alleged cultural, ethnic, or other "identities," life in mixed relationships is the rule, not the exception. The term *hybridity* underlines the productive value added by such mixed relationships, and it programmatically highlights the necessity for more in-depth study of such processes.[20] Thus it seems that while *hybridity*—as a heuristic term—calls attention to all kinds of conceivable culturally mixed relationships, it also helps us to see the value of such relationships in a positive light. Besides, what emerges is that hybridity is instantiated in very different ways depending on the context and that we need a more precise definition, since every metaphor used to explain the term considerably limits the semantic field the term is supposed to cover.

Transculturation or Transculturality?

The term *transculturation* was developed in the 1940s by Cuban cultural anthropologist Fernando Ortiz (1881–1969) in his book *Cuban Counterpoint: Tobacco and Sugar* (the Spanish original was published in 1940).[21] He describes the complex interaction of intercultural processes as reciprocal and

---

[20]"Hybridity is to culture what deconstruction is to discourse: The transcendence of binary categories." Ibid., 425.

[21]Fernando Ortiz, *Cuban Counterpoint: Tobacco and Sugar*, trans. Harriet de Onís (1947; 4th repr., Durham, NC: Duke University Press, 2003). For an introduction to Ortiz's thought, see Mathias Hildebrandt, "Von der Transkulturation zur Transdifferenz," in Allolio-Näcke, Kalscheuer and Manzeschke, *Differenzen anders denken*, 342-52.

often unexpected forms of exchange and reconfiguration, during which some cultural patterns are lost while others come into being. In his description, Ortiz criticizes the custom of classifying one culture as "dominant" and the other as "inferior." Ortiz's criticism is directed against the approach of US-American anthropologist Melville Herskovits (1895–1963), who had proceeded on the assumption of an obvious cultural disparity in his book *Acculturation*, published two years before (1938).[22]

Philosopher Wolfgang Welsch introduced the term *transculturality* (*Transkulturalität*) into the German debate as early as the 1990s, stating that he was dissatisfied with the hitherto customary cultural terminology.[23] Welsch believed that the disadvantage of Herder's concept of culture was that he had had to proceed on the assumption that cultures are homogenous units that need to define themselves over against one another. According to Welsch, Herder's was still the operative understanding of culture in the term *multiculturalism*, for it continued to presuppose a multicultural society consisting of constituent cultures—cultures imagined as different, yet nevertheless homogenous. Welsch argued that the same was true for the term *interculturality*, for here it was precisely the concept of culture as a homogenous unit that created the problem that the "inter-"action (of *interculturality*) was supposed to address: the constituent cultures are to be made to engage in an intercultural dialogue since it is difficult to understand one another—or so it is assumed. Welsch: "The hypothesis that individual cultures have 'their own' character creates the problem of the difficult coexistence of such cultures and their structural inability to communicate. Thus it is precisely the concept of interculturality that will be least able to provide the framework for the solution of the problem."[24]

In contrast, Welsch maintains, "'Transculturality' intends to demonstrate both: That we have moved beyond the classic definition of culture, and that the new forms of culture and the new way of life permeate these

---

[22]Melville J. Herskovits, *Acculturation: The Study of Culture Contact* (New York: J. J. Augustin, 1938).
[23]See Wolfgang Welsch, "Transkulturalität—Lebensformen nach der Auflösung der Kulturen," *Information Philosophie*, no. 2 (1992): 5-20; Welsch, "Transkulturalität: Zur veränderten Verfassung heutiger Kulturen," in Irmela Schneider and Christian W. Thomson, eds., *Hybridkultur: Medien, Netze, Künste* (Köln: Weinand, 1997), 67-90; Welsch, "Auf dem Wege zu transkulturellen Gesellschaften," in Allolio-Näcke, Kalscheuer and Manzeschke, *Differenzen anders denken*, 314-41.
[24]Welsch, "Auf dem Wege," 321.

old configurations almost as a matter of course."[25] Religious and mission studies scholar Klaus Hock believes this term to be a very useful one.[26] Indeed, there is a great deal to be said for the adoption of this approach. For Hock, the "significance of the concept of transculturation . . . consists in its emphasis that this process encompasses a set of diverse and complex spheres of interaction: Cultural elements are 'translated,' interpreted, re-adopted, transformed in the process, reconstituted, and developed further—and not just in an unilinear fashion, but in a multidirectional manner."[27] Because of the transparency emphasized in this concept of culture, Hock prefers this concept to older terms like *crosscultural, multicultural,* or *intercultural.* This seems to be a very sensible approach. At this point I will need to explain why this book is titled *Intercultural Theology* and not *Transcultural Theology.*

INTERCULTURAL THEOLOGY OR TRANSCULTURAL THEOLOGY?

Why then should we continue to speak of *intercultural* theology? I prefer to use the term *intercultural* in the concept of intercultural theology for two reasons: *First, the emphasis of this endeavor is to study forms of Christianity in other parts of the world, in other nations and ethnicities, and thus also in other cultures. Despite the effect of transcultural processes of assimilation—such as in the sphere of the media—these cultures and societies and their respective contexts continue to feature a sufficiently substantial difference from the German cultural configuration as to warrant the description intercultural theology. Second, the concept of interculturality is still a very meaningful one, since cultural differences are not only constituted by the artifacts that are used, nor only by different languages, behavioral patterns, and the like, i.e., areas in which assimilation, amalgamation, etc., may occur by means of processes of exchange. In the process, people also consciously attempt to preserve and stylize certain cultural differences, to shift and to reconfigure boundaries and border zones, but in so doing also to stylize, invoke, and—either consciously*

---

[25]Welsch, "Transkulturalität—Lebensformen," 5. On the one hand, the concept could allow for tendencies toward amalgamation and uniformity, and on the other, it could explain the emergence of diversity. See Welsch, "Transkulturalität," 79.

[26]Klaus Hock, "Religion als transkulturelles Phänomen. Implikationen eines kulturwissenschaftlichen Paradigmas für die Religionsforschung," *Berliner Theologische Zeitschrift* 19 (2002): 64-82.

[27]Ibid., 70.

or unconsciously—instrumentalize them. But this means that the continued use of the term intercultural *is justified also for the reason that in the minds of the actors, cultural differences play—and should continue to play—all kinds of roles.* In summary, as an *analytical concept,* the term *transculturality* is undeniably useful, but *as part of a subject title* it is of little use, for the reasons provided above.

24
....

So Much for Ecumenism!

Appreciating Christianity as a Global Formation

In the twentieth century, Christianity has undeniably become a global religious configuration. However, European theology does not yet seem to appreciate this fact. In most publications, when it comes to the subject of ecumenism people continue to orient themselves by the traditional set of confessions and denominations like the Orthodox churches, the Roman Catholic Church, and the Protestant churches, such as the Lutheran, Reformed, Baptist, Presbyterian, or Congregationalist churches. The founding of the World Council of Churches in 1948, which is headquartered in Geneva and to which 345 churches belong today, marked a significant milestone on the path to an improved awareness and exercise of Christian fellowship.[1] Yet as significant as the WCC is, it is naturally not synonymous with ecumenism as such. One of the tasks of intercultural theology is to treat Christianity as a *global religious configuration* and to help preempt simplified portrayals. For instance, a number of publications simply ignore numerically very significant segments of world Christianity—for whatever reason. We must vehemently protest against such ignorance. What is needed is a polycentric understanding of Christianity in all of its diverse variations; and it is perhaps precisely the demonstration of this plurality that will motivate others to establish, maintain, and cultivate contacts. Let us proceed by providing a brief sketch of the WCC.

---

[1] See the WCC homepage: The World Council of Churches, "World Council of Churches: A Worldwide Fellowship of Churches Seeking Unity, a Common Witness and Christian Service," www.oikoumene.org/en (accessed June 18, 2015). There is a wealth of literature on the history of the WCC. For an overview, see Ulrich Becker, "Ökumene," in Ulrich Becker and Udo Tworuschka, *Ökumene und Religionswissenschaft* (Stuttgart, Germany: Calwer, 2006), 13-90; and Willem Adolph Visser't Hooft, "Geschichte und Sinn des Wortes 'Ökumene': Ökumenischer Aufbruch," in *Hauptschriften* (Stuttgart, Germany: Kreuz-Verlag, 1967), 2:11-28.

THE WORLD COUNCIL OF CHURCHES

The World Council of Churches has its roots in the ecumenical movements of the end of the eighteenth century.[2] Beginning in the 1790s, these spiritual movements led to the founding of a whole series of mission societies that operated on an interdenominational level, such as the London Missionary Society (founded 1795), the Basel Mission (1815), or the Berlin Mission (1824).[3] One could also mention other initiatives, like the World Conference of Young Men's Christian Associations, founded in 1855 in Paris; the World Student Christian Federation, founded in 1895; the Christian Sunday School Movement; and others. The predecessors of the ecumenical movement of the twentieth century thus created a basis for ecumenism.[4] Four international organizations in particular provided the basis for the founding of the WCC, namely the World Mission Conferences, the movement for practical Christianity known as the Life and Work Movement, the Faith and Order Movement, and finally the World Sunday School Convention.[5]

The terrors of the First World War (1914–1918) that led to millions of casualties shook the way the allegedly so very Christian and enlightened Europe saw itself, down to its very foundations. After the war, the so-called League of Nations was founded in 1919 as a peace initiative on the level of global politics. At the conference of the World Alliance for International Friendship Through the Churches, which was held in the same year and at which sixty delegates from fourteen countries were present, Swedish Bishop Nathan Söderblom called for the founding of a World Council of Churches. However, this did not take place as yet. Instead, the first World Conference of Life and

---

[2]These in turn were preceded by Christian revival movements at the end of the eighteenth century. This refers to pietistic movements in the Anglo-Saxon world, especially North America and England, which would then spread to the European continent as well.

[3]Besides the mission societies founded in the early decades, many other mission societies would come into being during the course of the nineteenth century, especially in Great Britain, North America, Continental Europe, and Scandinavia.

[4]Becker and Tworuschka, Ökumene, 25-26.

[5]In terms of the mission conferences, we may note that after the commencement of mission work in many areas, the need for cooperation between various societies was generally recognized. Accordingly, from 1855 onwards *cooperative mission conferences* began to be held in overseas territories. *National mission councils* were formed in Europe and North America to serve as advisory bodies. Yet the first truly ecumenical conference only took place in 1910 in the form of the World Missionary Conference in Edinburgh.

Work was held in Stockholm in 1925. During the conference, a continuation committee was called into existence, which founded the Life and Work Movement in 1930. Here ecumenism was conceived of as the expression of an inner attitude that was supposed to contribute to practical cooperation. However, it proved impossible to engage in practical cooperation while ignoring doctrinal differences. This was demonstrated by the efforts of Anglican Bishop Charles Henry Brent from the United States, at whose initiative the so-called Faith and Order Movement was founded, with its first world conference taking place in Lausanne (Switzerland) in 1927.[6] Both of the movements held their second world conference virtually simultaneously in Oxford and Edinburgh in July/August 1937, and each elected delegates from among its ranks to serve on a joint committee to prepare for the founding of a World Council of Churches. However, World War II delayed the founding of the council for more than a decade. The Faith and Order Movement also worked toward ecumenism in another sense, namely in the sense of establishing relations among different churches in order to work toward unity.

While the Life and Work Movement and the Faith and Order Movement merged to form the WCC as a new institution in 1948, the two other ecumenical movements that would play an integral role in the development of the WCC continued to remain independent for some time. One of these was the World Council of Christian Education, founded in 1947 as the global association of World Sunday School Conferences. The other was the International Missionary Council, which had been founded in 1922 in the wake of the Edinburgh conference (1910) and which organized a series of world mission conferences—Jerusalem in 1928, Tambaram (India) in 1938, Whitby (Canada) in 1947, and Willingen (Germany) in 1952. Both institutions maintained long-standing ties of friendship with the WCC and were also associated with it on the personnel level. In 1961, the International Missionary Council was integrated into the WCC, and so was the World Council of Christian Education in 1972.

But let us return to the founding of the WCC in 1948. A total of 351 delegates from 147 churches participated in the first general assembly of the

---

[6]Even though the Roman Catholic Church did not participate in this conference, the other large denominational families were all represented, namely the Reformed, the Anglicans, the Lutherans, the Baptists, the Methodists, the Disciples of Christ, the Orthodox, and the Old Catholics.

WCC in Amsterdam. A theological formulation was agreed on, which was to serve as the criterion for membership in the WCC. It stated, "The World Council of Churches is a fellowship of churches which accept our Lord Jesus Christ as God and Saviour." This minimal consensus provided the basis on which the churches, about 80 percent of which still came from European and North American countries, were able to form a fellowship. Most of the participating churches were Protestant churches and Anglican churches, followed by a small minority of Orthodox churches. Over the following decades, a whole series of other churches joined. An especially significant event in this regard was when the Russian Orthodox Church became a member, followed eventually by most of the other Orthodox churches. In order for this step to be taken, however, the WCC's central committee was tasked with clarifying the ecclesiological position of the WCC. The committee carried out this task in Toronto in 1950.

It was especially the phrase "a fellowship of churches" that needed to be clarified. Under the title, "The Church, the Churches and the World Council of Churches: The Ecclesiological Significance of the World Council of Churches," the Toronto statement unmistakably limited the significance of the WCC:

> The World Council of Churches is not and must never become a superchurch. . . . The purpose of the World Council of Churches is not to negotiate unions between churches, which can only be done by the churches themselves acting on their own initiative, but to bring the churches into living contact with each other and to promote the study and discussion of the issues of Church unity. . . . The World Council cannot and should not be based on any one particular conception of the Church. It does not prejudge the ecclesiological problem. . . . Membership in the World Council of Churches does not imply that a church treats its own conception of the Church as merely relative. . . . Membership in the World Council does not imply the acceptance of a specific doctrine concerning the nature of Church unity. . . . Membership does not imply that each church must regard the other member churches as churches in the true and full sense of the word.[7]

These delimitations might come as a surprise, but they show that the WCC could only establish a broad base of member churches and become more

---

[7]The World Council of Churches, "Toronto Statement," www.oikoumene.org/en/resources/documents/central-committee/1950/toronto-statement (accessed June 18, 2015), passim.

representative by *leaving essential ecclesiological issues open in a virtually programmatic manner.* The statement asserts, first, that the negotiation of unions is left up to the individual churches; second, that the existence of the WCC does not presuppose any particular understanding of the nature of the church; third, that the membership of a church in the WCC does not automatically signify that this church thereby adopts any specific doctrine of the church; fourth, that membership does not mean that the church treats its own conception of the church as relative; and finally, fifth, that the membership of the church also does not mean that one church must automatically regard the other churches as churches in the full sense of the term.

At any rate, due to the influence of the Orthodox churches, the basis of the WCC was reformulated at its Third Assembly in New Delhi in 1961. Since then, it states, "The World Council of Churches is a fellowship of churches which confess the Lord Jesus Christ as God and Saviour according to the scriptures, and therefore seek to fulfill together their common calling to the glory of the one God, Father, Son and Holy Spirit."[8]

Naturally, this raises the question as to what ecclesiological status the World Council of Churches holds: Is it just a forum for debate, or can the WCC claim to be something like a church—and if yes, in what way? We can unambiguously affirm that the WCC is no superchurch, that it exercises no canonical authority, indeed, that it is not even an autonomous subject operating by various agencies, since a range of initiatives and efforts to reach agreement have not taken place under its aegis at all. The World Council of Churches is an institution that enables various churches to engage in theological exchange, an institution that coordinates interchurch initiatives by harnessing the cooperation of its member churches, that makes information available, and that develops materials through study processes that it makes available to the churches for additional consideration in their congregations. This bestows on the WCC what one may refer to as "sapiential authority" (*weisheitliche Autorität*) (D. Ritschl).

---

[8] It is very evident that the line about the "Lord Jesus Christ as God and Saviour" was expanded to include a trinitarian formulation ("to the glory of the one God, Father, Son and Holy Spirit") and a reference to Holy Scripture ("according to the scriptures"). It was also intensified by replacing the word *accept* with *confess*—it was now about confessing Jesus Christ along these lines.

The history of the WCC may be traced according to the various general assemblies that have been held over the years. Another insightful perspective is yielded by studying the assemblies held by the program units of the WCC, such as the World Mission Conferences, which have been held since 1963 under the aegis of the WCC, or the Faith and Order conferences,[9] to name just two. Beyond these, one could also point to the *programs* of the WCC, which are often short term in nature.[10] Unfortunately, we do not have the space to pursue this subject any further. We might mention in closing that the general assemblies of the World Council of Churches took place in Amsterdam (1948), Evanston (1954), New Delhi (1961), Uppsala (1968), Nairobi (1975), Vancouver (1983), Canberra (1991), Harare (1998), Porto Alegre (2006), and Busan, South Korea (2013).

The Pentecostal Movement and Pentecostal Churches as a Transcontinental Phenomenon

These remarks will suffice to show that the WCC is an extremely important institution when it comes to issues of Christian unity. But it is not the only such institution. So, as we transition to the next section, let us turn our attention to statistical data and some personal observations. Currently, the world's population exceeds 7 billion people. Of these, numerically speaking, Christianity is the largest religious configuration, with about 2.5 billion followers.[11] Among the Christian churches, the Roman Catholic Church is the largest, with more than 1 billion followers. Approximately 300 million people worldwide are Orthodox Christians, while the number of Protestants belonging to the traditional mainstream churches is significantly lower (with Reformed Christians numbering around 150 million and Lutheran Christians around 67 million). By comparison, the numerical size of the

---

[9]See the conferences held in Lund (1952), Montréal (1963), Aarhus (1964), Bristol (1967), Louvain (1971), Accra (1974), Bangalore (1978), Lima (1982), Stavanger (1985), Budapest (1989), and Crete (2009).

[10]Another possibility would be to study the biographies of important WCC personalities, such as the General Secretaries William A. Visser't Hooft from the Netherlands (1948–1966), Eugene C. Blake from the United States (1966–1972), Dr. Philip Potter from the Dominican Republic/Caribbean (1972–1984), Emilio Castro from Uruguay (1985–1992), Konrad Raiser from Germany (1993–2003), Samuel Kobia from Kenya (2004–2009), and Olav Fykse Tveit from Norway (since 2010).

[11]Followed by Islam, with about 1.5 billion followers, and the Hindu religions, with about seven hundred million to eight hundred million followers.

Pentecostal movement is striking, albeit—admittedly—difficult to estimate. Reliable estimates suggest that there are around 500 million followers world-wide.[12] Pentecostal churches exist in all parts of the world. They vary from multinational churches with a strong institutional character numbering millions of followers (like the Brazilian Igreja Universal do Reino Deus, currently numbering around 4.5 million members, the South Korean Yoido Full Gospel Church,[13] or the Aladura churches in West Africa, to name just a few examples) to Pentecostal movements in rural areas following illiterate prophets who cannot read the Bible and do not use it, preferring to live out a purely ritual form of Christianity. Thorough research from the field of religious and mission studies will be needed to be able to say whether movements of the latter type are *Christian*—and if so, from whose perspective.[14] In many parts of the world, the Pentecostal movement is among the most vibrant forms of religious praxis. This is very obvious when it comes to the African continent. But also in the case of, say, Latin America and the Caribbean, while the percentage of Protestants in these majority Roman Catholic areas was around 3.1 percent in 1960, it is estimated to have increased to more than 15 percent by the year 2000. In Brazil alone, of the current total national population of about 170 million, 26 million are Protestants, of which about 70 percent belong to Pentecostal churches. In the same time frame, the percentage of Catholics fell from 93 percent to 75 percent.[15] These few highlights will suffice for now.

Now if the phenomenon of "the" Pentecostal movement (would it not be better to speak of Pentecostal *movements*?) is already difficult to quantify, the many African Independent Churches (AICs) present a perhaps even

---

[12]For an overview of the literature, see the following limited selection: Stanley M. Burgess and Ed M. van der Maas, eds., *The New International Dictionary of Pentecostal and Charismatic Movements* (Grand Rapids: Zondervan, 2002); Ogbu Kalu, *African Pentecostalism: An Introduction* (Oxford: Oxford University Press, 2008); and Afeosemime Adogame, Roswith Gerloff, and Klaus Hock, eds., *Christianity in Africa and the African Diaspora: The Appropriation of a Scattered Heritage* (London: Continuum, 2011).

[13]Yoido Full Gospel Church, "Welcome to Yoido Full Gospel Church!," http://english.fgtv.com/ (accessed June 19, 2015).

[14]See, for example, Julie C. Ma and Wonsuk Ma, *Mission in the Spirit: Towards a Pentecostal/ Charismatic Missiology* (Eugene, OR: Wipf & Stock, 2010).

[15]See Martin Ufer, "Emotion und Expansion: Neopfingstlerische Bewegungen in Brasilien," in Alexander F. Gemeinhardt, ed., *Die Pfingstbewegung als ökumenische Herausforderung* (Göttingen: Vandenhoeck & Ruprecht, 2005), 93-128. For more on Brazil, see Paul Freston, "Pentecostalism in Brazil: A Brief History," *Religion* 25 (1995): 119-33.

greater ecumenical challenge. In sub-Saharan Africa alone there are currently about fifteen thousand different AICs, some of which number between one million and several million followers, such as, for instance, the South African Nazareth Baptist Church, founded by Isaiah Shembe.[16] We may note that in many places an observable (if limited) charismatization of many of the "traditional" churches (such as the Orthodox churches, the Roman Catholic Church and also the Protestant churches) is also taking place. But what does all of this mean as far as how Christianity is perceived as a global religious configuration? Two points deserve mention: First, it means that expertise in the area of religious and mission studies is needed to gain a better understanding of these phenomena through painstaking research. This is one of the important research fields of the subject of intercultural theology. Second, it means that the knowledge about the plurality of Christian churches, congregations, and lifeworlds in other cultural, religious, and political contexts must be incorporated into theological curricula (especially in Germany). This needs to be done in order for theology to remain relevant in the face of global challenges and to be able to meet and treat foreign brothers and sisters with respect—not only those overseas but also those we encounter in the many immigrant Christian congregations in Germany and Europe itself. After these preliminary remarks, let us now focus our attention on what we may call "the other ecumenism."

Few European theologians and congregation members seem to be aware that within the Pentecostal movement, various churches have grown to considerable size and have developed a complex institutional structure, often within the space of a few decades. Such an institutional structure may take the form of corporate holdings, radio stations, TV stations, private universities, hospitals, and the like.[17] Contrary to the Western prejudices held by many church bodies, the churches of the Pentecostal movement in other parts of the world were certainly not preponderantly founded or supported by US-American Pentecostals (such as the Assemblies of God).[18] For instance,

---

[16]It is currently split into four churches and said to have a combined total of about four million followers.

[17]In this regard, see for example the Yoido Full Gospel Church in South Korea or the Igreja Universal do Reino Deus in Brazil.

[18]See, for instance, the following study on South India: Michael Bergunder, *Die südindische Pfingstbewegung im 20. Jahrhundert* (Frankfurt: Peter Lang, 1998).

many of the Nigerian churches that were founded in the 1970s and 1980s, churches that could just as well be regarded as belonging to the AICs as to the Pentecostal movement, were founded solely by African initiatives. One example is the Redeemed Christian Church of God,[19] which has developed into a transnational Pentecostal church.[20] Another prejudice that needs to be corrected is that these churches do not care about social issues.[21] Of course examples exist of so-called neo-Pentecostal churches in which the prosperity gospel features large, while social work hardly features at all,[22] but these do not allow us to generalize and assume that this is always the case in "the" Pentecostal movement. Both the Roman Catholic Church[23] and the World Council of Churches[24] have recognized that some churches in the Pentecostal movement are indeed estimable dialogue partners. At any rate, there are good reasons for taking notice of the ecumenical scene in the Pentecostal movement, namely under the consideration of various aspects such as transnational networks, gender issues, the use of the media, social and ecological programs, interreligious relations, political engagement, and many others.

---

[19]Redeemed Christian Church of God, "Information Gateway of the Redeemed Christian Church of God," www.rccg.org (accessed June 19, 2015).

[20]Asonzeh F.-K. Ukah, *A New Paradigm of Pentecostal Power: A Study of the Redeemed Christian Church of God in Nigeria* (Trenten, NJ: Africa World Press, 2008). See also Olufunke Adeboye, "Transnational Pentecostalism in Africa: The Redeemed Christian Church of God, Nigeria," in Laurent Fourchard, André Mary and René Otayek, eds., *Entreprises religieuses transnationales en Afrique de l'ouest* (Paris: IFRA-Ibadan, 2005), 439-65; Olufunke Adeboye, "'Arrowhead' of Nigerian Pentecostalism: The Redeemed Christian Church of God, 1952–2005," *Pneuma* 29 (2007): 24-58; Olufunke Adeboye, "Running the Prophecy: The Redeemed Christian Church of God in North America; 1992–2005," *Missionalia* 36 (2008): 259-79; Afeosemime Adogame, "HIV/AIDS Support and African Pentecostalism: The Case of the Redeemed Christian Church of God (RCCG)," *Journal of Health Psychology* 12 (2007): 477; Asonzeh F.-K. Ukah, "Mobilities, Migration and Multiplication: The Expansion of the Religious Field of the Redeemed Christian Church of God (RCCG), Nigeria," in Afeosemime Adogame and Cordula Weissköppel, eds., *Religion in the Context of African Migration* (Bayreuth, Germany: Eckhard Breitinger, 2005), 317-41.

[21]In this regard, see the research overview in Michael Bergunder, "Pfingstbewegung in Lateinamerika: Soziologische Theorien und theologische Debatten," in *Pfingstbewegung und Basisgemeinden in Lateinamerika: Die Rezeption befreiungstheologischer Konzepte durch die pfingstliche Theologie*, Weltmission heute 39 (Hamburg: EMW, 2000), 7-42, 138-42.

[22]See for instance Karl Braungart, *Heiliger Geist und politische Herrschaft bei den Neopfingstlern in Honduras* (Frankfurt: Vervuert, 1995).

[23]A number of dialogues have taken place. For an overview, see Hans Gasper and Gerhard Bially, "Der pfingstlich/römisch-katholische Dialog," *Freikirchenforschung* 16 (2007): 164-91.

[24]Ever since the World Mission Conference in Athens in 2005, the WCC has increased its efforts to engage Pentecostal churches.

AFRICAN INITIATED CHURCHES AND THE SEARCH
FOR ECUMENICAL PARTNERSHIPS

In terms of African Initiated Churches,[25] it may be observed that a number of churches attempted to establish ecumenical contacts as early as the 1930s, albeit with a very specific intent, since they had heard that an *African* Christian church had existed ever since the days of the first Christians.[26] In terms of how these African-led churches—many of which had split off from mission churches led by white missionaries—viewed themselves, biblical references to an African Christianity were of great importance to them. One frequently cited example was Psalm 68:31, where it says, "Envoys will come out of Egypt; Ethiopia will quickly stretch out her hands to God" (NKJV). In the New Testament, the story of the Ethiopian eunuch (Acts 8:26-40) was considered the proof text warranting the existence of ancient African Christian traditions. Breakaway groups that separated from mission churches—a frequent occurrence in southern Africa between 1900 and 1940 or so—were often labeled by the term *Ethiopian movement.* In contrast, African churches founded by prophetic figures of their own were labeled *Zionist churches* due to the circumstance that they frequently named their church headquarters "New Zion," which led to the formulation of corresponding (and often very melodious) names for the churches themselves.

When leading personalities of such churches learned of the existence of the Coptic Orthodox Church in Egypt, many of them sent letters to the patriarch in Cairo, requesting membership in this church body.[27] This demonstrates the desire for (an initially African) ecumenism. Even though the letters went unanswered for years, the steady flow of requests continued. The Coptic churches finally made contact in the 1940s, but the attempts to establish fellowship failed. In contrast, the 1976 initiative by Coptic patriarch Shenouda III of installing a Coptic bishop for Africa did yield results. The

---

[25]Rufus Okikiolaolu Olubiyi Ositelu, *African Instituted Churches: Diversities, Growth, Gifts, Spirituality and Ecumenical Understanding of African Initiated Churches* (Münster: LIT Verlag, 2002); Dawid Venter, ed., *Engaging Modernity: Methods and Cases for Studying African Independent Churches in South Africa* (Westport, CT: Praeger, 2004).

[26]Michael Bergunder, "Die Afrikanischen Unabhängigen Kirchen und die Ökumene," *Ökumenische Rundschau* 47 (1998): 504-16.

[27]David B. Barrett and T. John Padwick, *Rise Up and Walk!: Conciliarism and the African Indigenous Churches* (Nairobi: Oxford University Press, 1989), 15. Reference drawn from Bergunder, "Die Afrikanischen Unabhängigen Kirchen," 512, 516.

seat of Bishop Antonious Markos was located in Nairobi. Traveling extensively, he established many contacts to AICs in various African countries. Further initiatives led to the establishing of an office in Nairobi with the intent to coordinate training programs for the education of preachers and leaders of participating AICs. The organization was registered with the Kenyan government in 1975 as the Organization of African Instituted Churches (OAIC).[28] The Coptic Orthodox Church, which had played a mediating role up until that point, now withdrew completely from the various boards. A widespread network is currently in place that also includes ties with the All Africa Conference of Churches (AACC), also headquartered in Nairobi.[29]

Meanwhile, the OAIC has established formal contact with the World Council of Churches. To date, only ten AICs have joined the WCC. In 2006, the membership of the OAIC was composed of about 298 churches.[30] The analysis of these churches also falls to the discipline of intercultural theology.[31] It is true that many churches have already been subjected to thorough research, such as the Kimbanguist Church[32] or the southern

---

[28]For more information, see the Organization of African Instituted Churches, www.oaic.org (accessed September 1, 2011). Also interesting is the holistic focus of the organization's activities; the goals for 2009–2013 are formulated as follows: "OAIC aims to:—Improve the livelihood opportunities of the rural and urban poor;—Support member churches and communities as they respond to health-related challenges, especially HIV and AIDS;—Promote economic justice and good governance in African communities;—Develop and implement appropriate theological education opportunities for its members;—Enable Africa's rural and urban poor to attain food security;—Empower women and youth as active leaders and participants in their communities;—Communicate the mission and vision of both AICs and OAIC to the broader public;—Ensure quality and accountability at all levels of the Organization;—Secure a sustainable and prosperous future for the OAIC."

[29]See All Africa Conference of Churches, "AACC: All Africa Conference of Churches," www.aacc-ceta.org. However, by the end of the 1990s, no more than a dozen AICS or so had been accepted into the AACC.

[30]See the World Council of Churches, "Organization of African Instituted Churches," www.oik oumene.org/en/church-families/african-instituted-churches/oaic (accessed June 19, 2015).

[31]Venter, *Engaging Modernity.*

[32]Marie-Louise Martin, "Afrikanische Gestalt des christlichen Glaubens: Die Kirche Jesu Christi auf Erden durch den Propheten Simon Kimbangu," *Evangelische Missionszeitschrift* 28 (1971): 16-29; Heinrich Balz, "Kimbanguisten am Kongo," in *Weggenossen am Fluss und am Berg: Von Kimbanguisten und Lutheranern in Afrika* (Neuendettelsau, Germany: Erlanger Verlag für Mission und Ökumene, 2005), 15-134; Balz, "Kimbanguismus auf Abwegen," *Interkulturelle Theologie/Zeitschrift für Missionswissenschaft,* no. 4 (2008): 438-45; Ngoy Kasukuti, *Recht und Grenze der Inkulturation* (Erlangen, Germany: Verlag der Ev.-Luth. Mission, 1991); and Joseph Ndi Okalla, "Historiographie indigener Christentumsbewegungen im Kongo-Becken: Der Kimbanguismus und seine Varianten; Eine afrikanische Initiative des 20. Jahrhunderts," in

African Shembe Church,[33] but there is still a tremendous need for research in this field.

Mergers Between Evangelicals and Fundamentalists

An ecumenism of intercultural and intercontinental scope demands that those streams of world Christianity that avoid contact with other churches should also enter the picture. This implies that an imperative exists to tolerate church bodies that seem offensive and eccentric, at least initially. One such example is constituted by the Christian fundamentalists. In the United States, a conservative Christian school of thought found a voice in *The Fundamentals*, a theological series first published in 1910.[34] The fundamentalists were intent on defending the fundamentals; they rejected progress and the academic (or rather critical) investigation of Scripture as well as other scientific advances. The movement included both postmillennialists, with an optimistic view of history, and premillennialists, with a pessimistic view of history. In 1917, the mission societies associated with the fundamentalists founded the Interdenominational Foreign Mission Association (IFMA), which includes more than fifty societies today. While the fundamentalist movement experienced a decline after 1948, the IFMA was not impaired. In 1948, the fundamentalists (the fundamentalist churches) joined under the leadership of Carl McIntire to found the International Council of Christian Churches, an association some might see as a counterpart to the World Council of Churches, founded the same year.

There is another school of thought that is far more receptive to critical research and to science as a whole and that is in favor of mission and cooperation

---

Klaus Koschorke, ed., *"Christen und Gewürze": Konfrontation und Interaktion kolonialer und indigener Christentumsvarianten* (Göttingen: Vandenhoeck & Ruprecht, 1998), 230-45.

[33]Edley J. Moodley, *Shembe, Ancestors, and Christ: A Christological Inquiry with Missiological Implications* (Eugene, OR: Pickwick, 2008); Gabriele Lademann-Priemer, *Heilung als Zeichen für die Einheit der Welten: Religiöse Vorstellungen von Krankheit und Heilung in Europa im vorigen Jahrhundert und unter den Zulu mit einem Ausblick in unsere Zeit* (Frankfurt: P. Lang, 1990); Lademann-Priemer, ed., *Traditionelle Religion und christlicher Glaube: Widerspruch und Wandel; Festschrift für Hans-Jürgen Becken zum 70. Geburtstag* (Ammersbek, Germany: Verlag an der Lottbek P. Jensen, 1993); and Andreas Heuser, *Shembe und die Soldaten Gottes* (Münster: Waxmann, 2003).

[34]For the following discussion, see Erich Geldbach, "Evangelikalismus: Versuch einer historischen Typologie," in Reinhard Frieling, ed., *Die Kirche und ihre Konservativen: Traditionalismus und Evangelikalismus in den Konfessionen* (Göttingen: Vandenhoeck & Ruprecht, 1984), 52-83.

with other churches. This school of thought exists within the worldwide evangelical movement—the so-called New Evangelicals, a movement that originated in the 1940s. The mission societies closely associated with this movement joined in 1940 to found the Evangelical Foreign Missions Association (EFMA). In 1968, its membership consisted of about seventy-five societies.[35] Both associations, the IFMA and the EFMA, see themselves as legitimate successors to the International Missionary Council. In 1966 they jointly organized first the Wheaton Congress and then also the World Congress on Evangelism in West Berlin. Also held at the instigation of Billy Graham was the Lausanne Conference,[36] which gave rise to the Lausanne Committee for World Evangelization.[37] Subsequent congresses were held in Manila in 1989 and in Cape Town in 2010.

In the 1970s and afterward, various schools of thought came into being within the evangelical movement, such as a group of "social-concern evangelicals," also known as the "radical evangelicals."[38] Members of this group include Orlando Costas (1942–1987), René Padilla (b. 1932) and Samuel Escobar (b. 1934) from Latin America; and Jim Wallis (b. 1948) and Ronald J. Sider (b. 1939) from the United States. Playing an important role for this stream of thought is the belief that the kingdom of God is already present in the world and is capable of transforming society. Meanwhile, a second evangelical school of thought called AD2000 and Beyond set its sights on the unreached peoples and places of the world. The focus is on the so-called 10/40 window, i.e., on those regions located approximately between ten degrees north and forty degrees north latitude and between the Atlantic and Pacific oceans. Here the emphasis is on those countries least reached by the gospel and that are the most difficult to reach. This area is dominated by Islam, the Hindu religions, and Buddhism. Many of these countries prohibit Christian mission, and Christians are frequently persecuted in this area.[39]

---

[35]This movement counted among its membership the likes of Billy Graham.

[36]Meanwhile, few fundamentalists attended the Lausanne Conference.

[37]Bernd Brandl, "Mission in evangelikaler Perspektive," in Christoph Dahling-Sander, Andrea Schultze, Dietrich Werner, and Henning Wrogemann, eds., *Leitfaden Ökumenische Missionstheologie* (Gütersloh, Germany: Gütersloher Verlagshaus, 2003), 178-99.

[38]See Erhard Berneburg, *Das Verhältnis von Verkündigung und sozialer Aktion in der evangelikalen Missionstheorie unter besonderer Berücksichtigung der Lausanner Bewegung für Weltevangelisation (1974–1989)* (Wuppertal, Germany: R. Brockhaus Verlag, 1997).

[39]Brandl, "Mission in evangelikaler Perspektive," 197.

The subject of intercultural theology/mission studies should pay attention to these movements in world Christianity for a number of reasons. *First*, the evangelical movement—which, as we have mentioned, is a very pluriform one—is *numerically* strong. *Second*, this movement features some internationally very influential *institutions of higher learning*, such as Fuller Theological Seminary in Pasadena, California, that exercise a globally significant influence through their international students. Material taught by some of those lecturing there often elicits favorable responses in countries like South Korea, Tanzania, or Nigeria. *Third*, once again we have to mention the subject of *international and transcontinental networks*, which is of considerable significance for the analysis of local forms of Christian praxis. It is also a fact that most of the churches in southern-hemisphere countries that were founded by northern-hemisphere missionaries are far more conservative than Christians in, say, Germany. Therefore, in order better to understand the praxis of these churches, it is imperative to study the influences of the evangelical and Pentecostal movements. *Fourth*, our intent is to foster a culture of theological dialogue that insists on engaging fellow Christians, even those who come across as foreign (and sometimes offensive), and to seek to understand them especially when we do *not* agree with their positions. That being said, how should we conceive of ecumenical solidarity in the face of such challenges? Along the lines of Christian unity? Fellowship? Cooperation? Or along the lines of a model that is altogether different?

THE ONE CHRISTIANITY? WHAT FORM SHOULD ECUMENICAL PARTNERSHIPS TAKE?

In the ecumenical discussions held in the course of the twentieth century, a wide variety of different concepts have been developed in answer to the question: How should we conceive of the visible unity of the churches?[40]

---

[40]Harding Meyer, *Ökumenische Zielvorstellungen* (Göttingen: Vandenhoeck & Ruprecht, 1996); for an English translation, see *That All May Be One: Perceptions and Models of Ecumenicity* (Grand Rapids: Eerdmans, 1999); Christoph Böttigheimer, "Ökumene ohne Ziel? Ökumenische Einigungsmodelle und katholische Einheitsvorstellungen," *Ökumenische Rundschau* 52 (2003): 174-87; Matthias Haudel, "Die Einheit der Kirchen als Koinonia (Gemeinschaft)? Chancen und Probleme des jüngsten ökumenischen Einheitskonzepts," *Ökumenische Rundschau* 55 (2006): 482-501; Reinhard Frieling, "Steht die Ökumenische Bewegung vor einem Pradigmenwechsel?," in *Im Glauben eins—in Kirchen getrennt?: Visionen einer realistischen Ökumene* (Göttingen: Vandenhoeck & Ruprecht, 2006), 228-55; Frieling, "Welche Einheit wollen wir? Zum Projekt 'Grund

Two basic options suggest themselves, each of which may again be divided into different submodels with distinctive emphases. The first basic option is preferred by most Protestant churches (the Lutherans, the Reformed, the Baptists, the Methodists, etc.), which see church unity as churches being in fellowship with one another. From the outset, then, the model allows for institutionally separate individual churches that join together in a way they are free to define—and the intent is not to merge the institutions, at least not initially. The second basic option is the model held essentially by the Roman Catholic Church and the Orthodox churches, which conceives of the *unity* of the one and indivisible church as institutionally manifested in the governance structure of the church. Thus while the Protestant churches proceed on the assumption of a *preexisting plurality* that is then (in a second step) incrementally transformed by the declaration of fellowship, the Roman Catholic Church and the Orthodox churches proceed on the assumption of a *preexisting ecclesiastical unity*—which continues to exist. For the latter churches, then, the task is to find ways to reintegrate those Christians who have separated themselves from the one church. In what follows, we will need to devote closer attention to these two basic options and to other models of *unity*, as opposed to models of *unification*.[41]

Let us now look back on the first few decades of discussions held in conjunction with the World Council of Churches. Our intent in doing so is to identify various models of ecclesiastical unification. We will initially describe the three models identified at the Second World Conference on Faith and Order held in Edinburgh in 1937: the cooperation model, the mutual recognition model, and the organic union model.[42]

(1) In brief, the first model focuses on cooperation and federation—on the *primacy of action*. Already at the first World Conference on Faith and Order, held in Lausanne in 1927, the idea of practical cooperation between churches that remained institutionally separate in all other respects played a significant role. It was expected that working together would give rise to impulses that could lead to greater unification of the churches. Here the

---

und Gegenstand des Glaubens' im Zusammenhang ökumenischer Einheitskonzeptionen," *Una Sancta* 64 (2009): 170-81.

[41]Meyer, *Ökumenische Zielvorstellungen*, 88ff. It must be noted that this distinction was only generally accepted in the 1970s.

[42]On the following discussion, see especially ibid., 88ff.

motto of Nathan Söderblom, "Doctrine divides—service unites," met with a favorable response. That being said, its adherents did also focus on the issue of unification by way of doctrine, faith life, and church governance structures. This model does not seek to identify a preexisting basis of mutual agreement; rather, it expresses the hope that joint efforts will lead to the development of an increasingly broad basis. The Conciliar Process for Justice, Peace and the Integrity of Creation that was launched in the 1980s also advocates this idea.

(2) In contrast, the mutual recognition model espouses the primacy of confessional plurality. Proponents of this model strive to achieve *mutual recognition in matters of doctrine*, seen to be a sign of unity, which makes it possible for the participating churches to celebrate unity by mutually participating in Holy Communion. While the presupposition is that the churches may continue to remain independent as institutions and denominations, a much stronger emphasis is placed on agreement in matters of doctrine and spiritual practice, as opposed to the cooperation model. In Edinburgh, it was stated with regard to this model: "Such [sacramental] intercommunion, as between two or more Churches, implies that all concerned are true Churches, or true branches of the one Church."[43]

The text of the Edinburgh Conference presupposes that with regard to this unification model, the churches involved must come to see themselves and each other in a new light, so that instead of dissociating themselves from and excluding other churches, they learn to recognize their value and to respect them. Old doctrinal differences need to be reexamined. The goal is to recognize other churches despite ongoing differences in denominational character and despite the ongoing structural separation into independent church organizations. The most prominent example of the mutual recognition model is the Leuenberg Concord, adopted in 1973. After many years of dialogue between Lutheran, Reformed, and United churches, old doctrinal condemnations were revoked. Along with the recognition of concord, full Communion fellowship was established.[44] The concord represents a joint formulation of core doctrinal statements concerning which there is unanimity. Nevertheless, the confessional

---

[43]Leonard Hodgson, ed., *The Second World Conference on Faith and Order Held at Edinburgh, August 3-18, 1937* (New York: Macmillan, 1938), 251.
[44]Meyer, *Ökumenische Zielvorstellungen*, 130.

documents specific to each denomination remain in effect. Although confessional plurality is maintained, the emphasis is on the recognition that a common basis exists, on the revocation of doctrinal condemnations, on the common goal of fellowship in word and deed, on the possibility of mutual communion fellowship, and on the recognition of ordination and the office of the ministry. The unity of the churches consists in these things, and their denominational and structural independence is not considered an impediment to unity. This church fellowship has not led to the institutional fusion of the individual churches, but it has led to the establishment of a common forum, the Community of Protestant Churches in Europe (CPCE). This must be seen as a significant step in the direction of the visible unity of the church.[45]

(3) Finally, the organic union model advocates the primacy of structural unity. In contrast to the "softer" models of fellowship by way of cooperation or unification in terms of mutual recognition, this model aspires quite literally to the *institutional fusion of various churches* into one church. This approach has been labeled the "organic union" approach. The aim is to bring about theological consensus on fundamental matters of Christian doctrine, a consensus that would enable the participants to live together in one church under a single church governance structure. In this way, different denominations would unite to form one church, i.e., to bring about an institutional innovation or simply an "organic union." In terms of the history of ecumenism, this model originated within the Anglican Church. The following statement was made in Edinburgh (1937):

> The third form in which the final goal of our movement may be expressed presents, from the standpoint of definition, the greatest difficulties. It is commonly indicated by such terms as "corporate union" or "organic unity." These terms are forbidding to many, as suggesting the ideal of a compact governmental union involving rigid uniformity. We do not so understand them, and none of us desires such uniformity. On the contrary, what we desire is the unity of a living organism, with the diversity characteristic of the members of a healthy body. The idea of "corporate union" must remain for the vast majority of Christians their ideal.[46]

---

[45]Frieling, "Welche Einheit," 172.
[46]The text went on to state, "In a Church so united the ultimate loyalty of every member would be given to the whole body and not to any part of it. Its members would move freely from one part to another and find every privilege of membership open to them. The sacraments would

The text shows that the conference wrestled with the topic of unity and diversity, and in this model specifically with diversity within unity, i.e., the unity of the constitutionally mandated resultant (new) church. The idea is for various individual churches to merge into one single church under joint leadership. The intent is not for churches merely to recognize one another but to merge and become united also with respect to church governance. The local churches are to become a local church. Many such unification processes have taken place in many countries in the twentieth century.[47]

(4) A fourth model exists, one that we may title "unity and diversity." In the 1980s, the Greek term *koinonia* was a key concept of the discussions held in conjunction with the WCC. For our purposes, we will leave the term *koinonia* untranslated, since the German word *Gemeinschaft*, the Latin word *communio*, or the English words *fellowship* or *communion* are not fully congruent with the semantic content of the Greek word.[48] Although the term had been used before, the concept itself was programmatically introduced as a new key concept at the seventh general assembly of the WCC in Canberra in 1991 and specifically in the document, "The Unity of the Church: Gift and Calling." The Canberra Statement reads,

> The unity of the Church to which we are called is a koinonia given and expressed in the common confession of the apostolic faith; a common sacramental life entered by the one baptism and celebrated together in one eucharistic fellowship; a common life in which members and ministries are mutually recognized and reconciled; and a common mission witnessing to all people to the gospel of God's grace and serving the whole of creation. The goal of the search for full communion is realized when all the churches are able to recognize in one another the one, holy, catholic and apostolic church in its fullness.[49]

---

be the sacraments of the whole body. The ministry would be accepted by all as a ministry of the whole body." Hodgson, *Second World Conference*, 252.

[47] The reference is to church unions, such as the United Church of Canada, founded in 1925 as a result of the merger of Methodist, Presbyterian, and Congregationalist churches; the Church of Christ in China, founded in 1927; the Church of South India, founded in 1947; or the Church of Christ in Zaire, founded in 1970. Meyer, *Ökumenische Zielvorstellungen*, 123.

[48] Haudel, "Die Einheit der Kirchen," 485.

[49] The Faith and Order Commission, "The Unity of the Church: Gift and Calling—The Canberra Statement; 20 February 1991," World Council of Churches, www.oikoumene.org/en/resources/documents/commissions/faith-and-order/i-unity-the-church-and-its-mission/the-unity-of-the-church-gift-and-calling-the-canberra-statement (accessed June 22, 2015). See also Dagmar

According to Harding Meyer, the term *koinonia* possesses an inherent "integrative power." He states, "The concept of koinonia has been accorded a high degree of acceptance in current ecumenical thinking and has become a key concept and guiding principle because it has given the understanding of the church a more elementary and more alive dimension."[50] According to Meyer, the following aspects of the term may be underscored: first, it combines church and unity; second, in terms of sharing in and enabling others to share, this combination has always had a tangible, visible dimension to it; third, this is about fellowship in faith; fourth, it also allows for service rendered to one another and to the world; fifth, the term *koinonia* prohibits standardization and mandatory uniformity; sixth, the term conversely also prohibits noncommitment by pointedly including structural aspects; and finally, seventh, it puts the existence of the church into perspective as but one aspect of the bigger picture of God's salvific action.[51] The term *koinonia* thus helps orient people. However, in my opinion the term cannot provide a convincing solution for the issue of what unity means, since *koinonia* does not define unity as such—meaning that the operative definition of unity depends on the way *koinonia* is interpreted.[52]

When it comes to the selection of terminology in this regard, at issue is always the relationship of unity and diversity and specifically the question as to how much diversity may and can be subsumed under the term *unity*. We will have to leave it at that, since we cannot devote any further attention to this issue here.

Catholic theologian Johannes Oeldemann correctly points out that when it comes to the issue of church fellowship in the ecumenical debate, a distinction must be made between the *understanding of unity*, on the one hand, and *unification models*, on the other.[53] He asserts that among the Orthodox churches and in the Roman Catholic Church there are models that would

---

Heller, ed., *Das Wesen und die Bestimmung der Kirche: Ein Schritt auf dem Weg zu einer gemeinsamen Auffassung* (Frankfurt: Lembeck, 2000).

[50]Meyer, *That All May Be One*, 67.

[51]Meyer, *Ökumenische Zielvorstellungen*, 82-84.

[52]See Haudel, "Die Einheit der Kirchen," 497. See also Walter Cardinal Kasper, *Wege der Einheit: Perspektiven für die Ökumene* (Freiburg im Breisgau, Germany: Herder, 2005).

[53]Johannes Oeldemann, "Gestufte Kirchengemeinschaft als ökumenisches Modell?: Überlegungen aus römisch-katholischer Perspektive," *Una Sancta* 60 (2005): 135-47, especially 137.

allow for *different levels of church fellowship*.[54] That being said, however, Oeldemann laments that the concept of different church fellowship levels is effectively being undermined in the Catholic domain.[55] For instance, newer initiatives by the Vatican limit the latitude of the liturgical independence of those Eastern churches that have entered into a union with Rome.[56] According to Oeldemann, there must be intermediate stages on the path toward unification. He alleges that while Leuenberg declared church fellowship in the same way as Meissen, Porvoo, Waterloo, and others had before, no follow-up action has actually been taken on an institutional level, at least not to date.[57]

TOWARD AN ECUMENICAL APPRECIATION OF PLURALITY: MAINTAINING CONTACT FROM A DISTANCE

These examples clearly show that the issue of the definition of unity and of unification concepts is fundamentally determined by the way one defines church. Yet we need to go one step further and ask: What form may Christian "fellowship" take when various churches lead the Christian life in fundamentally different ways? How are transcultural ecumenical ties possible when the conventional models of ecclesiastical unity are not workable— models like the Roman Catholic basic model of *church unity as ritual-institutional incorporation*, the Protestant basic model of *fellowship between churches by way of doctrinal consensus*, or the pragmatic basic model of *cooperation between churches according to the motto "doctrine divides—service unites"*? We would do well also to consider the basic model commonly used in both the Pentecostal movement and the African Initiated Churches,

---

[54]See ibid., 139-40.

[55]Medard Kehl, "Zum jüngsten Disput um das Verhältnis von Universalkirche und Ortskirchen," in Peter Walter et al., eds., *Kirche in ökumenischer Perspektive* (Freiburg im Breisgau, Germany: Herder, 2003), 81-101.

[56]Oeldemann points to "the ever-increasing number of Roman directives in recent years that keep limiting the independence of the Latin local churches." Oeldemann, "Gestufte Kirchengemeinschaft," 142-43.

[57]Oeldemann is thinking of going beyond the status quo instead of merely contenting oneself with holding ecumenical services and with the pastor from the other denomination participating in an "ecumenical wedding"—he is thinking of things like Protestants proclaiming the Word in Catholic worship services, or conceivably using bread that has been blessed (*antidoron*) as a sign of fellowship in the Orthodox domain, or some other ritual form of expression. Oeldemann, "Gestufte Kirchengemeinschaft," 145-47.

namely the model of *church as a force field*. When churches see themselves as force fields (even if this might be expressed using different metaphors), as fellowships in which people sense the power of God or of the Holy Spirit at work (often seen as being mediated by persons believed to be especially gifted), as fellowships in which people can pray for this power and stand a chance to receive it—then the result is a very specific model of association from a distance.

The verdict of Pastor Brown Oyitso, who ministers at an RCCG congregation in Germany, may serve as a typical example. He submits that affiliation between the RCCG and the Evangelical Church in Germany (EKD) is not possible, since EKD member churches do not practice speaking in tongues and since they take no clear position on heaven and hell. Oyitso states that cooperation may be possible to the extent of some joint projects, but no more than that, because "if I don't influence you, you will influence me. . . . So if I can't influence you to practise [speaking in tongues], I may begin to believe that what you are doing is right, and it can affect my belief."[58] Thus in this case, keeping one's distance appears to be an—entirely legitimate—protective strategy.[59]

Against this backdrop, models of ecumenical *unity* (in which it is unavoidable that the power of institutions will be brought to bear) should be called into question, as should models of ecumenical *fellowship*; even models of ecumenical *cooperation* have their limitations. Instead, I recommend the—far humbler—model of ecumenical *association* in the sense of maintaining contact.[60] *Association from a distance could serve as a model that combines the issue of ecumenical "unity" with the value of enduring plurality.* Here too we would need to ask what the hidden motives behind each instance of striving for unity may be, since fusions (may) always imply an increase in power for the larger institution in each case. The power factor plays a fundamental role for every kind of relationship and thus also for

---

[58]As cited in Anna D. Quaas, *Transnationale Pfingstkirchen: Christ Apostolic Church und Redeemed Christian Church of God* (Frankfurt: Lembeck, 2011), 362.

[59]We need to bear in mind that in Germany the EKD, with its twenty-five million members, is considerably larger than the RCCG, which consists of churches with a combined membership of a few thousand members from a sub-Saharan background.

[60]For a more detailed discussion of the subject, see Henning Wrogemann, "Einheit im Glauben? Ökumene und Toleranz," in *Das schöne Evangelium inmitten der Kulturen und Religionen* (Erlangen, Germany: Erlanger Verlag für Mission und Ökumene, 2011), 232-56.

transcultural ecumenism. For instance, due to their excellent financial situation and their successful dissemination efforts, various Pentecostal churches have no interest at all in establishing closer ties with older church bodies. Thus we may well ask: What motivates churches or congregations to seek stronger ecumenical ties?

25

Contexts

Contextual Theologies and Their Cultural Impregnation

In our deliberations thus far, we have discussed the core issues pertaining to the subject of intercultural theology/mission studies while only fleetingly addressing the subject of contexts. *In contrast to the concept of culture—however that may be defined—the concept of contexts is a more general one. It refers to societal, social, ecological, or medical frameworks that are not to be seen primarily as cultural forms of expression of the human existence.* Let us consider the issue of insufficient medical care as an example. The lack of sufficient institutions for the provision of medical care is common to many sub-Saharan countries, regardless of the cultural configuration concerned. This is a context—a *macro context*, if you will—in which not only people in general but also (more germane to our subject matter) religious and Christian movements and organizations have to position themselves. From this perspective, the context represents a transnational framework to which—and this is significant—each culture and religion may respond in its own unique way. More on that later. Another example might be the HIV/AIDS pandemic—this too is a kind of macro context, since the rate of infection is very high in many countries. Other contexts of this kind include corruption, the subject of justice, gender issues, and ecology (such as the growth of deserts due to the deforestation of rainforests). We will endeavor to demonstrate that contexts and cultural patterns must be seen as mutually interdependent: if the Christian message is to be relevant, then those who proclaim it must respond to the contexts; however, while there are many possible responses, all of them are culturally contingent.

JUSTICE AND DEVELOPMENT

Let us address this subject by discussing the concept of development. Up until the 1960s, development policies in the United States were determined by US national interests. For this reason, the government budgeted for development under the heading, "mutual defense." The intent was to supply "help to underdeveloped nations" in order to gain their allegiance in the course of the Cold War.[1] When decolonization ended toward the close of the 1960s, the Agency for International Development was founded in the United States, and the Federal Ministry for Cooperation (*Bundesministerium für Zusammenarbeit*) was founded in Germany. In the United Nations, because of the new national states the representatives of southern countries constituted a majority. They placed the topic of development on the agenda with corresponding emphasis. This led to the proclamation of so-called decades of development, from which we may deduce how the prevailing understanding of the term *development* changed. In the 1960s, the concept of development was seen predominantly in terms of *development through growth*. At least four aspects are fundamental in this regard.

According to this concept, first, the initial *cause* of the economic problems in many countries was their *lack of capital*. All that was needed for these countries to develop—the thinking went—was for capital to be made available to them. Second, according to the same thinking, wherever investments were made, modernization would ensue, jobs would be created, and the resulting *"trickle-down" effect* would be felt throughout the surrounding area. Thus by means of the effects of modernization and industrialization, remote and still underdeveloped areas would be reached indirectly. Third, once local production had increased, developing countries would be integrated into the world markets more and more, and consumption would pick up as a result, to the benefit of all concerned. Fourth and finally, this model was predicated on the assumption that other *nations worldwide would follow*—and would have to follow—*the same path of modernization and industrialization* as the industrialized nations. In other words, development was seen as playing catch-up according to a fixed scheme of economic and societal processes.

---

[1]For the following discussion, see Franz Nuscheler, "Entwicklungspolitik im Gezeitenwandel," in *Lern- und Arbeitsbuch Entwicklungspolitik*, 6th ed. (Bonn, Germany: Dietz, 2005), 76-97, particularly 78.

Meanwhile, at the end of the 1960s the president of the World Bank, Robert McNamara, commissioned a report from the "Commission on International Development." This so-called Pearson Report, which was presented in 1969, examined twenty years of development work and came to a very critical conclusion: despite a certain amount of economic growth, the development policies of the time had not been able to forestall the increase of global mass poverty. As a result, in the second decade of development, which took place during the 1970s, a new strategy was followed: the *basic needs strategy*. Many conferences held during this decade were characterized by fierce debates. Calls for a new world economic order became ever more strident. However, in this decade too the results did not match the expectations. Increased help was provided only to the very poorest countries.

This greater political context is very clearly reflected in the debates about theological issues, both in the work of the World Council of Churches and in the analyses of liberation theologians. In general, the latter blamed the dependency of the so-called developing countries on the industrialized nations for the perpetuation of the disparity.[2] This is known as the "dependency theory."[3] The analysis concluded that the structures were "sinful" since they helped perpetuate "neocolonial" relationships. This accusation was often made, and especially so during the World Mission Conference in Bangkok in 1973, convened under the theme "Salvation Today." Here representatives of the churches of the south pilloried the churches of the north. But let us return to the subject of development policies. Representatives of the different contexts entered into critical disputes with each other. For instance, Asian theologians accused Latin American liberation theologians of acting in hegemonic ways and of claiming that their own position was universally valid—even though it did not apply to other religio-politico-cultural contexts, as shown by the following example: they pointed out that contextual theologians in Indonesia did not speak of liberation theology as such, but rather very specifically of a *theology of development*, which included aspects of liberation.

---

[2] See Kurt Zaugg-Ott, *Entwicklung oder Befreiung? Die Entwicklungsdiskussion im Ökumenischen Rat der Kirchen von 1968 bis 1991* (Frankfurt: Lembeck, 2004), 53.

[3] See Dieter Senghaas, ed., *Peripherer Kapitalismus: Analysen über Abhängigkeit und Unterentwicklung* (Frankfurt: Suhrkamp, 1974), 37-67. Although he based his theory on analyses drawn from Latin America, he universalized his approach and expanded it to formulate a theory of a peripheral capitalism, which he claimed was valid for the entire Third World.

The third decade of development took place from 1981–1990. This was a time marked by serious economic crisis. The growth rates of most developing countries fell, exacerbated by a decline in the price of raw materials. As a result, the debt crisis became the biggest problem for the national economies of many developing countries. While a few countries did succeed in keeping their success stories going—such as the Asian countries of Taiwan, Singapore, South Korea, and Hong Kong, as well as China—other countries that had formerly enjoyed good results, like Brazil, now suffered severe setbacks, as did some oil-exporting countries such as Mexico, Venezuela, Algeria, or Nigeria. After 1982, the so-called interest rate shock did the rest: the combination of low prices for raw materials and the high interest rate forced many countries into a debt trap, with the result that from 1982 until the end of the decade or so, many countries had to pay more in interest than they could receive in the form of new credits. Also, attempts to export more raw materials yielded no results, since the subsequent glut in the world markets led to prices falling even further.

As a counterstrategy, a new economic policy was implemented in the industrialized nations in the form of Reaganism in the United States and of Thatcherism in Great Britain. What followed in the wake of these reforms was less a new "strategy" of development policies than it was a *neoliberal reform policy*, one that was prescribed to many developing countries. The agenda of this economic policy was, first, *to lower inflation*, which was contingent, second, on the *denationalization of the economy*, i.e., the suppression of government intervention in the economic sector; also, third, the *deregulation of the market*, i.e., the abolition of governmental restrictions, of bureaucracy, etc.; fourth, the *liberalization of trade*; and, fifth, an increased emphasis on *promoting private enterprise*.

This means that in the 1980s, a time many observers see as the "lost decade" of development policies, indebted developing countries were made to comply with certain reforms before they could receive development aid. The International Monetary Fund, the World Bank, and the donor countries made debtor nations comply with certain reforms, which were summarized in the "Washington Consensus." At the insistence of the United States, the catchphrase "new world economic order" disappeared from the orders of business of the north-south conferences. The debt crisis showed quite plainly the limitations of state-led economic development: ineffecient public enterprises, corrupt bureaucracies, the paralysis of private enterprise, etc. As an antidote to these problems, the free market was prescribed, propped up by conditional requirements intended to guarantee legal certainty and the free flow of capital. Meanwhile, in the face of the situation on the ground in many countries, sooner or later the question had to be asked: What effect was denationalization supposed to have on an already weak state? How was economic liberalization supposed to benefit countries in which the prerequisites for capitalistic development were not met, either in terms of infrastructure, mental readiness, or education? Was the shock therapy not too much for many states, even if the direction proved to be the correct one overall? Should neoliberal politics not be accompanied and undergirded by development initiatives? More and more, the aim became to implement a "global structural policy" (Nuscheler), i.e., sustainable global development.

So much for the sketch. What is interesting as far as the subject of intercultural theology/mission studies is concerned is that people interpreted these phenomena very differently. Some blamed the mentalities of southern-hemisphere populations (corruption, tribalism, no long-term planning) for the misery; others held the injustices of the world market as well as—and especially—those of the industrialized nations responsible. In this regard at least, the two perspectives have something in common: in furnishing these interpretations, both tacitly reproduce cultural stereotypes. In summary, theological interpretations and religious motivations are closely linked with the problems at issue here. In terms of Pentecostal churches, for instance, we may ask: How do these churches operate in the context we have sketched here? Which religio-lifeworldly answers do they supply? Do they contribute unilaterally to consumerism? Where do they stand on discourses on justice, on secular activities, on politics?

Healing, Reconciliation, Gender, Ecology

We will address the other contexts only briefly. The hypothesis states that it is precisely by analyzing both contextual frameworks and specific cultural reaction patterns that the subject of intercultural theology/mission studies makes an important contribution to the ecumenical-intercultural dialogue. For instance, in the macro context of insufficient medical care, issues related to wholeness, salvation, and healing tend to be expressed within very specific cultural patterns. It is imperative that we first understand the various medical systems before we can analyze the theological content of Christian behavioral patterns and the situation in the church. In this regard, it is particularly the HIV/AIDS pandemic that constitutes a macro context.[4] What is the relationship between various traditional medicine paradigms, on the one hand, and medical requirements from the perspective of Western medicine, on the other? How do various churches interpret the pandemic, and what are the consequences of the various interpretations? What are the possibilities for communal, ecumenical, and interreligious cooperation? Which political demands are made as a result of the interplay of local constellations?

The same applies to the topic of *reconciliation*.[5] In various states around the world during the past decades, people have been brutalized: genocides have taken place in countries such as Rwanda and Burundi; political mass murders have been committed in places such as Cambodia; dictatorships have carried out abductions, torture, and murder for decades; and millions of people have been traumatized in civil-war areas such as the Congo or South Sudan. Such contexts, marked by the reign of violence, also pose a challenge, one that is common—tragically—to many countries and regions. Yet here too the specific religiocultural patterns must be considered, such as certain rites of reconciliation or a certain understanding of fellowship. Here we may recall Geertz's "thick description" and the cultural-semiotic approach. While it is true that contextual theologies find expression in theological reflections, they do so to a far more comprehensive extent in ritual actions and in ritual-symbolic-liturgical innovations and practices.

It is no coincidence that global discourses have come into being concerning such phenomena as truth and reconciliation commissions around

---

[4]Hansjörg Dilger, *Leben mit AIDS: Krankheit, Tod und soziale Beziehungen in Afrika* (Frankfurt: Campus, 2005); Katja Heidemanns and Marco Moerschbacher, eds., *Gott vertrauen? AIDS und Theologie im südlichen Afrika* (Freiburg im Breisgau, Germany: Herder, 2005); Isabel Apawo Phiri, Beverley Haddad, and Madipoane Masenya, *African Women, HIV/AIDS and Faith Communities* (Pietermaritzburg, South Africa: Cluster Publications, 2003); Sonja Weinreich and Christoph Benn, *AIDS—Eine Krankheit verändert die Welt: Daten—Fakten—Hintergründe*, 3rd ed. (Frankfurt: Lembeck, 2005).
[5]See Robert J. Schreiter, *Wider die schweigende Anpassung: Versöhnungsarbeit als Auftrag und Dienst der Kirche im gesellschaftlichen Umbruch* (Lucerne, Switzerland: Edition Exodus, 1993).

the globe, especially in South Africa after the fall of the apartheid regime[6] as compared to similar commissions—in entirely different contexts—in Latin America. In addition to the specific cultural-contextual differences (such as political, social, economic, or religious ones), this raises yet again the question about binding standards for justice, about a global discourse and comparable standards, such as provided by, say, the 1948 United Nations declaration of human rights. Or are these values also "contextual"? At any rate, these things are widely debated, both interculturally and intercontinentally. It goes without saying that the same is true for gender issues, since each cultural configuration has its own pattern, its own unique way of defining the relationship between the sexes. These patterns are constantly changing, and it is only possible to develop relevant contextual theologies if proper attention is paid to the influence of culture in each case. The same is also true for issues of ecology and creation spirituality.

Churches in Cultures and Contexts: Yearning for the Kingdom of God

The questions we have raised direct our attention back to that referential factor that is downright essential for contextual theologies: Christian forms of communitization. Churches in Africa, Asia, Latin America, and elsewhere are frequently interwoven into the cultural fabric and the contexts in which they exist. The pursuit of intercultural theology is about the issue of communal Christian existences in the face of challenges. Again, theologies manifest themselves in forms of communitization, in the "dialogues" of the lifeworld, in proverbs, in subtle forms of resistance, and in ritual-liturgical models that empower the lives of people. Life in the church—the life of the church—is suffused, in spite of all its brokenness, with the yearning for the kingdom of God, the yearning for wholeness in the form of healing, health, reconciliation, dignity, justice, freedom, abundance in

---

[6]John W. de Gruchy, "Die Vergangenheit in Südafrika erlösen," *epd-Dokumentation* 32 (1997): 28-37; Tinyiko Sam Maluleke, "Truth, National Unity and Reconciliation in South Africa: Aspects of the Emerging Theological Agenda," *Missionalia* 25 (1997): 59-86; Tinyiko Sam Maluleke, "The South African Truth and Reconciliation Discourse," in Laurenti Magesa and Zablon John Nthamburi, eds., *Democracy and Reconciliation: A Challenge for African Christianity* (Nairobi: Action, 1999), 215-41; Dirkie J. Smit, "The Truth and Reconciliation Commission: Tentative Religious and Theological Perspectives," *Journal of Theology for Southern Africa* 90 (1995): 3-15.

this life, and consummation in the next. And for this reason, as we engage Christian existence in all its many facets worldwide, we must continually focus our attention on the fact that *theology* is manifesting itself in the various existences at the grassroots level, at the level of the church and of the community. As long as this is not recognized, intercultural misunderstanding is bound to occur. We must emphasize this in the face of an elitist, bookish, and sometimes didactic-systematic understanding of theology. We do not dispute the rightfulness of the pursuit of systematic theology, but at the same time we want to pay tribute to Christian community as the locus for the "production" of theology.

LIBERATION, THEOLOGY OF RECONSTRUCTION, SUSTAINABILITY

Mission studies scholar Robert Schreiter (b. 1947) has pointed out that while in the 1970s and 1980s there was a global theological discourse about liberation theologies, since the 1990s a reorientation has taken place due to the fall of military dictatorships in Latin America, the fall of apartheid in South Africa, and the fall of socialism.[7] The focus has shifted to a *theology of reconstruction*, to a theology of the reconstruction of societies that have been traumatized.[8] Charles Villa-Vicencio has proposed that the biblical image of the exodus (of the emigration of the people of God from servitude in Egypt), which had long been definitive for liberation theology, should now be supplemented with the *image of the return from exile* or with the image of the *reconstruction of the temple* in Jerusalem. Villa-Vicencio believes that these theological images are capable of formulating the theological task of introducing a Christian, public theology into those societies searching for their own identity. Ecological issues make for an additional widening of the perspective. The aim in many places today is to engage in theological reflection and to find a church praxis that creates the parameters for sustainable living conditions.

---

[7]Robert J. Schreiter, *Die neue Katholizität: Globalisierung und die Theologie* (Frankfurt: IKO-Verlag für Interkulturelle Kommunikation, 1997).

[8]For more on this subject, see for instance Charles Villa-Vicencio, *A Theology of Reconstruction: Nation-Building and Human Rights* (Cambridge: Cambridge University Press, 1992).

26

Theology and Interculturality

Walking the Path Together

Since Christianity is a religious configuration that is as global as it is multifaceted, it is highly likely that it will continue to diversify. Of the various theological disciplines, it falls to the subject of intercultural theology/mission studies to describe these processes of localization, globalization, and diversification. This of course raises the question: With all this diversity, what serves as the unifying factor? So, in closing, we will discuss some of the theological challenges facing the most disparate variants of Christianity, which they will need to address. Due to the scope of this book, we will only be able to do so in brief. Some of the issues we raise here will need to be addressed in greater detail in the following volumes.

The One Gospel amid a Plurality of Christianities?
Identity

In part, what makes intercultural ecumenism such a volatile subject is the issue of the theological interpretive sovereignty. Whereas some believe that the basic data of Christian identity may only be understood from the perspective of the history of Christian tradition, others see this as an attempt to defend the hegemonic claims of the West. They generally respond by proposing an understanding of the Bible predicated on their own culture, which they believe to be a contextually *authentic* understanding of the biblical message. This again raises the issue of power and influence. Now, while some churches deal with these issues against the backdrop of a transcontinental hierarchy (Roman Catholic, Anglican), in other churches the situation is very different. Yet this search for meaning is carried out not only between different cultures within the same church but also between various churches. It concerns such issues as the interpretation of poverty, an appropriate reaction to HIV/AIDS (such as preventive efforts), sexual ethics (such as homosexuality or, in many places, the issue of polygamy), ritual issues (such as dietary rules), the appropriate attitude toward other religions, and many others.

However, if churches and movements are unable to agree as to which traditions are authoritative, then only the Bible itself remains as a normative source of faith. Yet as we have seen people read the Bible with very different eyes. How then can a joint search process come about? What type of hermeneutics is appropriate? Which of the following (somewhat generalized) models is the right one: the biblicist approach (seeing the Bible as inerrant or infallible), higher criticism (the Western academic model), understanding the Bible by the inspiration of the Spirit (the Pentecostal model), or the hermeneutics of suspicion (the liberation theological model)?[1]

A whole series of suggestions have been made in the course of the debate as to appropriate reference points. Thus, for instance, US-American theologian George A. Lindbeck (b. 1923) has identified three regulative principles that allegedly characterize the Christian grammar of faith.[2] The first rule states that there is only one Creator God. The second rule asserts that Jesus of Nazareth was a historical human being. The third rule correlates the first two, declaring that "every possible importance is to be ascribed to Jesus that is not inconsistent with the first rules."[3] Thus Jesus is conceived of as being extremely close to God, while at the same time always being perceived as a human being. It will need to be shown whether these rules of Christian grammar always hold true. Heidelberg New Testament scholar Gerd Theissen (b. 1943) has submitted a different proposal.[4] Theissen argues for the existence of a series of "basic motifs" that feature throughout the New Testament writings.[5] The task is to become aware of these and to use them

---

[1]Of course, each of these models may be subdivided into a range of different schools of thought. To describe each of these would, however, demand a separate study.

[2]George A. Lindbeck, *The Nature of Doctrine: Religion and Theology in a Postliberal Age* (Philadelphia: Westminster, 1984).

[3]Ibid., 94.

[4]Gerd Theissen, "Die Einheit der Kirche: Kohärenz und Differenz im Urchristentum," *Zeitschrift für Missionswissenschaft* 20 (1994): 70-86.

[5]Theissen identifies the following fifteen basic motifs: exodus, faith, repentance, *agape*, vicarious

as a yardstick to determine whether various local theologies reflect the basic motifs of the New Testament or not. Regardless of what one may think about these suggestions, the fact remains that the area of biblical hermeneutics presents an ongoing challenge.

JESUS CHRIST: THE INCARNATION OF THE CRUCIFIED ONE: CHRISTOLOGY

Another challenge comprises the understanding of Jesus Christ as the crucified and risen one. No one disputes the centrality of Jesus Christ for the twenty-seven books of the New Testament. At the same time, a substantive argument is raging between the different cultural variants of Christianity, on the one hand, and the various piety movements within these variants, on the other—an argument about how the centrality of Jesus Christ is to be interpreted. Here the opinions vary considerably. We will address this in a theology of religions, or more specifically in a theology of interreligious relationships (vol. 3). At this point we will merely point out that Christology becomes a central issue when, for instance, in some parts of the Pentecostal movement the experiences of the Holy Spirit gradually become separated from the New Testament witness about the person of Jesus Christ, or when in some African Initiated Churches a particular prophet or his descendants position themselves as a spiritual hierarchy between God and the believers and in so doing effectively usurp Christ's mediator role for themselves. As it is, Christology is heavily debated among the various forms of Christianity that hold different positions in various dialogue constellations. We might also consider the Christian-Muslim dialogue, in which many Muslims demand that Christians affirm that the prophet Isa (Jesus) was nothing more than a human being, or the Christian-Hindu dialogue, in which people might well affirm the divinity of Jesus as an avatar of the god Vishnu, but not his crucifixion.[6] These few examples suffice to show that dogmatic issues are by no means insignificant for the domain of intercultural relationships, since the practice of piety in everyday life, i.e., life on the grassroots level, in

---

substitution, incarnation, self-stigmatization, change of position, creation, wisdom, miracle, hope, judgment, justification, and distance.

[6]See Henning Wrogemann, "Wem gehört Jesus? Interreligiöse Streifzüge und dogmatische Wegmarken," in *Das schöne Evangelium inmitten der Kulturen und Religionen* (Erlangen, Germany: Erlanger Verlag für Mission und Ökumene, 2011), 10-22.

general is characterized by theological interpretations, on the one hand, while it also demands theological explanations, on the other. This may seem strange considering the backdrop of Western societies, where a certain religious arbitrariness has become the hallmark of societal majorities in various countries. In other contexts, however, observers will quickly notice major differences in this regard.

The Holy Spirit and Unholy Spirits: Pneumatology

Another challenge lies in experience-oriented forms of the exercise of religion. In many religious configurations, a large contingent of followers distinguish between acceptable and unacceptable forms of the practice of faith, and these forms are again subjected to religious interpretation for their part. From a Christian perspective, in the intercultural-ecumenical scene nowadays we often come across interpretive models of Satan and evil spirits, on the one hand, and of the Holy Spirit, on the other. This is a dynamic that we need to address. We need to pay especially careful attention in those instances when religious interpretive models lead to diastatic thought patterns, to binary classifications as good or evil, friend or foe, etc.[7] Conversely, the example of pneumatology clearly shows that this domain of Christian doctrine and praxis opens up a wealth of possibilities for the development of new forms of intercultural and interreligious relationship models.[8]

Faith Communities as Force Fields: Ecclesiology

It may be a mark of globalization that religious configurations that successfully establish themselves are characterized, first, by the facilitation of experience; second, by the social formation of small groups; and third, by stylizing their own religious identities. As far as Christian churches and movements are concerned, this means that Christian community is often experienced as a type of force field: in simple terms, "it has something to offer"—orientation, purpose, community, healing, economic benefits, and many other things. But

---

[7]It may be noted that dualistic interpretive models are also found in the revitalization movements of other religions—among Muslims or Hindus, for example, to name just two large religious configurations. They are, however, also found in many new religious movements. These interpretive models and the contexts in which they arise are important objects of future research.
[8]See for instance Amos Yong, *Hospitality and the Other: Pentecost, Christian Practices, and the Neighbor* (Maryknoll, NY: Orbis Books, 2008).

what does this mean for the way Christian community is perceived above and beyond one's own group, movement, or church? Which new interpretive models, and specifically which *theological* interpretive models, are out there to help us understand and respect these phenomena? Future research in the field of mission and religious studies will need to devote greater attention to how religious reality is *effectively* constituted.

Plurality Between Appreciation and Stylization: Society

Another challenge concerns the issue of the legitimacy and the limitations of plurality. Many might censure the increase in plurality as a one-way path to chaos and confusion, i.e., into unpredictability and uncontrollability. Others again might sing the praises of plurality and commend it for promoting cultural diversity, similar to the way in which one might approve, say, of the increased range of products offered by a large supermarket. Yet these interpretations fall short because they underestimate yet again the power and stylization factor. Some might well draw attention to the plurality of a society in order to justify apartheid systems. In such cases, the acceptance of plurality serves as a pretext for the implementation of systems of plural discrimination. Then again, drawing attention to justice might well result in the implementation of equal treatment for all, which in turn might threaten the existence of cultural plurality because people are pressured to conform to a certain norm. Again, our framework does not allow us to do more than to allude to these issues. At any rate, the Christian perspective gives rise to an intrareligious and intercultural mandate to be aware of religiocultural plurality, to value it, and to engage in a constructive debate about which forms of expression are beneficial and comply with the witness of the New Testament—against the backdrop of the entire Bible. But not only that. It also raises politico-societal questions as to the most appropriate and desirable form of plurality for a given society, the way in which minorities should be protected, and many others.

Intercultural Theology/Mission Studies: Fields of Learning

Under this heading, the subject of intercultural theology/mission studies also makes an important contribution to the processes in which Christians see themselves within the pluralized societies of Europe and around the globe. Various forms of Christianity are analyzed from an intercultural perspective according to their particular characteristics, according to what they take for granted both culturally and contextually, according to what they view as problematic, and according to their particular assumptions and priorities. In this way, they become part of the discourse of theology and of the church. This helps us, on the one hand, better to understand our foreign brothers and sisters in the faith; on the other hand, it also helps us to gain a new perspective of ourselves, of what we take for granted, possibly also of our own blind spots, strengths, and weaknesses.

The purpose of all of this, hermeneutically speaking, is to practice changing our perspective, to listen to others, and critically to observe what happens when intercultural encounters take place. Whether in the area of academic teaching, in the life and activity of churches and congregations, or in the domain of education in schools and universities (to mention just a few examples), intercultural theology and intercultural hermeneutics will need to make a considerably stronger contribution in order for the abovementioned processes of interaction between representatives of different cultures and religions to be observed, analyzed, critically appraised, and promoted.

Bibliography

Abraham, K. C., ed. *Third World Theologies: Commonalities and Divergences, Papers and Reflections from the Second General Assembly of the Ecumenical Association of Third World Theologians, December, 1986, Oaxtepec, Mexico.* Maryknoll, NY: Orbis Books, 1990.

Adeboye, Olufunke. "'Arrowhead' of Nigerian Pentecostalism: The Redeemed Christian Church of God, 1952–2005." *Pneuma* 29 (2007): 24-58.

———. "Running the Prophecy: The Redeemed Christian Church of God in North America; 1992–2005." *Missionalia* 36 (2008): 259-79.

———. "Transnational Pentecostalism in Africa: The Redeemed Christian Church of God, Nigeria." In Laurent Fourchard, André Mary, and René Otayek, eds., *Entreprises religieuses transnationales en Afrique de l'ouest,* 439-65. Paris: IFRA-Ibadan, 2005.

Adogame, Afeosemime. "Aladura." In *Religion in Geschichte und Gegenwart.* 4th ed.

———. "HIV/AIDS Support and African Pentecostalism: The Case of the Redeemed Christian Church of God (RCCG)." *Journal of Health Psychology* 12 (2007): 475-84.

Adogame, Afeosemime, Roswith Gerloff, and Klaus Hock, eds. *Christianity in Africa and the African Diaspora: The Appropriation of a Scattered Heritage.* London: Continuum, 2011.

Ahn, Byung-Mu. *Draußen vor dem Tor: Kirche und Minjung in Korea; Theologische Beiträge und Reflexionen.* Theologie der Ökumene 20. Göttingen: Vandenhoeck & Ruprecht, 1986.

Aklé, Yvette, et al., eds. *Der schwarze Christus: Wege afrikanischer Christologie.* Translated by Ursula Faymonville. Freiburg im Breisgau, Germany: Herder, 1989.

Allolio-Näcke, Lars, Britta Kalscheuer, and Arne Manzeschke, eds. *Differenzen anders denken.* Frankfurt: Campus, 2005.

Altena, Thorsten. *"Ein Häuflein Christen mitten in der Heidenwelt des dunklen Erdteils": Zum Selbst- und Fremdverständnis protestantischer Missionare im kolonialen Afrika 1884–1918.* Münster: Waxmann, 2003.

Amanze, James. "History and Major Goals of Regional Associations of Theological Schools in Africa." In Dietrich Werner et al., eds., *Handbook of Theological Education in World Christianity*, 346-67. Oxford: Regnum note, 2010.

Amoah, Elizabeth, and Mercy Amba Oduyoye. "The Christ for African Women." In Virginia Fabella and Mercy Amba Oduyoye, eds., *With Passion and Compassion: Third World Women Doing Theology*, 35-46. Maryknoll, NY: Orbis Books, 1988.

Anderson, Allan. "The Newer Pentecostal and Charismatic Churches: The Shape of Future Christianity in Africa?" *Pneuma* 24 (2002): 167-84.

Anderson, Allan, et al., eds. *Studying Global Pentecostalism: Theories and Methods*. Berkeley: University of California Press, 2010.

Appiah-Kubi, Kofi, et al., eds. *African Theology en Route: Papers from the Pan-African Conference of Third World Theologians, December 17-23, 1977*. Maryknoll, NY: Orbis Books, 1979.

Assmann, Aleida. "Geschmack an Zeichen: Homo interpres und die Welt als Text." *Zeitschrift für Semiotik* 12, no. 4 (1990): 359-70.

———. "Kultur als Lebenswelt und Monument." In Aleida Assmann and Dietrich Harth, eds., *Kultur als Lebenswelt und Monument*, 11-25. Frankfurt: Fischer Taschenbuch Verlag, 1991.

Assmann, Aleida, and Heidrun Friese, eds. *Identitäten*. Vol. 3 of *Erinnerung, Geschichte, Identität*. 2nd ed. Frankfurt: Suhrkamp, 1999.

Assmann, Jan, ed. *Die Erfindung des inneren Menschen. Studien zur religiösen Anthropologie*. Gütersloh, Germany: Gütersloher Verlagshaus, 1993.

Assmann, Jan, and Theo Sundermeier. *Das Fest und das Heilige*. Gütersloh, Germany: Gütersloher Verlagshaus, 1991.

Aymoré, F. Amado, and Michael Müller. "Die Globalisierung des Christentums durch die Überseemission der Jesuiten: Das Beispiel zentraleuropäischer Missionare in Südamerika im 17. / 18. Jahrhundert." In Artur Bogner, Bernd Holtwick, and Hartmann Tyrell, eds., *Weltmission und religiöse Organisationen*, 137-61. Würzburg, Germany: Ergon Verlag, 2004.

Ayrookuzhiel, A. M. Abraham. "Dalit Theologie: Bewegung einer Gegenkultur." In Johanna Linz, ed., *Gerechtigkeit für die Unberührbaren: Beiträge zur indischen Dalit-Theologie*, 51-68. Weltmission Heute, Studienheft 15. Hamburg: Evangelisches Missionswerk in Deutschland, 1995.

Ayuk, A. Ausaji. "The Pentecostal Transformation of Nigerian Church Life." *Asian Journal of Pentecostal Studies* 5, no. 2 (2002): 189-204.

Azzi, Riolando, et al., eds. *Lateinamerika*. Translated by Karl Baumgart. Vol. 4

of *Theologiegeschichte der Dritten Welt*. Edited by Theo Sundermeier and Norbert Klaes. Munich: Chr. Kaiser, 1993.

Bachmann-Medick, Doris. *Cultural Turns. Neuorientierungen in den Kulturwissenschaften*. 3rd ed. Hamburg: Rowohlt, 2009.

Balz, Heinrich. "Kimbanguismus auf Abwegen." *Interkulturelle Theologie/ Zeitschrift für Missionswissenschaft*, no. 4 (2008): 438-45.

———. "Kimbanguisten am Kongo." In *Weggenossen am Fluss und am Berg: Von Kimbanguisten und Lutheranern in Afrika*, 15-134. Neuendettelsau, Germany: Erlanger Verlag für Mission und Ökumene, 2005.

"Barrett, David B., and T. John Padwick. *Rise Up and Walk! Conciliarism and the African Indigenous Churches*. Nairobi: Oxford University Press, 1989.

Barth, Boris, and Jürgen Osterhammel, eds. *Zivilisierungsmissionen: Imperiale Weltverbesserung seit dem 18 Jahrhundert*. Konstanz, Germany: UBK Verlagsgesellschaft, 2005.

Barthes, Roland. *Mythen des Alltags*. Frankfurt: Suhrkamp, 1964.

———. *Mythologies*. Paris: Éditions du Seuil, 1957.

———. *Mythologies: The Complete Edition, in a New Translation*. Translated by Richard Howard and Annette Lavers. New York: Hill and Wang, 2012.

Bateye, Bolaji O. "Paradigmatic Shifts: Reconstruction of Female Leadership Roles in the New Generation Churches in South-Western Nigeria." In Adogame, Gerloff and Hock, *Christianity in Africa*, 113-25.

Baumann, Gerd. "Ethnische Identität als duale diskursive Konstruktion: Dominante und demotische Identitätsdiskurse in einer multiethnischen Vorstadt von London." In Aleida Assmann and Heidrun Friese, eds., *Identitäten*, 288-313. Vol. 3 of *Erinnerung, Geschichte, Identität*. 2nd ed. Frankfurt: Suhrkamp, 1999.

Beck, Hartmut. *Brüder in vielen Völkern: 250 Jahre Mission der Brüdergemeine*. Erlangen, Germany: Verlag der Ev.-Luth. Mission, 1981.

Becken, Hans-Jürgen. "Christliche Kirchen und Bewegungen im neuen Südafrika." *Zeitschrift für Missionswissenschaft* 20 (1994): 19-26.

———. "Die Entstehung einer prophetischen Großkirche in Südafrika." *Zeitschrift für Missionswissenschaft* 18 (1992): 99-108.

———. "Isaiah Shembe und der Heilige Geist." *Zeitschrift für Missionswissenschaft* 20 (1994): 145-52.

———. *Theologie der Heilung: Das Heilen in den Afrikanischen Unabhängigen Kirchen in Südafrika*. Hermannsburg, Germany: Missionshandlung, 1972.

———. *Wo der Glaube noch jung ist: Afrikanische Unabhängige Kirchen im Südlichen Afrika*. Erlangen, Germany: Verlag der Mission Erlangen, 1985.

Becker, Ulrich. "Ökumene." In Ulrich Becker and Udo Tworuschka, *Ökumene und Religionswissenschaft*, 13-90. Stuttgart, Germany: Calwer, 2006.

Bediako, Kwame. "Biblical Christologies in the Context of African Traditional Religions." In Vinay Samuel and Chris Sugden, eds., *Sharing Jesus in the Two-Thirds World: Evangelical Christologies from the Contexts of Poverty, Powerlessness, and Religious Pluralism*, 81-122. Grand Rapids: Eerdmans, 1984.

———. *Christianity in Africa: The Renewal of a Non-Western Religion*. Edinburgh: Edinburgh University Press, 1995.

———. *Jesus in African Culture: A Ghanaian Perspective*. Accra, Ghana: Asempa Publishers, 1990.

Benedict, Ruth. *Patterns of Culture*. New York: Penguin Books, 1934.

Berglund, Axel-Ivar. *Zulu Thought Patterns and Symbolism*. London: C. Hurst, 1976.

Bergunder, Michael. "Die Afrikanischen Unabhängigen Kirchen und die Ökumene." *Ökumenische Rundschau* 47 (1998): 504-16.

———. *Die südindische Pfingstbewegung im 20. Jahrhundert*. Frankfurt: Peter Lang, 1998.

———. "Umkämpfte Vergangenheit: Anti-brahmanische und hindu-nationalistische Rekonstruktionen der frühen indischen Religionsgeschichte." In Michael Bergunder and Rahul Peter Das, eds., *"Arier" und "Draviden": Konstruktionen der Vergangenheit als Grundlage für Selbst- und Fremdwahrnehmungen Südasiens*, 135-80. Halle, Germany: Verlag der Franckeschen Stiftungen zu Halle, 2002.

———. "Zur Einführung—Pfingstbewegung in Lateinamerika: Soziologische Theorien und theologische Debatten." In *Pfingstbewegung und Basisgemeinden in Lateinamerika: Die Rezeption befreiungstheologischer Konzepte durch die pfingstliche Theologie*, 7-42, 138-42. Weltmission heute 39. Hamburg: EMW, 2000.

Berneburg, Erhard. *Das Verhältnis von Verkündigung und sozialer Aktion in der evangelikalen Missionstheorie unter besonderer Berücksichtigung der Lausanner Bewegung für Weltevangelisation (1974–1989)*. Wuppertal, Germany: R. Brockhaus Verlag, 1997.

Berner, Ulrich. *Untersuchungen zur Verwendung des Synkretismus-Begriffes*. Wiesbaden, Germany: Harrassowitz, 1982.

Beyerhaus, Peter, and Lutz von Padberg, eds. *Eine Welt—Eine Religion? Die synkretistische Bedrohung unseres Glaubens im Zeichen von New Age*. 2nd ed. Asslar, Germany: Schulte & Gerth, 1989.

Bhavnani, Kum-Kum. "Rassismen entgegnen: Querverbindungen und Hybridität." In Kossek, *Gegen-Rassismen*, 186-201.

Bimwenyi-Kweshi, Oscar. *Alle Dinge erzählen von Gott: Grundlegung afrikanischer Theologie.* Freiburg im Breisgau, Germany: Herder, 1982.

———. *Discours Théologique Négro-Africain: Problème des Fondements.* Paris: Présence Africaine, 1981.

Bochinger, Christoph. *Ganzheit und Gemeinschaft: Zum Verhältnis von theologischer und anthropologischer Fragestellung im Werk Bruno Gutmanns.* Frankfurt: P. Lang, 1987.

Boff, Leonardo. *Gott kommt früher als der Missionar: Neuevangelisierung für eine Kultur des Lebens und der Freiheit.* Translated by Horst Goldstein. Düsseldorf, Germany: Patmos Verlag, 1991.

———. *Jesus Christ Liberator: A Critical Christology for Our Time.* Maryknoll, NY: Orbis Books, 1978.

———. *Kirche: Charisma und Macht.* Düsseldorf, Germany: Patmos Verlag, 1985.

Boff, Leonardo, and Clodovis Boff. *Wie treibt man Theologie der Befreiung?* Translated by Michael Lauble. Düsseldorf, Germany: Patmos Verlag, 1986.

Böttigheimer, Christoph. "Ökumene ohne Ziel? Ökumenische Einigungsmodelle und katholische Einheitsvorstellungen." *Ökumenische Rundschau* 52 (2003): 174-87.

Boulaga, Fabien Eboussi. *Christianisme sans Fétiche: Révélation et Domination.* Paris: Présence Africaine, 1981.

———. *Christianity Without Fetishes: An African Critique and Recapture of Christianity.* Maryknoll, NY: Orbis Books, 1984.

Brachmann, Wilhelm. "Die Ostasien-Mission in Vergangenheit und Gegenwart." *Zeitschrift für Missions- und Religionswissenschaft* 46 (1931): 238-53.

Brandl, Bernd. "Mission in evangelikaler Perspektive." In Christoph Dahling-Sander, Andrea Schultze, Dietrich Werner, and Henning Wrogemann, eds., *Leitfaden Ökumenische Missionstheologie*, 178-99. Gütersloh, Germany: Gütersloher Verlagshaus, 2003.

Bujo, Bénézet. *African Theology in Its Social Context.* Maryknoll, NY: Orbis Books, 1992.

Büker, Markus. *Befreiende Inkulturation—Paradigma christlicher Praxis: Die Konzeptionen von Paulo Suess und Diego Irarrázaval im Kontext indigener Aufbrüche in Lateinamerika.* Freiburg, Switzerland: Universitätsverlag, 1999.

Bultmann, Rudolf. *Jesus Christ and Mythology.* 1958. Reprint, London: SCM Press, 2012.

———. *Jesus Christus und die Mythologie: Das Neue Testament im Licht der Bi-belkritik.* 5th ed. Gütersloh, Germany: Gütersloher Verlagshaus, 1980.

Burgess, Stanley M., and Ed M. van der Maas, eds. *The New International Dictionary of Pentecostal and Charismatic Movements.* Grand Rapids: Zondervan, 2002.

Buss, Ernst. *Christliche Mission, ihre principielle Berechtigung und practische Durchführung.* Leiden: E. J. Brill, 1876.

Cabrita, Joel. "Texts, Authority, and Community in the South African 'Ibandla lamaNazaretha' (Church of the Nazaretha), 1910–1976." *Journal of Religion in Africa* 40 (2010): 60-95.

Callaway, Helen. "Dressing for Dinner in the Bush: Rituals of Self-Definition and British Imperial Authority." In Ruth Barnes and Joanne Bubolz Eicher, eds., *Dress and Gender: Making and Meaning,* 232-47. Oxford: Berg Publishers, 1993.

Camps, Arnulf, OFM. "Begegnung mit indianischen Religionen: Wahrnehmung und Beurteilung in der Kolonialzeit." In Sievernich et al., *Conquista und Evangelisation,* 348-72.

———. "Die ökumenische Vereinigung von Dritte-Welt-Theologen (EATWOT)." In Giancarlo Collet, ed., *Theologien der Dritten Welt: EATWOT als Herausforderung westlicher Theologie und Kirche,* 183-200. Immensee, Switzerland: Neue Zeitschrift für Missionswissenschaft, 1990.

Cartledge, Mark J., and David Cheetham, eds. *Intercultural Theology: Approaches and Themes.* London: SCM Press, 2011.

Cayota, Mario. "Die franziskanischen Missionen: Prophetische Alternative oder kolonialistische Kollaboration?" In Sievernich et al., *Conquista und Evangelisation,* 373-412.

Chidester, David. "Anchoring Religion in the World: A Southern African History of Comparative Religion." *Religion* 26 (1996): 141-60.

Cho, David Yonggi. *A Bible Study for New Christians.* Seoul: Seoul Logos, 1997.

Chung, Hyun Kyung. "Come Holy Spirit, Renew the Whole Creation." In Michael Kinnamon, ed., *Signs of the Spirit: Official Report, Seventh Assembly, Canberra, Australia, 7-20 February 1991,* 37-47. Geneva: WCC Publications, 1991.

Collet, Giancarlo. "'Wir aber schätzen das Leben und die Seele eines Indianers höher ein als alles Gold und Silber': Kontext, Ziele und Methoden der Mission." In Sievernich et al., *Conquista und Evangelisation,* 223-41.

Comaroff, John, and Jean Comaroff. *Of Revelation and Revolution: Christianity,*

Colonialism and Consciousness in South Africa. 2 vols. Chicago: Chicago University Press, 1991–1997.

Corten, André, and Ruth Marshall-Fratani, eds. *Between Babel and Pentecost: Transnational Pentecostalism in Africa and Latin America.* Bloomington: Indiana University Press, 2001.

Cragg, Kenneth. "Abduh, Muhammad." In *The Oxford Encyclopedia of the Modern Islamic World.*

Crais, Clifton C. "South Africa and the Pitfalls of Postmodernism." *South African Historical Journal* 31 (1994): 274-79.

Crapanzano, Vincent. "Das Dilemma des Hermes: Die verschleierte Unterwanderung der ethnographischen Beschreibung." In Doris Bachmann-Medick, ed., *Kultur als Text. Die anthropologische Wende in der Literaturwissenschaft*, 161-93. Frankfurt/M.: Fischer Verlag, 1996.

D'Arcy May, John. *Christus Initiator: Theologie im Pazifik.* Theologie Interkulturell 4. Düsseldorf, Germany: Patmos Verlag, 1990.

Delgado, Mariano. "Inkulturation oder Transkulturation? Der missionstheologische Charakter der Evangelisierung der altamerikanischen Kulturen am Beispiel der Übertragung des abendländisch geprägten trinitarischen Gottesbegriffs." *Neue Zeitschrift für Missionswissenschaft* 48 (1992): 172.

Derrida, Jacques. *Grammatologie.* Frankfurt: Suhrkamp, 1974.

Dickson, Kwesi. *Theology in Africa.* Maryknoll, NY: Orbis Books, 1984.

Dietrich, Stefan. "Mission, Local Culture and the 'Catholic Ethnology' of Pater Schmidt." *Journal of the Anthropological Society of Oxford* 23, no. 2 (1992): 111-25.

Dilger, Hansjörg. *Leben mit AIDS: Krankheit, Tod und soziale Beziehungen in Afrika.* Frankfurt: Campus, 2005.

Dohi, Aki, et al. *Japan.* Translated by Martin Repp and Frank Biebinger. Vol. 2 of *Theologiegeschichte der Dritten Welt.* Edited by Theo Sundermeier and Norbert Klaes. Munich: Chr. Kaiser, 1991.

D'Sa, Francis X. "Inkulturation oder Interkulturation? Versuch einer Begriffsklärung." In Michael Heberling, ed., *Inkulturation als Herausforderung und Chance*, 21-54. Aachen, Germany: Riese Springer, 2001.

Dussel, Enrique. "Christliche Kunst des Unterdrückten in Lateinamerika: Eine Hypothese zur Kennzeichnung einer Ästhetik der Befreiung." *Concilium* 16 (1980): 106-13.

———. "Chronologische Darstellung der Entstehung und Entwicklung der Theologie der Befreiung in Lateinamerika (1959–1989)." In Riolando Azzi et al.,

Theologieschichte der Dritten Welt, 268-364. Munich, Germany: Chr. Kaiser, 1993.

Eco, Umberto. *Theory of Semiotics*. Bloomington: Indiana University Press, 1979.

Eger, Wolfgang. "Zur Geschichte der Ostasien-Mission." In Ferdinand Hahn, August Bänziger, and Winfried Glüer, eds., *Spuren . . . Festschrift zum hundertjährigen Bestehen der Ostasien-Mission*, 56-61. Stuttgart, Germany: Evangelisches Missionswerk in Südwest-deutschland, 1984.

Ela, Jean-Marc. *Ma Foi d'Africain*. Paris: Karthala, 1985.

———. *My Faith as an African*. Maryknoll, NY: Orbis Books, 1988.

Elizondo, Virgil. "Unsere Liebe Frau von Guadelupe als Kultursymbol: Die Macht der Machtlosen." *Concilium* 13 (1977): 73-78.

Ellacuría, Ignacio, and Jon Sobrino, eds. *Mysterium Liberationis: Fundamental Concepts of Liberation Theology*. Maryknoll, NY: Orbis Books, 1993.

———. *Mysterium Liberationis: Grundbegriffe der Theologie der Befreiung*. 2 vols. Lucerne, Switzerland: Exodus, 1995–1996.

Elphick, Rodney. "South African Christianity and the Historian's Vision." *South African Historical Journal* 26 (1992): 182-90.

England, John C., et al., eds. *Asian Christian Theologies: A Research Guide to Authors, Movements, Sources*. 3 vols. Maryknoll, NY: Orbis Books, 2002–2004.

Erdheim, Mario. "Die Repräsentanz des Fremden: Zur Psychogenese der Imagines von Kultur und Familie." In *Psychoanalyse und Unbewußtheit in der Kultur*, 237-51. Frankfurt: Suhrkamp, 1988.

Feldtkeller, Andreas. "Der Synkretismusbegriff im Rahmen einer Theorie von Verhältnisbestimmungen zwischen Religionen." *Evangelische Theologie* 52 (1993): 224-45.

———. "Mission aus der Perspektive der Religionswissenschaft." *Zeitschrift für Missionswissenschaft und Religionswissenschaft* 85 (2001): 99-115.

Fiedler, Klaus. *Christentum und afrikanische Kultur: Konservative deutsche Missionare in Tanzania, 1900 bis 1940*. Gütersloh, Germany: Gütersloher Verlagshaus, 1983.

Fischer, Moritz. *Maasai gestalten Christsein: Die integrative Kraft traditionaler Religion unter dem Einfluss des Evangeliums*. Erlangen, Germany: Erlanger Verlag für Mission und Ökumene, 2001.

Foucault, Michel. *The Archaeology of Knowledge*. London: Routledge, 1989.

———. *Archäologie des Wissens*. Frankfurt: Suhrkamp, 1981.

Frei, Fritz, ed. *Inkulturation zwischen Tradition und Modernität: Kontexte—Begriffe—Modelle*. Freiburg, Switzerland: Universitätsverlag, 2000.

Freston, Paul. "Pentecostalism in Brazil: A Brief History." *Religion* 25 (1995): 119-33.

———. "The Universal Church of the Kingdom of God: A Brazilian Church Finds Success in South Africa." *Journal of Religion in Africa* 35 (2005): 33-65.

Freud, Sigmund. "Das Unheimliche." In *Werke aus den Jahren 1917–1920.* Vol. 12 of *Gesammelte Werke: Chronologisch geordnet,* edited by Anna Freud and Marie Bonaparte, 229-68. London: Imago, 1947.

Friedli, Richard, et al. *Intercultural Perceptions and Prospects of World Christianity.* Studies in the Intercultural History of Christianity 150. Frankfurt: Peter Lang, 2010.

Friedman, Jonathan. "The Hybridization of Roots and the Abhorrence of the Bush." In Mike Featherstone and Scott Lash, eds., *Spaces of Culture: City-Nation-World,* 230-55. London: SAGE Publications, 1999.

Frieling, Reinhard. "Steht die Ökumenische Bewegung vor einem Pradigmenwechsel?" In *Im Glauben eins—in Kirchen getrennt? Visionen einer realistischen Ökumene,* 228-55. Göttingen: Vandenhoeck & Ruprecht, 2006.

———. "Welche Einheit wollen wir? Zum Projekt 'Grund und Gegenstand des Glaubens' im Zusammenhang ökumenischer Einheitskonzeptionen." *Una Sancta* 64 (2009): 170-81.

Gabbert, Wolfgang. "Phasen und Grundprobleme protestantischer Mission im kolonialen Afrika—Die Brüdergemeine bei den Nyakyusa in Tansania." In Artur Bogner, Bernd Holtwick, and Hartmann Tyrell, eds., *Weltmission und religiöse Organisation,* 517-40. Würzburg, Germany: Ergon Verlag, 2004.

Gadamer, Hans-Georg. *Truth and Method.* Rev. ed. London: Bloomsbury Academic, 2013.

———. "Vom Zirkel des Verstehens." In *Variationen.* Vol. 4 of *Kleine Schriften,* 54-61. Tübingen: J. C. B. Mohr, 1977.

———. *Wahrheit und Methode: Grundzüge einer philosophischen Hermeneutik.* 3rd ed. Tübingen: Mohr, 1972.

Gasper, Hans, and Gerhard Bially. "Der pfingstlich/römisch-katholische Dialog." *Freikirchenforschung* 16 (2007): 164-91.

Gebhardt, Jürgen. "Interkulturelle Kommunikation: Vom praktischen Nutzen und theoretischen Nachteil angewandter Sozialwissenschaft." In Allolio-Näcke, Kalscheuer, and Manzeschke, *Differenzen anders denken,* 275-86.

Geertz, Clifford. "Common Sense as a Cultural System." In *Local Knowledge,* 73-93. New York: Basic Books, 1983.

———. "'From the Native's Point of View': On the Nature of Anthropological Understanding." *Bulletin of the American Academy of Arts and Sciences* 28, no. 1 (1974): 26-45.

———. "Thick Description: Toward an Interpretive Theory of Culture." In *The Interpretation of Cultures*, 3-32. 1973. Reprint, New York: Basic Books, 2000.

Geldbach, Erich. "Evangelikalismus: Versuch einer historischen Typologie." In Reinhard Frieling, ed., *Die Kirche und ihre Konservativen: Traditionalismus und Evangelikalismus in den Konfessionen*, 52-83. Göttingen: Vandenhoeck & Ruprecht, 1984.

Gifford, Paul. "Ghana's Charismatic Churches." *Journal for Religion in Africa* 24 (1994): 241-65.

Goffman, Erving. *Frame Analysis: An Essay on the Organization of Experience.* New York: Harper & Row, 1974.

———. "The Interaction Order." *American Sociological Review* 48, no. 1 (1983): 1-17.

Goldmann, Stefan. "Wilde in Europa: Aspekte und Orte ihrer Zuschaustellung." In Thomas Theye, ed., *Wir und die Wilden*, 243-69. Reinbek bei Hamburg, Germany: Rowohlt, 1985.

Görgens, Manfred. *Kleine Geschichte der indischen Kunst.* Cologne: DuMont, 1986.

Greive, Wolfgang, and Raul Niemann, eds. *Neu glauben? Religionsvielfalt und neue religiöse Strömungen als Herausforderung an das Christentum.* Gütersloh, Germany: Gütersloher Verlagshaus Mohn, 1990.

Gruchy, John W. de. "Die Vergangenheit in Südafrika erlösen." *Epd-Dokumentation* 32 (1997): 28-37.

Gründer, Horst. "'Bin ich nicht ein Mensch und ein Bruder?'—Vom Sklavenhandel der Christen zur christlichen Antisklavereibewegung." In *Christliche Heilsbotschaft und weltliche Macht: Studien zum Verhältnis von Mission und Kolonialismus; gesammelte Aufsätze*, 175-88. Münster: LIT Verlag, 2004.

———. "Conquista und Mission." In *Christliche Heilsbotschaft und weltliche Macht: Studien zum Verhältnis von Mission und Kolonialismus; gesammelte Aufsätze*, 23-46. Münster: LIT Verlag, 2004.

———. "Der 'Jesuitenstaat' in Paraguay: 'Kirchlicher Kolonialismus' oder 'Entwicklungshilfe' unter kolonialem Vorzeichen?" In *Christliche Heilsbotschaft und weltliche Macht: Studien zum Verhältnis von Mission und Kolonialismus; gesammelte Aufsätze*, 47-70. Münster: LIT Verlag, 2004.

Gutiérrez, Gustavo. *Theologie der Befreiung.* Translated by Horst Goldstein. 8th ed. Munich: Kaiser, 1985 (1972).

———. *A Theology of Liberation: History, Politics, and Salvation.* Translated by Caridad Inda and John Eagleson. Maryknoll, NY: Orbis Books, 1973.

Gutmann, Bruno. *Freies Menschentum aus ewigen Bindungen*. Kassel, Germany: Bärenreiter Verlag, 1928.

———. "Urtümliche Bindungen und Sünde." *Neue Evangelische Missionszeitschrift* (1934): 20-31.

Habermas, Jürgen. *Der philosophische Diskurs der Moderne*. Frankfurt: Suhrkamp, 1985.

Haddad, Yvonne. "Muhammad Abduh." In 'Alī Rāhnamā, ed., *Pioneers of Islamic Revival*, 30-63. London: Zed Books, 1994.

Hahn, Ferdinand. "Das theologische Programm von Ernst Buss." In Ferdinand Hahn, August Bänziger, and Winfried Glüer, eds., *Spuren . . . Festschrift zum hundertjährigen Bestehen der Ostasien-Mission*, 10-18. Stuttgart, Germany: Evangelisches Missionswerk in Südwestdeutschland, 1984.

Hansen, Klaus P. *Kultur und Kulturwissenschaft: Eine Einführung*. 3rd ed. Tübingen: A. Francke Verlag, 2003.

Hasselblatt, Gunnar. "Herkunft und Auswirkungen der Apologetik Muhammed Abduhs (1849–1905), untersucht an seiner Schrift: Islam und Christentum im Verhältnis zu Wissenschaft und Zivilisation." PhD diss., University of Göttingen, 1968.

Hastings, Adrian. "Afrika. III. Christentumsgeschichte." In *Religion in Geschichte und Gegenwart*, 4th ed.

Haudel, Matthias. "Die Einheit der Kirchen als Koinonia (Gemeinschaft)? Chancen und Probleme des jüngsten ökumenischen Einheitskonzepts." *Ökumenische Rundschau* 55 (2006): 482-501.

Haussmann, Thomas. *Verstehen und Erklären: Zur Theorie und Pragmatik der Geschichtswissenschaft*. Frankfurt: Suhrkamp, 1991.

Heidemanns, Katja, and Marco Moerschbacher, eds. *Gott vertrauen? AIDS und Theologie im südlichen Afrika*. Freiburg im Breisgau, Germany: Herder, 2005.

Heller, Dagmar, ed. *Das Wesen und die Bestimmung der Kirche: Ein Schritt auf dem Weg zu einer gemeinsamen Auffassung*. Frankfurt: Lembeck, 2000.

Herder, Johann Gottfried. *Auch eine Philosophie der Geschichte zur Bildung der Menschheit*. 1774. Reprint, Frankfurt: Suhrkamp, 1967.

Herskovits, Melville J. *Acculturation: The Study of Culture Contact*. New York: J. J. Augustin, 1938.

Hesselgrave, David J., and Edward Rommen. "Contemporary Understandings of and Approaches to Contextualization: Africa; John S. Mbiti and Byang H. Kato." In *Contextualization: Meanings, Methods, and Models*, 96-112. Leicester, UK: Apollos, 1989.

Heuser, Andreas. "Die sakralisierte (Kon-)Version eines Kriegstanzes." In *Shembe, Gandhi und die Soldaten Gottes: Wurzeln der Gewaltfreiheit in Südafrika,* 224-37. Münster: Waxmann, 2003.

———. "'Odem einzuhauchen in verdorrtes Gebein . . . ': Zum Missionsverständnis ausgewählter afrikanischer Kirchen in Hamburg." In *Theologie— Pädagogik—Kontext: Zukunftsperspektiven der Religionspädagogik; Wolfram Weisse zum 60. Geburtstag,* 269-85. Edited by Ursula Günther et al. Münster: Waxmann, 2005.

———. "'Put on God's Armour Now!'—The Embattled Body in African Pentecostal-Type Christianity." In Sebastian Jobs and Gesa Mackenthun, eds., *Embodiments of Cultural Encounters,* 115-40. Münster: Waxmann, 2011.

Hexham, Irving. "Violating Missionary Culture: The Tyranny of Theory and the Ethics of Historical Research." In Ulrich van der Heyden and Jürgen Becker, eds., *Mission und Gewalt,* 193-206. Stuttgart, Germany: Franz Steiner Verlag, 2000.

Hildebrandt, Mathias. "Von der Transkulturation zur Transdifferenz." In Allolio-Näcke, Kalscheuer, and Manzeschke, *Differenzen anders denken,* 342-52.

Hinga, Teresa M. "Jesus Christ and the Liberation of Women in Africa." In Mercy Amba Oduyoye and Rachel Angogo Kanyoro, eds., *The Will to Arise: Women, Tradition, and the Church in Africa,* 183-94. Maryknoll, NY: Orbis Books, 1992.

Hock, Klaus. *Das Christentum in Afrika und im Nahen Osten.* Leipzig: Evangelische Verlagsanstalt, 2005.

———. *Einführung in die Interkulturelle Theologie.* Darmstadt, Germany: Wissenschaftliche Buchgesellschaft, 2010.

———. "'Jesus-Power—Super-Power!' Annäherungen an die Schnittstellen zwischen christlichem Fundamentalismus und Neuen Religiösen Bewegungen in Afrika." *Zeitschrift für Missionswissenschaft* 21 (1995): 134-50.

———. "Religion als transkulturelles Phänomen. Implikationen eines kulturwissenschaftlichen Paradigmas für die Religionsforschung." *Berliner Theologische Zeitschrift* 19 (2002): 64-82.

Hoekendijk, Johannes Christiaan. *Kirche und Volk in der deutschen Missionswissenschaft.* Munich: Chr. Kaiser Verlag, 1965.

Hollenweger, Walter J. *Interkulturelle Theologie.* 3 vols. Munich: Chr. Kaiser Verlag, 1979–1988.

Hourani, Albert. *Arabic Thought in the Liberal Age: 1798–1939.* Oxford: Oxford University Press, 1962.

Huff, Toby E., and Wolfgang Schluchter, eds. *Max Weber and Islam.* New Brunswick: Transaction Publishers, 1999.

Idowu, E. Bolaji. *African Traditional Religion: A Definition*. London: SCM Press, 1973.

Johnstone, Patrick. *Gebet für die Welt: Handbuch: Umfassende Informationen zu über 200 Ländern*. Holzgerlingen, Germany: Hänssler, 2003.

Kalliath, Antony. "A Call to Liberative Praxis of the Gospel: A Discourse on Inculturation in India with Special Reference to the Catholic Church." In Lalsangkima Pachuau, ed., *Ecumenical Missiology: Contemporary Trends, Issues, and Themes*, 204-36. Bangalore: United Theological College, 2002.

Kalu, Ogbu. *African Pentecostalism: An Introduction*. Oxford: Oxford University Press, 2008.

Kapteina, Detlef. *Afrikanische Evangelikale Theologie*. 2nd ed. Nuremberg, Germany: VTR, 2001.

Kapur, Anuradha. "Deity to Crusader: The Changing Iconography of Ram." In Gyanendra Pandey, ed., *Hindus and Others: The Question of Identity in India Today*, 74-109. New Delhi: Viking, 1993.

Kasper, Walter. *Wege der Einheit: Perspektiven für die Ökumene*. Freiburg im Breisgau, Germany: Herder, 2005.

Kasukuti, Ngoy. *Recht und Grenze der Inkulturation*. Erlangen, Germany: Verlag der Ev.-Luth. Mission, 1991.

Kato, Byang H. *Biblical Christianity in Africa: A Collection of Papers and Addresses*. Achimota, Ghana: Africa Christian Press, 1985.

———. *Theological Pitfalls in Africa*. Kisumu, Kenya: Evangel Publishing House, 1975.

Kehl, Medard. "Zum jüngsten Disput um das Verhältnis von Universalkirche und Ortskirchen." In Peter Walter et al., eds., *Kirche in ökumenischer Perspektive*, 81-101. Freiburg im Breisgau, Germany: Herder, 2003.

Keilhauer, Anneliese, and Peter Keilhauer. *Die Bildersprache des Hinduismus: Die indische Götterwelt und ihre Symbolik*. Cologne: DuMont, 1983.

Kim, Younhee. "Interkulturation: Der immerwährende Missionsauftrag der Kirche." In Richard Brosse et al., eds., *Für ein Leben in Fülle. Visionen einer missionarischen Kirche*, 223-32. Freiburg im Breisgau, Germany: Herder, 2008.

Knoll, Arthur J. "Die Norddeutsche Missionsgesellschaft in Togo 1890–1914." In Klaus J. Bade, ed., *Imperialismus und Kolonialmission*, 165-88. Wiesbaden, Germany: Steiner, 1982.

Kohl, Karl-Heinz. "Ethnizität und Tradition aus ethnologischer Sicht." In Assmann et al., *Identitäten*, 269-87.

———. "Ethnologische Theorien." In *Ethnologie—die Wissenschaft vom kulturell Fremden: Eine Einführung*, 129-66. Munich: C. H. Beck, 1993.

Konetzke, Richard. "Die Bedeutung der Sprachenfrage in der spanischen Kolonisation Amerikas." *Jahrbuch für Geschichte von Staat, Wirtschaft und Gesellschaft Lateinamerikas* 1 (1964): 72-116.

———. *Süd- und Mittelamerika.* Vol. 1. Frankfurt: Fischer, 1988.

Koschorke, Klaus, et al., eds. *Außereuropäische Christentumsgeschichte: Asien, Afrika, Lateinamerika 1450–1990.* Neukirchen-Vluyn, Germany: Neukirchener Verlag, 2004.

Kossek, Brigitte, ed. *Gegen-Rassismen: Konstruktionen—Interaktionen—Interventionen.* Hamburg: Argument, 1999.

Kraft, Charles H. "Contemporary Trends in the Treatment of Spiritual Conflict." In A. Scott Moreau et al., eds., *Deliver Us from Evil: An Uneasy Frontier in Christian Mission,* 177-202. Monrovia, CA: World Vision International, 2002.

Kroeber, Alfred L., and Clyde Kluckhohn. *Culture: A Critical Review of Concepts and Definitions.* Papers of the Peabody Museum of American Archaeology and Ethnology 47. Cambridge, MA: The Museum, 1952.

Küster, Volker. *Einführung in die Interkulturelle Theologie.* Göttingen: Vandenhoeck & Ruprecht, 2011.

Lademann-Priemer, Gabriele. *Heilung als Zeichen für die Einheit der Welten: Religiöse Vorstellungen von Krankheit und Heilung in Europa im vorigen Jahrhundert und unter den Zulu mit einem Ausblick in unsere Zeit.* Frankfurt: P. Lang, 1990.

———, ed. *Traditionelle Religion und christlicher Glaube: Widerspruch und Wandel; Festschrift für Hans-Jürgen Becken zum 70. Geburtstag.* Ammersbek, Germany: Verlag an der Lottbek P. Jensen, 1993.

Lindbeck, George A. *The Nature of Doctrine: Religion and Theology in a Postliberal Age.* Philadelphia: Westminster, 1984.

Lüsebrink, Hans-Jürgen. "Geschichtskultur im (post-)kolonialen Kontext: Zur Genese nationaler Identifikationsfiguren im frankophonen Westafrika." In Assmann et al., *Identitäten,* 401-26.

Lux, Thomas. "Zur Rezeption des Fremden in der Medizin: Der Begriff Malaria bei einem Beniner Krankenpfleger." In Theo Sundermeier, ed., *Den Fremden wahrnehmen: Bausteine einer Xenologie,* 76-98. Gütersloh, Germany: Gütersloher Verlagshaus, 1992.

Ma, Julie C., and Wonsuk Ma. *Mission in the Spirit: Towards a Pentecostal/Charismatic Missiology.* Eugene, OR: Wipf & Stock, 2010.

Mahlke, Reiner. "Nazareth Baptist Church (Shembe Church)." In *Prophezeiung und Heilung: Das Konzept des Heiligen Geistes in Afrikanischen Unabhängigen Kirchen (AIC) in Südafrika,* 194-215. Berlin: D. Reimer, 1997.

Malinowski, Bronislaw. *Eine wissenschaftliche Theorie der Kultur: Und andere Aufsätze*. Frankfurt: Suhrkamp, 1975.

———. "A Scientific Theory of Culture." In *A Scientific Theory of Culture*, 1-144. 1944. Reprint, Chapel Hill: University of North Carolina Press, 1977.

Mall, Ram Adhar. *Philosophie im Vergleich der Kulturen*. Darmstadt, Germany: Wissenschaftliche Buchgesellschaft, 1995.

Maluleke, Tinyiko Sam. "The South African Truth and Reconciliation Discourse." In Laurenti Magesa and Zablon John Nthamburi, *Democracy and Reconciliation: A Challenge for African Christianity*, 215-41. Nairobi: Action, 1999.

———. "Truth, National Unity and Reconciliation in South Africa: Aspects of the Emerging Theological Agenda." *Missionalia* 25 (1997): 59-86.

Manzeschke, Arne. "Introduction." In Allolio-Näcke, Kalscheuer, and Manzeschke, *Differenzen anders denken*, 355-60.

Martin, Marie-Louise. "Afrikanische Gestalt des christlichen Glaubens: Die Kirche Jesu Christi auf Erden durch den Propheten Simon Kimbangu." *Evangelische Missionszeitschrift* 28 (1971): 16-29.

Mbiti, John. *African Religions & Philosophy*. New York: Praeger, 1969.

———. *African Religions and Philosophy*. Nairobi: Heinemann, 1969.

———. *Concepts of God in Africa*. London: SPCK, 1970.

Melià, Bartomeu. "Und die Utopie fand ihren Ort . . . Die jesuitischen Guaraní–Reduktionen von Paraguay." In Sievernich et al., *Conquista und Evangelisation*, 413-29.

Meyer, Birgit. "Beyond Syncretism: Translation and Diabolization in the Appropriation of Protestantism in Africa." In Charles Stewart and Rosalind Shaw, eds., *Syncretism/Anti-Syncretism: The Politics of Religious Synthesis*, 45-68. London: Routledge, 1994.

———. "Christian Mind and Worldly Matters: Religion and Materiality in Nineteenth-Century Gold Coast." *Journal of Material Culture* 2, no. 3 (1997): 311-37.

———. "Christianity and the Ewe Nation: German Pietist Missionaries, Ewe Converts and the Politics of Culture." In Artur Bogner, Bernd Holtwick, and Hartmann Tyrell, eds., *Weltmission und religiöse Organisationen*, 541-69. Würzburg, Germany: Ergon Verlag, 2004.

———. "Christianity in Africa: From African Independent Churches to Pentecostal-Charismatic Churches." *Annual Review of Anthropology* 33 (2004): 447-74.

Meyer, Harding. *Ökumenische Zielvorstellungen*. Göttingen: Vandenhoeck & Ruprecht, 1996.

————. *That All May Be One: Perceptions and Models of Ecumenicity.* Grand Rapids: Eerdmans, 1999.

Michaels, Axel. *Der Hinduismus: Geschichte und Gegenwart.* Munich: C. H. Beck, 1998.

————. *Hinduism: Past and Present.* Princeton, NJ: Princeton Universtiy Press, 2003.

Miyamoto, Ken Christoph. "A Response to 'Mission Studies as Intercultural Theology and Its Relationship to Religious Studies.'" *Mission Studies* 25 (2008): 109-10.

Möller, Horst. *Vernunft und Kritik: Deutsche Aufklärung im 17. und 18. Jahrhundert.* Frankfurt: Suhrkamp, 1986.

Moltmann, Jürgen. "Is the Filioque Addition to the Nicene Creed Necessary or Superfluous?" In *The Spirit of Life: A Universal Affirmation.* Translated by Margaret Kohl, 306-9. Minneapolis: Fortress, 1992.

Moodley, Edley J. *Shembe, Ancestors, and Christ: A Christological Inquiry with Missiological Implications.* Eugene, OR: Pickwick, 2008.

Moore, Basil, ed. *Black Theology: The South African Voice*: London: C. Hurst, 1973.

Moreau, A. Scott. "A Survey of North American Spiritual Warfare Thinking." In A. Scott Moreau et al., eds., *Deliver Us from Evil: An Uneasy Frontier in Christian Mission,* 117-27. Monrovia, CA: World Vision International, 2002.

Morgan, Lewis Henry. *Ancient Society: Or, Researches in the Line of Human Progress from Savagery Through Barbarism to Civilization.* London: Macmillan, 1877.

Müller-Funk, Wolfgang. *Kulturtheorie: Einführung in Schlüsseltexte der Kulturwissenschaften.* Tübingen: Francke, 2006.

Nebel, Richard. *Altmexikanische Religion und christliche Heilsbotschaft: Mexiko zwischen Quetzalcóatl und Christus.* Immensee, Switzerland: Neue Zeitschrift für Missionswissenschaft, 1983.

Nederveen Pieterse, Jan. "Globale/lokale Melange: Globalisierung und Kultur; Drei Paradigmen." In Brigitte Kossek, ed., *Gegen-Rassismen: Konstruktionen—Interaktionen—Interventionen,* 167-85. Hamburg: Argument, 1999.

————. "Hybrid Modernities: Mélange Modernities in Asia." *Sociological Analysis* 1, no. 3 (1998): 75-86.

————. "Hybridität, na und?" In Allolio-Näcke, Kalscheuer, and Manzeschke, *Differenzen anders denken,* 396-430.

Nehring, Andreas. "Hinduismus und Christentum: Begegnung, Konflikte, Brüche."

In Mariano Delgado and Guido Vergauwen, eds., *Interkulturalität: Begegnung und Wandel in den Religionen*, 247-63. Stuttgart, Germany: Kohlhammer, 2010.

———. "Reinheit und Bekehrung. Hindu-Nationalismus, Säkularer Staat und die Anti-Bekehrungsgesetze in Indien." *Zeitschrift für Missionswissenschaft und Religionswissenschaft* 88, no. 3/4 (2004): 232-49.

———. "Religion, Kultur und Macht: Auswirkungen des kolonialen Blicks auf die Kulturbegegnung am Beispiel Indiens." *Zeitschrift für Missionswissenschaft und Religionswissenschaft* 87 (2003): 200-217.

Ngobese, B. E. "The Concept of the Trinity Among the AmaNazaretha." In Gerhardus C. Oosthuizen and Irving Hexham, eds., *Empirical Studies of African Independent/Indigenous Churches*, 91-109. Lewiston, ME: E. Mellen, 1992.

Niebuhr, Richard. *Christ and Culture*. New York: Harper, 1951.

Nietzsche, Friedrich. "On the Uses and Disadvantages of History for Life." In *Untimely Meditations*. Translated by R. J. Hollingdale. Edited by Daniel Breazeale, 104-5. Cambridge Texts in the History of Philosophy. 2nd ed. 1997. Reprint, Cambridge: Cambridge University Press, 1999.

Nirmal, Arvind P. "Towards a Christian Dalit Theology." In R. S. Sugirtharajah, ed., *Frontiers in Asian Christian Theology: Emerging Trends*, 27-40. Maryknoll, NY: Orbis Books, 1994.

Nuscheler, Franz. "Entwicklungspolitik im Gezeitenwandel." In *Lern- und Arbeitsbuch Entwicklungspolitik*, 76-97. 6th ed. Bonn, Germany: Dietz, 2005.

Nyamiti, Charles. "African Christologies Today." In J. N. Kanyua Mugambi et al., eds., *Jesus in African Christianity: Experimentation and Diversity in African Christology*, 17-39. Nairobi: Initiatives, 1989.

———. "African Christologies Today." In Schreiter, *Faces of Jesus in Africa*, 3-23.

———. *Christ as Our Ancestor: Christology from an African Perspective*. Gweru, Zimbabwe: Mambo Press, 1984.

Oborji, Francis Anekwe. "Missiology in Its Relation to Intercultural Theology and Religious Studies." *Mission Studies* 25 (2008): 113-14.

Oduyoye, Mercy Amba. "Christianity and African Culture." *International Review of Mission* 84 (1995): 77-89.

———. "Churchwomen and the Church's Mission." In John S. Pobee and Bärbel von Wartenberg-Potter, eds., *New Eyes for Reading: Biblical and Theological Reflections by Women from the Third World*, 68-80. Geneva: WCC, 1986.

———. "A Critique of Mbiti's View of Love and Marriage in Africa." In Jacob Obafemi Kehinde Olupona and Sulayman S. Nyang, eds., *Religious Plurality in Africa: Essays in Honour of John S. Mbiti*, 341-65. Berlin: Mouton de Gruyter, 1993.

———. *Hearing and Knowing: Theological Reflections on Christianity in Africa.* Maryknoll, NY: Orbis Books, 1986.

———. "Naming the Women: The Words of the Akan and the Words of the Bible." *Bulletin of African Theology* 3 (1981): 81-97.

Oeldemann, Johannes. "Gestufte Kirchengemeinschaft als ökumenisches Modell? Überlegungen aus römisch-katholischer Perspektive." *Una Sancta* 60 (2005): 135-47.

Ohlig, Karl-Heinz. *Fundamentalchristologie: Im Spannungsfeld von Christentum und Kultur.* Munich: Kösel, 1986.

Ojo, Matthews A. "Deeper Life Bible Church of Nigeria." In Paul Gifford, ed., *New Dimensions in African Christianity*, 161-81. Ibadan, Nigeria: Sefer, 1993.

———. "Deeper Life Christian Ministry: A Case Study of the Charismatic Movements in Western Nigeria." *Journal of Religion in Africa* 18 (1988): 141-62.

———. "Transnational Religious Networks and Indigenous Pentecostal Missionary Enterprises in the West African Coastal Region." In Adogame, Gerloff, and Hock, *Christianity in Africa*, 167-79.

Okalla, Joseph Ndi. "Historiographie indigener Christentumsbewegungen im Kongo-Becken: Der Kimbanguismus und seine Varianten; Eine afrikanische Initiative des 20. Jahrhunderts." In Klaus Koschorke, ed., *"Christen und Gewürze": Konfrontation und Interaktion kolonialer und indigener Christentumsvarianten*, 230-45. Göttingen: Vandenhoeck & Ruprecht, 1998.

Okure, Teresa. "Inculturation: Biblical/Theological Bases." In Teresa Okure et al., *32 Articles Evaluating Inculturation of Christianity in Africa*, 55-86. Spearhead 112-114. Eldoret, Kenya: AMECEA Gaba Publications, 1990.

———. "Jesus, der Mann, der in der Art der Frauen wirkte." *Jahrbuch Mission* (1993): 53-62.

———. "The Significance Today of Jesus' Commission to Mary Magdalene (John 20:11-18)." *International Review of Mission* 81 (1992): 177-88.

Oliveros, Roberto. "History of the Theology of Liberation." In Ellacuría and Sobrino, *Mysterium*, 1:3-32.

Omenyo, Cephas N. "African Pentecostalism and Theological Education." In Dietrich Werner et al., eds., *Handbook of Theological Education in World Christianity: Theological Perspectives—Regional Surveys—Ecumenical Trends*, 742-49. Oxford: Regnum Books International, 2010.

Onyinah, Opoku. "Deliverance as a Way of Confronting Witchcraft in Modern Africa: Ghana as a Case History." *Asian Journal for Pentecostal Studies* 5, no. 1 (2002): 107-34.

Oosthuizen, Gerhardus C. "Diviner-Prophet Parallels in the African Independent and Traditional Churches and Traditional Religion." In Gerhardus C. Oosthuizen and Irving Hexham, eds., *Empirical Studies of African Independent/Indigenous Churches*, 163-94. Lewiston, ME: E. Mellen, 1992.

———. "Isaiah Shembe and the Zulu World View." *History of Religion* 8 (1968): 1-30.

———. "Wie christlich ist die Kirche Shembes?" *Evangelische Missionszeitschrift* n. 31 (1974): 140-41.

Oosthuizen, Gerhardus C., and Irving Hexham, eds. *Afro-Christian Religion at the Grassroots in Southern Africa*. Lewiston, ME: E. Mellen, 1991.

Oosthuizen, Gerhardus C., et al., eds. *Afro-Christian Religion and Healing in Southern Africa*. Lewiston, ME: E. Mellen, 1989.

Ositelu, Rufus Okikiolaolu Olubiyi. *African Instituted Churches: Diversities, Growth, Gifts, Spirituality and Ecumenical Understanding of African Initiated Churches*. Münster: LIT Verlag, 2002.

Pannenberg, Wolfhart. "Erwägungen zu einer Theologie der Religionsgeschichte." In *Grundfragen systematischer Theologie: Gesammelte Aufsätze*, 252-95. 2nd ed. Göttingen: Vandenhoeck & Ruprecht, 1971.

Parratt, John K. *Afrika*. Translated by Klaus-Dieter Stoll. Vol. 1 of *Theologiegeschichte der Dritten Welt*. Edited by Theo Sundermeier and Norbert Klaes. Munich: Chr. Kaiser, 1991.

Parrinder, Edward Geoffrey. *African Traditional Religion*. 2nd ed. London: SPCK, 1962.

Pauly, Wolfgang. "Mission—Inkulturation—Reziproke Interkulturation: Aspekte zur Begegnung zwischen Christentum und anderen Kulturen." *Orientierung* 73, no. 11 (2009): 123-25.

Peel, John D. Y. "The Cultural Work of Yoruba Ethnogenesis." In Elizabeth Tonkin, Malcolm Chapman, and Maryon McDonald, eds., *History and Ethnicity*, 198-215. London: Routledge, 1989.

———. *Religious Encounter and the Making of the Yoruba*. Bloomington: Indiana University Press, 2003.

Phiri, Isabel Apawo, Beverly Haddad, and Madiopoane Masenya. *African Women, HIV/AIDS and Faith Communities*. Pietermaritzburg, South Africa: Cluster Publications, 2003.

Pieris, Aloysius. *Fire and Water: Basic Issues in Asian Buddhism and Christianity*. Maryknoll, NY: Orbis Books, 1996.

Pobee, John S., ed. *Exploring Afro-Christology*. Frankfurt: P. Lang, 1992.

———. *Toward an African Theology*. Nashville: Abingdon, 1979.

Porter, Andrew. "Christentum, Kontext und Ideologie: Die Uneindeutigkeit der 'Zivilisierungsmission' im Großbritannien des 19. Jahrhunderts." In Barth and Osterhammel, *Zivilisierungsmissionen*, 125-47.

———. "Religion and Empire: British Expansion in the Long Nineteenth Century 1790–1914." *Journal of Imperial and Commonwealth History* 20, no. 3 (1992): 370-90.

Priest, Robert J., Thomas Campbell, and Bradford A. Mullen. "Missiological Syncretism: The New Animistic Paradigm." In Edward Rommen, ed., *Spiritual Power and Missions*, 9-87. Pasadena, CA: W. Carey Library, 1995.

Pulsfort, Ernst. *Christliche Ashrams in Indien: Zwischen dem religiösen Erbe Indiens und der christlichen Tradition des Abendlandes*. 2nd ed. Altenberge, Germany: Oros, 1991.

Puthanangady, Paul. "Die Inkulturation der Liturgie in Indien seit dem Zweiten Vatikanum." *Concilium* 19 (1983): 146-51.

Quaas, Anna D. *Transnationale Pfingstkirchen: Christ Apostolic Church und Redeemed Christian Church of God*. Frankfurt: Lembeck, 2011.

Quadflieg, Dirk. "Roland Barthes: Mythologe der Massenkultur und Argonaut der Semiologie." In Stephan Moebius and Dirk Quadflieg, eds., *Kultur: Theorien der Gegenwart*, 17-29. Wiesbaden, Germany: Verlag für Sozialwissenschaft, 2006.

Ranger, Terence. "The Local and the Global in Southern African Religious History." In Robert W. Hefner, *Conversion to Christianity*, 65-98. Berkeley: University of California Press, 1993.

Räthzel, Nora. "Hybridität ist die Antwort, aber was noch mal die Frage?" In Kossek, *Gegen-Rassismen*, 204-19.

Raupp, Werner, ed. *Mission in Quellentexten*. Erlangen, Germany: Verlag der Ev.-Luth. Mission, 1990.

Reckwitz, Andreas. "Multikulturalismustheorien und der Kulturbegriff: Vom Homogenitätsmodell zum Modell kultureller Interferenzen." *Berliner Journal für Soziologie* 11 (2001): 179ff.

Renan, Ernest. *Der Islam und die Wissenschaft*. Edited by Klaus H. Fischer. Schutterwald/Baden, Germany: Wissenschaftlicher Verlag, 1997.

———. *L'Islam et la Science*. 1883. Reprint, Apt, France: L'Archange Minotaure, 2007.

Richebächer, Wilhelm. *Religionswechsel und Christologie: Christliche Theologie in Ostafrika vor dem Hintergrund religiöser Syntheseprozesse*. Neuendettelsau, Germany: Erlanger Verlag für Mission und Ökumene, 2003.

Robertson, Roland. "Glocalization: Time-Space and Homogeneity-Heterogeneity." In Mike Featherstone, Scott Lash, and Roland Robertson, eds., *Global Modernities*, 25-44. London: SAGE Publications, 1995.

Roser, Markus. *Hexerei und Lebensriten: Zur Inkulturation des christlichen Glaubens unter den Gbaya der Zentralafrikanischen Republik.* Erlangen, Germany: Erlanger Verlag für Mission und Ökumene, 2000.

Rücker, Heribert. "'Afrikanische Theologie': Charles Nyamiti, Tansania." In Hans Waldenfels, ed., *Theologen der Dritten Welt: Elf biographische Skizzen aus Afrika, Asien und Lateinamerika*, 54-70. Munich: Beck, 1982.

Rüther, Kirsten. "Heated Debates over Crinolines: European Clothing on Nineteenth-Century Lutheran Mission Stations in the Transvaal." *Journal of Southern African Studies* 28 (2002): 359-78.

———. *The Power Beyond: Mission Strategies, African Conversion and the Development of a Christian Culture in the Transvaal.* Münster: LIT Verlag, 2002.

Rzepkowski, Horst. *Lexikon der Mission.* Graz, Austria: Verlag Styria, 1992.

Sahlins, Marshall David. *Culture and Practical Reason.* Chicago: University of Chicago Press, 1976.

———. *Kultur und praktische Vernunft.* Frankfurt: Suhrkamp, 1981.

Said, Edward. *Orientalism.* New York: Vintage Books, 1978.

Salamone, Frank A. "Colonialism and the Emergence of Fulani Identity." *Journal of Asian and African Studies* 20 (1985): 193-202.

———. "Indirect Rule and the Reinterpretation of Tradition." *African Studies Review* 23 (1980): 1-14.

Sanon, Titianma Anselme. *Das Evangelium verwurzeln: Glaubenserschließung im Raum afrikanischer Stammesinitiationen.* Freiburg im Breisgau, Germany: Herder, 1985.

———. "Jesus, Meister der Initiation." In Yvette Aklé et al., eds., *Der schwarze Christus: Wege afrikanischer Christologie*, 87-107. Translated by Ursula Faymonville Freiburg im Breisgau, Germany: Herder, 1989.

Scannone, Juan Carlos. *Weisheit und Befreiung.* Düsseldorf, Germany: Patmos, 1992.

Schiffauer, Werner. "Der cultural turn in der Ethnologie und der Kulturanthropologie." In Friedrich Jäger and Jürgen Straub, eds., *Handbuch der Kulturwissenschaften*, 2:502-17. Stuttgart, Germany: J. B. Metzler, 2004.

Schmidt, Wilhelm. "Die Bedeutung der Ethnologie und Religionskunde für Missionstheorie und Missionspraxis." *Zeitschrift für Missionswissenschaft* 18 (1992): 117-31.

———. *Philosophie der Lebenskunst.* Frankfurt: Suhrkamp, 1998.

Schreiner, Peter. *Im Mondschein öffnet sich der Lotus: Der Hinduismus*. Düsseldorf, Germany: Patmos, 1998.

Schreiter, Robert J. *Constructing Local Theologies*. Maryknoll, NY: Orbis Books, 1985.

———. *Die neue Katholizität: Globalisierung und die Theologie*. Frankfurt: IKO-Verlag für Interkulturelle Kommunikation, 1997.

———, ed. *Faces of Jesus in Africa*. Maryknoll, NY: Orbis Books, 1991.

———. *The Ministry of Reconciliation: Spirituality and Strategies*. 6th ed. Maryknoll, NY: Orbis Books, 2004.

———. "Synkretismus und duale Religionssysteme." In *Abschied vom Gott der Europäer*, 220-40. Salzburg, Austria: Anton Pustet, 1992.

———. *Wider die schweigende Anpassung: Versöhnungsarbeit als Auftrag und Dienst der Kirche im gesellschaftlichen Umbruch*. Lucerne, Switzerland: Edition Exodus, 1993.

Sellin, Volker. "Nationalbewusstsein und Partikularismus in Deutschland im 19. Jahrhundert." In Jan Assmann and Tonio Hölscher, eds., *Kultur und Gedächtnis*, 241-64. Frankfurt: Suhrkamp, 1988.

Senghaas, Dieter, ed. *Peripherer Kapitalismus: Analysen über Abhängigkeit und Unterentwicklung*. Frankfurt: Suhrkamp, 1974.

Setiloane, Gabriel M. *Der Gott meiner Väter und mein Gott: Afrikanische Theologie im Kontext der Apartheid*. Wuppertal, Germany: Peter Hammer, 1988.

Shaw, Rosalind. "The Invention of 'African Traditional Religion.'" *Religion* 20 (1990): 339-53.

Shimada, Shingo, and Jürgen Straub. "Relationale Hermeneutik im Kontext interkulturellen Verstehens: Probleme universalistischer Begriffsbildung in den Sozial- und Kulturwissenschaften—erörtert am Beispiel 'Religion.'" *Deutsche Zeitschrift für Philosophie* 47, no. 3 (1999): 449-77.

Sievernich, Michael. "Von der Akkomodation zur Inkulturation. Missionarische Leitideen der Gesellschaft Jesu." *Missionskunde und Religionswissenschaft* 86 (2002): 260-76.

Sievernich, Michael, et al., eds. *Conquista and Evangelisation*. Mainz, Germany: Matthias-Grünewald-Verlag, 1992.

Silber, Stefan. "Inkulturation und Befreiung in der Politik des Vatikan." In "Die Befreiung der Kulturen: Der Beitrag Juan Luis Segundos zur Theologie der inkulturierten Evangelisierung," 152-75. PhD diss. University of Würzburg, 2001.

———. "Typologie der Inkulturationsbegriffe: Vier Aporien; Eine Streitschrift für einen neuen Begriff in einer notwendigen Debatte." *Jahrbuch für Kontextuelle Theologien* 97 (1997): 117-36.

Siller, Hermann Pius, ed. *Suchbewegungen: Synkretismus—kulturelle Identität und kirchliches Bekenntnis.* Darmstadt, Germany: Wissenschaftliche Buchgesellschaft, 1991.

Six, Clemens. *Hindu-Nationalismus und Globalisierung: Die zwei Gesichter Indiens: Symbole der Identität und des Anderen.* Frankfurt: Brandes & Apsel, 2001.

Smit, Dirkie J. "The Truth and Reconciliation Commission: Tentative Religious and Theological Perspectives." *Journal of Theology for Southern Africa* 90 (1995): 3-15.

Smith, Susan. "A Response to Re-naming Mission as 'Intercultural Theology' and Its Relationship to Religious Studies." *Mission Studies* 25 (2008): 111-12.

Song, Choan-Seng. *Third-Eye Theology: Theology in Formation in Asian Settings.* Maryknoll, NY: Orbis Books, 1979.

Souga, Thérèse. "Das Christusereignis aus der Sicht afrikanischer Frauen—Eine katholische Perspektive." In Regula Strobel, *Leidenschaft und Solidarität: Theologinnen der Dritten Welt ergreifen das Wort*, 51-61. Lucerne, Switzerland: Edition Exodus, 1992.

Stauth, Georg. *Islam und westlicher Rationalismus.* Frankfurt: Campus, 1993.

Steigenga, Timothy J., and Edward L. Cleary, eds. *Conversion of a Continent: Contemporary Religious Change in Latin America.* New Brunswick, NJ: Rutgers University Press, 2007.

Stein, Jürgen. *Christentum und Kastenwesen: Zum Verhältnis von Religion und Gesellschaft in Indien.* Frankfurt: Verlag O. Lembeck, 2002.

Strahm, Doris. *Vom Rand in die Mitte: Christologie aus der Sicht von Frauen in Asien, Afrika und Lateinamerika.* 2nd ed. Lucerne, Switzerland: Edition Exodus, 1997.

Straub, Jürgen. "Personale und kollektive Identität: Zur Analyse eines theoretischen Begriffs." In Assmann et al., *Identitäten*, 73-104.

Suess, Paulo. "Inkulturation." In Ellacuría and Sobrino, *Mysterium Liberationis*, 1011-59.

Sundermeier, Theo. *Christliche Kunst weltweit: Eine Einführung.* Frankfurt: Otto Lembeck, 2007.

———. *Den Fremden verstehen.* Göttingen: Vandenhoeck & Ruprecht, 1996.

———, ed. *Den Fremden wahrnehmen: Bausteine einer Xenologie.* Gütersloh, Germany: Gütersloher Verlagshaus, 1992.

———. "Die Daseinserhellung durch Kunst übersteigt immer die des Wortes." In *Jahrbuch Mission 1990*, 29-41. Hamburg: Evangelisches Missionswerk in Deutschland, 1990.

——. *The Individual and Community in African Traditional Religions.* Beiträge zur Missionswissenschaft/Interkulturellen Theologie 6. Münster: LIT, 1998.

——. "Inkulturation und Synkretismus: Probleme einer Verhältnisbestimmung." *Evangelische Theologie* 52 (1992): 192-209.

——. *Religion—Was ist das? Religionswissenschaft im theologischen Kontext.* 2nd ed. Frankfurt: Lembeck, 2007.

——. "Zum Verhältnis von Religionswissenschaft und Theologie." In Sundermeier, *Religion—Was ist das?*, 273-306.

Sundkler, Bengt G. M. *Bantupropheten in Südafrika.* Stuttgart, Germany: Evangelisches Verlagswerk, 1964.

Tajfel, Henri. *Human Groups & Social Categories: Studies in Social Psychology.* Cambridge: Cambridge University Press, 1981.

Tappa, Louise K. *Das Christus-Ereignis aus der Sicht afrikanischer Frauen.* Lucerne, Switzerland: Edition Exodus, 1992.

——. "Ein Gott nach dem Bild des Mannes." In John Pobee et al., eds., *Komm, lies mit meinen Augen: Biblische und theologische Entdeckungen von Frauen aus der Dritten Welt*, 135-42. Offenbach, Germany: Burckhardthaus-Laetare-Verlag, 1987.

——. "Woman Doing Theology." *Ministerial Formation* 48 (1990): 29-30.

Theissen, Gerd. "Die Einheit der Kirche: Kohärenz und Differenz im Urchristentum." *Zeitschrift für Missionswissenschaft* 20 (1994): 70-86.

——. "Tradition und Entscheidung: Der Beitrag des biblischen Glaubens zum kulturellen Gedächtnis." In Jan Assmann and Tonio Hölscher, eds., *Kultur und Gedächtnis*, 170-96. Frankfurt: Suhrkamp, 1988.

Thiel, Josef Franz. *Grundbegriffe der Ethnologie.* 4th ed. Berlin: Reimer, 1983.

Thomas, Madathilparampil Mammen. "The Absoluteness of Jesus Christ and Christ-Centred Syncretism." *The Ecumenical Review* 37 (1985): 387-97.

Tibi, Bassam. *Islam and the Cultural Accommodation of Social Change.* Boulder, CO: Westview Press, 1990.

Tiénou, Tite. "Indigenous African Christian Theologies: The Uphill Road." *International Bulletin of Missionary Research* 14, no. 2 (1990): 73-77.

——. "The Theological Task of the Church in Africa: Where Are We Now and Where Should We Be Going?" *East Africa Journal of Evangelical Theology* 6, no. 1 (1987): 3-11.

——, ed. *The Theological Task of the Church in Africa.* 2nd ed. Achimota, Ghana: Africa Christian Press, 1990.

Todorov, Tzvetan. *Die Eroberung Amerikas: Das Problem des Anderen.* Frankfurt: Suhrkamp, 1985.

Troeltsch, Ernst. "Über historische und dogmatische Methode in der Theologie." In *Zur religiösen Lage: Religionsphilosophie und Ethik*. 2nd ed. Vol. 2 of *Gesammelte Schriften*, 729-53. Tübingen: J. C. B. Mohr, 1922.

Ufer, Martin. "Emotion und Expansion: Neopfingstlerische Bewegungen in Brasilien." In Alexander F. Gemeinhardt, ed., *Die Pfingstbewegung als ökumenische Herausforderung*, 93-128. Göttingen: Vandenhoeck & Ruprecht, 2005.

Ukah, Asonzeh F.-K. "Mobilities, Migration and Multiplication: The Expansion of the Religious Field of the Redeemed Christian Church of God (RCCG), Nigeria." In Afeosemime Adogame and Cordula Weissköppel, eds., *Religion in the Context of African Migration*, 317-41. Bayreuth, Germany: Eckhard Breitinger, 2005.

———. *A New Paradigm of Pentecostal Power: A Study of the Redeemed Christian Church of God in Nigeria*. Trenten, NJ: Africa World Press, 2008.

Ustorf, Werner. *Die Missionsmethode Franz Michael Zahns und der Aufbau kirchlicher Strukturen in Westafrika (1862–1900)*. Erlangen, Germany: Verlag der Ev.-Luth. Mission, 1989.

Venter, Dawid, ed. *Engaging Modernity: Methods and Cases for Studying African Independent Churches in South Africa*. Westport, CT: Praeger, 2004.

Vester, Heinz-Günter. "Erving Goffman's Sociology as a Semiotics of Postmodern Culture." *Semiotica* 76, nos. 3-4 (1989): 191-203.

Villa-Vicencio, Charles. *Gottes Revolution: Gesellschaftliche Aufgaben der Theologie am Beispiel Südafrikas*. Freiburg im Breisgau, Germany: Herder, 1995.

———. *A Theology of Reconstruction: Nation-Building and Human Rights*. Cambridge Studies in Ideology and Religion. Cambridge: Cambridge University Press, 1992.

Visser't Hooft, Willem Adolph. "Geschichte und Sinn des Wortes 'Ökumene': Ökumenischer Aufbruch." In *Hauptschriften*, 2:11-28. Stuttgart, Germany: Kreuz-Verlag, 1967.

Wagner, Peter. "Fest-Stellungen: Beobachtungen zur sozialwissenschaftlichen Diskussion über Identität." In Assmann et al., *Identitäten*, 44-72.

Waldenfels, Bernhard. *Der Stachel des Fremden*. Frankfurt: Suhrkamp, 1990.

Warneck, Gustav. *Evangelische Missionslehre*. 2nd ed. Gotha, Germany: F. A. Perthes, 1897.

Weber, Max. "Die protestantische Ethik und der Geist des Kapitalismus." In *Gesammelte Aufsätze zur Religionssoziologie*, 1:17-206. 9th ed. Tübingen: J. C. B. Mohr, 1988.

———. *The Protestant Ethic and the Spirit of Capitalism: With Other Writings on the Rise of the West*. Translated by Stephen Kalberg. 4th ed. Oxford: Oxford University Press, 2008.

Weinreich, Sonja, and Christoph Benn. *AIDS—Eine Krankheit verändert die Welt: Daten—Fakten—Hintergründe.* 3rd ed. Frankfurt: Lembeck, 2005.

Welsch, Wolfgang. "Auf dem Wege zu transkulturellen Gesellschaften." In Allolio-Näcke, Kalscheuer, and Manzeschke, *Differenzen anders denken,* 314-41.

———. "Transkulturalität—Lebensformen nach der Auflösung der Kulturen." *Information Philosophie,* no. 2 (1992): 5-20.

———. "Transkulturalität: Zur veränderten Verfassung heutiger Kulturen." In Irmela Schneider and Christian W. Thomson, eds., *Hybridkultur: Medien, Netze, Künste.* Köln: Weinand, 1997.

Werner, Dietrich, et al., eds. *Handbook of Theological Education in World Christianity.* Oxford: Regnum, 2010.

Wessel, Carola. "'Es ist also des Heilands sein Predigtstuhl so weit und groß als die ganze Welt': Zinzendorfs Überlegungen zur Mission." In Martin Brecht and Paul Puecker, eds., *Neue Aspekte der Zinzendorf-Forschung,* 163-73. Göttingen: Vandenhoeck & Ruprecht, 2006.

Wilfred, Felix, et al., eds. *Indien.* Translated by E. Anneliese Gensichen, Hans-Werner Gensichen, and Theodora Karnasch. Vol. 3 of *Theologiegeschichte der Dritten Welt.* Edited by Theo Sundermeier and Norbert Klaes. Munich: Chr. Kaiser, 1992.

Will, Paul, J. "Swami Vivekananda and Cultural Stereotyping." In Ninian Smart and B. Srinivasa Murthy, eds., *East-West Encounters in Philosophy and Religion,* 377-87. Mumbai: Popular Prakashan Pvt., 1996.

Wissenschaftliche Gesellschaft für Theologie and Deutsche Gesellschaft für Missionswissenschaft. "Mission Studies as Intercultural Theology and Its Relationship to Religious Studies." *Mission Studies* 25, no. 1 (2008): 103-8.

Witte, Johannes. "Was veranlasst die Ostasien-Mission zur Bitte um Aufnahme in den Deutsch-Evangelischen Missionsbund?" *Zeitschrift für Missions- und Religionswissenschaft* 46 (1931): 225-38.

Wittgenstein, Ludwig. *Tractatus Logico-Philosophicus.* Edited by David Pears and Brian McGuinness. London: Routledge, 2001.

Wrogemann, Henning. *Das schöne Evangelium inmitten der Kulturen und Religionen.* Erlangen, Germany: Erlanger Verlag für Mission und Ökumene, 2011.

———. "Einheit im Glauben? Ökumene und Toleranz." In *Das schöne Evangelium,* 232-56.

———. *Mission und Religion in der Systematischen Theologie der Gegenwart.* Göttingen: Vandenhoeck & Ruprecht, 1997.

———. *Missionarischer Islam und gesellschaftlicher Dialog: Eine Studie zu Begründung und Praxis des Aufrufes zum Islam (da'wa) im internationalen sunnitischen Diskurs.* Frankfurt: Lembeck, 2006.

———. "Wem gehört Jesus? Interreligiöse Streifzüge und dogmatische Wegmarken." In *Das schöne Evangelium*, 10-22.

Yong, Amos. *Hospitality and the Other: Pentecost, Christian Practices, and the Neighbor*. Maryknoll, NY: Orbis Books, 2008.

Zahn, Franz Michael. "Die Muttersprache in der Mission." *Allgemeine Missions-Zeitschrift* (1895): 337-60.

Zaugg-Ott, Kurt. *Entwicklung oder Befreiung? Die Entwicklungsdiskussion im Ökumenischen Rat der Kirchen von 1968 bis 1991*. Frankfurt: Lembeck, 2004.

Zimmerling, Peter. *Nikolaus Ludwig Graf von Zinzendorf und die Herrnhuter Brüdergemeine*. Holzgerlingen, Germany: Hänssler, 1999.

———. "Zinzendorf und die Brüdermission." In *Pioniere der Mission im älteren Pietismus*, 30-45. Giessen, Germany: Brunnen Verlag, 1985.

Name Index

Subject Index

MISSIOLOGICAL ENGAGEMENTS

Series Editors: Scott W. Sunquist, Amos Yong, and John R. Franke

Missiological Engagements: Church, Theology, and Culture in Global Contexts charts interdisciplinary and innovative trajectories in the history, theology, and practice of Christian mission at the beginning of the third millennium.

Among its guiding questions are the following: What are the major opportunities and challenges for Christian mission in the twenty-first century? How does the missionary impulse of the gospel reframe theology and hermeneutics within a global and intercultural context? What kind of missiological thinking ought to be retrieved and reappropriated for a dynamic global Christianity? What innovations in the theology and practice of mission are needed for a renewed and revitalized Christian witness in a postmodern, postcolonial, postsecular, and post-Christian world?

Books in the series, both monographs and edited collections, will feature contributions by leading thinkers representing evangelical, Protestant, Roman Catholic, and Orthodox traditions, who work within or across the range of biblical, historical, theological, and social scientific disciplines. Authors and editors will include the full spectrum from younger and emerging researchers to established and renowned scholars, from the Euro-American West and the Majority World, whose missiological scholarship will bridge church, academy, and society.

Missiological Engagements reflects cutting-edge trends, research, and innovations in the field that will be of relevance to theorists and practitioners in churches, academic domains, mission organizations, and NGOs, among other arenas.

Finding the Textbook You Need

The IVP Academic Textbook Selector
is an online tool for instantly finding the IVP books
suitable for over 250 courses across 24 disciplines.

www.ivpress.com/academic/